Victor Cousin

BSHP NEW TEXTS IN THE HISTORY OF PHILOSOPHY

The aim of this series is to encourage and facilitate the study of all aspects of the history of philosophy, including the rediscovery of neglected elements and the exploration of new approaches to the subject. Texts are selected on the basis of their philosophical and historical significance and with a view to promoting the understanding of currently under-represented authors, philosophical traditions, and historical periods. They include new editions and translations of important yet less well-known works which are not widely available to an Anglophone readership. The series is sponsored by the British Society for the History of Philosophy (BSHP) and is managed by an editorial team elected by the Society. It reflects the Society's main mission and its strong commitment to broadening the canon.

General editors

Maria Rosa Antognazza (†2023)
Michael Beaney
Mogens Lærke (managing editor)

ALSO PUBLISHED IN THE SERIES

Leibniz: *General Inquiries on the Analysis of Notions and Truths*
Edited with an English translation by Massimo Mugnai

Félix Ravaisson: *French Philosophy in the Nineteenth Century*
Translated by Mark Sinclair

Amalia Holst: *On the Vocation of Woman to Higher Intellectual Education*
Edited by Andrew Cooper

Johann Gottlieb Fichte: *The Doctrine of the State*
Edited by Jeffrey Church and Anna Marisa Schön

Victor Cousin

Philosophical Fragments

Edited by
DELPHINE ANTOINE-MAHUT
AND
DANIEL WHISTLER

Translated by
DANIEL WHISTLER

OXFORD
UNIVERSITY PRESS

Great Clarendon Street, Oxford, OX2 6DP,
United Kingdom

Oxford University Press is a department of the University of Oxford.
It furthers the University's objective of excellence in research, scholarship,
and education by publishing worldwide. Oxford is a registered trade mark of
Oxford University Press in the UK and in certain other countries

© Delphine Antoine-Mahut and Daniel Whistler 2025

© Chapter 2 Félix Barancy and Sarah Bernard-Granger 2025
© Chapter 3 Pierre-François Moreau 2025
© Chapter 4 Lucie Rey 2025

The moral rights of the authors have been asserted

All rights reserved. No part of this publication may be reproduced, stored in a retrieval system, transmitted, used for text and data mining, or used for training artificial intelligence, in any form or by any means, without the prior permission in writing of Oxford University Press, or as expressly permitted by law, by license or under terms agreed with the appropriate reprographics rights organization. Inquiries concerning reproduction outside the scope of the above should be sent to the Rights Department, Oxford University Press, at the address above.

You must not circulate this work in any other form
and you must impose this same condition on any acquirer

Published in the United States of America by Oxford University Press
198 Madison Avenue, New York, NY 10016, United States of America

British Library Cataloguing in Publication Data
Data available

Library of Congress Control Number is on file at the Library of Congress

ISBN 978–0–19–886626–8

DOI: 10.1093/actrade/9780198866268.001.0001

Printed and bound by
CPI Group (UK) Ltd, Croydon, CR0 4YY

The manufacturer's authorised representative in the EU for product safety is Oxford University Press España S.A. of el Parque Empresarial San Fernando de Henares, Avenida de Castilla, 2 – 28830 Madrid (www.oup.es/en).

Contents

Editors' Preface: Victor Cousin, Eclectic Philosophy, and Its Legacies Delphine Antoine-Mahut and Daniel Whistler	vii
Note on Editions, Abbreviations, and Translations	xxiii

I.	INTRODUCTIONS	1
	Cousin and French Philosophy *Delphine Antoine-Mahut*	3
	Cousin and the Politics of Philosophy *Félix Barancy and Sarah Bernard-Granger*	14
	Cousin and the History of Philosophy *Pierre-François Moreau*	25
	Cousin and the Eighteenth Century *Lucie Rey*	34
	Cousin and the Problem of Metaphysics *Daniel Whistler*	45
II.	THE THREE PREFACES	57
	Preface to the 1826 Edition of *Philosophical Fragments*	59
	Preface to the 1833 Edition of *Philosophical Fragments*	91
	Prefatory Note to the 1838 Edition of *Philosophical Fragments*	124
III.	1816–1818	139
	On the Moral Law and Freedom	141
	On the True Meaning of the *cogito, ergo sum*	144
	Attempt at a Classification of Philosophical Questions and Schools	150
	On the Fact of Consciousness	159
	On the Clear and the Obscure in Knowledge, or On Spontaneity and Reflection	166
	On Real Beauty and Ideal Beauty	172
IV.	1826–1830	179
	On the True Beginning of the History of Philosophy	181
	Plato: Language of the Theory of Ideas	185
	Plato	191
	Prefatory Note to *New Philosophical Fragments*	197
	Preface to the Translation of Tennemann's *Manual of the History of Philosophy*	200
	From Review of Reiffenberg's *On Eclecticism*	209

V. AFTER 1833 213
    Introduction to the Posthumous Works of Maine de Biran 215
    From Abelard 237
    From Foreword to *On Pascal's Pensées* 242
    Foreword to *Fragments of Cartesian Philosophy* 250

Appendix: Two Edicts Issued by the Royal Council of Public Education 257
Index 263

Editors' Preface

Victor Cousin, Eclectic Philosophy, and Its Legacies

Delphine Antoine-Mahut and Daniel Whistler

1. The Spectre of Cousin

Victor Cousin's standing has remained consistently low among Anglophone historians of philosophy over the past fifty years. He is portrayed as an "academic entrepreneur" and "derivative philosopher," a "naïve" thinker whose philosophy is "empty" and "flawed," since it constitutes little more "than an opportunistic interplay between ideas and politics."[1] The consensus view presents Cousin as a mediocre philosopher who happened to be in the right place at the right time to wield immense political and institutional power, as an administrator who worked more for the state and his own glory than for truth, and who subordinated ideas to expediency and opportunism. On this line of interpretation, he has been consigned "to the scrapheap of intellectual history."[2]

And yet, this is an image of Cousin that has become—to some extent—increasingly outdated outside of the English-speaking world. In France, modern Cousin-scholarship began after May '68 failed—after, that is, it failed to overthrow the bourgeois structure of philosophical practice instituted in Cousin's image. The reasons for this failure—for the stubborn persistence of Cousinianism in the methods and structures of French philosophy—demanded a return to Cousin's writings, and this project ("Victor Cousin after May '68") occupied, among others, Stéphane Douailler, Christiane Mauve, Danielle Rancière, and, above all, Patrice Vermeren, whose 1995 *Victor Cousin: Le Jeu de la philosophie et l'État* was

---

[1] These quotations are taken from B. Bâcle, "Victor Cousin and Eclecticism," in M. Moriarty and J. Jennings (eds), *The Cambridge History of French Thought* (Cambridge: Cambridge University Press, 2019), pp. 323, 330; J. Goldstein, *The Post-Revolutionary Self: Politics and Psyche in France, 1750–1850* (Cambridge, MA: Harvard University Press, 2005), p. 139; D. Leopold, "Victor Cousin (1792–1867)," in *Routledge Encyclopedia of Philosophy* (1998 version). This line of interpretation is long-standing in twentieth-century Anglophone research: take e.g. Wilcox's 1953 remarks that Cousin "smothered his ignorance with eloquence," "made jejune efforts to refute Kant before he was able to read him," "hid his opportunism under an easy eclecticism," and "dazzled [with] metaphysical banalities [that] passed for the new revelation." John Wilcox, "The Beginnings of *l'Art Pour l'Art*," *Journal of Aesthetics and Art Criticism* 11.4 (1953), pp. 366–7.

[2] A. B. Spitzer, *The French Generation of 1820* (Princeton: Princeton University Press, 1987), p. 74.

its culmination.[3] In its wake there has emerged further interest in Cousin's role in the development of history of philosophy as a discipline,[4] in his pivotal position in Franco-German and Franco-British cultural transfers[5] and, most recently, in his shaping of a French philosophical conversation over the value and nature of empiricist methodology, psychology, metaphysics, and Cartesianism.[6] None of this work ends up glorifying or redeeming Cousin (indeed, much of it takes place under the rubric, "Know thy enemy!"); however, what these new waves of scholarship share is a refusal to flinch before the fact that *Victor Cousin invented modern French philosophy*. Precisely because he appears in this tradition as both founding father and "skeleton in the closet," to return to Cousin is to reckon with what philosophers have owed him and what they owe him still. Pierre Macherey sums this up in the following reminder to his fellow French philosophers:

> We must dare tell ourselves: Cousin haunts [our philosophies] in the manner of a theoretical unconscious, as something unthought which precedes all our thoughts and orients them in a certain sense.... We have not yet gone beyond the nineteenth century.[7]

---

[3] P. Vermeren, *Victor Cousin: Le Jeu de la philosophie et de l'État* (Paris: L'Harmattan, 1995). This group had initially congregated around the journals, *La Doctrinal de Sapience* and, to a lesser extent, *Les Révoltes logiques*, during the 1970s. See further Vermeren's introductory essays. "Victor Cousin, l'État et la révolution," *Corpus* 18/19 (1991), pp. 3–13; "Venir après l'histoire de la philosophie, la *Reforma universitaria* de 1918 et Mai 68?," *Le Télémaque* 54.2 (2018), pp. 37–42; the introduction by Vermeren and S. Douailler to J. Ferrari, *Les Philosophes salariés* (Paris: Payot, 1983); D. Rancière, "L'État et la philosophie," in V. Cousin, *Défense de l'université et de la philosophie* (Paris: Solin, 1977); and the anthology, *La Philosophie saisie par l'État*, ed. S. Douailler et al. (Paris: Aubier, 1992). This approach also forms the background to François Châtelet's references back to Cousin in *La Philosophie des professeurs* (Paris; Grasset, 1970) and "La question de l'histoire de la philosophie aujourd'hui," in D. Grisoni (ed.), *Politiques de la philosophie* (Paris: Grasset, 1976), pp. 29–54, as well as Jacques Derrida's allusions to Cousin in *Who's Afraid of Philosophy? Right to Philosophy 1*, trans. J. Plug (Stanford: Stanford University Press, 2002). Related projects that returned to Cousin's politics of philosophy are J.-P. Cotten, *Autour de Victor Cousin: une politique de la philosophie* (Paris: Les Belles Lettres, 1992); P. Macherey, *Études de philosophie "française"* (Paris: Publications de la Sorbonne, 2013); and the collection *Victor Cousin: Homo theologico-politicus*, ed. E. Fauquet (Lyon: Kimé, 1988).

[4] See L. Rey, *Les Enjeux de l'histoire de la philosophie au XIXe siècle: Pierre Leroux contre Victor Cousin* (Paris: L'Harmattan, 2013); P.-F. Moreau, "Victor Cousin, la philosophie et son histoire," *Le Télémaque* 54.2 (2018), pp. 57–66; C. König-Pralong, *La colonie philosophique: écrire l'histoire de la philosophie aux XVIIIe–XIXe siècles* (Paris: EHESS Éditions, 2019); D. Couzinet and M. Meliadó (eds), *L'Institution française et la Renaissance: L'époque de Victor Cousin* (Leiden: Brill, 2022). See also D. R. Kelley, *The Descent of Ideas: The History of Intellectual History* (London: Routledge, 2002), pp. 31–64.

[5] See e.g. M. Espagne and M. Werner, *Lettres d'Allemagne: Victor Cousin et les hégéliens* (Tusson: Du Lérot, 1990); E. Arosio and M. Malherbe, *Philosophie écossaise et philosophie française (1750–1850)* (Paris: Vrin, 2007).

[6] See esp. D. Antonie-Mahut, *L'Autorité d'un canon philosophique: le cas Descartes* (Paris: Vrin, 2021), pp. 261–314, as well as D. Antoine-Mahut and D. Whistler (eds), *Une arme philosophique: l'éclectisme de Victor Cousin* (Paris: Éditions des archives contemporaines, 2019).

[7] P. Macherey, *Histoires de dinosaure: faire de la philosophie, 1965–1997* (Paris: Presses Universitaires de France, 1999), p. 197.

Nevertheless, Cousin's legacy is not a parochial matter for French philosophers alone, for his eclecticism was an international event. Its effects were notably felt in Belgium, in Germany (by Hegelians and Schellingians, in particular), in Italy, and then, later in the century, in Latin America.[8] In fact, its most visible effects were on English-speaking philosophers in the mid-nineteenth century: from Sarah Austin and William Hamilton in Britain to Orestes Brownson and George Ripley in New England, Cousin was a constant point of reference.[9] A flurry of English translations appeared between 1832 and 1854,[10] and Cousin's ideas were incorporated into the work of Ralph Waldo Emerson and W. T. Harris, among many others. One contemporary noted of Emerson and Brownson in particular: "So far as I can judge, they have merely taken up the philosophy of Victor Cousin."[11]

What is more, Cousin lives on outside France in traditions dependent on modern French philosophy, such as Anglophone "European philosophy" or the "theory" of Humanities departments. For example, the Cousinian structure of the *dissertation de philosophie générale* compulsory in France, in which the history of philosophy is incorporated into philosophical reflection by means of a personal trajectory of thinking constructed out of a choice between historically identifiable philosophical positions,[12] is reproduced in Anglophone applications of the history of philosophy. To pick out what is valuable from a series of diffuse past thinkers

---

[8] On Belgium, see pp. 209–11 below; on Germany and Italy, see pp. 91, 124–5 below; on Latin America, see M. A. Molano Vega, "L'éclectisme philosophique en Nouvelle-Grenade (Colombie): circulation du discours et usages politiques," in Antoine-Mahut and Whistler (eds), *Une arme philosophique*, pp. 135–42, as well as J. Canhada, *O discurso e a historia. A filosofia no Brasil no século XIX* (Sao Paolo: Ediçoes Loyola Jesuitas, 2020).

[9] See pp. 125–6 below; J. Urbas, "In Praise of Second-Rate French Philosophy: Reassessing Victor Cousin's Contribution to Transcendentalism," *Revue française d'études américaines* 140.3 (2014), pp. 37–51; C. König-Pralong, "Une French theory au XIXe siècle: l'éclectisme de Cousin en Grande-Bretagne et aux États-Unis d'Amérique," in Antoine-Mahut and Whistler (eds), *Une arme philosophique*, pp. 111–24; as well as, more generally, C. Bolus-Reichert, *The Age of Eclecticism: Literature and Culture in Britain, 1815–85* (Columbus, OH: Ohio State University Press, 2009).

[10] There were seven major translations between these dates, including translations of Cousin's 1828 lecture course, his lectures on the true, the beautiful, and the good and his lectures on Kant—for full details, see König-Pralong, "Une French theory," pp. 114–15. Several of the texts translated within this volume were first translated in George Ripley's *Philosophical Miscellanies* (1838), as noted in our translators' endnotes. Ripley also translates two "fragments" not included in this volume: "The Idea of Cause and of the Infinite" (pp. 163–5) and "Religion, Mysticism, Stoicism" (pp. 166–70).

[11] J. Murdock, *Sketches of Modern Philosophy* (Hartford, Wells, 1842), p. 177. See König-Pralong, "Une French theory," p. 117. One example of this initially enthusiastic reception-history is Henry Reeve's paean on meeting Cousin in February 1832: "You know what I thought of [Cousin's] lectures when I was reading them some twelve months ago; they have influenced in no slight degree the opinions and conceptions I have formed in the last year.... How anything so cynical [as] ordinary life can co-exist with a soul and a faith so platonical and so refined is, and ever will be, to me a subject of great wonder.... His *Nos*! and *Has*! his gesticulations, his wit, his vanity, his malice, and his philosophy are all—I mean no disrespect to Mr. Emmanuel Kant—transcendental." J. Knox Laughton (ed.), *Memoirs of the Life and Correspondence of Henry Reeve*, vol. 1 (London: Longmans, 1893), pp. 15–16.

[12] This is the argument made by Moreau (in "La philosophie et son histoire"), as well as in more polemical fashion by Châtelet (in *La philosophie des professeurs*). Strictly speaking, the *dissertation de philosophie générale* is a post-Cousinian institution but remains very much determined by the eclectic spirit beyond the nineteenth century. See e.g. Claude Lévi-Strauss' critical account of his preparation for the *agrégation*. *Tristes Tropiques*, trans. J. Russell (New York: Criterion, 1961), p. 54.

for the purposes of the present is an eclectic gesture codified most rigorously by Cousin. As Wallach Scott puts it, contemporary practices of theoretical pick-and-mix have "resemblances with and perhaps even roots in" Cousin's project.[13] In other words, Cousin haunts contemporary theory every time the latter operates according to logics of accumulation and reconciliation—that is, according to a principle of "more of the same."[14]

Cousin is still with us. He haunts the past and the present of French philosophy, as well as all philosophical traditions impacted by it. To read Cousin (again) is to acknowledge the scars contemporary philosophy still carries, in its doctrines, its controversies, and its institutions. The present volume is intended to make this reading possible and to contribute to the project of *re-introducing* Cousin into Anglophone history of philosophy by making accessible (once more) some of his more exemplary philosophical writings. It includes not only two of his philosophical "manifestos" (the 1826 and 1833 prefaces to *Philosophical Fragments*), but also additional "fragments" that exemplify his practice of psychological analysis, his ethics, aesthetics, and philosophy of religion, as well as his interventions in the historiography of ancient, medieval, and modern philosophy. Our reintroduction begins with five preliminary essays reconstructing Cousin's philosophy: Delphine Antoine-Mahut outlines Cousin's role in a French philosophical conversation proceeding from Descartes through Condillac and Maine de Biran; Félix Barancy and Sarah Bernard-Granger provide the institutional and pedagogical context to Cousin's "politics of philosophy"; Pierre-François Moreau details Cousin's contribution to the genesis of the historiography of philosophy, in which—in a fateful gesture—philosophy comes to be mediated through its history; Lucie Rey shows how Cousin reacts to the French Revolution and its intellectual sources by offering philosophers a post-revolutionary settlement; and, finally, Daniel Whistler analyses Cousin's attempt to secure the conditions of possibility of a secularized metaphysics of morals in a post-Kantian context. What then follows are Cousin's texts themselves—both his programmatic prefaces and his various interventions on particular philosophical and historical questions from 1815 through to the 1840s. Finally, a short appendix gives two examples of Cousin's political reform of philosophical pedagogy.

To provide some orientation to the reader new to Cousin and to provide global context to the introductory essays that follow, the rest of this preface provides three brief overviews of (i) Cousin's eclectic project as a whole, (ii) his intellectual biography, and (iii) the *Philosophical Fragments* themselves.

---

[13] J. Wallach Scott, "Against Eclecticism," *differences* 16.3 (2005), pp. 116–17.
[14] It is on the basis of this principle that commentators are quick to emphasize that "eclectics is the contrary of dialectics" (Macherey, *Études*, p. 288).

2. Eclecticism: An Overview

Cousin does philosophy under "the banner" of *eclecticism*—a term drawn from the late Alexandrian idea of a "secta non secta," as well as various early modern eclectic critics from Christian Thomasius to Denis Diderot.[15] Just as J. J. Brucker characterizes eclectics as those who "extract from all sects what they see fit to concur with their own thought and reasoning, and make it into a system"[16] and just as Diderot defines "eclectic method" as "forming a solid whole, which is genuinely one's own work, out of a great number of collected parts that belong to others,"[17] so too Cousin describes his own project in terms of both independence from all pre-existing systematic positions and hospitality to them all:

[My] ambition to reject no system nor to accept any in its entirety, [but] to choose what appears true and good and therefore durable in everything—this, in a word, is eclecticism. (p. 202 below)

The later Cousin is adamant that he "belongs to no school, but to common sense,"[18] where "common sense" comprises a set of eternal truths proper to every sound reason. He continues that eclectic philosophy will become "the natural ally of all good causes, sustain religious feeling, defend genuine art … ground the law, repel demagoguery and tyranny in equal measure, teach all men to respect and love one another, and gradually lead human society to the true republic."[19]

To achieve these lofty ends, Cousin conceives philosophy primarily as a form of education—in particular, as a pedagogy that inculcates a series of epistemic virtues in the minds of his students and readers. Four such virtues give some idea of his aims:

1. *The Virtue of Impartiality*: First and foremost, Cousin's ambitions are to be realized through the choice of an appropriate method (for "philosophy is and can be, properly speaking, solely a method"),[20] and this method is that of the introspective observation of one's own consciousness—or "psychology." Psychological

---

[15] See M. Albrecht, *Eklektik: eine Begriffsgeschichte mit Hinweisen auf die Philosophie- und Wissenschaftsgeschichte* (Stuttgart: Frommann-Holzboog, 1994); U. J. Schneider, "L'éclectisme avant Cousin: la tradition allemande." *Corpus* 18/19 (1991), pp. 15–28; G. Barroux, "Le XVIIIe siècle: Moment d'une renaissance de l'éclectisme philosophique," in Antoine-Mahut and Whistler (eds), *Une arme philosophique*, pp. 3–18. For a further introductory overview of Cousin's eclecticism that also focuses on its reception among his contemporaries, see D. Antoine-Mahut, "Eclecticism and Its Discontents," in M. Sinclair and D. Whistler (eds), *The Oxford Handbook of Modern French Philosophy* (Oxford: Oxford University Press, 2024), pp. 43–54.
[16] U. J. Schneider, "The Problem of Eclecticism in the History of Philosophy," *Intellectual History Review* 26.1 (2016), p. 121.
[17] D. Diderot, "Éclectisme," in Diderot and D'Alembert (eds), *Encyclopédie, ou dictionnaire raisonné des sciences, des arts et des métiers, etc.* (http://encyclopedie.uchicago.edu/), vol. 5, p. 271.
[18] Cousin, *Défense*, p. 28.
[19] V. Cousin, *Du Vrai, du Beau et du Bien*, 8th edn (Paris: Didier, 1860), pp. iii–iv.
[20] V. Cousin, *Cours de philosophie: introduction à l'histoire de la philosophie*, ed. P. Vermeren (Paris: Fayard, 1991), p. 119.

method "constitutes the fundamental unity" of all his writings (p. 64 below) and came to symbolize his philosophical reforms: its popular success can be gleaned from Comte's complaint about a "psychological mania" sweeping France[21] and Stendhal's jibe that philosophy had become little more than the instruction: "Close your eyes and search your consciousness!"[22]

According to Cousin, what distinguishes his empiricist method from his predecessors is its "impartiality," which prevents it from being skewed by systematic prejudice. In the wake of a modernity of the "exclusive system" that "observes only the facts that agree with it ... corrupt[ing] the experimental method with systematic views," Cousin offers "a freer philosophy,"[23] one that "employs the method of observation alone, but applied to all the facts, whatever they may be, as long as they exist" (p. 63 below). This is a commitment to recording observed truths wherever they might take you—even, Cousin suggests, beyond the empirical realm into the speculative recesses of metaphysics, the moral law, and the divine. In other words, such is Cousin's metaphysical empiricism: a posteriori method ultimately discovers and determines what is purely a priori.[24] Philosophy thus ascends to its traditional heights, but now does so in a rigorous, impartial, and "severe" manner ("severity" constituting another aspect of Cousin's virtue-talk).

2. *The Virtue of Extensity*: Impartiality entails a philosophy of the unconditioned: "The exactness [of my method] is in its impartiality, and its impartiality is found solely in its extensity" (p. 63 below). In other words, the measure of success for impartial observation is its ability to philosophize about everything, to resist exclusivism through maximal range or inclusivity—that is (in the ethical register in which all philosophy culminates for Cousin): *absolute tolerance*. Since, according to Cousin, "the incomplete and therefore the exclusive is philosophy's unique vice" (p. 159 below), the task of any reformed philosophy is to "exclude nothing, accept everything and understand everything."[25] In psychology, this takes the form of an open form of observation which "reproduces every fact of consciousness" (p. 225 below). In the history of philosophy, it takes the form of the cumulative addition of everything true in past philosophies—an accumulation of true "fragments [scattered] here and there within all systems" into an ever-expanding whole (p. 113 below). That is, Cousin formulates an absolute historiography that is also intended as a historiography of the absolute: all philosophies find a home within eclecticism,

---

[21] A. Comte, *Cours de philosophie positive*, ed. M. Serres et al. (Paris: Hermann, 1975), pp. 853–4. On Comte's critique of Cousin's psychology, see J.-F. Braunstein, "L'invention française du 'psychologisme' en 1828," *Revue d'histoire des sciences* 65.2 (2012), pp. 197–212.

[22] Stendhal, in Douailler et al. (eds), *La Philosophie saisie par l'État*, p. 183.

[23] V. Cousin, "A propos de l'ouvrage de M. Degérando, *Histoire comparée des systèmes de philosophie* (1823)," *Journal des Savans* (July 1825), p. 438.

[24] On Cousin's "metaphysical empiricism" in the context of other syntheses of empiricism and rationalism at the period, see D. Whistler, "'True Empiricism': The Stakes of the Cousin-Schelling Controversy," *Perspectives on Science* 27.2 (2019), pp. 129–45.

[25] Cousin, *Introduction à l'histoire de la philosophie*, p. 38.

such that what he articulates as the rediscovery of truth in every system ultimately converts into the idea that the truth of every system is Cousinianism. Eclecticism positions itself, in short, as the fulfilment of philosophical history precisely by accumulating and reconciling everything.

One way in which this virtue is cashed out is in an imperative *to proliferate one's teachers* ("Far from claiming that I have had no masters, I confess that I have had many" [p. 103 below][26]). The eclectic should learn from all intellectual traditions, no matter how alien they might seem at first. This accounts for Cousin's tendency to flit between philosophies: from Scottish common-sense philosophy, to Kantianism, to Cartesianism, to Platonism, to Hegelianism—or, in his own words, "to pass through more than one school, trying to account for the attraction each of them in turn had for me" (p. 203 below). It also accounts for the "internationalist" strand in Cousin's thinking which led him to "open the gates" to French interest in German philosophies, in particular (p. 103 below), even if this strand sits alongside an equally forceful "nationalist" tendency that casts his own project as the "union of patriotic spirit and philosophical spirit."[27]

3. *The Virtue of Moderation*: "Eclecticism is moderation in the philosophical order"[28]—it puts an end to fanaticism in the realm of ideas by always taking the middle path—what König-Pralong dubs, "Cousinian centrism."[29] It is here that Cousin's proximity to his *doctrinaire* allies, like François Guizot and Pierre-Paul Royer-Collard, is most manifest: he transposes the doctrine of the *juste milieu* onto the philosophical plane, proposing a "peace treatise" between warring parties (p. 203 below) by representing them as irrational extremisms between which Cousin himself takes up a position of reasonable common sense. In other words, what the eighteenth century (as anarchic) supposedly lacked, but the nineteenth century possesses in Cousin himself is an intellectual authority able to moderate between competing extremes, just as the seventeenth century possessed such a figure in Descartes, the twelfth century did in Abelard and (outside of this French lineage) the fourth century BCE did in Plato—avatars who forestalled revolutionary excess through eclectic good sense. The late Cousin concludes:

The very perspective of fanaticism, to which an exclusive opinion can lead, recommends to me more than ever [the need for] moderation and wisdom; and it is

---

[26] On this point, Cousin stands opposed to Diderot's characterisation of the eclectic philosopher as having no master ("The sectarian is someone who has embraced a philosopher's doctrine; the eclectic, on the contrary, is someone who recognises no master." [in Diderot, "Eclectisme", 270]), and this forms part of the post-Hegelian twist to his rehabilitation of the early modern eclectic tradition: philosophical schools are not so much sources of partial errors than of partial truths.
[27] Cousin, *Du Vrai, du Beau et du Bien* (1860 edn), p. 129. See the discussion of nationalism and internationalism in Cousin's development in Macherey, *Études*, pp. 271-94.
[28] Cousin, *Du Vrai, du Beau et du Bien* (1860 edn), p. 363.
[29] König-Pralong, *La colonie philosophique*, p. 71.

my express wish, if not my hope, that eclecticism will serve as a guide for French philosophy during the nineteenth century. (p. 204 below)

Moreover, as the references to Descartes, Abelard, and Plato suggest, the "wisdom" gained by those living after the French Revolution consists in the recovery of perennial truths—the "patrimony of human reason."[30] Hence, while Cousin might speak in his early lectures of providing "the principles of the future,"[31] this future is primarily a "regeneration"[32] or "rehabilitation"[33] of traditional ideas: future investigations are not meant to find anything new, but to operate on the principle of "more of the same." It is for this reason he ends up presenting his philosophy as "both a return to the past and an effort towards the future."[34]

4. *The Virtue of Timeliness*: Cousin frequently desires to speak to and for his time—to write *the* philosophy of the nineteenth century. He presents eclecticism as "the idea of the century in philosophy" (p. 196 below), "the necessary philosophy of the century."[35] Yet, as mentioned above, what the nineteenth century embodies is not innovation, but the becoming self-conscious of a perennial philosophical tradition. He exclaims, "The spirit of the nineteenth century has come to recognize itself in eclecticism: the two of them can now undertake their journey together over all obstacles." (p. 115 below)

For Cousin, the timeliness of eclectic philosophy is further demonstrated by its successes, particularly its rise to orthodoxy under the July Monarchy. It became more than a doctrine; it became "a banner" under which Cousin's "regiment" of students, allies, and readers marched towards a conciliary future that would put an end to warring intellectual factions. Ultimately, the timeliness of eclecticism is manifest in its ideological functions, in its use in regulating institutions, syllabi, teaching practices, political reforms, appointments, debates, and publications. In these respects, Cousin did indeed come to personify the spirit of his age.

3. The Five Ages of Cousin

To help provide some further orientation to the reader, the present section provides a very brief intellectual biography in line with the chronology of the "fragments" translated in what follows.

---

[30] Cousin, *Défense*, p. 28.
[31] V. Cousin, *Cours de philosophie sur le fondement des idées absolues du Vrai, du Beau et du Bien*, ed. A. Garnier (Paris: Hachette, 1836), p. 8.
[32] Cousin, *Du Vrai, du Beau et du Bien* (1836 edn), p. 11.
[33] Cousin, *Du Vrai, du Beau et du Bien* (1860 edn), p. 9.
[34] Cousin, *Du Vrai, du Beau et du Bien* (1836 edn), p. 9. See further F. Barancy, "Politiques de l'éclectisme en situation de crise: Damiron promoteur d'une école philosophique," in Antoine-Mahut and Whistler (eds), *Une arme philosophique*, pp. 81–92.
[35] Cousin, *Du Vrai, du Beau et du Bien* (1860 edn), p. 364.

1. *Teacher, Psychologist, Liberal (1815–20)*: Born in 1792 into a working-class Parisian family, Victor Cousin came—by a happy accident[36]—to attend the prestigious *lycée* Charlemagne, winning the *prix d'honneur* in the *Concours général*, and this, in turn, led to entry into the École Normale in 1810 (as part of the first cohort after the Revolution). He obtained the *agrégation* at 21 and a year later defended a doctoral thesis on analytic method. By 1815, Cousin was giving lecture courses at the Faculty of Letters of the University of Paris and teaching at the École Normale, as Royer-Collard's *suppléant*. A regular visitor to the Auteuil salon, Cousin came to be dubbed by Maine de Biran the "hope of the true philosophy among us."[37]

Cousin's early courses were exploratory and experimental, but also very successful. Together he worked closely with his students for the revival of a post-revolutionary philosophy[38]—a collaboration made possible, above all, by Cousin's charismatic teaching style: Adolphe Garnier speaks of "the timbre of his voice, the fire of his gaze, the majesty of his gestures," continuing that Cousin's early lectures "grasped his listeners through all their senses."[39] In terms of content, Cousin's lectures soon became known for their openness to foreign philosophical trends as material for the construction of a "new French philosophy": his two visits to Germany in 1817–18—and the friendships he forged there with G. W. F. Hegel and F. W. J. Schelling—gave Cousin the aura of an insider to German philosophical developments.[40]

The early lecture courses would go on to provide the building blocks for many of Cousin's publications over the next fifty years. Yet, prior to 1826, these courses on Scottish philosophy and the moral law (1815–16), facts of consciousness and the history of their analysis (1816–17), the true, the beautiful, and the good (1818),

---

[36] This episode was the first in a series from Cousin's life (culminating in his arrest in Dresden) to be mythologized by himself and his school. Here e.g. is Jules Simon's rendition of it: "One day early in October 1803, at half-past four in the afternoon, the children rushed tumultuously from the lycée Charlemagne, pursuing with loud cries a schoolmate [Epagomène Viguier] clad in a great coat, which made him, in their eyes at least, look ridiculous.... While he was being hustled, pushed, and beaten, an urchin [i.e. Cousin] of eleven years, who had been playing in the gutter, rushed into the thick of the mob and scattered the band of persecutors, by giving the ringleaders a shower of blows. Madame Viguier was informed of this act of heroism that very evening.... She declared that she would defray the expenses of his education. He entered the *lycée* Charlemagne and advanced with giant strides.... Had it not been for that shower of blows just at the right moment, perhaps France might still be conning the amusing and witty philosophy of Laromiguière." J. Simon, *Victor Cousin*, trans. M. B. Anderson and E. P. Anderson (Chicago: McClurg, 1888), pp. 14–15.

[37] P. Maine de Biran, *Journal*, vol. 2, ed. H. Gouhier (Neuchatel: La Baconnière, 1955), p. 303.

[38] See V. Cousin, *Premiers essais de philosophie*, 4th edn (Paris: Didier, 1862), p. 409.

[39] Adolphe Garnier, quoted in R. Ragghianti and P. Vermeren, "Introduction," in V. Cousin, *Philosophie morale*, ed. S. Matton (Paris: Garnier, 2019), p. 9. Ragghianti's and Vermeren's introduction as a whole provides a detailed reconstruction of Cousin's philosophical development from 1815 to 1820.

[40] Cousin's self-proclaimed "discovery" of Hegel in Heidelberg (pp. 105–6 below) was another of the mythologized events from his early life that contributed to his aura of expertise. See further D. Whistler, "Becoming Cousin: Eclecticism, Spiritualism and Hegelianism," in K. Chepurin et al. (eds), *Hegel and Schelling in Early Nineteenth-Century France* (Dordrecht: Springer, 2023), vol. 2, and, in more detail, A. Bellantone, *Hegel in Francia, 1817–1941*, vol. 1 (Soveria Mannelli: Rubbettino, 2006).

sensualist philosophy (1818–19), Scottish philosophy (1819), moral philosophy (1819–20), and Kant's philosophy (1820) were only published as occasional extracts in the *Journal des savants* and the *Archives philosophiques*.

2. *Philology outside the Academy (the early 1820s)*: A victim of the Duc de Richelieu's reactionary Government of 1821 owing to his liberal sympathies, Cousin was banned from public teaching and exiled from institutional philosophy. In 1824, he was then arrested in Dresden and held on parole in Berlin for the same kind of reasons.[41] These moments of "exile" coincided, moreover, with a shift in his own philosophical interests: he began to understand his work less in terms of direct interventions in contemporary psychology and metaphysics than in terms of the recovery of past truths. As Cousin's biographer, Jules Barthélemy-Saint-Hilaire, put it, "Philosophy was no longer to be science, but history."[42] Or, in Cousin's own words:

> I quit speculation for some time, or rather I pursued it and realized it by applying it more particularly that I had yet done to the history of philosophy. Always faithful to the psychological method, I transposed it onto history. (p. 81 below)

Philosophy was to be mediated through the history of philosophy to the extent that—at the culmination of this trajectory in 1828—Cousin proclaimed "the identity of philosophy and the history of philosophy."[43]

This marks the origin of "the fruitful alliance of philology and philosophy" in Cousin's work (p. 205 below). The reconstruction of lost or neglected texts, the compiling of fresh editions of canonical works, and the issuing of new translations became prerequisites of philosophical understanding, such that erudition and reflection were to be undertaken in tandem. In this vein, from 1821 Cousin began compiling a 6-volume edition of Proclus' work, an 11-volume edition of Descartes' work, and a 13-volume translation of Plato's dialogues. He would go on to prepare editions of Abelard, Aristotle, and Maine de Biran, alongside archival manuscripts on the history of Cartesianism.[44]

3. *The Returning Hero (the late 1820s)*: By 1825, Cousin had become a famous liberal martyr. Yet, to those who happened not to have been in the right lecture room during the late 1810s, he was a cult hero without a legible philosophy: beyond his Proclus edition, all that existed in print were a series of short extracts in

---

[41] On these events and their role in Cousin's self-mythologization as a persecuted philosopher, see P. Vermeren, "Les vacances de Cousin en Allemagne: La raison du philosophe et la raison d'État," *Raison présente* 63: 77–97 / 64: 101–19.

[42] J. Barthélemy-Saint-Hilaire, *Victor Cousin: Sa vie et sa correspondance* (Paris: Hachette, 1895), vol. 1, p. 303.

[43] Cousin, *Introduction à l'histoire de la philosophie*, p. 103.

[44] On the philosophical significance of this editorial work, see Moreau's essay below, as well as F. Barancy, "Pourquoi édite-t-on les philosophes 'classiques' en France au XIXe siècle?," *Astérion* 26 (2022).

scholarly journals. It was to remedy this lack that the 34-year-old philosopher published the first edition of *Philosophical Fragments* in 1826, collecting together those previously published extracts from the early lectures with a few unpublished ones, alongside a fifty-page systematic preface that served as a manifesto, a "long profession of faith in which all the basic elements of eclecticism are expressed."[45]

Then, in January 1828, the Vicomte de Martignac formed a less repressive government which was quick to reinstate Cousin to his official teaching positions. A few months later, Cousin took to the podium in the Sorbonne and lectured to an enthusiastic, overflowing audience on the history of philosophy. As one contemporary put it, "The room could not contain the number of young people avid to either see their teacher once more or to get to know this eloquent professor."[46] Each lecture of his 1828 course was rushed separately to press to be circulated across France. Once again, Cousin's charismatic style was central: he "spoke like a high priest; his rich intonation, his mobile features, his weighty and cadenced diction ... everything he did favoured the impression made on his audience."[47]

Popularity was transformed into power following the July Revolution in 1830. As part of Guizot's inner circle during the uprising, Cousin received appointments as full Professor at the Sorbonne, Director of the École Normale, State Counsellor, controlling member of the Royal Council of Public Instruction and fellow of the Académie française. In 1832, he became a Pair de France and a fellow of the Académie des sciences morales et politiques (following his own recommendation to Guizot to reinstate this institution). Several years later Cousin was further appointed Minister of Public Education for eight months during Adolphe Thiers' second government and, more permanently, President of the philosophy *agrégation* jury. Philosophical successes during the late 1820s were translated into very visible political successes. As Jules Simon would later remark, "The 1830 Revolution which made Louis Philippe king of the French made Cousin king of the philosophers. But Louis Philippe was only a constitutional king; Cousin was an absolute king."[48]

4. *State-Philosopher (the 1830s)*: Paul Janet's remark that "Cousin did for the teaching of philosophy what Descartes had done for philosophy itself"[49] holds good for the 1830s and early 1840s above all, since this was the period when political power gave Cousin the opportunity to shape French education institutions in his own image. When Sarah Austin comes to translate one of Cousin's works in 1834, he is characterized less as a practising philosopher than as "Peer of

---

[45] B. Mélès, *Les classifications des systèmes philosophiques* (Paris: Vrin, 2016), p. 134.
[46] Editor of the *Lycée* journal, quoted in S. Nicolas, "Introduction," to V. Cousin, *De la méthode en psychologie* (Paris: L'Harmattan, 2010), p. 13.
[47] A. Marrast, quoted in Goldstein, *The Post-Revolutionary Self*, p. 155.
[48] Archive "fonds Jules Simon" 87 1P 16; cited in P. Vermeren, *Victor Cousin*, p. 176.
[49] P. Janet, *Victor Cousin et son œuvre* (Paris: Calmann-Lévy, 1885), p. 270.

France, Councillor of State, Professor of Philosophy, Member of the Institute, and of the Royal Council of Public Instruction"[50]—a politician first and a teacher of philosophy second. Likewise, Schelling worries in a letter to Cousin from 1833 whether "your political career has not taken you from science."[51]

Correspondingly, Cousin's philosophical publications of the period are increasingly just re-publications—repetitions in which the same works appear in different configurations, under different titles and with frequent textual revisions and omissions. What is "new" typically consists in prefaces, interpolated footnotes, and appendices, reinterpreting the original writings in light of new demands. Far from the experimental attitude of the 1810s and 1820s, the 1830s witness a growing defensiveness on Cousin's part—the construction of an orthodoxy in response to proliferating criticisms. Hence, Azar remarks that the 1826 Preface and the 1833 Preface to *Philosophical Fragments*—despite covering the same content—were "not written with the same pen."[52] Cousin also begins publishing a new genre of works in the 1830s: political speeches and reports, collected as various volumes of "political discourses," as well as studies on educational institutions across Western Europe. Political concerns are entangled with intellectual analysis.

5. *Retreat (the 1840s onwards)*: Times changed: by the mid-1840s, Cousin had passed from the great hope of liberal France to an unpopular representative of an unpopular regime. With the coming of the 1848 Revolution, Cousin was now a spokesman for the old world—as one contemporary noted, "The mere name of democracy never reached his ears without causing him obvious displeasure."[53] Soon after the installation of the anti-philosophical Second Empire, Cousin retired to Cannes where he remained until his death in January 1867.

While one or two major philosophical works date from this period—notably, the reworking of *On the True, the Beautiful, and the Good* into a spiritualist textbook in 1853 and the reframing of his 1829 lecture course on the history of philosophy as a *General History of Philosophy* in 1863—Cousin's most significant publications were studies of female intellectuals from the seventeenth century: Anne Geneviève de Bourbon (Madame de Longueville), Marie de Hautefort, Jacqueline Pascal, Marie de Rohan (Madame de Chevreuse), Madeleine de Scudéry, and Madeleine de Souvré (Madame de Sablé). These studies both signal a retreat from contemporary philosophical debate and, at the same time, also perhaps suggest some interest on Cousin's part in opening up the limits of philosophy through focus on a more "literary" and less obviously canonical subject matter.

---

[50] V. Cousin, *Report on the State of Public Instruction in Prussia*, trans. S. Austin (London: Effingham, 1834), title page.

[51] V. Cousin and F. W. J. Schelling, "Correspondance, 1818–1845," ed. C. Mauve and P. Vermeren, *Corpus* 18/19 (1991), p. 222.

[52] A. A. Azar, "Le cas Victor Cousin, un étrange observateur de la pensée germanique pendant le début du XIXe siècle," *Critique* 473 (1986), p. 987.

[53] A. Franck, quoted in Goldstein, *The Post-Revolutionary Self*, p. 149.

Generally, however, the later publications reveal a new rendition of eclecticism, now reduced to the mere enumeration of "all of the principal elements of the human race's eternal belief" (p. 100 below)—what Cotten calls, "a kind of catalogue of 'good doctrines.'"[54] While, as Mélès notes, Cousin was at the best of times "able to resist the temptation to argumentation," in his later works "one looks in vain for the least attempt at demonstration."[55] It is this kind of position that Félix Ravaisson criticizes as Cousin's "half-spiritualism"[56] and Taine mocks as the philosophical version of a "relaxing tepid bath."[57]

4. The Genres of Cousin's Philosophy

The prominence Cousin gives to the concept of the "fragment" is intriguing. He does not intend by it the Jena Romantic idea of the necessary incompleteness of all philosophical presentation, nor the Kierkegaardian sense of "crumbs" as Socratic resistance to systematic wholes—and certainly not the Pascalian fragment he elsewhere associates with a scepticism destructive of philosophical rationality. Rather, roughly following his understanding of Leibniz's productions, the fragment in Cousin's philosophy constitutes a "detached piece" awaiting incorporation into a larger whole. In this vein, eclecticism is to be defined as "the formation of a great whole out of all the particular pieces."[58]

Nevertheless, to write in fragments as Cousin so often did was also, in part, an admission of (temporary) failure, a deferral of the achievement of this "great whole." The very appearance of *Philosophical Fragments* revealed that the great synthetic work into which all such fragments should be subsumed had not yet been completed. Hence, Cousin was repeatedly chastised for failing to publish a comprehensive treatise, system, or compendium—even Garnier, Cousin's student and editor, speaks of his production as "entirely fragmentary, fine apercus on a large number of philosophical topics but no developed system."[59] Candidates from Cousin's oeuvre to fill this absence have sometimes been suggested by his commentators (the 1818 lectures on the true, the beautiful, and the good, the 1819–20 lectures on moral philosophy, the 1826 preface to *Philosophical Fragments*);[60] however, more often than not, the absence of *the*

---

[54] Cotten, *Autour de Victor Cousin*, p. 194.
[55] Mélès, *Classification*, pp. 162–4.
[56] F. Ravaisson, *French Philosophy in the Nineteenth Century*, ed. and trans. M. Sinclair (Oxford: Oxford University Press, 2022), p. 32.
[57] H. Taine, *Les philosophes du XIXe siècle en France* (Paris: Hachette, 1857), p. 311. See Spitzer, *The French Generation of 1820*, p. 75.
[58] Cousin, *Du Vrai, du Beau et du Bien* (1860 edn), p. 302.
[59] A. Garnier, quoted in Goldstein, *The Post-Revolutionary Self*, p. 140.
[60] Commentators have also attempted to reconstruct Cousin's system out of its "fragments"—most notably, Janet, who extracts thirteen systematic theses from the 1826 Preface to *Philosophical Fragments*: 1. "the method of observation taken as starting point"; 2. "ontology or metaphysics

work of eclecticism has been taken to be indicative of Cousin's status as philosopher manqué.[61]

Alongside the fragment, the primary genre in which Cousin worked was the lecture. His lecture courses are intended to be "general"—that is, to furnish students with a bird's-eye view of the narrative of philosophy through the presentation of as many particular instances as possible for comparison. They give outlines of the eclectic whole, in order to initiate students and lay-readers into professional philosophizing and give them practice in the eclectic art of sifting the true from the false. The fragments, on the other hand, are pieces cut out from this eclectic whole—isolated, treated in more detail, and addressed to specialists; they form Cousin's attempt "to show his working" (i.e. to provide justifications for the broad historical narratives presented in the lecture courses), as well as possessing an exemplary function—as representative of Cousin's own philosophical interests and the key foci in any eclectic assemblage. This symbiosis of the generalist (lectures) and the specialist (fragments) is important to Cousin: for instance, in his 1828 lectures, he insists, "It is my perfect conviction that one must above all and without cease mix focused studies of details with the generalization of ideas." This will ideally result, he continues, in a kind of rhythm of "decomposition" and "re-composition" in the production of histories of philosophy.[62]

In addition to the genres of the lecture and the fragment, there is also—particularly from the 1830s onwards—the genre of the preface. The 1838 edition of *Philosophical Fragments* has almost 150 pages of prefatory material preceding the fragments themselves (as well as two further prefaces included as "fragments" proper). These prefaces have an apologetic function which is clear from their autobiographical excursions (*apologiae sua vita* mimicking Descartes' *Discourse on Method*) and from their polemical intent, situating Cousin's thought in the middle of the contemporary intellectual landscape between competing doctrines. The

---

defended ... but given as a consequence of psychology"; 3. "the transition from psychology to ontology by means of the absolute principles of reason"; 4. "the theory of the three classes of facts: sensible facts, intellectual facts and voluntary facts"; 5. "the reduction of all the categories to two fundamental ones: substance and cause"; 6. "the theory of pure apperception to save the objectivity of reason"; 7. "the highest ground of things posited in the laws of thought"; 8. "the I residing in the will"; 9. "causality residing in the pure will and not solely in muscular effort"; 10. "the theory of absolute freedom"; 11. "the doctrine of the consubstantial unity of man, nature and God"; 12. "the reconciliation of philosophy and common sense in the doctrine of spontaneity"; 13. "the reconciliation of all systems—or eclecticism" (Janet, *Victor Cousin*, pp. 169–77).

[61] Counterintuitively, it is here that some of Cousin's lasting philosophical significance can be located—in his decentring of the philosopher's fundamental activity: not just the late Cousin's political transformation of philosophy into an apparatus for regulating the production of ideas, but equally his displacement of the ideal of a published system into philological erudition, on the one hand, and into the virtuosity of oral performance, on the other. See König-Pralong, *La colonie philosophique*, pp. 72–3 and C. Mauve et al., "Introduction," in V. Cousin, *Platon*, ed. C. Mauve et al. (Paris: Vrin, 2016), pp. 17–18.

[62] Cousin, *Introduction à l'histoire de la philosophie*, p. 340. See further pp. 197–8 below.

prefaces ward off criticism by instructing the reader in advance how to draw the "right"—that is, commonsensical—truths from his own writings.

Ultimately, what is most striking about Cousin's *Philosophical Fragments* is the work's success: it went through six major French editions during Cousin's lifetime (1826, 1833, 1838, 1846–7, 1855, 1865), expanding from one volume in 1826, to two in 1838, to four in 1847, and to five in 1855. It was further supplemented by ancillary and supplementary volumes on specialist subjects, such as the *New Philosophical Fragments* of 1829 on ancient philosophy, the *Scholastic Fragments*, and the *Fragments of Cartesian Philosophy*. These additional volumes were afterwards absorbed back into later editions of the primary work. In short, *Philosophical Fragments*—in all its variants—was a statement of Cousin's philosophy that was representative in its scope, widely read and often taken for a definitive presentation of his output—and for this reason, among others enumerated above, it here serves to reintroduce Anglophone readers to Cousin's philosophy.[63]

---

[63] See the "Note on Editions, Abbreviations and Translations" below for more details on *Philosophical Fragments* and our selections from it.

Note on Editions, Abbreviations, and Translations

Philosophical Fragments is less a discrete work than a depository of ever-changing "fragments." Each time Cousin published a new edition, it was born anew with different contents and a different structure, in response to the different contexts within which Cousin was philosophizing.

There were, in general, three levels of revision continually at work across the various editions of *Philosophical Fragments*. First, the text of the fragments was subject to constant alteration, resulting sometimes in substantial omissions: the 1826 Preface loses around twenty pages of text over the course of forty years, including the loss of some of its central doctrines, like that of absolute freedom.[64] Moreover, these changes are in no way indicated by Cousin in later editions—in 1833, for example, he talks of making "some corrections that are not worth the trouble to enumerate" (p. 91 below).[65] In other words, no reader would necessarily notice the variations unless they placed the different editions side by side. Secondly, this process of revision included the reordering and redistribution of texts within *Philosophical Fragments* itself as it increased in volume number: fragments that had been central in the first few editions (including the 1826 and 1833 Prefaces) were gradually marginalized to the final *Contemporary Philosophy* volume as Cousin came to stress the historical nature of his interventions. Finally, many of the fragments were replaced, migrating to other collections (often, from 1846, *First Essays in Philosophy*) or disappearing entirely, while other short works that had originally appeared elsewhere were included in their place. As Azar describes it, "In Cousin's work, the collection of 'fragments' is a kind of makeshift shelter from which texts are subsequently redistributed to other destinations judged more appropriate."[66] Ultimately, within the five volumes of fragments published in 1865 only three texts were retained from the original 1826 edition.

In order to gain some understanding of the genesis of Cousin's philosophy across this baroque publication history, the following translation provides the first ever attempt to track in detail the significant changes Cousin made to the text of

---

[64] See P. Janet, *Victor Cousin et son œuvre* (Paris: Calmann-Lévy, 1885), p. 174.

[65] Charles Secrétan comments that such disguising of the revision process is an attempt to give the instability of Cousin's development "the appearance of immutable thought." *La Philosophie de Victor Cousin* (Paris: Grassart, 1868), p. 52.

[66] A. A. Azar, "Le cas Victor Cousin, un étrange observateur de la pensée germanique pendant le début du XIXe siècle," *Critique* 473 (1986), p. 992. See further J. Simon, *Victor Cousin*, trans. M. B. Anderson and E. P. Anderson (Chicago: McClurg, 1888), p. 90.

xxiv NOTE ON EDITIONS, ABBREVIATIONS, AND TRANSLATIONS

some of his fragments between 1826 and 1865. Only through a genetic approach to Cousin's texts—through the history of their composition and revision—do they ultimately make sense. Hence, the translators' endnotes contain a list of these textual and structural revisions across editions of *Philosophical Fragments*.[67] Cousin still awaits a critical edition and, until that appears, we hope these endnotes will provide some orientation.

The endnotes therefore register the changes Cousin made to texts in each of the editions of *Philosophical Fragments*, which are referred to and catalogued according to the following abbreviations:[68]

1826	*Fr. phil. 1826*	*Fragments philosophiques* (Paris: Sautelet).
1828	*Nouv. fr. phil.*	*Nouveaux fragments philosophiques* (Paris: Pichon and Didier).
1833	*Fr. phil. 1833*	*Fragments philosophiques*, 2nd edn (Paris: Ladrange).
1838	*Fr. phil. 1838*	*Fragments philosophiques*, 3rd edn, 2 vols (Paris: Ladrange).
1840	*Fr. phil. schol.*	*Fragments philosophiques. Philosophie scholastique* (Paris: Ladrange).[69]
1840	*Fr. phil. anc.*	*Fragments philosophiques. Philosophie ancienne* (Paris: Ladrange).[70]
1845	*Fr. phil. cart.*	*Fragments de philosophie cartésienne* (Paris: Charpentier).
1847	*Fr. phil. 1847*	*Fragments philosophiques pour faire suite aux cours de l'histoire de la philosophie*, 4 vols, Œuvres de Cousin, 3rd series (Paris: Ladrange and Didier):[71] Vol. 1: *Philosophie ancienne*; Vol. 2: *Philosophie scholastique*; Vol. 3: *Philosophie moderne*; Vol. 4: *Philosophie contemporaine*.

---

[67] One exception where we do not track the changes between editions of *Philosophical Fragments* in detail concerns Cousin's practice of self-citations in footnotes, since the texts he cites are themselves constantly republished under different names with altered contents. Hence, we provide solely an indicative description of the cited passages.

[68] In this list, we include only those editions published in Paris (Cousin often released parallel Belgian editions published in Brussels). For full bibliographical details of Cousin's works, see P. Vermeren, *Victor Cousin: la jeu de la philosophie et de l'État* (Paris: L'Harmattan, 1995), pp. 359–66.

[69] This volume repeats the editorial material from the 1834 *Abélard: ouvrages inédits, pour servir à l'histoire de la philosophie scolastique*, and for that reason Cousin designates it a "second edition."

[70] This volume approximately repeats the contents of the 1828 *Nouveaux fragments philosophiques* (with a couple of alterations), and for that reason Cousin designates it a "second edition."

[71] In the preface to this edition (p. iii), Cousin explicitly designates the 1845 *Fragments de philosophie cartésienne* a further component of this series of volumes, even if it is not formally incorporated until 1855: it "is united to this series and ought to be considered as the first volume of *Philosophie moderne*."

1855–6 Fr. phil. 1855   *Fragments philosophiques*, 5 vols, *Œuvres de Cousin*, 3rd series, 2nd edn (Paris: Ladrange et Didier):
Vol. 1: *Fragments de philosophie ancienne*;
Vol. 2: *Fragments de philosophie du moyen âge*;
Vol. 3: *Fragments de philosophie cartésienne*;
Vol. 4: *Fragments de philosophie moderne*;
Vol. 5: *Fragments de philosophie contemporaine*.

1865–6 Fr. phil. 1865   *Fragments philosophiques pour servir l'histoire de la philosophie*, 5 vols, *Œuvres de Cousin*, 3rd series, 3rd edn (Paris: Durand and Didier):
Vol. 1: *Philosophie ancienne*;
Vol. 2: *Philosophie du moyen âge*;
Vol. 3: *Philosophie moderne I*;
Vol. 4: *Philosophie moderne II*;
Vol. 5: *Philosophie contemporaine*.

Cousin also uses the moniker, "fragments," when naming related volumes, most notably: *Fragments littéraires* (Paris: Didier, 1843) and *Fragments et souvenirs* (Paris: Didier, 1857).

In selecting texts for this anthology from the multiple editions and multiple volumes of *Philosophical Fragments*, we have attempted to be as representative as possible, in order to provide a global sense of the sorts of fragments that came and went from the collection. This includes representing the range of Cousin's disciplinary interests: psychology, metaphysics, ethics, philosophy of religion, aesthetics, and the history of philosophy; the range of his historical interests: Descartes, Plato, Abelard, Condillac, Leibniz; and the range of his contemporary engagements: Maine de Biran, Laromiguière, Lamennais, Royer-Collard, Reid, Kant and Fichte, Schelling and Hegel. However, the present volume is less representative of the entire span of Cousin's career, simply because fewer of Cousin's later shorter works were ever included in *Philosophical Fragments* and those that were are typically too long to fit easily within a one-volume anthology (e.g. *Souvenirs d'Allemagne*). We have, however, attempted to include a representative sample from the 1840s through, in particular, the addition of a preface on Pascal which was not strictly included within the volumes of *Philosophical Fragments* themselves. Nevertheless, our selection does still have its limits: for instance, it is regrettable that there is no suitable "fragment" detailing Cousin's interpretation of Scottish philosophy and that Cousin's commentaries on Laromiguière and Degérando are fairly inaccessible to Anglophone readers without detailed knowledge of the original works.

We have taken as the basis for our translations the earliest available publication of each text, identifying later revisions in the endnotes as described above. Footnotes in the translation denoted by asterisks and cognate symbols (*) are

Cousin's own; our translators' endnotes (which follow at the end of each piece) are indicated by Arabic numerals. In these endnotes, we have attempted to keep interpretative material to a minimum, as well as to avoid disrupting the flow by explaining well-known philosophical names or concepts.

Cousin's philosophical language is thoroughly gendered—not only in its appeal to "virtues" like virility, but in explicit comments such as his 1828 condemnation of a "cowardly spiritualism, good for children and for women, fatal to science," or the contrast he draws between his own "virile" approach and an obscure metaphysics "for children and for women."[72] As Anabelle Bonnet has pointed out, Cousin's educational reforms were no less sexist, confining women to a very meagre education; he reportedly exclaimed when challenged, "Woman, incomplete entity condemned to eternal childhood, now you aspire to philosophy! From what blindness are you suffering? You are not animated by the same spirit as man: it falls only to him to contemplate truth."[73] Accordingly, in the translations that follow, we have not attempted to disguise or dilute the gendered language, except where neutral language is particularly unobtrusive (e.g. "humankind" in place of "mankind").

Other significant translation decisions we have made include:

(a) *l'aperception*: Maine de Biran had distinguished between perception in the generic sense as "la perception" and the specific act of self-intuition as "l'aperception." Cousin, however, ignores this distinction entirely and uses "apercevoir" and "l'aperception" indiscriminately to refer to all acts of perception. Since in standard French these terms can indeed mean "to perceive" and "perception," we have translated them as such throughout. Nevertheless, Cousin is presumably occasionally (at least) drawing on the more technical, Leibnizo-Kantian sense of "apperception" employed by Maine de Biran— and this should be borne in mind.

(b) *développer*: the French *développer*—and particularly in Cousin's employment of it—possesses more of a connotation of "to express" and "to actualize" than the English equivalent, and, on a few occasions, we have employed the English "to express" to translate it, although this meaning should be born in mind more generally.

(c) *l'esprit*: As in all philosophical French, *l'esprit* possesses a semantic range that approximates to no word in English. Therefore, we translate it variously as "spirit" and "mind" depending on context.

---

[72] V. Cousin, *Cours de philosophie. Introduction à l'histoire de la philosophie*, ed. P. Vermeren (Paris: Fayard, 1991), pp. 212, 227. On these passages, see further J. Goldstein, *The Post-Revolutionary Self: Politics and Psyche in France, 1750–1850* (Cambridge, MA: Harvard University Press, 2005), p. 173. Goldstein further tracks Cousin's correspondence with his female "disciples" like Caroline Angebert (*The Post-Revolutionary Self*, pp. 174–9, 222–8).

[73] See A. Bonnet, *La Barbe ne fait pas le philosophe: les femmes et la philosophie en France (1880–1949)* (Paris: CNRS Editions, 2022), pp. 17–19.

(d) *l'étendue*: As described in our Preface above, the eclectic virtue of *l'etendue* is central to Cousin's project. We have used the term "extensity" (as in "range") to translate it, where possible, but at times (indicated in the texts below with the French original) "comprehensiveness" comes closer to Cousin's meaning.
(e) *général*: Cousin frequent use of the term "general" in place of "universal" may sometimes seem awkward but is philosophically motivated by his attempt to reconceive philosophical truth as *extensive* and *generalist*, rather than intensive. He typically reserves the adjective "universal" for describing the properties of the Kantian categories.
(f) *le moi*: As Cousin notes at the beginning of "On the Clear and the Obscure in Knowledge," much of his early work is responding in detail to Fichte, and to this extent we have retained the Fichtean resonance of "le moi" by translating it as "the I" throughout (and correlatively, "le non-moi" as "the not-I"). However, unlike Fichte (and Kant), Cousin is keen to emphasize the substantive nature of "le moi," so "the self" would have been an equally possible translation, and one which, moreover, would have emphasized Cousin's place more firmly in a French spiritualist tradition that runs through to Ricoeur's *Soi-même comme un autre*.
(g) *la sévérité*: Another eclectic virtue mentioned in the Preface above is *la severité* which Cousin often uses in a way that approximates to the English "rigour" and we have translated it as such on one or two occasions, while indicating the original French.

I
INTRODUCTIONS

Cousin and French Philosophy

Delphine Antoine-Mahut

1. Introduction: Victor Cousin, the "Politics of Philosophy" and the "New French Philosophy"

Today, Victor Cousin's work sits at a crossroads between two interpretations: a more institutional and political interpretation and a more philosophical one. The first interpretation—largely dominant since the 1970s—insists on the incontestably authoritarian and regal dimension of Cousin's activity. On the basis of his adherence to the constitutional Charter and to a politics that one might today label centre-right, this reading reconstructs his "philosophy of State," a form of spiritualist eclecticism which borrows from both British "empiricism" and German "Idealism," without necessarily understanding them and, certainly, without always admitting it; an eclecticism which is distrustful of, even hostile to the knowledge of the positive sciences, which instrumentalizes the history of philosophy and serves as the unthematizable norm for French educators and so for what François Guizot designated as "the government of minds." The second, more recent interpretation does not deny the intrinsic relations between Cousin's philosophy and his political project; however, it focuses above all on delineating the limits (what it includes and what it excludes) of this very philosophy, as well as on the reason why it was able to stimulate such passion and fill the lecture theatres of the Sorbonne during the 1820s, on why it was then progressively abandoned, even by its most fervent partisans,[1] and on why it continues to "haunt" us today, even if we cannot determine precisely how. In sum, what is now at stake in Cousin-research is understanding the ways in which this philosophy "*à la française*" that emerges from the first interpretation is articulated in the name of a demand for a "*philosophie française*" emergent from the second one.

That is, Cousin certainly claimed to be giving France a philosophy, to be founding a new French philosophy. And his contemporaries characterized his work precisely in terms of this specifically *French* project, whether they embraced it as embodying "the French spirit *par excellence*"[2] or did not (as when Jean Saphary responds to the national, even nationalist rhetoric of Cousin's writing with the wish—citing the early, more internationalist Cousin against himself— "that, in philosophy as in geometry, there would be neither French, nor Scottish, nor German").[3] The question, then, becomes what philosophical sense can be made of this Cousinian demand for a *French* philosophy, as well as its visible reception. After reconstructing Cousin's philosophical "family tree" (its living and dead ancestors),[4] I will describe the principal theses of this French philosophy "*à la Cousin*" (the primacy of the experimental method, a metaphysics of facts of consciousness, and the demand to apply it). To conclude, I will consider its effects—effects which are occasionally paradoxical—that still make Cousin relevant today.

2. The Family Tree of "French Philosophy"

For Cousin, the ambition to become the king of French philosophy is understood in terms of a need to be recognized as the king of French philosophers. These French philosophers wrote and thought in the past, of course—and so, through becoming a historian of philosophy, he intends to identify them, categorize them, and evaluate them. Nevertheless, this project to give the French a new philosophy is present in his work from its very beginnings (prior to his turn to the history of philosophy). This is a project aimed at repairing the post-revolutionary moral and political faults generated by the *Idéologues*' problematic "sensualist" metaphysics without running to the other theological extreme.[5] Moreover, at this early date the project is articulated in relation to four philosophers that Cousin immediately acknowledges as his "masters": Pierre Laromiguière, Pierre-Paul Royer Collard, Pierre Maine de Biran, and Joseph-Marie Degérando. In order to emancipate himself from their influence and ascend to the throne alone, he must therefore commit a quadruple parricide.[6]

2.1 The Initial Quadruple Parricide

Cousin's positioning in relation to these four figures, at the threshold between Ideology and spiritualism,[7] is a matter of the distinctively *French* constellation that determines his philosophical project, and what results from this constellation is a philosophical operation that filters what Cousin labels "facts of consciousness" through three successive sieves: that of sensation (Laromiguière), that of the intellect (Royer-Collard), and that of the will (Maine de Biran), so as to denounce the exclusivism of using just one of them or of placing them in a mistaken hierarchy. Degérando, the author of the vast *Comparative History of Systems of Philosophy*, can, in the wake of this operation, be reclaimed insofar as he began to overturn Ideology in the name of a genuine spiritualism and initiated a salutary and entirely French reckoning with an idealism from Germany. Each of the four potential fathers of the new "French philosophy" can thus, at the same time, be integrated into Cousin's project and superseded. Hence, Cousin summarizes:

By separating attention from sensation Laromiguière had already made one fruitful distinction. The superior good sense and virile dialectic of Royer-Collard overcame sensation by striking yet more violent blows against it: my illustrious predecessor has the honour of being the first person to introduce the wise doctrines of Scottish philosophy into France. A man [Maine de Biran] who is no longer with us and who should be known as the greatest metaphysician to have honoured France since Malebranche, achieved much without almost any knowledge of contemporary German thinking. Led by the instinct of a superior wisdom, he gradually arrived—through various metamorphoses—at a perspective which lacks only more consistency, extensity and audacity to resemble Fichte's. Far from sensation, in the depths of voluntary and free activity which constitutes all personality, Biran sought the origin of the highest ideas which today form part of consciousness. He re-established the authority of these ideas, and—in place of borrowing them from the outside and from the external world—he drew them from the I itself, so as to transport them into nature on the strength of an induction whose evident subjectivity seems a pale reflection of Fichte's subjective and personal idealism. Finally, in the second edition of the *Comparative Systems of Philosophy*, Degérando began to pay more attention to idealist theories which had until then been disdained, and was completely astonished to find in it something attractive for French philosophers. Why should I not also say that there has also emerged from the École Normale students who are today teachers and who in their lectures and their writings have increased and expanded this new philosophical movement? In sum, it is an incontestable fact that, in the face of Condillac's philosophy, a new, much more idealist philosophy has now been established.[8]

Hence, if the "new philosophical movement" that accompanied Cousin's institutional ascent is "much more idealist" than previously fashionable philosophies, it is also not strictly Cousin's own philosophy, for he believes it to be too idealist or idealist in a bad way. The problem for Cousin is that such a new "movement" postulates ontology in place of securing the means to attain it. In this sense, it risks returning to the abstruse metaphysics rightly denounced by Condillac,[9] instead of renewing it. In consequence, what Cousin is compelled to clarify is the ways in which the rediscovery of Descartes's seventeenth-century psychological innatism can restore the symbolic prestige of the experimental method, promulgated by Condillac in the wake of Bacon and Locke, so as to found a philosophy that is "equitable" (non-exclusive), non-idealist and new.

2.2 Ancestors of a "Common Blood"

Cousin searches throughout the history of modern French philosophy for the arguments and precursors capable of establishing his own modernity and establishing his own legitimacy. His treatment of Condillac and Descartes is decisive in this respect, and I begin with Condillac.

Despite his severe criticisms, Cousin recognizes that in Condillac "the metaphysician dominates."[10] What is more, he does not hesitate to present Condillac as "the only, the true French metaphysician of the eighteenth century."[11] Alongside A. R. J. Turgot—"this universal and profound mind who penetrated all human knowledge, and who wrote the best piece of metaphysics published in that century, the author of the article *Existence* [in Diderot and d'Alembert's *Encyclopédie*]"— Condillac, as a metaphysician-psychologist (and so as a philosopher), is transformed into a positive example for the French philosophical school over which Cousin claims to rule.

Cousin distinguishes two periods in Condillac's work: that of the *Essai sur l'origine des connaissances humaines* and that of the *Traité des sensations*. In the first period, in which, in a certain way, Condillac merely reproduces Locke, the most interesting point is the distinction Cousin draws between the spirit and the letter of the *Essai*. The more one progresses through the text, the more the distinction between the materials provided by sensations and the faculty working upon them (reflection) disappears. Yet, this essential activity of the mind remains present beneath the surface, and it is in this way that the first Condillac provides everything needed to found a healthy and true psychology. However, in this initial period, he already flirts dangerously with the position of the *Traité des sensations*—the turning point between the two Condillacs. Cousin emphasizes the extent to which in the *Traité* Descartes is attacked and "openly sacrificed to Locke,"[12] such that the *Traité des systèmes* then becomes a "manifesto for the school of Locke, pitting the philosophy of the eighteenth century against the philosophy of the seventeenth century."[13] This intermediate Condillac is characterized as abandoning experience and succumbing to abstraction. As a result, the Condillacian principle of "the necessity of observation and experience" can now become "our weapon turned against him," for Condillac "finally becomes himself"[14] in the *Traité des sensations*. He abuses hypotheses in the very way he had himself denounced in the *Traité des systèmes*. He dreams of a primitive human nature, because he is unable to observe the human's current nature.[15] In short, Condillac "completely ignores the spirit of experimental philosophy."[16] Reflection, with which Locke saved the activity of the soul (and finds its residue in the writing of the first Condillac), ends up being reduced to just another of the numerous transformations of the kind of sensation experienced by this fictitious and abstract subject, represented by the symbol of the statue. It is on this point Cousin goes on to contrast at length the passivity, fatality and involuntary character of sensation, on the one hand, with the activity, liberty, and voluntary character of his own position, on the other. He emphasizes that sensation itself requires an active consciousness from within the subject. Finally, the basic distinction between the spirit and the letter of Condillac's doctrine, between his "admitted method" and what he really does, culminates in a particular insistence on the disfigurations of Condillac by those who later claimed his lineage (the *Idéologues*).

By recovering a "genuine" Condillac conducive to the project of the new French philosophy, Cousin is able to identify a positive eighteenth-century French tradition—that of the "*sens intime*," of common sense and of moral sense. This tradition passes through Turgot, as mentioned above, but also through Père Buffier, Lelarge de Lignac, and even the Rousseau of the *Savoyard Vicar*.[17]

Nevertheless, it is above all Descartes who Cousin identifies, more and more exclusively, as the uncontested father of modernity. And he does so to the point of defining earlier figures in relation to him: "philosophy before Descartes" is significant solely in preparing (or blocking) the way for him, and, in this way, Abelard becomes "the Descartes of the twelfth century" (p. 240 below), etc.[18] Likewise, philosophy after Descartes would never have been what it is—and might perhaps never have existed—without him. In other words, Descartes' legacy is one of a lasting and uncontested philosophical supremacy within France:

> Descartes invented everything. He is without precursor or, at least, without model. The school he founded owes nothing to any foreign inspiration. It is a fruit of the earth, a work which, at bottom and in its form, is profoundly and exclusively French—and perhaps even more so, if I may say, than the poetry and arts of this great and incomparable epoch.
>
> Moreover, to what movements did Cartesian philosophy give rise from one end of Europe to the other! Let us mention just one aspect: it is Descartes who produced Spinoza, Leibniz, Clarke and Locke himself. (p. 252 below)

To recover the symbolic prestige of his renowned ancestor, Cousin goes so far as to link his own intellectual trajectory with that of a Descartes unjustly persecuted for defending free thinking (despite not effecting any political revolution whatsoever). Two essential moments in Cousin's biography are at stake here. On the one hand, the moment in 1828 when he returns to lecturing, after being barred for his liberal ideas: Cousin returns armed with his completely new edition of Descartes' *Œuvres complètes* in eleven volumes (1824–6) which transforms the seventeenth-century philosopher into the champion of modern psychology and free thinking. On the other hand, the moment of his 1844 speeches to the Chambre des Pairs of the national legislature: Cousin stands on the podium holding in his hands the rationalist Descartes of the proofs of the existence of God, in order to defend the necessary separation between philosophy and religion—against the theologians.[19] Some months beforehand in 1843, Cousin had recovered Père André, Malebranche's biographer, as someone who, in the eyes of his persecutors, had only one fault—his resolution "to not betray his conscience and to not abjure the Cartesian doctrine."[20] The last lines of "On the Persecution of Cartesianism" can—without any difficulty—be transposed onto Cousin himself, especially through its use of a royal metaphor:

> Vain despotism! The very rigour exercised against the new philosophy worked in its favour, because [this rigour] bestowed on all [its persecutors] an open mind and a well-trained one; and despite the efforts of Louis XIV, the Father Confessor and the Archbishop, the great persecuted [Descartes] was and remained the teacher of intellects, the spiritual sovereign of the seventeenth century, while another persecuted man, Voltaire, was soon to become the true king of the following century.[21]

What, then, is the precise philosophical content associated with Descartes' name that makes such an affiliation possible?[22]

Cousin develops an increasingly more ontological and metaphysical—and so an increasingly less empiricist—interpretation of the *cogito*. In his first lecture course,[23] succeeding Royer-Collard and having freshly defended a Latin thesis on Condillac's analytic method,[24] he shows his students the Descartes of the *cogito* both as a promise (the promise of an empirical psychology establishing the self as principle of knowledge and freedom) and as a danger (the danger of scepticism, rooted in doubt).[25] Following Cousin's editorial work on the *Œuvres complètes*, the sense of danger disappears. From now on, Descartes' name will refer to a rational psychology issuing from the enthymeme, "I think, therefore I am," articulated as "I am, I exist" in the second of the *Meditations* and then exemplarily articulated in the *Discourse on Method*, which, moreover, Cousin edits and envisages as a text independent of the three scientific essays (the *Dioptrics*, the *Geometry*, and the *Meteors*) which had for Descartes himself constituted its indissociable application.[26]

On this basis, what can we deduce from this interpretation of the history of modern French philosophy for the reconstruction of Cousin's own philosophy?

3. The Contents of a Philosophy Made for France

If Cousin did not write one treatise or essay that set down what he might consider *the* philosophy and preferred instead to publish his lecture courses and work on critical editions, this is not solely because he considered eclecticism to be primarily a resource for teaching. It is rather because of the importance he accorded to method. On the one hand, both the seventeenth and eighteenth centuries had articulated this need for methodology—and so the development of method alone is capable of bringing back together what they had pulled apart and even overthrown. On the other hand, a good method is the condition of true progress, from the metaphysical roots of philosophy to its most diverse practical applications.

What, then, is this method? And for what metaphysics and what applications does it call for?

3.1 The Primacy of the "Experimental" Method

Cousin's principal concern is to restore the epistemological prestige of the "philosophy of experience" derived from Bacon's natural philosophy, identified with analysis by Condillac and applied to the study of facts of consciousness by Reid. The great attraction of this method is its grounding on a universally shared demand for observation:

> [It] is always a matter of observation and experience. Across Europe and the world, everywhere it was the same spirit, everywhere the same method—this is the real unity of the century, since this unity is to be found within such major differences. (p. 61 below)

What is at stake, then, is demonstrating how well-directed psychological observation can lead to a kind of progress as successful as that of the post-seventeenth-century natural sciences:

> With a little bit of attention, will and practice, one will succeed in internal observation as in external observation. Though it is indeed more difficult than physics, by its nature psychology is in the end, like [physics], a science of observation, and thus it has the same right to the rank and title of genuine science.[27]

This primacy of observation turns psychology into the experimental basis of metaphysics. Psychology is defined by the observation of three sorts of facts of consciousness: sensible facts, volitional facts, and rational facts—and not just one of them; hence, its scientific value is grounded on this integrative perspective. How does Cousin argue from this psychological basis?

3.2 A Metaphysics of Facts of Consciousness: Ontology Preserved, but "Adjourned"

Cousin's principal philosophical argument is the following: if ontology cannot be presupposed by the experimental method, or if Condillac and his followers are right to affirm that "no substantial existence falls under observation" (p. 65 below), it is still the case that the salutary enlargement of observation's domain of application permits the rediscovery of ontology. Ontology is thus not so much abolished as adjourned.[28] It is by traversing the path of observation to its end that one progresses along what seems, in appearance, to be most opposed to it, but what ultimately can strengthen observation itself. What was disqualified in the new metaphysics as pertaining to hypothesis is thus found to be legitimate when treated as fact. Every fact of consciousness is, as a consequence, "both psychological and ontological" (p. 100 below).

This "transition from psychology to idealism" is described in more detail in Whistler's essay below, but the key point for present purposes is that, by this move, Cousin is not somehow erasing Condillac and his heirs from the map of French philosophy by turning back to the old metaphysics. Rather, through illuminating two laws of subjectivity (substance and causality) in observation and working on volitional facts to get at the very heart of the action of the will on itself, ontology is rediscovered without idealism. That is, the point of departure remains observation. Moreover, Cousin's focus on the link between observation and laws enables him to definitively turn the sensualist project against itself. Not only are the physical sciences not materialist (which would have constituted an argument that was both run of the mill and critically ineffective), but they are, in reality, spiritualist without knowing it. This is another way to say that they are empirical in a bad way, in contrast to which a good way is possible. The alliance of the metaphysical and physical sciences is thus achieved by a complete subordination of the latter to the former.

3.3 The Demand for Application

What Cousin finds most significant in this return to the Baconian tree of knowledge[29] and in grounding the sciences on a spiritualist metaphysics is its fruits. The demand for application found in Descartes and his "relatives" is common to all modernity. Recovered first by the *Encyclopédistes* and the *Idéologues*, this Baconian turn results in the development of method and metaphysics for the sake of morality and politics. For example, Cousin does not hesitate to assert that, on the political and moral plane of its applications,[30] Condillac's metaphysics of the sensible fact—systematized by a Helvetius nourished on the ideas of Hobbes and Spinoza—"necessarily" engendered the morality of self-interest and despotism.[31] This notion of application also includes the arts: in the tenth lecture of his popular work, *On the True, the Beautiful and the Good*, Cousin shows that "French art of the seventeenth century."[32] expresses metaphysical and moral beauty in a way that will from then on be designated under the name of classicism. Finally, the connection between politics and philosophy to which I alluded in the introduction cannot be understood without taking into account this conception of the co-ordination of the different orders of knowledge in which their practical stakes are always dominant.

4. Conclusion: Is Cousin the Forgotten King of "French Philosophy"?

In the institutional and political (in the broadest sense) domain, Cousin incontestably bequeathed to the French his "philosophy of State," his "administration" of thinking. But whether one can also affirm without question that he bequeathed to the French a way of thinking, or a philosophy, is something a number of his successors did not hesitate to contest. In 1860, Ernest Renan describes this phenomenon in terms that are both critical and clear:

> The idea did not come from anywhere else but France that a teacher [*professeur*] teaching is the State teaching, that his doctrine should be considered that of the State and that it necessarily follows that the State has the right to dictate it to him. The evident consequence of such a system is that the State—that is, in the case we are concerned with, the minister of public instruction—possesses a philosophy, a science. It is inadmissible, as a result, for the professor to lend the State his own philosophy, and if the State is responsible for all that is said by its professors [*chaires*], the administrative order will be perfected only when its departments teach, that is, distribute to their teachers ready-made course books to be regurgitated.[33]

And yet, Cousin also bequeathed to the French tools (e.g. critical editions), educational practices (e.g. the dissertation of general philosophy, specific to the French system), as well as the series of competitions necessary to be become a philosophy teacher in France (the Capes and the *agrégation*) and the curricula and objectives of philosophy programmes for all final-year classes in French *lycées* which determine the trajectories and the type of "freedoms" available to the student and the teacher. The paradox of Cousin's spiritualist eclecticism is thus to have, at the same time, bequeathed to the French both their canonical norms and the means of contesting them.

Notes

1. When he attempts to write the history of the French philosophical school Cousin sought to found, Paul Dubois describes this enthusiasm for Cousin's lectures during "the most fateful years of the century." But this is done so as to then denounce "the successive dilution of his ideas" which "led Cousin, in the editions he himself published, to efface all of their initial features, all the boldness, all the fantasies of a youthful and faithful vigour." P. Dubois, *Cousin, Jouffroy, Damiron. Souvenirs, avec une introduction par Adolphe Lair* (Paris: Perrin, 1904), p. 37.
2. To use Joseph Willm's expression from his "Essai sur la nationalité des philosophes" which prefaces Willm's own 1835 translation of Schelling's "judgment" on Cousin. Willm also qualifies the encounter between Schelling and Cousin as that between the "successor to Kant and Fichte" and the "successor to Descartes and Condillac." See S. Bernard-Granger, "Universel philosophique et particularités nationales: Willm, entre Schelling et Cousin," *Schelling Studien* 10 (2023), pp. 129–52.

3. J. Saphary, *L'École éclectique et l'école française* (Paris: Joubert, 1844), p. 17. Saphary is here citing Cousin's 1833 Preface—see pp. 96–7 below.
4. See D. Antoine-Mahut, "Is the History of Philosophy a Family Affair? The Examples of Locke and Malebranche in the Cousinian School," in M. Laerke et al. (eds), *Philosophy and Its History. New Essays on the Methods and Aims of Research in the History of Philosophy* (New York: Oxford University Press, 2013), pp. 159–77.
5. He thereby differentiates his project from other spiritualists, labeled as "theologians" and retrospectively designated as "anti-moderns" and "reactionaries" (Joseph de Maistre; Louis de Bonald; Félicité de Lammenais; Pierre-Simon Ballanche; Louis Eugène Marie Bautain).
6. The most representative references for the positions of the four "fathers" with whom Cousin is engaging are: for Royer-Collard, Cousin's *Discours prononcé à l'ouverture du cours de l'histoire de la philosophie, le 13 décembre 1815*; for Laromiguière, the commentary on the *Examen des Leçons* in *Journal des Savants* (April/October 1819/February 1821); for Biran, the two posthumous editions Cousin prepared as well as their prefaces (see pp. 215–36 below); and, for Degérando, the review of the second edition of *L'histoire comparée des systèmes de philosophie* in the *Journal des Savants*.
7. On Cousin and Maine de Biran, see D. Antoine-Mahut, "Maine de Biran's Places in French Spiritualism: Occultation, Reduction and Demarcation," in P. Maine de Biran, *Relation of the Physical and the Moral in Man*, ed. D. Meacham and J. Spadola (London: Bloomsbury, 2016), pp. 33–46; "L'éclectisme de Victor Cousin: une philosophie *française* sans *philosophie* française", in *Ad argumenta. Quaestio* 1 [2019], pp. 149–68. On Royer-Collard, see J.-P. Cotten, *Autour de Victor Cousin. Une politique de la philosophie* (Paris: Belles Lettres, 1992) and "La redécouverte de Reid par Royer-Collard: état des sources et des interprétations," in *Philosophie écossaise et philosophie française (1750–1850)*, ed. E. Arosio and M. Malherbe (Paris: Vrin, 2007), pp. 53–74. On Cousin and Scottish philosophy, see C. Etchegaray, "La réception de la philosophie écossaise chez Victor Cousin," in *Philosophie écossaise et philosophie française*, pp. 95–114, and M. Malherbe, "La réception de la philosophie écossaise chez le jeune Cousin (1815–1829)," in *Philosophie écossaise et philosophie française*, pp. 115–36. On Royer-Collard, Cousin and Théodore Jouffroy, see S. Chignola, "A Philosophy before Philosophy: Royer-Collard, Jouffroy, Cousin," *Rivista di Storia della Filosofia* 66.3 (2011), pp. 471–504. For a global presentation of Royer-Collard, see C. Doria, *Pierre-Paul Royer-Collard (1763–1845). Un philosophe entre deux révolutions* (Rennes: Presse universitaire de Rennes, 2018), pp. 119–56. On Degérando, see J.-L. Chappey et al. (eds), *J.-M. de Gérando (1772–1842). Connaître et réformer la société* (Rennes: Presse universitaire de Rennes, 2014); on his relationship to empiricism, see S. Manzo, "Historiographical Approaches on Experience and Empiricism in the Early Nineteenth Century: Degérando and Tennemann," *Perspectives on Science* 27.5 (2016), pp. 655–72; and on his comparatism, see S. Lézé, "Contrôler le territoire philosophique à coups de canon: l'éclipse de 'l'histoire comparée' de Joseph-Marie de Gérando (1772–1842) à l'orée d'une juridiction de l'incomparable," *Ad argumenta. Quaestio* 1 (2019), pp. 223–44. On Laromiguière, see P. Brouillet, "Condillac Restored: The Paradox of Attention in Pierre Laromiguière's *Lessons on Philosophy* (1815)," in D. Antoine-Mahut and A. Waldow (eds), *Condillac and His Reception* (London: Routledge, forthcoming) and A. Prosper, *Laromiguière et son école. Étude biographique avec quatre portraits* (Paris: Belles Lettres, 1929).
8. See V. Cousin, *Philosophie de Locke*, 4th edn (Paris: Didier, 1861).
9. Condillac distinguishes "two sorts of metaphysics"—one with the ambition "to pierce all the mysteries; the nature [and] the essence of beings, the most hidden causes," and the other which "knows how to contain itself within the limits traced for it." É. Bonnot de Condillac, *Essai sur l'origine des connaissances humaines*, ed. J.-C. Pariente and M. Pécharman (Paris: Vrin, 2014), pp. 59–60.
10. Cousin, *Philosophie de Locke*, p. 29. For a description of the decisive and complex role attributed to the figure of Condillac in the attempts to found a "French school" of philosophy in the first half of the nineteenth century, see D. Antoine-Mahut, "'The Only, the True French Metaphysician of the Eighteenth Century': Condillac, Cousin and the 'French School,'" in *Condillac and His Reception*. On Cousin's criticisms of Condillac, see also Rey's essay below.
11. V. Cousin, *Philosophie sensualiste au XVIIIe siècle*, 5th edn (Paris: Didier, 1866), pp. 47–8.
12. Cousin, *Philosophie sensualiste*, p. 65.
13. Cousin, *Philosophie sensualiste*, p. 67.
14. Cousin, *Philosophie sensualiste*, p. 69.
15. Cousin, *Philosophie sensualiste*, p. 73. Royer Collard is the source of the attribution to Condillac of a form of idealism, the principle of which was supposedly posited by Descartes.
16. Cousin, *Philosophie sensualiste*, p. 51.
17. For an analysis of Cousin's work on Buffier, see L. Rouquayrol "Un livre 'utile en ce moment': l'édition de Buffier comme pratique idéologique au XIXe siècle," *Astérion* 26 (2022).

18. On Cousin and the Renaissance, see D. Couzinet and M. Meliadò (eds), *L'institution philosophique française et la Renaissance. L'époque de Victor Cousin* (Leiden: Brill, 2022).
19. From this perspective, his Cartesian policing of the philosophy/theology boundary is radical: "The philosophy which came before Descartes was theology. Descartes' philosophy is the separation of philosophy and theology; it is, so to speak, the introduction of philosophy onto the world stage under its proper name." V. Cousin, *Cours de l'histoire de la philosophie. Introduction à l'histoire de la philosophie*, rev. edn (Paris: Pichon et Didier, 1841), p. 405.
20. Père André, *Œuvres philosophiques*, ed. V. Cousin (Paris: Adolphe Delahays, 1843), p. xcviii.
21. Jean-Pierre Cotten was the first to speak of "the politics of the use of Cartesianism in Cousin" (see "La philosophie écossaise en France avant Victor Cousin. Victor Cousin avant sa rencontre avec les Ecossais," in *Victor Cousin. Les idéologues et les Ecossais* [Paris, PENS, 1985], p. 133).
22. On Cousin's Descartes, see further D. Antoine-Mahut, *L'autorité d'un canon philosophique. Le cas Descartes* (Paris: Vrin, 2021), pp. 261–314; "Figures de Descartes dans l'historiographie française au XIXe siècle," *XVIIe Siècle* 26.3 (2022), pp. 485–94; "Philosophizing with a Historiographical Figure. Descartes in Degérando's *Comparative History* (1804 and 1847)," *British Journal for the History of Philosophy* 28.3 (2020), pp. 533–52; and "Bien reçu? Trois éditions de Descartes au XIXe siècle en France," in T. Roger and S. Zékian (eds), *Accuser réception*, fabula.org (2020).
23. On this young Cousin full of promises, filling the lecture rooms of the Sorbonne, see Ragghianti's and Vermeren's introduction to V. Cousin, *Philosophie morale (1819–20)* (Paris: Classiques Garnier, 2019), pp. 5–57.
24. V. Cousin, *Dissertatio philosophica de methodo sive de analysi, quam ad publicam disceptationem proponit, ad doctoris gradum promovendus. Victor Cousin, Scolae Normalis Alumnus, in Facultate Litterarum jam Licenciatus* (Paris: Imprimerie de Fain, 1814).
25. In the 1855 edition of his 1815 "Opening Lecture," Cousin makes explicit his own development in a note: "These views on Descartes' sceptical role in modern philosophy are borrowed from Reid and from Royer-Collard. They were abandoned and disavowed by me the very same year at the end of the lectures, as we can see ... in the programme of the lecture course on the question of personal existence, and in the first fragment on Descartes, where the true meaning of the Cartesian enthymeme, 'I think, therefore I am' is reestablished and defended." V. Cousin, *Premiers essais de philosophie*, 3rd edn (Paris: Librairie Nouvelle, 1855), pp. 41–2. See further pp. 144–9 below.
26. Eugène Lerminier's words—which borrow a citation first attributed to Théodore Jouffroy when explaining the impact of Cousin's Descartes following the publication of the *Œuvres complètes*—are revealing: "The *Discourse on Method* is the preface to modern philosophy; the *Meditations* is its first chapter." "Du cartésianisme et de l'éclectisme," *Revue des deux Mondes* 4 (1843), p. 929.
27. Cousin, *Philosophie de Locke*, p. 82.
28. On this point, see P.-F. Moreau, "'Ajourner l'ontologie'. Le cartésianisme relu par Victor Cousin," in *Qu'est-ce qu'être cartésien?*, ed. D. Kolesnik-Antoine (Antoine-Mahut) (Lyon: ENS Editions, 2013), pp. 521–30.
29. It is a return to the Baconian tree of knowledge, but also an inversion of it, since the tree now has metaphysics at its root.
30. On the Condillacian method of analysis as a political instrument of the French Revolution, see W. R. Albury, "The Order of Ideas: Condillac's Method of Analysis as a Political Instrument in the French Revolution," in *The Politics and Rhetoric of Scientific Method*, ed. J. A. Schuster and R. R. Yeo (Dordrecht: Reidle Publishing, 1986), pp. 203–25.
31. Cousin, *Philosophie morale*, p. 31.
32. By this phrase, Cousin includes: Pierre Corneille, Jean Racine, Molière, Jean de la Fontaine, and Nicolas Boileau in poetry; Jean-François Lesueur, Nicolas Poussin, Claude Gellée le Lorrain, and Philippe de Champaigne in painting; Jacques Sarrazin, Michel and François Anguier, François Girardon, and Pierre Puget in sculpture and engraving; and also André Le Nôtre in architecture.
33. E. Renan, "De la métaphysique et de son avenir," *Revue des Deux Mondes* 25, 2nd series 2 (1860), pp. 365–92.

Cousin and the Politics of Philosophy

Félix Barancy and Sarah Bernard-Granger

The idea of a philosophy put at the service of a political project—a "politics of philosophy" in a generic sense—has haunted philosophical discourse since May '68, as well as since the most recent attempt at the professionalization of philosophy departments.[1] And, in many ways, Victor Cousin's work appears to be an archetype of this "politics of philosophy."[2] However, following a suggestion by Lucie Rey,[3] we wish to argue in this introductory essay that things are not quite that simple in Cousin's work. That is, we want to interrogate the relationship between philosophy and politics in Cousin and especially the relationships between Cousin's theoretical discourse and his political action. If the idea of a "politics of philosophy" is generally understood as the exploitation of the latter by the former, we should also be able to turn the question around: what, in Cousin's politics, is philosophical? Our study of this intertwining of politics and philosophy will follow three lines of inquiry: the effects that Cousin's formal political roles had on philosophy as an institution and as a school discipline, his desire to produce a *French* philosophy, and the conflict that set him against the Catholic clergy in this undertaking.

1. The Effects of Cousin's Political Roles

Cousin is a unique figure in the French history of philosophical institutions: he was granted full political and administrative powers in matters of public education during the July Monarchy (1830–48). Such a dominant position enabled him to reform philosophical education and, more broadly, the discipline of philosophy in France in ways that accorded with his own theoretical views. To this extent, he takes on the role of a kind of philosopher-king who does not just have a responsibility to "know for himself" but also to know "for others" through his entanglement with the life of the State, as Cousin writes in his commentary on Plato's *Laws*.[4]

1.1 Cousin as Professor and His Early Disciples

Cousin began his career as a teacher: after distinguishing himself at the lycée Charlemagne, he enrolled at the École Normale at the age of eighteen. It was customary at the time for students of the École Normale to teach as well as learn, and Cousin began by assisting the Professor of Greek, and then, from 1813, the Professor of the History of Philosophy, Pierre-Paul Royer-Collard. It was at this early moment that he also attracted his first disciples: Paul Dubois, Philibert Damiron, and Théodore Jouffroy. Alongside them (and sometimes via them), he would go on to train a whole generation of French intellectuals. His role was first and foremost that of a *"passeur"* ("broker"): inexperienced in philosophy himself (since he had not taken any philosophy courses at school), he began by disseminating the philosophy of his own teachers to his public, popularizing interpretations of Scottish and German philosophers, in a spirit of shared emulation. As his biographer and follower, Jules Simon, put it, his "students" were also his "classmates."[5] But, as early as 1818, Cousin would go on to distance himself from Royer-Collard, and lecture on topics he was more personally invested in. All this occurred, however, without full institutional recognition: without a chair, he worked under the auspices of his teachers at the École Normale, until, in 1821, these teachers fell out of favour and the school was closed. Officially suspended, Cousin nevertheless continued teaching clandestinely from his Paris apartment.

It is thus, in part, precisely because of his lack of real institutional recognition at the beginning of his career that Cousin was able to establish a personal and intimate bond with his students. What is more, it also allowed him to identify with the figure of the "persecuted philosopher" in his early work,[6] which, in turn, gave his classes the aura of political resistance, and, when he returns to the lecture theatre after a ministerial reshuffle in 1828, his courses attracted a large public. His return is triumphant, but short-lived, as the revolution of July 1830 takes Cousin away from teaching post and marks the end of his teaching career.

1.2 Reforms of the Education System

The decade that followed the 1830 July Revolution put Cousin in a position to test his philosophical framework in reality. Indeed, he left the Sorbonne not because of a dismissal, but a promotion: Cousin was appointed to the Royal Council for Public Instruction—a commission that reported to the Ministry of Public Instruction but actually functioned in almost complete independence. Under the July Monarchy, this Council exercised the real administrative and political power in the field of education.[7] And within this Council, Cousin took all the decisions on the faculties of letters and the École Normale (and even beyond). As Simon noted, "he used to meddle in everything."[8] His work focused primarily on the form and content of philosophical teaching in the lycées, but he also, more generally, organized how future citizens were to be educated according to a systematic framework in which all elements were to be controlled by the State, from the education of young children to the recruitment of teachers.

Among the most significant measures are those that transform the *agrégation* from merely a recruitment competition for secondary school teachers into a prestigious and very demanding examination which permitted those who passed it—the *agrégés*—to work in higher education too. In addition, Cousin reformed the *baccalauréat* by introducing a series of written tests (instead of short oral ones) and standardized the curriculum on a national scale. Finally, he drew up civil regulations on primary education—something which had previously been left in the hands of the Church.

1.3 Cousin and His "Regiment"

Cousin's work for the government was, however, just the tip of the iceberg. The most striking aspect of his work—at least in the eyes of his contemporaries—was his activity directing philosophical education in various institutions: as president of the jury of the philosophy *agrégation* from 1830 to 1850; as director of the École Normale from 1835 to 1840; as a decisive voice on the Royal Council for Public Instruction, which ruled on promotions and transfers between institutions; and as an influential member of the Académie des sciences morales et politiques onto which Cousin ensured his protégés and allies were also elected. These positions gave Cousin the ability to rule over philosophical education as over a "regiment," to quote the military metaphor used by Simon[9]—for example, Cousin sat on all doctoral defences, often having previously imposed the subject of the thesis on the candidate; he also personally met all *agrégation* candidates, managed the appointments of teachers and even, at the Académie and Royal Council, granted pensions. And it should be emphasized that, without a post in a lycée or a seat at the Académie, it was very difficult, if not impossible, for a philosopher to make a living.

However, Cousin did not only possess the power to make careers; he also had the power to break them, when he felt anyone strayed too far from the official position. One of his very first official acts on joining the Royal Council was to commission a series of reports on the teaching of philosophy in the Parisian lycées, in order, in part, to keep close watch over his regiment. Hence, Simon writes to Damiron:

> If Cousin were only my former teacher, and if he allowed me to write to him, it would be a real pleasure for me, whenever I did so. But, when writing to him, one can hardly forget that he is the leader and autocrat of the philosophy teachers [...].[10]

Nevertheless, Simon is keen to reassure Damiron (as Cousin's right-hand man) that he remains loyal to their shared master: "I will follow the tradition of the École [Normale] in my teaching, and will try not to depart from it in any way."

2. The Regulation of Philosophical Practice

Cousin's control over philosophical institutions might have consigned his influence to something ephemeral, for, in 1851, the advent of the authoritarian Second Empire, which was hostile to philosophy, left him with no other function than member of the Académie. And yet, he still succeeded in reshaping the way philosophy has been practised in France—both in its form and in its content—for far longer than his moment of institutional power might suggest.

2.1 The Pedagogies of Eclecticism

When Cousin took on responsibility for public education in France, he inherited a system that had not yet been organized from the perspective of either the recruitment and training of teachers or curriculum and teaching practices. From his position on the Royal Council, Cousin strove to reform the latter by instituting two exercises—considered the foundation of French teaching practice and still in use today: the *dissertation* and the *explication de texte* (although these names were not fully fixed until after the 1880s).[11]

Both are grounded in Cousin's eclecticism. Their underlying philosophical principle is the following: empirical study shows that the history of philosophy is nothing but the cyclical clash of recurrent philosophical "systems," associated with "fundamental ideas" of human reason.[12] What Cousin thus proposed to do in the two "topical exercises" of the *dissertation* and the *explication de texte* is to acknowledge this repetition and consequently refocus philosophical study around the identification of "what is true in each of these systems," requisite for the "compos[ition of] a philosophy superior to all systems, which governs them all by dominating them all, which is no longer this or that philosophy, but philosophy itself in its essence and unity" (p. 200 below). On this basis, philosophy essentially becomes a *history* of philosophy, and its scientific character depends on an objective relation to the past. In other words, Cousin's eclectic methodology has direct pedagogical implications. Since philosophy is identified with the history of philosophy, there is nothing more to do in a philosophy class than study the philosophers of the past: "it is not about making philosophy, but observing it."[13] And, since all past philosophies contain a portion of "the truth," and since the philosophy-student is tasked with extracting these "true" elements from past systems, then this results in a marginalization of the *rédaction*, which had previously been dominant (as an exercise in which students reproduces the lecture of their teacher philosophizing in front of them) and a parallel promotion of the *composition*, which consists in combining the ideas of different authors to generate a synthetic response to transhistorical questions.

Correlate to this restructuring of pedagogic forms, Cousin effectuates several reforms that promote the construction of lessons around past authors elevated to the status of philosophical *authorities*. The "true rule of philosophical study," he writes, is that of "imposing authorities." Moreover, the textbook, he adds, should be replaced by "a choice of monuments that science and religion enshrined in their most beautiful memories": these will ensure that teaching "always remains irreproachable, without being any less free or comprehensive."[14]

2.2 Canon-Formation

Cousin also undertakes to reform the very content of what is taught in philosophy classes in France by forming what has come to be called the "canon"—that is, the *problems*, *authors* and *texts* that are used to frame its activity.

In 1832, Cousin wrote the first philosophy program for the *baccalauréat*, which is translated in the Appendix to this volume.[15] Although he largely takes inspiration from the *questions* written by his predecessor, Denis Frayssinous, Cousin breaks with him on several fronts. The first is by establishing a mandatory order within the syllabus: the philosophy teacher is no longer free to begin with the part that seems most appropriate to them, but must—after a brief "introduction"— have students study "psychology." This is, once again, the pedagogical expression of eclecticism's principles, where the study of the "facts of consciousness" is considered "the condition and the vestibule of philosophy" (p. 64 below). In this vein, the first lesson from this psychology course is even intended to demonstrate the "necessity of beginning the study of philosophy with psychology." In addition, Cousin swaps around the lessons on morality and theodicy, so that the latter is now to be understood as a consequence of the former. In other words, religion appears as a part of morality, and not the other way round. Finally, Cousin adds a lesson on "the history of philosophy" as a conclusion.

Alongside this work on the set problems of a philosophy curriculum, Cousin set out to establish a canon of authors whose texts, when read in class, would provide solutions to these problems.[16] This is also translated in the Appendix to this volume. His choices are again motivated by the spiritualist imperatives of his philosophy: he removes from the previous list all philosophers too close to "sensualism" (Bonnet, Condillac) and to "scepticism" (Pascal) and replaces them with allies from the tradition (Buffier, Reid, Ferguson, Bossuet). In a circular sent to philosophy teachers, Cousin explains that his reform is built on the progress philosophical knowledge has undergone over the last few centuries: it results in a demand for the teaching of philosophy to become universal in scope. Nevertheless, it is clear that the prevalence of French authors on this list suggests something different—a connection to the project of constructing a *French philosophy*.

3. The Construction of a *French Philosophy*

At the beginning of the nineteenth century, Europe no longer possessed any more philosophical unity than it did political unity. It is in this context of political, institutional, and spiritual instability that the need to create a new *French philosophy* was felt. Indeed, as early as 1815, when Cousin gives his first lectures at the Sorbonne, he argues that European philosophy is at a philosophical impasse, and so requires a new French philosophy that can restore the nation's spiritual and moral unity and impose itself on the European philosophical scene. Hence, Cousin's project of re-founding philosophy in France exceeds a strictly national framework, so as to coincide with a framework in which *French* philosophy is always *also* the only universal philosophy. It is for this reason Cousin presents his eclectic philosophy as a historical necessity (and this, in turn, legitimates both his own political position of power and the newly instituted constitutional monarchy in general).

3.1 Eclecticism as Philosophical Necessity

According to Cousin, particular and exclusive philosophical systems that mutually "destroy each other" (p. 200 below) proliferated in eighteenth-century Europe, making philosophy's universalist ambitions impossible.[17] French eclecticism is thus understood as a philosophically necessary response to this state of affairs imposed by the latent universalist character of philosophy, which risks extinction in the struggle between particular systems. Indeed, for Cousin, the nineteenth century began with Europe divided into three major philosophical schools, each exclusive of the other: one resulting from Locke's "sensualism" which was brought to completion by Condillac in France; a second resulting from Reid's philosophy of common sense in Scotland; and a third resulting from Kant's critical philosophy and brought to completion in Fichte's subjective idealism in Germany. These schools are, however, "limited and incomplete in [themselves]" (p. 157 below), because they consider philosophy from a particular point of view which makes no claim to universality. "After Kant's subjective idealism, Locke's empiricism and sensualism developed and exploited as far as possible," Cousin sees "no other" possibility "than the union of these two systems in the centre of a vast and powerful eclecticism."[18] Although a specifically *French* philosophy, eclecticism is nonetheless conceived as necessary to save the universality of philosophy from European fragmentation. It is on this basis that Cousin presents himself as "the legislator of philosophy" (p. 133 below), reconciling and unifying opposed intellectual camps. Thus, to save the philosophical requirement for universality, philosophy has to be unified in French eclecticism which then imposes itself as a philosophical, historical, and political necessity.

3.2 Eclecticism as Historical Necessity

Cousin considers philosophy as the fullest expression of society's spiritual and political state: after industry, politics, and art, it is in philosophy that "the complete development of thought"[19] is embodied. Hence, he continues, eclecticism is also the result of European social and political history: it is "the necessary philosophy of the century" because "it is the only one which conforms to its needs and spirit."[20] Hence, eclecticism emerges "necessarily out of the general movement of society across Europe, and especially in France," where all "is mixed, complex, blended," where "all contraries live and live very well together."[21] More precisely, eclecticism arises as a historical need in the wake of the late eighteenth-century "fight between the old society and the new society," which "is fundamentally nothing but the fight between absolute monarchies and democracy."[22] Out of this struggle emerged constitutional monarchy, embodied in the constitutional Charter of 1814. Eclecticism, which "has its necessary foundation in the present state of society in Europe"[23], is intended to parallel the success of this Charter on the philosophical level.[24]

For Cousin, eclecticism is necessitated historically by the spiritual state of the European nineteenth century and the function of constitutional monarchy in post-revolutionary France.

3.3 Politics Justified by Philosophy

The presentation of eclecticism as the necessary philosophy of the century is based on European political and philosophical history; however, it also allows Cousin to justify the French political system as the best political system. Like eclecticism in philosophy, constitutional monarchy is the best form of government, "the one that best assures freedom" (p. 250 below). Eclecticism has the additional function, therefore, of providing a theoretical justification for Cousin's own liberal political position: to understand eclecticism as a historical and philosophical necessity is at the same time to understand constitutional monarchy as a political necessity.

That is to say, by preserving "on the one hand an element of the old regime, and on the other hand an element of revolutionary democracy,"[25] the Charter of 1814 "contains all the opposed elements melted in a more or less perfect harmony," and it is, from this perspective, "a true eclecticism."[26] It grounds "the sole true government for all civilized peoples" since 1789 (p. 250 below).

Cousin justifies French politics philosophically by eclecticism. The history of philosophy, which necessarily leads to eclecticism, makes it possible to justify postrevolutionary French politics—and, at the same time, this political situation attests to the historical necessity of eclecticism. Eclecticism is thus not only a philosophical and pedagogical method, but a way of positioning oneself on both the national and international political stage.

4. The Secularization of Philosophy

Cousin's eclectic project can further be understood as a philosophical attempt to establish a secular jurisdiction over "the universal." That is, Cousin conceives a universal scientific method on the basis of observing the facts of consciousness, rather than the data of Christian Revelation, and, in so doing, he wages a twofold polemic: with the "sensualists," on the one hand, and with the Catholic clergy, on the other.

4.1 Eclecticism as Metaphysical Project

When Cousin takes on the task of reforming the university system, he finds it in a state of "ruin" brought about by the confrontation of contradictory systems, particularly the conflict between German subjective idealism and French antimetaphysical materialism, with the consequence that philosophers have become unable to produce an ontological discourse on metaphysical objects such as the nature of God. Eclecticism as a conciliatory project aims "to return metaphysics to France—a metaphysics so discredited by eighteenth-century philosophy"[27] as Paul Janet puts it—and, to do so, not by returning to the "philosophy of the clergy," but by developing a *new French philosophy*. Here, again, the aim is to find a middle ground between the atheism of the materialists and the dogmatism of the Catholics. This new philosophy is thus conceived as *independent* of Catholic dogma but still *compatible* with Christianity—that is, a rational theology grounded on eclectic psychological method and inheritor of Cartesianism through its "separation of philosophy and theology."[28]

Cousin's project is therefore presented as a "conciliation" between a Catholic faith and a reason understood as independent from each other. It implies that faith is liberated from any philosophical ground and philosophy is, in turn, emancipated from theology. It is in this sense that the Cousinian project can be understood as a secularization of philosophy, despite its declared wish to preserve a "State religion."[29]

Moreover, the basis for this secularization project is to be found in an ambiguity that exists in the Constitutional Charter of 1814, renewed in 1830. Both versions of the Charter make the double of affirmation of, on the one hand, the defence of individual liberties, notably religious freedom (art. 5), and, on the other hand, a national religion defined as Roman Catholic in 1814 and then Christian in 1830. Noticeably, it is on this basis that Cousin stands up for the independence of philosophy teachers:

> University professors of philosophy do not teach religion; they have no right to; for they do not speak in the name of God; they speak in the name of reason. They should, rather, teach a philosophy which, so as not to betray reason itself, society, and the state, should contain nothing which is opposed to religion. (p. 247 below)

In concrete terms, this means that, for Cousin, "religion" is reduced to a set of moral precepts that should not be contradicted, but rather confirmed by good philosophy. It also ensures that the teaching of religion retains a privileged position in primary education—that is, during that period when children are initiated into morality without yet being able to access philosophy.

4.2 Between Metaphysics and Politics: Pantheism

Far from actually bringing about a "conciliation" of philosophy and theology, Cousin's eclectic project found itself at the origin of a vast controversy that shook the French intellectual world of the nineteenth century repeatedly and in which political and philosophical stakes are mixed—the pantheism controversy. Cousin came to be accused of pantheism on the basis of the argument that any rationalism which affirms one unique substance necessarily results in pantheism. Such a philosophy would conflict with church doctrine, from the true conception of God, and from a robust moral system: "If All is One, there is neither good nor evil."[30]

The first attacks on this pantheistic rationalism were formulated by Félicité de Lamennais, but then become more systematic from 1833 onwards under the impetus of the Abbé Bautain. 1833 marked the promulgation of the Guizot law (28 June 1833), which was the result of Cousin's work on the best form of primary education and which also positioned the State as guarantor of teachers' morality through the issuing of certificates of good character and the control of official textbooks.

This was the context behind the attempt by Cousin's critics among the Catholic clergy to reduce eclecticism to a morally unacceptable pantheism and symptomatic of the "illness of the century,"[31] in danger of spreading among the young. Pantheism thus becomes a tool to denounce the "monopoly" of both Cousin and the State over education. Finally, the accusation of pantheism justifies for these critics a return to the ecclesiastical control of education—a pre-revolutionary structure in which the Church is recognized as the only institution capable (in opposition to the "particularism" of the eclectics) of reaching the universal. Théodore Combalot, for example, writes:

> The Church has a philosophy. Only she determines by indisputable and positively taught dogmas what are, in the present state of man, the bases of reason, what is the principle of our knowledge, the rule of our judgments, and the *criterium* of truth.[32]

Cousin's critics therefore aim to denigrate as pantheist and atheist any rational metaphysics not grounded in Catholic dogmas. Nevertheless, during the late 1830s and early 1840s, Cousin did not cede any ground, but strove instead to establish his secularized French philosophy capable of doing ontology and based on Cartesian-psychological method. His project of secularizing philosophy in the form of a rational theology thus forms an inextricable part of a more general political project of secularizing the education system.

5. Conclusion

Cousin entangles politics and philosophy in a singular fashion: his "politics of philosophy" is based on spiritualist eclecticism as a philosophy of politics. That is, in addition to a philosophical system that makes metaphysical, universal claims, Cousin's eclecticism (particularly as *the* new French philosophy) allows him to justify both his political and pedagogical projects, for which it provides both model and method. It must therefore be understood as much as an ambition to construct a *French* philosophy that endows the French nation with a spiritual identity as an ambition to make a French *philosophy* that safeguards the universality and autonomy of philosophy as a science.

Notes

1. See K. Ross, *May '68 and Its Afterlives* (Chicago: Chicago University Press, 2004); P. Vermeren, "Venir après l'histoire de la philosophie, la *Reforma universitaria* de 1918 et Mai 68?," *Le Télémaque* 54.2 (2018), pp. 37–42.
2. J. Goldstein, *The Post-Revolutionary Self. Politics and Psyche in France, 1750–1850* (Cambridge, MA: Harvard University Press, 2005). See, more generally, J.-P. Cotten, *Autour de Victor Cousin: une politique de la philosophie* (Paris: Les Belles Lettres, 1992); P. Vermeren, *Victor Cousin, le jeu de la philosophie et de l'État* (Paris: L'Harmattan, 1995).
3. L. Rey, "Victor Cousin et l'instrumentalisation de l'histoire de la philosophie," *Le Télémaque* 54.2 (2018), p. 43.
4. V. Cousin, "Argument philosophique," in *Œuvres de Platon*, trans. V. Cousin, vol. 7: *Les Lois* (Paris: Pichon et Didier, 1831), p. cxxi.
5. J. Simon, *Victor Cousin* (Paris: Hachette, 1887), p. 13.

6. See Cousin's *Frag. ph. cart.* generally, as well as his essay; "De la persécution du cartésianisme en France," in *Fr. phil. 1833*, pp. 174–206.
7. See P. Gerbod, "L'administration de l'instruction publique, 1815–1870," in *Histoire de l'administration de l'enseignement en France, 1789–1981*, ed. Pierre Bousquet et al. (Geneva: Droz, 1983), pp. 19–36.
8. Simon, *Victor Cousin*, p. 105.
9. Simon, *Victor Cousin*, pp. 77, 118.
10. Letter from Jules Simon to Philibert Damiron, 23 December 1836 (Paris, Bibliothèque de la Sorbonne, MS 2665, f. 15).
11. See B. Poucet, "De la rédaction à la dissertation. Évolution de l'enseignement de la philosophie dans l'enseignement secondaire en France dans la seconde moitié du XIXe siècle," *Histoire de l'éducation* 89 (2001), pp. 95–120.
12. V. Cousin, *Introduction à l'histoire de la philosophie* (Paris: Pichon et Didier, 1828), lecture IV.
13. V. Cousin, *Cours de l'histoire de la philosophie. Histoire de la philosophie du XVIIIe siècle* (Paris: Pichon et Didier, 1829), vol. 2, p. 29.
14. V. Cousin, "Circulaire relative à la liste des livres classiques adressée aux recteurs d'académie," *Bulletin universitaire de l'instruction publique* 11.34 (1842), p. 121. This circular was co-written with the Minister of Public Instruction, Abel Villemain.
15. V. Cousin, "Questions de philosophie sur lesquelles seront interrogés les aspirants au grade de bachelier ès-lettres," *Bulletin universitaire de l'instruction publique* 3.47 (1832), pp. 78–84.
16. V. Cousin, "Catalogue des ouvrages qui seront employés pour l'enseignement dans les collèges […] pendant l'année 1842-1843," *Bulletin universitaire de l'instruction publique* 11.31 (1842), pp. 80–1. This catalogue remained unchanged until 1851.
17. On this point, see especially G. Piaia and R. Pozzo (eds), *Identità nazionale e valori universali nella moderne storiografica filosofica* (Padua: CLEUP, 2008); S. Bernard-Granger, "Universel philosophique et particularités nationales: Willm, entre Schelling et Cousin," *Schelling-Studien* 10 (2023), pp. 129–51.
18. Cousin, *Introduction à l'histoire de la philosophie*, lecture XIII, p. 13.
19. Cousin, *Introduction à l'histoire de la philosophie*, lecture I, p. 25.
20. Cousin, *Introduction à l'histoire de la philosophie*, lecture I, p. 43.
21. Cousin, *Introduction à l'histoire de la philosophie*, lecture XIII, pp. 42–3.
22. Cousin, *Introduction à l'histoire de la philosophie*, lecture XIII, p. 36.
23. Cousin, *Introduction à l'histoire de la philosophie*, lecture XIII, p. 30.
24. See Rey's essay, Chapter 4 below.
25. Cousin, *Introduction à l'histoire de la philosophie*, lecture XIII, pp. 39–40.
26. Cousin, *Introduction à l'histoire de la philosophie*, lecture XIII, p. 42.
27. P. Janet, *Victor Cousin et son œuvre* (Paris: Calmann Lévy, 1885), p. 82.
28. Cousin, *Introduction à l'histoire de la philosophie*, lecture XIII, p. 9.
29. Cousin, *Introduction à l'histoire de la philosophie*, lecture XIII, p. 40.
30. L. Bautain, *Philosophie du Christianisme* (Paris/Strasbourg: Dérivaux/Février, 1835), vol. 2, p. 166.
31. See Bautain, *Philosophie du Christianisme*, p. 148.
32. T. Combalot, *Mémoire adressé aux évêques de France et aux pères de famille sur la guerre faite à l'Église et à la société par le monopole universitaire* (Paris: Sirou, 1843), p. 16.

Cousin and the History of Philosophy

Pierre-François Moreau

Before Victor Cousin, French philosophers paid little attention to the history of philosophy, or only occasionally—and, even then, often solely to deny it. Or, more precisely, they were interested in history in different ways: they might polemicize against a predecessor or an adversary; they might claim a spiritual precursor or denounce the resurgence of a current of ideas which seemed to them to have erred (usually in order to refute their opponent's arguments); they might also use their ancient and modern readings as a repertoire of arguments. But all this tended to isolate ideas, not to trace the continuity or different steps of a history. In short, the history of philosophy was at most a setting; it did not appear as an autonomous object with its own laws and consistency. A sure sign of this absence of history is to be found in the publications of the early modern period: neither Descartes nor Rousseau seemed to feel the need to publish or translate the texts of their predecessors. Those who did were more likely to be disciples, scholars, or epigones—or else it was a young philosopher's first production, such as Diderot's adaptation of Shaftesbury. This contrasts with the situation in Germany, where, already in the eighteenth century, there had arisen a clear historiographical consciousness, as evidenced, for example, by the work of J. J. Brucker.[1] In France, works were published such as that of André-François Boureau-Deslandes,[2] or the articles of the *Encyclopédie* (which often content themselves with translating—sometimes modifying—chapters of Brucker's work), but they had no immediate impact on the works of philosophers. Thus, philosophy in France before 1789 seems to have been done without any internal relationship to its own history: even those who wrote this history did not conceive of it as itself constituting philosophical reflection.

Everything changed between the beginning and the middle of the nineteenth century, and it is the name of Victor Cousin which is primarily associated with this change. It now goes without saying in France, at least, that, in order to be a philosopher, one must be a historian of philosophy. For reasons related to university politics, but with effects and implications that went far beyond that institution, the history of philosophy was integrated within philosophy itself. Henceforth, philosophy appeared to be engaged in a perpetual dialogue with itself—with its own past and with its foreign present (distance in space replacing distance in time), whether German or British—a foreign present that was called upon, and first and foremost translated in response to the needs of the French philosophical debate.

From 1820 onwards, those who chose to pursue a career in philosophy often felt obliged to engage in editing either the works of the philosophers whose disciples they claimed to be, or, on the contrary, of those with whom they did not want to be confused, in order to maintain the right distance (a situation which also explains certain delays in translation as well as certain errors of judgement and certain misinterpretations). Readers were confronted with "sensualism," "pantheism," "scepticism," and, symmetrically, with the "philosophy of the clergy"; and what remained standing after these confrontations was the "philosophy of the University,"[3] which was nothing more than what remained after a process of criticizing all errors and retaining what was valid. And this process gave rise to lecture courses and books on the history of philosophy.[4] They seem to have been a fundamental activity for the whole group of Cousin's close relations and pupils, and at the same time, an immense enterprise of textual edition and translation: Cousin published Descartes and Proclus and translated Plato; Barthélemy Saint-Hilaire translated Aristotle; Auguste Véra translated Hegel; Théodore Jouffroy translated Dugald Steward and Thomas Reid; Amédée Jacques edited Leibniz; Saisset translated Spinoza—and this latter translation[5] was very explicitly a polemical machine against those who accused Cousin and his followers of being pantheists.

How did this change come about? If the history of philosophy became a priority, this change had been made possible by the philosophy of history. The proof of this can be found at the beginning of the lectures given by Cousin in 1829: "History, gentlemen, is not pursued simply to satisfy scholarly curiosity or to provide pictures for the imagination of the artist; it is above all a lesson for the future; a serious man does not engage in the study of the past simply to learn what was, but to extract from it what should be; and a history of philosophy which seeks to be truly philosophical must lead to positive conclusions about the future destinies of philosophy."[6] The "scholarly curiosity" that is dismissed here is erudition—that is, the activity of the Académie des inscriptions et belles-lettres in the eighteenth century—while the reference to pictures for the imagination concerns the creation of past heroes by poets and painters, and perhaps also by court historians. So, what then does it mean it to be "truly philosophical"? It means admitting that the past has a meaning—that is, that we must situate ourselves in relation to this past. It is a return to the old idea of *historia magistra vitae*, but much changed: no longer a question of individuals and singular examples, but of centuries and the general movement of history. The French Revolution, with the upheavals it caused throughout Europe, is a landmark in this context. So too is Cousin's reading of Hegel, although it is true that this movement of history is rarely grasped by Cousin with Hegelian breadth. When he uttered the above words in 1829, his gaze was above all fixed on the eighteenth century: "On the stage of the world, every century that passes, and more than any other the eighteenth, filled with such great events, leaves behind it a long legacy of conflicting interests. The eighteenth century therefore necessarily has ardent and sceptical admirers and adversaries: in this conflict of opposing passions, philosophical independence would be ill at ease if it did not find in itself its strength and its reward." Philosophy is here asserting a claim to independence, and this is in part based on the fact that it has found a new object: no longer God, the soul, or the physical world, no longer civil society or the passions, but the meaning of great historical events. Or, in Cousin's terms: the "mission" of each age. He thus declares to his audience: "The general mission of the eighteenth century: to put an end to the Middle Ages; hence the two great characteristics of the eighteenth century: the generalization and dissemination of the principle of freedom."[7] Thus, the eighteenth century is so prominent in Cousin's reflection not just because it was the closest century, but first and foremost because it was partly the home of a moderate freedom, as far removed from despotism as it was from revolutionary Terror.

To take stock of the eighteenth century is therefore to write the history of freedom. But it is a paradoxical balance-sheet, since this century of generalization and diffusion of freedom concludes in the Terror and the irreligion of the Revolution. Freedom turned into its opposite, and this political paradox is accompanied by a philosophical paradox: the thinkers who should have legitimized human freedom within the framework of rational religiosity followed a path which led them to the negation of God, of the immortality of soul, and of free will, that is, to atheism, materialism, and "fatalism." Such an inversion of values could only ruin the social order instead of reforming it peacefully. Then, by an extreme reversal, the Revolution was followed by Napoleonic despotism and, under the Restoration, by the temptation to turn the clock back, with its nostalgia for the *ancien régime*. Political reaction also found philosophical expression: the beginning of the nineteenth century saw the appearance of doctrines which denied the power of Reason and which attempted to defend the social structure by basing religion solely on Revelation. In the eyes of Cousin and his generation, both these dangers had to be countered. In defending true freedom in politics, equidistant from despotism and disorder, a happy medium in philosophy had to be found: against the "philosophy of the clergy," the battle for Enlightenment had to be pursued; and against the materialists, resistance was necessary against the excesses of that same Enlightenment.

The strategy of Cousin and his group is therefore clear in the face of attacks coming, on the one hand, from the last of the *Idéologues*, relayed by materialist physicians and socialists (the danger on their left, in short) and, on the other hand, from those nostalgic for the *ancien régime* and from the clergy who accused them of undermining the foundations of the Church, as well as of the State which should, the clergy claimed, be founded on the Church (the danger on their right). The best means of defence, then, was to construct a sort of cartography of thought, determining both the place of each of these doctrines in history and the catastrophes to which they could lead. And this philosophical historiography was in no way an appendix to philosophy itself, but a constituent part of it, since the place and content of true philosophy were determined by the choices it made among opposing doctrines. Rather than Hegelian dialectic, it is therefore eclecticism that was to regulate philosophy according to the golden mean.

On the one hand, this new philosophy focused on the history of Christian origins, to show what they owed to ancient philosophy (and thus to the reconciliation of faith and human reason)—hence the research on the School of Alexandria, which sparked memorable controversies with representatives of the Catholic Church. On the other hand, it fought against "sensualism," which involved a reckoning with the legacy of the Enlightenment.

What is "sensualism"? This was a word invented after the event in order to designate anything that reduces the origin of thought to sensation, thereby risking diminishing the role attributed to reflection, to free will, and to the mind. Such a reduction was quickly accused of leading to a disastrous materialism, since, by giving such weight to sensation, it seems to deny human activity, and so (perhaps) free will and everything that escapes matter. It was claimed that this tendency had reigned over philosophy during the eighteenth century (and even at the end of the seventeenth century). In fact, everything that did not belong to Descartes' legacy was included haphazardly: Locke, Condillac, Helvétius, the *Idéologues*—not because they all defended the above precise theses, but because their own theses, even if they were more nuanced, were supposed to lead to materialism.

The fight against sensualism began before Cousin: the Spirit had to be saved. In this vein, Pierre Laromiguière tried to oppose attention to sensation; P. P. Royer-Collard imported the "philosophy of common sense" from Scotland. By scrutinizing the human mind, he sought to escape the perilous reduction of the superior to the inferior. However, his learned and rather bourgeois thinking was insufficient to arouse the enthusiasm of young liberals. Cousin, who had also begun by teaching "common sense," soon tired of it, discovered Kant and travelled to Germany. It was there that he was struck by Hegel's and Schelling's thinking, which was far more profound and exciting. It was there that Cousin discovered history, and with it the speculative meaning of the history of philosophy. As a result, he began constructing a new approach, where history came to support the analysis of the mind. Back in Paris, when he taught it, Cousin unleashed both the enthusiasm of his listeners and the attacks of the two opposing camps. Accused of importing obscure thoughts from across the Rhine, Cousin defended himself by looking for a national precursor. His solution was to base his spiritualism on a reinterpretation of Descartes. Indeed, while Cousin defined political modernity in terms of the spirit of freedom, in seeking a philosophical emblem for that modernity, he turned to Cartesianism—"the spirit which characterizes it is the very one which distinguishes Descartes from all his predecessors, that is to say the spirit of method."[8] The great drama of the history of philosophy was now to be played out against a backdrop of Cartesianism—a rewritten Cartesianism reduced fundamentally to the *cogito* (understood as the internal exploration of the human mind) and reinforced by the fact that it brings together, in Cousin's version, all that is positive in other doctrines. This is therefore a Cartesianism based on the historical exploration of the adventures of thought—which is somewhat paradoxical in the case of a philosopher who claimed to owe nothing to the past (*nemo ante me...*).

In establishing the above history of philosophy, the French of the period were quite familiar with Latin and Greek. They were less conversant with philology, and so it had to be imported. German universities had developed rigorous historiographical and philological methods, resulting in publications that the French would have been hard pressed to equal. Cousin and his colleagues were therefore content to exploit them and learn from them, until a time when they were able to compete with them. It was therefore not only speculative content that came from across the Rhine, but also scientific research, scholarly references and criteria of objectivity. Cousin's school thus implanted German historiography wholesale into French thought, for example in 1829 Cousin translated (or, rather, had translated) Tennemann's *Manual of the History of Philosophy*. However, he exploited it for his own ends—that is, for the inscription of historical moments within a framework of the mind's experience—not Mind with a capital letter, but individual psychology. The use (or misuse, if you prefer) of the history of thought is based on internal description of figures of consciousness that Cousin discovered in all periods of history: just as the individual mind first receives impressions from the outside world, then turns its attention to itself, and is seized with doubt in the face of these contradictory experiences and—to escape this fluctuation—throws itself into blind faith, likewise the collective human mind produces philosophies which in turn lapse into sensualism, idealism, scepticism, and mysticism. Philosophy itself—the true one, the one that must now be taught—would, in a sense, bring nothing new; it would evaluate and adopt whatever was true in each movement, "abstract[ing] what is true in each of these systems and out of it compos[ing] a philosophy superior to all such systems, which governs them all by subordinating them all, which is not merely a particular philosophy, but philosophy itself in its essence and in its unity" (p. 200 below). It is precisely in the Preface to Tennemann's *Manual* translated below that Cousin set out his programme.

What is the instrument employed to effectuate this sorting of doctrines? It is not so much a specific philosophical content as a certain virtuous "attitude." In the face of fanaticism and theocracy, there remained "no other resources for a philosophy ... than fairness, moderation, impartiality, wisdom." This sounds more like rhetoric than demonstration, but such rhetoric was commonplace among academics at the beginning of the nineteenth century. Moreover, Cousin himself admits: "It is, I agree, a fairly desperate resource, but I see no other. It would be absurd if in the present day anything but common sense could have any effect on men's imagination. However, it is certain that every other form of prestige seems exhausted" (p. 202 below). So, what will henceforth be the philosopher's task? He has *both* to write the history of philosophy *and* engage in an analysis of the human mind—the goal being to show that the two coincide:

> It is as if [the philosopher] has been condemned to a new role, humbler in appearance, but in reality the best and the grandest—[the role] of being just towards all systems and the dupe of none; of studying them all, instead of becoming the disciple of one of them, converting them all to its banner, and marching at their head in the discovery and conquest of truth. This ambition to reject no system nor to accept any in its entirety, to cast off one aspect and to take on another, to choose what appears true and good and therefore durable in everything—this, in a word, is eclecticism. (p. 202 below)

Thus, no initial content is posited, for it is by traversing prior systems that one is led to the conclusive truth. This traversal coincides with the "golden mean" of Cousin's renewed Cartesianism. Indeed, while he sketched vast schemas for the philosophical currents of every era, it was only ever to discover more and more clearly that the same drama was being played out: philosophy reflects "the stability of the laws of the human mind."[9]

Thus, the eighteenth century—which, as described above, was alternately hailed as a century of freedom and criticized as a century of sensualism and materialism—was also discovered to possess the four fundamental figures of sensualism, idealism, scepticism, and mysticism. This is why, alongside sensualism (in the majority at this period) and its adversary, Rousseau's and Turgot's idealism, Voltaire must be included within the description of scepticism and Saint-Martin within that of mysticism. Despite its originality, the Enlightenment came to be integrated into a general movement of philosophies: the final word on the eighteenth century involved reading into it the repetition of the same drama in four acts which was eternally played out by the human mind.

This accounts for Cousin's late interest in Eastern philosophies. Beyond Cousin's efforts to reconstruct them—notably, thanks to the work of Indologists—they serve to demonstrate the fixity of the human mind. If we equally find the same four moments of reflection in India, we are sure not to be mistaken in finding them at each stage of Western history. As a result, this mechanism can be put to the service of Cousin's university politics and his politics in general.

The fact that Cousin's historiography is more concerned with spotting trends than with rigorously describing systems makes sense of one of its more striking features: investigating not only what a thought says, but what it leads to—as if despite itself—when the logic of its arguments is pushed to the extreme. In other words, the history of philosophy is also the identification of aberrations. Locke, despite his honesty, led to Voltaire's scorn; and Voltaire, despite his belief in God, led to materialism. The history of philosophy is, in this way, perpetually out of step with itself: in deciphering a doctrine, we are less concerned with its meaning than with its truth, and its truth is its posterity; we therefore seek less to establish what the author really said than to establish the disastrous consequences that others may draw from what was said. What results is a fairly common motif in the writings of

Cousin and his disciples: the praise of a philosopher's character, followed immediately by the condemnation of their doctrine because of the seeds it contains.

There is another dimension to Cousin's work in the history of philosophy that should be underlined: its institutional aspect. He was not content to create this combination of analysis of consciousness and history of doctrines; he disseminated it extremely effectively by taking control of the French school and university system. Each year, he set the programme for the *agrégation*; his pupils, whom he familiarly called his "regiment," were placed in *lycées* where they taught eclecticism; and, once their thesis had passed their viva, the best of them came to occupy positions at the University and at the Académie des sciences morales et politiques. The Académie, moreover, played an essential role in defining what could be called, anachronistically, a research policy: the Académie, where Victor Cousin presided over the philosophy section, proposed a subject for competition each year, which was just as significant as the *agrégation* programme. The competition typically involved a critical question on the history of philosophy: How should we read the philosophers of the eighteenth century and what can be retained of what they wrote? How can we write the history of the Cartesian school and what can be retained of it, etc.? For example, the first of these competitions in 1833 had as its subject a "critical examination of Aristotle's work entitled *Metaphysics*" and its "programme" was explained as follows: "1. To make this work known by an extensive analysis and to determine its structure. 2. To write its history, point out its influence on later systems in antiquity and in modern times. 3. To investigate and discuss the portion of error and the portion of truth which it contains, and to designate the ideas which survive today or which could usefully enter into the philosophy of our century."[10]

In other words, the normal career of a philosopher, in the first half of the nineteenth century (as well as afterwards, with some variations), consisted in listening to the lectures of Cousin or his successors at the École Normale, then in passing the *agrégation* according to a programme established by Cousin, as well as according to a jury which he chaired; then, once in post, possibly undertaking a translation and submitting a manuscript for a competition of the Académie des sciences morales et politiques. Of course, Cousin and those of his disciples who sat on juries that evaluated these manuscripts rejected those that came from materialist or sensualist authors and crowned ... the young Cousinians—that is, those in whom they rediscovered their own ideas. The system was finely tuned. The prize-winning dissertations would then find a publisher and would contribute to a series of works that established a sort of historical encyclopaedia of controversial issues. To all of this were added articles published in periodicals (in particular, the *Revue des Deux Mondes*) which, among other things, praised precisely these published works.

It would be wrong, however, to see this as nothing more than a system of administrative and publishing authoritarianism. The system could only work because it was underpinned by Cousin's two weapons of legitimation—on the one hand, genuine scientific and philological work: editions of and commentaries on texts by previous philosophers, enlisted both as precursors and objects of study (including of negative analysis) in the name of the affirmation of current philosophy; on the other hand, the constitution of an imaginary memory, the memory by which the philosophical institution acquires a past that justifies it (through that past's accomplishments as well as its erratic wrong-turns).

We can clearly see all that is open to criticism in Cousin's works and in those of his disciples: the quasi-mythological reconstruction of the history of thought, with Descartes as the first psychologist and national philosopher (i.e. a philosopher because he was a psychologist); eclecticism at the service of a highly motivated policy; the fight against a "sensualism," which is a catch-all term and which condemns more than it nuances; the institution of an authoritatively determined "philosophy of the University"; rhetoric that is too often a substitute for demonstration. All that is certainly true, but—even without recalling that this institutionalization made it possible to defend the autonomy of philosophy against the influence of the clergy—Cousin is also the one who imported philological concerns into France as the basis of any serious attempt at philosophy: editions, translations, dictionaries, the choice of curricula. This was no mean feat, even if, taken to extremes, such a choice entailed consequences that turned against Cousin's interpretation itself— precisely because there is a positivity in philological and interpretative work which led his successors to question his simplistic readings and his hasty amalgams. It is also interesting to note that philosophical controversies (as well as religious controversies) came to be linked to publishing problems. The discovery and publication of texts, their translation, and their commentary play a fundamental role in the effort to legitimize a philosophical point of view or to situate the great figures of past eras (those whose doctrines are still acclaimed or contested today). The relationship works both ways: ideological controversy encourages textual work, and the latter in turn sees its results enlisted in the service of controversy. Thus, the birth of academic philology did not take place on neutral ground: it was both motivated and exploited by the intellectual conflicts of the time and each adversary sought to discredit the other by emphasizing that he himself had superior historiographical documents or that he used them with a better methodology.

Victor Cousin was forgotten, overtaken at the end of his own century by positivism, neo-Kantianism, and forms of spiritualism that were more refined and less rhetorical than his own. In the twentieth century, phenomenology, existentialism, Marxism, and structuralism prolonged this oblivion. However, whether they have been conscious of it or not, all his successors have had to fit into the institutional forms he invented. They have all learned to closely combine their philosophical reflection with the history of philosophy, so that the French proponents of these successive movements resemble each other precisely in this dimension and are thus distinguished from foreign representatives of their doctrines. They have learned this because they have been trained in exercises that bring this close interweaving into play, like all young French people who have been taught philosophy in their final school year. Both the lectures of the professors and the dissertations of the students have contributed to this ventriloquism in which one is supposed to think for oneself while allowing the accents of Plato, Descartes or Kant to pierce through one's own voice, which, in turn, constitutes the various moments of a supposedly spontaneous reflection. So much so that the author of these lines remembers having heard one of the most prestigious and energetic trainers of these teachers give them this advice, which was also a confession: "When I am teaching, I no longer know if it is Spinoza who speaks or if it is me."

Notes

1. See, for example, Johann Jakob Brucker, *Historia critica philosophiae a mundi incunabuli ad nostrum usque aetatem deducta* (1742–4).
2. Boureau-Deslandes published in 1737 (a century after the *Discourse on Method*) a *Histoire critique de la philosophie* whose full title can be translated as: *Critical History of Philosophy in which we deal with its origin, its progress, and the various revolutions that have happened to it up to our time*.
3. This is how Cousin qualifies his own position.
4. And at the most systematic level: the *Dictionnaire des sciences philosophiques*, ed. A. Franck (Paris: Hachette, 1844).
5. B. Spinoza, *Œuvres*, 2 vols, trans. E. Saisset (Paris: Charpentier, 1842), republished in three volumes in 1860.
6. V. Cousin, *Cours de l'histoire de la philosophie. Histoire de la philosophie au XVIIIe siècle* (Paris: Pichon and Didier, 1829), vol. 1, p. 5.
7. Cousin, *Cours de l'histoire de la philosophie*, vol. 1, p. 5.
8. V. Cousin, *Cours de philosophie sur le fondement des idées absolues du Vrai, du Beau et du Bien*, ed. Adolphe Garnier (Paris: Hachette, 1836), p. 2.
9. V. Cousin, *Histoire générale de la philosophie* (Paris: Librairie académique, 1864), p. 483.
10. In *Mémoires de l'Académie royale des sciences morales et politiques*, 2nd ser., vol. 2 (Paris: Firmin Didot, 1839).

Cousin and the Eighteenth Century

Lucie Rey

1. Philosophizing after the Revolution

To philosophize in France during the early nineteenth century necessitated working through the trauma of the French Revolution, whether one ended up affirming its principles, qualifying them, attacking them, or even consigning them to oblivion. A political strategy was needed to navigate France's immediate intellectual past and to quell anxiety over whether the interests of the present were best served by continuing the project of eighteenth-century radicalism or changing course (which was equally, of course, an anxiety over the value of the Restoration and its intellectual legitimacy). The question of nineteenth-century philosophy's relation to the French Revolution—and so to the eighteenth-century philosophies which were seen to prepare it—was particularly acute for a global historian of philosophy like Victor Cousin, who was required to write about the eighteenth century. And it is a question that became even more acute for a historian of philosophy like Cousin who did philosophy out of a will to construct an official, national doctrine—a distinct, "French" philosophical tradition—to which he would position himself and the constitutional monarchy of Louis Philippe as true heirs.[1]

It is, then, Cousin's closest historical predecessors in France that caused him most trouble in the history of philosophy and forced him to repeatedly ask the question: what relationship should contemporary philosophy have to the legacy of the eighteenth century and the Revolution? As Renzo Ragghianti has helpfully noted: "The problem to which Cousin seeks the solution by uniting eclecticism with [Louis XVIII's constitutional] Charter comes back to the idea of putting an end to the Revolution."[2] This, one can provisionally conclude, is a problem that motivates a large part of eclecticism's philosophical strategy and its odd treatment of eighteenth-century French philosophy, much of which—as I will show—is passed over in silence and the rest reduced to a metaphysics based on faculty-psychology.

To make sense of Cousin's approach to the eighteenth century, it is necessary to put it in context of what he was trying to do in and for the nineteenth century. That is, as previous essays in this introductory section have described, Victor Cousin's philosophy marks the site at which the institutionalization of French philosophy began, and this process of institutionalization was made possible by the fact that his philosophy is subjected to an external political project, which is played out in his work, particularly in his instrumentalization of the history of philosophy for extrinsic ends. Moreover, Cousin is not alone among early nineteenth-century French philosophers in politicizing the history of philosophy: in reaction to his work, a series of interpretations of the history of philosophy are offered that differ precisely on the basis of their attitude to contemporary political life (i.e. on the basis of whether the author wishes to legitimate the nineteenth century or not), as well as their attitude to a tradition entitled "French" philosophy.

In this short introductory essay, I want to describe Cousin's various political strategies in the history of philosophy by focusing on how they shape, determine, and in some cases deform what eighteenth-century philosophy looked like to him. I will thus describe the key features of the Cousinian reading of the eighteenth century as a way of showing how it participates in the transformation of philosophy which—from its eighteenth-century role as critique of the established order—becomes an instrument for legitimizing the political apparatus of the present. Then, in conclusion, I will briefly contrast this vision of the eighteenth century with the equally politically motivated history of philosophy of Pierre Leroux, Cousin's most vocal radical critic, whose 1839 *Refutation of Eclecticism* stands as a powerful anti-eclectic manifesto of the period.

2. Features of the Eighteenth Century in Cousin's Project

2.1 The Reduction of Philosophy to Metaphysics

To begin, before turning to Cousin's explicit critique of the eighteenth century, it is useful to examine how Cousin's general methodological tendencies in the history of philosophy have the effect of obscuring moral and political philosophy. Indeed, by making psychology the ground of all philosophy and then by assimilating the rest of philosophy to metaphysics, Cousin excludes a whole current of eighteenth-century thought and thereby insists on the absolute invalidity of much philosophy from that century. For example, in the foreword to the *Fragments of Cartesian Philosophy*, he writes, "Let me dare utter the truth: the eighteenth century in France—so rich in great men—did not produce one in philosophy, at least if one understands philosophy to be metaphysics." (p. 251 below).

The most visible effect of this assimilation of philosophy to metaphysics is the immediate exclusion from philosophy of the writings of Montesquieu, Voltaire, Diderot, Rousseau, and Condorcet. They are solely cited for their work outside the eighteenth-century philosophical void—as naturalists, economists, and historians (pp. 251–2 below). This is a result not just of Cousin's choices in relation to the eighteenth century in particular but of the very method of eclecticism as such—a brief rehearsal of the principles of this method will therefore be useful.

2.2 The Reduction of the History of Philosophy to the Repetition of Four Systems

Cousin's most fundamental, if implicit thesis on the history of philosophy is, paradoxically, that of its *non-historicity*. As Pierre-François Moreau has helpfully shown,[3] Cousin refuses to turn the history of philosophy into mere narrative and, instead, transforms it into a collection of hypotheses, a set of possible philosophical positions and ideas. It is in one of his longer works, his lecture course on the history of philosophy from 1829[4] (reissued in the later *General History of Philosophy*)[5] that Cousin is most explicit on this point—and his position there can be reconstructed in terms of two theses:

(a) the identification of philosophy with psychology: philosophy or metaphysics is nothing but the study of the human mind;
(b) the construction of the history of philosophy as material for the verification of this psychological method.

These theses rest on the underlying affirmation that "philosophy has no history."[6] Of course, such an affirmation seems odd coming from an author and professor who used the expression "history of philosophy" in most of his lecture courses and publications and who is hailed, even by his detractors, for having given his contemporaries a taste for erudite studies in the history of philosophy.[7] Yet, this is the fundamental position on which the whole of Cousinian history of philosophy is founded and which orients all his interpretations of past philosophies.

This thesis can be explained as followed: the history of philosophy is, for Cousin, not the description of an evolution in human thought over the course of time; rather, it manifests numerous variations on a few necessary, basic positions, the origins of which are to be found in the common operations of the human mind. This repetition allows very little space for any historical evolution, but, on the contrary, takes as its model something like the cyclical repetition of the natural seasons and applies it to "natural laws" to the mind. The Cousinian history of philosophy is presented as a theory of the eternal return of a cycle of four systems which repeat themselves and can only repeat themselves continuously and in the same order. Moreover, since these different systems in the history of philosophy are nothing but the manifestation of general laws of the human mind, understanding them is less a matter of the study of history and its systems than of the study of the human mind itself.

What is more, according to Cousin, this study of the human mind—that is, psychology—is grounded in the activity of reflection, which is itself oriented towards a prior activity: spontaneous thought. Spontaneous thought is confused and multiple: in order to discern its features, reflection undertakes analytic work which isolates them and puts them under the microscope. Reflection is the sole genuinely philosophical mode of thinking. However, such an analytic operation brings risks, notably that of confounding the part with the whole—that is, the analysed part or faculty of the mind with the whole of the mind.[8] This necessary error—inherent to the very workings of the human mind—engenders each basic type of system that recurs in the history of philosophy.[9] Every time a mind falls into this fault and transforms one isolated moment of analysis into the starting point for a system, other minds react by turning to those elements of the mind that have been unjustly neglected—ending up, in turn, committing the same fault.

According to Cousin, then, analysis of the spontaneity-reflexivity binary gives rise to four systems which succeed each other inexorably in the history of human thought: sensualism, idealism, scepticism, and mysticism. As a result, the task of the historian of philosophy consists in rediscovering the cycle of these systems and describing the ways in which they recur century after century.

2.3 The Application of this Reduction to the Eighteenth Century

In the tenth lecture of the *General History of Philosophy*, Cousin applies this reductive methodology to the eighteenth century. In the preceding lectures, he had successively studied all the major philosophical epochs, and he professes himself certain that this method of reducing the history of philosophy to four recurrent systems does not omit any important school: "History has constantly resolved itself into the same four systems, holding them closely together without confusing them, developing them harmoniously and always with marked progress."[10] Moreover, to be able to confirm that such an approach is faithful to a genuine law of history, Cousin must now further apply it to the eighteenth century, which will thereby demonstrate his complete description of the history of philosophy. In short, the eighteenth century must in its turn be resolvable into four systems. And for Cousin this is never in doubt: the historical data guarantee his inference from human psychology. Therefore, Cousin does indeed go about applying his schema to the eighteenth century—but with what results?

Cousin's schema leads to:

(a) the disappearance of all those philosophies which do not, in the first instance, treat the question of psychology;
(b) retaining solely secondary features of the remaining philosophies.

For example, Cousin presents Jean-Jacques Rousseau as one representative of the idealist system in France during the eighteenth century, to the extent that he defends conscience and disinterested virtue, alongside the freedom and immateriality of the soul. However, at the same time, Cousin makes a number of moves that completely devalue Rousseau's status as a philosopher, for he is unable to fit very neatly into this idealist system—as becomes clear from Cousin's comparison of Rousseau with Turgot, who was "also the declared adversary of sensualism and utterly inferior to the author of *Emile* as a writer, but very much his superior as a philosopher."[11] The only one of Rousseau's texts mentioned in the *General History of Philosophy* is the *Profession of Faith of the Savoyard Vicar*: the *Social Contract* and the *Discourses* or even Rousseau's overarching project in *Emile* is omitted entirely.

More generally, the political stakes so important to eighteenth-century philosophers are avoided by Cousin. For instance, Montesquieu is praised in passing by Cousin as the greatest mind of the century,[12] but his name does not appear once in the general presentation of eighteenth-century philosophy; Voltaire is merely presented as one of Locke's disciples and a representative of a superficial good sense vulnerable to scepticism; and the *Encyclopédie* project, mentioned by chance in a passage on Turgot,[13] is otherwise given no room in Cousin's account.

In sum, Cousin's classification ends up obscuring much of the particular value of French eighteenth-century philosophy—insofar as it differs from other centuries—and it certainly obscures all of its claims to intellectual originality:[14]

> Our observations have confirmed the theory. We made an induction, based on the entire history of the past, which divided eighteenth-century philosophy in advance into four schools, and we have found that this epoch of the history of philosophy is in fact so divided in this way. This division, which in itself would merely be a real but arbitrary fact, is transformed into a necessary fact in relation to the entire history which it repeats, and so it does indeed express a law.[15]

2.4 Rewriting the Philosophical Eighteenth Century

The only idiosyncrasy that Cousin does recognize in the eighteenth century lies in the preponderant place it accords to sensualism (whereas the seventeenth century was instead the century of idealism), even if all four currents are *necessarily* present in each century. While I do not have the space to reconstruct all of the systems of the eighteenth century from Cousin's perspective, a look at the eighteenth-century idealists is helpful. They include:

(a) Kant, who produced an idealism that was precisely turned against the idealisms of the seventeenth century, to the extent that all his work is concerned with positing the limits of human reason by means of critique;

(b) Rousseau and Turgot in France, as mentioned above;
(c) And above all, the Scottish philosophers, particularly Reid and his philosophy of common sense.

The legitimacy of positioning the Scottish philosophers on the side of the idealists may well, of course, be questioned: it, at least, shows the extent to which Cousin's classifications are simplifications. Reid's philosophy, for instance, is opposed to both sensualism and empiricism, because of his theory of common sense, and so he ends up being associated with the idealists, despite his fairly violent critique of any philosophy founded solely on reason. Ultimately, Cousin's extended discussion of Reid is primarily used to distract his reader's attention from French eighteenth-century thinkers—those whom Cousin considers "impious"—whom he deliberately banishes to the margins of his account. In short, analysing the faults of a "secondary" thinker like Reid gives Cousin the latitude to reconstruct an eighteenth century in which and through which his own spiritualism can recognize itself and orient itself:

> The spiritualist philosophy of the nineteenth century is of course associated with Descartes, and it is this great name—bound entirely to one nation, France—for whom we bear the flag; but we would be very ungrateful if we did not acknowledge that we also owe much to Reid, for we owe him to Royer-Collard.[16]

Cousin goes on to construct the figure of Reid as a discreet, retiring defender of good sense—introduced by Royer-Collard into France—and the purpose of such a construction is to refocus eighteenth-century philosophy around the psychological analysis of the individual self and thereby downplay its concern with social ideas of humanity and political rights and responsibilities. It is for this reason that the following description of Reid is intended to become emblematic of eighteenth-century philosophical developments: "After spending fifteen years studying by himself and retreating from the world, this modest and hard-working pastor of a poor Scottish parish amassed a full account of the operations of his mind, as well as the sentiments and convictions of his heart."[17] Crudely put, Cousin turns Reid into the Socrates of the eighteenth century.

What this example hopefully shows is the extent to which Cousinian doctrine strays from its purported ambition to constitute a neutral history of philosophy when it comes to the eighteenth century. However, in the end, what is perhaps even more remarkable is the extent to which Cousin describes the eighteenth century in very broad brushstrokes—that is, in a hasty and superficial manner. He claims that lack of time has resulted in a lack of detail when compared to his reading of the seventeenth century. But this excuse just masks what is the real impossibility underlying his account—the impossibility of describing the eighteenth century using the general methodological categories he has elsewhere derived.

3. To Have Done with the Eighteenth Century: The Philosophical Function of the Charter

Notwithstanding the above, what is interesting about Cousin's account of the eighteenth century is its ambivalence. For, alongside this classificatory reduction which suppresses any claim it might make to originality, elsewhere Cousin is keen to make use of the eighteenth century to draw conclusions about what nineteenth-century thought ought to become.

For example, in the *General History of Philosophy*, Cousin's evaluation of the eighteenth century is twofold. First, he deplores its destructive character, understanding it primarily in terms of a spirit of dissolution that ends in revolution. This is what the nineteenth century must resist. That is, the eighteenth century is a period marked by the decline of old political powers, the weakening of ecclesiastical might and of religion, but also by moral and artistic decline[18]—and this is something Cousin regrets. He laments the dissolution of old values—notably, chivalric values—which were replaced by a general spirit of "feebleness," "scepticism," and "licence" and resulted in a widespread loosening of mores. And while he does still recognize the appearance of new virtues in the eighteenth century, they are not enough. And it is for this reason Cousin emphasizes, in order to reject, the spirit of dissolution in the eighteenth century.[19]

Nevertheless and secondly, this rejection does not prevent Cousin from judging the eighteenth century as a success insofar as it accomplished the "tragic mission"[20] bestowed upon it—the mission of finally putting an end to the legacy of the Middle Ages. And it is in this context Cousin makes the following significant, if gnomic claim: "In the abyss of that immense revolution which it began and which it finished, the eighteenth century has left scarcely anything but abstractions, yet these abstractions are eternal truths which envelop the future."[21] This reference to "eternal truths which envelop the future" is startling: such a phrase could have originated from Leroux, although it would have had an entirely different meaning.

On the one hand, for Pierre Leroux (to whom I return at length in the conclusion below), the present has not yet taken in hand the slogan carved in stone by the Revolution—Liberty, Equality, Fraternity. The difficulties experienced implementing this slogan constitute, in Leroux's opinion, the fundamental problem for the nineteenth century.[22] Nineteenth-century philosophy is thus charged with coming to terms with these revolutionary principles, so as to create a properly new society. On the other hand, for Cousin, something different is at stake in the eighteenth century's anticipation of the future. For him, it is not a matter of continuing the legacy of the eighteenth century, but of honouring it, of rendering it homage—and, in so doing, transforming the eighteenth century into something finished and that has necessarily ended. Cousin might always declare himself in favour of the Revolution (see p. 250 below), but that does not prevent him hastening beyond it so as to not remain bound up in its errors. He writes, "Let us study it with discernment and equity so as to draw salutary lessons from it; let us honour it and not continue it. Imitate it only by serving the same cause—that of freedom and civilization—by different means."[23]

This is an argumentative strategy that Cousin tends to present in his writings as a median position between two extremes. So, on the other hand, Cousin responds to the fanatic partisans of the eighteenth century that it is necessary to judge theories by their practical consequences, such that one cannot legitimate an act with "horrible" effects. However, on the other hand, Cousin responds to the counter-revolutionaries in an indirect way. That is, instead of directly and explicitly embarking on a defence of the principles of the Revolution, Cousin explains to the counter-revolutionaries what is implied in their stance of refusal: even if Cousin thinks nothing in the eighteenth seems to be worth defending, he stills wants to diagnose the counter-revolutionary refusal of the eighteenth century as a symptom of a larger and misguided position—the refusal of modernity in favour of a return to the Middle Ages. While Cousin shares with the counter-revolutionaries a feeling of revulsion when confronted with the excesses of the Revolution, he also presents the Revolution as the logical conclusion of a modern history motored by Providence. As a result, he gives the enemies of the French Revolution an ultimatum: Condemn the Revolution and "you will condemn the three great centuries which have prepared it, which it represents and which it completes, and you will instead attach yourself to the Middle Ages. Condemn the march and progress of modern civilization, and you oppose yourself to History, you oppose yourself to the designs of Providence."[24]

In the end, Cousin himself refuses to make any kind of judgment on the Revolution; rather, he cedes to the figure of Louis XVIII, who had underwritten his institution of monarchical power by the Charter, a compromise constitutional document that attempted to mediate between sovereign power and revolutionary principles. Louis XVIII and his Charter are invoked by Cousin as superior authorities which have settled the question of the legacy of the Revolution; he writes, "He who made the Charter [i.e. Louis XVIII] thereby made a peremptory judgment about the French Revolution, he made clear what was good and what was bad; he condemned what was condemnable and conserved what was legitimate."[25] Cousin thus conceives the Charter as itself a form of historical recurrence, which synthesizes the past, so as to form an official position that makes space for all that is essential.

But what did the Charter in fact recognize? And what did it synthesize?

To begin, according to Cousin, the Charter recognizes the pre-eminence of Christianity and royalty and brings about their legitimate return. However, at the same time, the Charter absorbs some of the general principles and results of the French Revolution (as well as what preceded it in modernity) by introducing different legislative chambers into the royal government and allowing for the participation of the people in the nation's affairs. In short, the French government becomes a representative government modelled on the post-1688 British form.

Likewise, the principles of liberty and equality are, according to Cousin, "consecrated" by various articles in the Charter, which gives them their dues. So, equality is "consecrated by the article which recognizes that all Frenchmen have access to all vocations, and which establishes true equality, the only possible and legitimate equality—equality before the law."[26] Freedom is equally recognized, according to Cousin, in the general principle of freedom of the press: "What is freedom of the press in fact if not the unlimited freedom of reasoning, the right of inquiry in all its scope, that is, the principle of freedom in his highest generality?"[27] The principles of the French Revolution now come to be—through Louis XVIII's Charter—acquisitions of French society that are inalienable:

> The Charter itself has adopted the religious and political reforms of the sixteenth and seventeenth centuries, as well as the great revolution of the eighteenth century. The final result of the achievements of humanity are here represented and protected. It is under this authority that I place my wishes for the future, my opinions on the past, and all my teaching.[28]

The legacy of the Revolution is only to be understood when taken out of the eighteenth century and placed in the context of the July Monarchy. In other words, Cousin's philosophy affirms the principles of the Revolution only in the horizon of the present and as a doctrine to accompany and legitimate monarchy.

Conclusion: Pierre Leroux and the *Réfutation de l'éclectisme*

There is an apparent tension within Pierre Leroux's attack on Cousin's history of philosophy in his 1839 *Réfutation de l'éclectisme*. On the one hand, Leroux accuses Cousin of not having his own philosophy, of not thinking in the present, but contenting himself with retreating to past philosophies and assembling them. By creating nothing new, Cousin's work does not merit the name philosophy. However, on the other hand, Leroux equally accuses eclecticism of being a doctrine without tradition[29]—cut off from the past, Cousin elaborates a philosophy glued to the present. These two claims stand in tension; yet, they make sense when understood in terms of the very different relationship between the history of philosophy and the past tradition of philosophy in Leroux's writings.

Leroux describes Cousin's history of philosophy as a great edifice which claims to be objective but which crushes thinking in the present, since it is weighed down by a dead weight, unable to create anything new. The eclectic system consists in an activity of sifting without discernment, a flattened catalogue in which all solutions are already given a priori, before history is even studied.[30] The application of a pre-established interpretative grid radically denatures the doctrines studied by depriving them of all singularity and of the very force which characterizes them, by considering them just as recurrent manifestations of a general classificatory mechanism. In this sense, while drawing all his thought from past doctrines, Cousin is a philosopher without tradition, for he does not make use of any of the potential force found in past philosophies. Instead, this weight of the past that disables Cousin's philosophy can actually become a productive force for present philosophizing by offering it a strong, stable foundation by which to raise itself towards the future.

For Leroux true philosophy is not neutral and should not claim to be. It must rediscover the meaning of tradition, not to repeat it but to take it back, reactivate it by making sense of past facts subjectively. All of Leroux's efforts are directed at showing that his philosophy is inscribed within a long tradition which constitutes the basic movement of modern philosophy, and that by reactivating this tradition, by understanding past facts subjectively, he can reinvent them as new vibrant material responsive to the needs of contemporary action and knowledge. Leroux uses the metaphor of generation[31] to get at the difference between his synthetic conception of the history of philosophy and Cousin's act of composition: Leroux's synthesis engenders; it is productive and gives birth to new thought; whereas eclecticism is a eunuch: its theoretical emptiness is a symptom of its sterility.

What follows from this for Leroux is that Cousin's relates to the past as something closed. For Cousin, the present completes history, ends it by fulfilling it, by imposing a final result. Cousin's philosophy takes the form of the construction of a definitive doctrine which attempts to resume all past truths while also transcending them. It presupposes that all possible combinations have already been realized by the human mind, and this authorizes the activity of sifting and summation which puts in place its rigid edifice.

On the contrary, in Leroux, interpreting the past is not oriented towards the present as a time of closure, but is entirely a matter for the future: philosophy is conceived as force and tradition provides material for a bursting forth towards novelty. And novelty is, indeed, a fundamental requirement for Leroux's vital thinking, his "science of life"—not an absolute novelty, but one that arises out of centuries of germination.[32] To be a living science in both content and form, philosophy must be endowed with purposiveness: life is not pure mechanism but presupposes internal orientation. Hence, Leroux opposes any conception of philosophy, like Cousin's, as a descriptive science; rather, philosophy is normative: it has practical stakes, and, as a result, a telos. Tradition provides the instruments, the means, to realize this telos, and so, while this concept might at first blush seem to stand in tension with his future-oriented philosophizing, what it actually shows is the originality of Leroux's use of the term: tradition is not placed in the service of reaction or even of the status quo, but of emancipation.

Notes

1. See further, on this and the below, L. Rey, *Les Enjeux de l'histoire de la philosophie au XIXe siècle. Pierre Leroux contre Victor Cousin* (Paris: L'Harmattan, 2013); "Victor Cousin et l'instrumentalisation de l'histoire de la philosophie," *Le Télémaque* 54.2 (2018), pp. 43–55.
2. R. Ragghianti, "Victor Cousin, fragments d'une nouvelle théodicée," *Corpus* 18/19 (1991), p. 105.
3. P.-F. Moreau, "Spinozisme et matérialisme au XIXe siècle," *Raison Présente* 52 (1979), pp. 85–94.
4. V. Cousin, *Cours de l'histoire de la philosophie* (Paris: Pichon et Didier, 1829).
5. V. Cousin, *Histoire générale de la philosophie* (Paris: Librairie académique, 1864).
6. Moreau, "Spinozisme et matérialisme," p. 86.
7. For example, even in his polemic against Cousin in the 1832 *Lettres philosophiques adressées à un Berlinois*, Eugène Lerminier still notes in passing "the incontestable services Cousin has performed for the history of philosophy" (Paris: Paulin, 1832, p. 75).
8. "It is to be feared that by operating on one sole part of the primitive synthesis, they take the part for the whole and neglect or do not perceive the other parts equally worthy of attention and interest. From this emerges an incomplete psychology which, in turn, gives rise to a defective metaphysics, particular and exclusive systems, in place of a vast doctrine that reflects all natural knowledge with all its parts, the human soul with all its principles, all its tendencies and all its features." Cousin, *Cours de l'histoire de la philosophie*, p. 9.
9. See e.g. Cousin, *Cours de l'histoire de la philosophie*, p. 136.
10. Cousin, *Histoire générale*, p. 509.
11. Cousin, *Histoire générale*, p. 515.
12. Cousin, *Histoire générale*, p. 528.
13. This is merely a mention of Turgot's article on existence in the *Encyclopédie*. Cousin, *Histoire générale*, p. 515.
14. Of course, it is also puzzling that this interpretative schema divides philosophical history into centuries so neatly: why is the manifestation of the law of the human mind in history to be calculated in centuries? Cousin never addresses this.
15. Cousin, *Histoire générale*, p. 520.
16. Cousin, *Histoire générale*, p. 544.
17. Cousin, *Histoire générale*, p. 544.
18. Cousin, *Histoire générale*, pp. 12–14.
19. See Cousin, *Histoire générale*, p. 21.
20. Cousin, *Histoire générale*, p. 28.
21. Cousin, *Histoire générale*, p. 28.
22. See e.g. P. Leroux, *Réfutation de l'éclectisme, où se trouve exposée la vraie définition de la philosophie, et où l'on explique le sens, la suite, et l'enchaînement des divers philosophes depuis Descartes* (Paris: Honoré Champion, 1979), p. 48.
23. Cousin, *Histoire générale*, p. 30.
24. Cousin, *Histoire générale*, p. 26.
25. Cousin, *Histoire générale*, p. 26.
26. Cousin, *Histoire générale*, p. 27.
27. Cousin, *Histoire générale*, p. 27.
28. Cousin, *Histoire générale*, p. 28.
29. Leroux, *Réfutation*, pp. 304–7.
30. On this point, see further Rey, *Les Enjeux de l'histoire de la philosophie*, pp. 36–8.
31. Leroux, *Réfutation*, p. 346.
32. See e.g. Leroux, *Réfutation*, p. 22.

Cousin and the Problem of Metaphysics

Daniel Whistler

"Is there or is there not absolute truth?"[1] Such is one of the more pressing questions at issue in Victor Cousin's philosophy; indeed, it expresses one of his most long-standing philosophical ambitions: to secure metaphysical good sense for the nineteenth century as Descartes had for the seventeenth. His passion for absolute truth both enthused and confused his contemporaries in equal measure: as well as "running to Cousin's lectures the way people run to the opera,"[2] they were at times puzzled by his "metaphysical fever,"[3] his "singular disorder ... for dreaming philosophy,"[4] and his "all-too-ardent mind" which sought truths beyond the self "in the unity of substance."[5] For his own part, Cousin recognized that "my taste for grand speculation"[6] went against the grain, since, after Hume, he acknowledges, "indifference to metaphysics had become total throughout Europe" (p. 203 below). It is for this reason he took Kant's awakening from his dogmatic slumber as one of his models, "living two whole years as if buried within the subterranean passages of Kantian psychology ... occupied solely with the transition from psychology to ontology" (p. 104 below). However, Cousin understood Kant's question *quid juris?* as but one instance of a modern tradition running from Descartes that confronted the problematic status of metaphysics in the name of securing "a firm basis for science" (*VBB* 1853, p. 441). Just like previous centuries, the nineteenth century was in sore need of "fixed, immutable and eternal principles which possess absolute authority and on which we can found a science" (*PM*, p. 82)—and this is what he set out to provide in a "complete theory of absolute truths" (p. 187 below). The following essay reconstructs Cousin's theory as set out in his early lecture courses, summarized and revised in the Prefaces to *Philosophical Fragments*, and then repurposed in his later spiritualist manuals.[7]

1. What Is Cousinian Metaphysics?

Cousin's programme for his 1818 lecture course, *On the True, the Beautiful, and the Good* (*Du Vrai, du Beau et du Bien*), summarizes his "introduction to all science, or the science of science" that takes as its "fundamental axiom": "the absolute as the scientific element."[8] That is, it is devoted to "the problem of the absolute" (p. 153 below), where the term "absolute" exhibits three overlapping features that together constitute a robust notion of universality:

(a) Absolute truths are true in themselves, not just for us;
(b) Absolute truths therefore hold good for mind-independent states of affairs;
(c) Absolute truths are also "independent of all circumstances of time and place" (*VBB* 1836, p. 133) and so universal.

The various "parts" of this science of the absolute are then enumerated in the 1818 programme as follows:

(a) On the absolute, as idea, or in its relation to reason—*Rational Psychology*;
(b) On the absolute, outside of reason, in its relation to existence—*Ontology*;
(c) On the legitimacy of the transition from the idea to being, from rational psychology to ontology—*Logic*.[9]

Rational psychology—which in 1817 Cousin had labelled "phenomenology" or "subjective science"[10]—is further described as the self observing itself as it scales a series of "degrees" towards "the perspective of pure reason" in which "all relativity, all subjectivity, all reflexivity expires."[11] It is thus the complement to logic: the former describes the subject's experiential ascent to the highest faculty of mind, while the latter demonstrates the correlation of this psychological ascent to actual knowledge of being, to absolute truths.

Ontology is the object of metaphysics. The later Cousin will typically list its contents as the two dogmas of spiritualism (freedom of the will and immateriality of the will), a philosophy of nature (or the causal principles that structure nature), and a theodicy (a doctrine of God as "the centre and source of all truths" [*VBB* 1836, p. 129] and a doctrine of Providence).[12] In his early lectures, Cousin likewise defines ontology in terms of three questions "which concern the totality of things" and which pertain to the present, past, and future respectively: "What is the universe and what are its features? Where does it come from; is it eternal or accidental; has it always existed? What is the end of this universe; where is it heading; what will it become; must something come after it?" (*PM*, p. 151). These are, of course, traditional, "dogmatic"[13] lists: the upshot of Cousinian metaphysics is a body of immutable truths—"expressions of eternal reason" (*VBB* 1836, p. 24)—that purport to accurately represent supersensible states of affairs. In this manner, Cousin maps his project very closely onto a scholastic *metaphysica specialis* consisting of a *psychologia rationalis*, a *cosmologia rationalis*, and a *theologia rationalis*—or, in Cousin's own terms: the willing self as personal cause; dynamic natural forces as impersonal causes; and God as the absolute substance-cause. Moreover, this is a list which prioritizes the defence of moral norms (as a particularly urgent post-revolutionary task), since

Cousin collapses any distinction between theoretical and practical reason (see *PM*, p. 193). The theoretical justification of absolute truths must be understood practically—or, in Cousin's words, "All philosophy which does not culminate in morality is scarcely worthy of the name" (*VBB* 1853, p. 258). The supreme end of metaphysics is the moral law, "a sovereign and absolute truth which commands us all" (*VBB* 1836, p. 16; see *PM*, p. 302), and, as a result, the only possible ethics is a metaphysics of morals. Indeed, since law, politics, and religion rest, in turn, on morality (see *PM*, pp. 155–6, 248), they too are only properly comprehensible on the basis of this metaphysics.

The building blocks of Cousin's metaphysics are rational "principles" or "laws," irreducible propositional judgements, such as "every effect has a cause" and "every quality presupposes a substance." In positing these principles as fundamental, Cousin rejects logical atomism as "a false theory of judgement" (*VBB* 1836, p. 178): principles, not their constituent ideas, are "primitive" (although not innate). These principles are further transposed onto Kant's table of judgements, which Cousin then refigures as two parallel hierarchies atop of which sit the principle of cause and the principle of substance (see p. 170 below). These two principles provide the ineluctable representational framework that determines all knowledge. In Cousin's own words, "There is no thought in the human mind that is not reducible to one or other of these forms" (*VBB* 1836, p. 33).

The possibility of metaphysics ultimately rests on the principle of cause and the principle of substance fulfilling three conditions that will structure the rest of this essay:

(a) They must be *real* or *true* (in opposition to the use of hypotheses by the absolute idealists);
(b) They must be *certain* or *necessary* (in opposition to Hume's scepticism);
(c) They must be *absolute* (in opposition to the "refined" scepticisms of Kant and Reid).

What is deliberately omitted from this list of the conditions of possibility of metaphysics is any appeal to faith, dogma, or theological expertise. Cousin undertakes a thoroughgoing secularization of the absolute. Knowledge of God, Providence, the immortal soul, and the moral law can be obtained independently of particular religious beliefs and practices. The ascent of this "liberal"[14] doctrine to state orthodoxy after 1830 provides some of the theoretical background to Cousin's secular reforms of education and the controversies that ensued.

2. The Reality of Metaphysical Principles

"I call 'real' everything which immediately falls under observation" (*VBB* 1853, p. 32). For Cousin, truth is a function of perception: all metaphysical principles must be empirically verified, where this verification-procedure is not intended to discount metaphysical truths, but to legitimate them. Cousin is a speculative verificationist. This position directly results from his programmatic refusal to equate the experimental method with the receipt of external sense-data. Instead, drawing on Locke's distinction between sensation and reflection, empiricism becomes for Cousin an introspective procedure of attending to the contents of one's own consciousness: "I have often said and will repeat it: the starting point of philosophy is psychology or description, the history of the internal phenomena of humanity" (*PM*, p. 248).

This reformed empiricism becomes speculative via its ability to describe more than just sensations—that is, its commitment to a more comprehensive notion of experience inclusive of rational principles posited in consciousness. Empiricism here attains maximal extensity as an empiricism of reason. To put it another way: Cousin's major innovation to traditional *metaphysica specialis* is to mediate it through a more fundamental *psychologia empirica*—this displacement structures Cousin's project: the foundations of metaphysics are moved outside itself—i.e. ontology is adjourned.

One motivation for Cousin's verificationism is a "horror of hypothesis" (*VBB* 1853, p. 8). Cousin will ultimately subvert the motif of *hypotheses non fingo* against eighteenth-century renditions of it; however, initially, his "horror" is framed according to a traditional empiricist concern: every hypothesis—that is, every unperceived truth-claim, even the most likely—is "scientifically void" as long as it remains unperceived (p. 93 below). In other words, "All science must rest solely on facts" (*PM*, p. 170). Rationalist and absolute idealist metaphysicians fall foul of precisely this reality-condition: they "place themselves straightaway at the pinnacle of speculation; me, I begin from experience. To escape the subjective character of inductions from an imperfect psychology, they begin with ontology, which is then nothing but a hypothesis; I begin with psychology, and it is psychology itself which leads me to ontology and saves me from ... hypothesis" (pp. 107–8 below). Structurally, what Hegel, Schelling, and their ilk do wrong is presume metaphysics to be a self-sufficient science without an external supplement in psychological reflection.

Metaphysics is empiricist all the way down: "By way of observation, we arrive at the threshold of the absolute" (*VBB* 1836, p. 150).[15] This has two key consequences. First, metaphysical argument does not require the apparatus of transcendental deduction or dialectical critique but comprises analytic description and an appeal to virtuosity in introspection. Cousin is interested in "facts that I record, not beliefs that I propose" (*PM*, p. 84) and, as such, the contents of philosophy should be immediately present to any sufficiently practised observer. Secondly, since rational principles not only form part of the apparatus of knowing (qua *noēsis*) but also constitute objects of perception (qua *noēma*), they take on a double role in reflection.[16] This is why Cousin speaks of them so often as "facts of consciousness": their factuality or objecthood as *noēma* is foregrounded by way of consciousness turning back on itself. As a result, the metaphysician is tasked with the description of the properties, laws, tendencies, and causal behaviour of mental facts, in loose analogy to any physical fact.[17]

3. The Certainty of Metaphysical Principles

Of the truths observed within and by consciousness, some are contingent and open to doubt, others are necessary and indubitable. As Cousin puts it, "Among true propositions, I have discovered some are marked with the character of necessity" (*VBB* 1836, p. 120). Necessity is not disclosed to the philosopher as the result of a transcendental argument (or, indeed, any argument), but as the result of observing mental entities (as the immediate data of reflective consciousness). Necessary principles are "preliminary given[s]" (p. 67 below), "incontestably in our mind" (*VBB* 1853, p. 440): necessity is immediately visible to any sufficiently well-directed act of reflection. In consequence, the establishment of metaphysical certainty is one more "victory for the method of observation" (p. 67 below).[18] In so claiming, Cousin attempts to refute Hume as one empiricist pitted against another: even if Hume was indeed right not to perceive any evidence of necessity in sensation, things change when an empiricism of sensation becomes an empiricism of reflection. Hume's "scepticism ... is shattered before [the perceived fact of] rational principles" (*VBB* 1836, p. 134).[19] The two conditions of metaphysical truth considered so far—the reality and the certainty of principles—thus open up a middle path for Cousin between the rationalist excess of hypothesis and the sensationalist excess of scepticism.

Nevertheless, this is not yet enough. More is still needed to secure metaphysics. Its truths must be more than just necessary—such is Cousin's constant refrain: "Necessity is not the end in which metaphysics culminates, it is not the ground of the absolute" (*VBB* 1836, p. 121). This is because necessity is "merely relative to the intellect": it supplies "the relative criterion" for metaphysical truth, so an additional "absolute criterion" is required (*VBB* 1836, p. 113). Necessity is posited by the individual subject—*I affirm* that two and two necessarily make four: "If you affirm the truth solely because it is necessary for you to conceive it, you only ever have your own conception as guarantee or criterium of truth, and therefore you never escape yourself." Cousin continues, "Every time we wish to demonstrate the existence of a truth by the necessity by which we perceive it, we enclose it in the I, we subjectivize the absolute" (*VBB* 1836, pp. 122, 125). The experience of necessity is determined by the structure of our individual consciousness and, on its own, does little to resist the kind of subjectivism Cousin opposes to true metaphysics. This gives rise to Cousin's fundamental challenge, "the *objective* problem par excellence" (p. 153 below)— "to pass from necessity to the absolute" (*VBB* 1836, p. 125).

4. Pre-Reflexive Reason

In Kant's *Critique of Pure Reason*, the necessary and the universal are typically bundled together; Cousin, on the contrary, subjects them to individual analysis, such that they come to represent two "degrees" or stages which observation must pass through on the way to the absolute. The ascription of necessity to truth-claims is but one staging post—one which Kant, in particular, wrongly takes as a terminus, thereby "making the absolute descend into the relative" (*VBB* 1836, p. 116). According to Cousin, Kant's partial focus on necessity gives rise to a "refined scepticism," which is, he concedes, "new and original," "the wisest, most moral there ever was," but nevertheless still scepticism (*VBB* 1853, pp. 14, 433): Kant rendered the categories of the understanding "impotent" (p. 68 below) by failing "to go beyond the limits of a *relative criterion* and [instead] retreating before the *absolute criterion*" (*VBB* 1836, p. 116). To put it slightly differently, Cousin considers Kant's inference from necessity to objectivity a failure because necessity is unable to escape mind-dependence. The kind of objectivity secured by the Transcendental Deduction is too weak to ground metaphysics properly: it is not "absolute." Hence, in its place, Cousin himself insists on "absoluteness" as a far stronger, "dogmatic" criterion of objectivity, one that justifies the mind-independent validity of rational principles.

Cousin finds evidence for this dogmatic version of objectivity in his foundational distinction between spontaneous and reflective rationality (correlated to a distinction between spontaneous and voluntary acts of will). In the face of this distinction, "Reid's and Kant's system is destroyed" (*VBB* 1836, p. 124)[20] and, by means of it, "the problem of the absolute" is to some extent resolved.

Spontaneous rationality is pre-reflexive, variously described as "an intellectual intuition," "instinct" and "a simple perception of being" (*VBB* 1853, pp. 66, 140, 55). It is opposed to reflection, which doubles the contents of consciousness, mediates intuitions through structures of knowing, and always comes too late. Three features of spontaneity are pertinent. First, spontaneity is still rational; it involves no mystical excess of feeling or inspired premonition; it expresses the same thing as reflection but immediately. Secondly, while reflective judgement affirms truths only by distinguishing them from what they are not (according to a complex interplay of antithesis and synthesis), spontaneous intuition is purely thetic, "an affirmation accompanied by absolute security and without even the sliver of a possible negation" (*VBB* 1853, p. 62). Spontaneity is "consciousness in its state of purity" (*PM*, p. 141), and, in consequence, does not involve the labour of the subject or any of its categorial apparatus. Thirdly and as a result, "subjectivity expires" in spontaneity: there are no "subjective wrappings," but solely a "pure perception of truth" (*VBB* 1836, pp. 121–2). Pre-reflexive reason is *impersonal*—from this claim emerges the doctrine of impersonal reason canonized as eclectic dogma in Francisque Bouillier's 1844 *Théorie de la raison impersonnelle*.[21] That is, spontaneous truths are indifferent to the subject, indifferent to the consciousness in which they appear: they are "within the I but do not belong to the I" (*VBB* 1853, p. 30). Consequently, the subject might bear witness to such truths in consciousness but has little power over them.

Therefore, impersonal spontaneous intuition provides one clue how to get beyond the "relative criterion" or necessity. The expiration of subjectivity in spontaneity is equally the expiration of necessity (as part of the conceptual apparatus of the subject): "In spontaneous perception there is no feeling of necessity, nor therefore the character of subjectivity" (*VBB* 1853, p. 59). Spontaneous truths are absolute in a way that reflective truths can never be: they are more than necessary, they are universal and impersonal—and so they fulfil the absolute criterion and guarantee a robust form of objectivity. They open up a space for metaphysics by making possible a negative response to the question, "Are all [our judgements] marked by this necessity which subjectivizes the truth?," as well as to the question, "Does our understanding only ever act under the law of reflection?" (*VBB* 1836, p. 123).

5. Logic

Yet even this is not enough. The existence of spontaneity may well provide evidence for the possibility of absolute truths, but it does not furnish *the philosopher*—that is, she who *reflects*—with access to them. Cousin's reform of empiricism makes philosophy fundamentally reflective, but "spontaneity expires in reflection" (p. 169 below).[22] The philosopher is seemingly stuck with necessity, stuck at the stage of the "relative criterion"—stuck, that is, within subjectivism. Cousin is well aware of this difficulty. "It seems contradictory," he writes, "for a philosopher to speak of the spontaneous state: for he can grasp it only with the instrument of philosophy, that is, with reflection, and reflection destroys spontaneity." However, there is no trace of tragedy or futility here, for he continues: "But this difficulty is not insurmountable: we can regrasp the spontaneous fact by the most legitimate logical inductions" (*VBB* 1836, p. 53). That is, Cousin is confident that there is a further solution to the more specific problem of the *reflective* "transition from psychology to ontology"— or, what he calls "logic." Ultimately, "logic alone can lead to ontology."[23]

Nevertheless, Cousin's contemporaries were less confident in his logic. For example, on the initial publication of *Philosophical Fragments*, Hector Poret confided to him:

> The fundamental idea of your system ... if I am not mistaken, is found entirely in your method by which you try to pass from psychology to ontology and to arrive at unity and the absolute by the experimental path. It is on the logical possibility of this method that all my doubts bear.... Your psychology enchants me; it appears to me a masterpiece of analysis.... What I don't yet understand is how you

exit from psychology to arrive at ontology; this appears to me the point of utmost danger in your whole system.[24]

Equally, in his 1834 commentary, F. W. J. Schelling also worries about this possibility of transition from "the first" part of Cousin's philosophy which "remains completely within the sphere of psychology and therefore subjectivity" to "a second part, a dogmatic and objective part, [which] claims to prove the existence of the external world, that of our own personality and that of God."[25] Schelling interprets this purported transition as a failed ontological argument: an introspective analysis of ideas *in intellectu* is supposed to give us access to existences *in re*, despite the "unbridgeable chasm" separating the two domains.[26]

The difficulty both Poret and Schelling identify is that of justifying a strong form of objectivity (absoluteness) at the same time as restricting metaphysical method to psychological reflection. Nevertheless, Cousin keeps on talking about the possibility of precisely such a logical transition in a number of ways—all of which cumulatively contribute to his account of the possibility of metaphysics.

The first model for logic found in his writings involves the "capture" of spontaneity at the origins of reflection. Spontaneous intuition may well be "a fugitive act" (*VBB* 1836, p. 122) that resists linguistic expression (since languages "are fully determinate, that is, profoundly reflective"), but the philosopher can still "grasp the spontaneous viewpoint ... by catching it ... at the dawn of reflection, at the almost indivisible moment when the primitive gives way to the present, when spontaneity expires in reflection" (p. 169 below). A residue of absoluteness can be extracted even from philosophical thinking by taking natural spontaneity "by surprise" in the act of becoming reflective (p. 169 below).

A similar model for logic rests on the notion of "immediate abstraction," as the reflective correlate to spontaneous intuition. Immediate abstraction is distinguished from "comparative abstraction," which compares similar objects to isolate what is general in them (see pp. 176–7 below). On the contrary, according to Cousin, metaphysics can be constituted by means of the immediate and total elimination of particularity from phenomena through abstraction without any need for comparison: as soon as one experiences a causal chain, one can "eliminate the determinate and obtain the pure principle of causality" (*VBB* 1836, p. 169). The empirical component of knowledge is done away with, so as to form an idea of the absolute.

Cousin also toys with the idea of a description of the dynamics of rational facts—a "phenomenology," as he puts it in 1817. On this model, consciousness acts as "witness" to the tendency of these facts to transcend consciousness. Cousin's empiricism of reason here comes into its own, following mental entities wherever they lead: "[Within] consciousness where there are only phenomena, there are also concepts whose further development transcends the limits of consciousness and reaches existences. Do you hinder the development of these concepts? If so, you arbitrarily limit the scope of a fact" (p. 65 below). Consciousness cannot stop observing until it has faithfully observed rational facts (treated here in their factuality as posited objects of perception) pass beyond the mind.

Finally, there are two further and increasingly frequent models for logic in Cousin's later publications. His endless appeals to common sense (as well as the eclectic virtues of extensity and generality) are to be understood as part of a strategy for justifying metaphysics: since absoluteness and universality are synonymous, it follows that ideas common to humans across nations and epochs (i.e. truths of common sense) are particularly good candidates for absolute ideas. However, more explicit in this context is Cousin's rewriting of the Cartesian trademark argument. According to his reconstruction of the argument, Descartes "recognized himself as imperfect, full of faults, of limitations, of suffering—and at the same time he conceived of something infinite and perfect. He possessed the idea of the infinite and of the perfect; but this idea is not his own work, for he is imperfect; thus [the idea] must have been placed in him by another being endowed with perfection—this being is God" (*VBB* 1853, p. 77).[27] Through psychological analysis, the metaphysician comes to recognize that her principles must express a mind-independent source whose truths she "borrows": she recognizes the mark of an external, absolute ground to her ideas. This model is intimately linked to the doctrine of impersonal reason, for it effectuates the philosophical realization that "although you are making [some judgement], you know that you do not constitute it, and so the truth it expresses appears to you universal, invariable, absolute, infinite" (p. 172 below).

6. Conclusion: The Absolute in History

Cousin's metaphysics ends in a paean to the powers of impersonal reason, "the bridge thrown between psychology and ontology, between consciousness and being," "extend[ing] into the infinite and attain[ing] the being of beings" (pp. 78, 100 below). At this point metaphysics becomes philosophy of religion: absolute truths presuppose absolute substance as their ground; reason is to be reconceived as *Logos*; the principle of cause and the principle of substance become divine attributes; and metaphysical knowledge is understood as a kind of participation in divine reason.[28] In Cousin's eyes, this is no renunciation of the experimental method, but its final apotheosis as a rationalism-empiricism totality, "the conciliation of reason and observation" (*VBB* 1836, p. 151), in which "the a priori and the a posteriori are reunited" (*PM*, p. 88). Such a concordance between the rational and the empirical defines Cousin's metaphysical empiricism: its "peculiarity," as William Hamilton first noted, "consists in the attempt to combine the philosophy of experience and the philosophy of pure reason into one."[29]

This harmonious co-ordination of rational and empirical methodologies defines Cousin's historical research too.[30] His interest in the historical is no retreat from the problematic of the absolute, for, in line with the strict analogy he establishes between psychology and history (psychology is to individual consciousness what history is to "the consciousness of humanity as a whole" [VBB 1836, p. 45]), Cousin now looks to historical facts for evidence of absoluteness. Just like in psychological introspection, he here isolates the rational principles or laws which structure history, empirically verifies them and traces their origin back to an impersonal source (divine Providence). Cousin's philosophy of history and history of philosophy become, therefore, a "living demonstration" (p. 113 below) of a metaphysics in action.

Notes

1. V. Cousin, *Cours de philosophie sur le fondement des idées absolues du Vrai, du Beau et du Bien*, ed. A. Garnier (Paris: Hachette, 1836), p. 111. There are two very different versions of *On the True, the Beautiful, and the Good* (*Du Vrai, du Beau et du Bien*) that should be considered independent works: the 1836 reconstruction of Cousin's original 1818 lectures based on student notes, and the complete rewrite Cousin made in 1853 as a manual for his later spiritualism (V. Cousin, *Du Vrai, du Beau et du Bien*, 8th edn [Paris: Didier, 1860]). Along with many of the "fragments" translated below and his 1819–20 lecture course (V. Cousin, *Philosophie morale*, ed. S. Matton [Paris: Garnier, 2019]), these texts contain his most extended reflections on metaphysics. I henceforth reference them in-text as *VBB* 1836, *VBB* 1853, and *PM*, respectively.
2. H. Taine, *Les philosophes du XIXe siècle en France* (Paris: Hachette, 1857), p. 102. See J. Goldstein, *The Post-Revolutionary Self: Politics and Psyche in France, 1750–1850* (Cambridge, MA: Harvard University Press), p. 156.
3. P. Janet, *Victor Cousin et son œuvre* (Paris: Alcan, 1885), p. 92. Janet's remark reads in full, "For eighteen years from 1815 to 1833, Cousin possessed to the highest degree the metaphysical fever. Like Plato, like Malebranche, like Hegel, he believed in the power and virtue of speculative thought."
4. F. Dubois, quoted in R. Ragghianti and P. Vermeren, "Introduction" to Cousin, *Philosophie morale*, p. 14.
5. P. Maine de Biran, *Journal*, vol. 2, ed. H. Gouhier (Neuchatel: La Baconnière, 1955), p. 303.
6. V. Cousin, *Souvenirs d'Allemagne*, ed. D. Bourel (Paris: CNRS édition, 2011), p. 56. See also Cousin's comment to F. W. J. Schelling in July 1821: "I hope you will find in my work proof that Germany has not been completely useless to me and that, in France, we are also beginning to view things from the perspective of Platonic philosophy, the deepened study of which—along with that of German philosophy—can reanimate among us a taste for high speculation." V. Cousin and F. W. J. Schelling, "Correspondance, 1818–1845," ed. C. Mauve and P. Vermeren, *Corpus* 18/19 (1991), p. 202.
7. In what follows, I attempt to minimize the use of proper names as reference points for interpreting Cousin's metaphysics, despite the evident echoes and analogies to other philosophers palpable in the particularly (and unfashionably) "Germanic" Cousin I present. This is in part to allow Cousin's texts to speak for themselves without being reduced in advance to a set of pre-established positions (even if "eclecticism" often encourages this operation) and in part because there is no space in this introduction to tackle the thorny problematic of "influence," which becomes especially thorny when it comes to Cousin's relationship with German thinkers (for some discussion in the English-language literature, see K. Chepurin et al. (eds), *Hegel and Schelling in Early Nineteenth-Century France*, 2 vols [Dordrecht: Springer, 2023]).
8. V. Cousin, "Programme du cours de philosophie de année 1818," in *Fr. phil. 1826*, p. 264.
9. Cousin, "1818 Programme," p. 266.
10. V. Cousin, "Programme du cours de philosophie de année 1817," in *Fr. phil. 1826*, p. 229.
11. Cousin, "1818 Programme," p. 270.
12. See e.g. V. Cousin, *Défense de l'université et de la philosophie*, ed. D. Rancière (Paris: Solin, 1977), pp. 29, 42, 60. Whereas in 1818 (above) Cousin makes a distinction between rational psychology

and ontology, in his later work rational psychology—as a doctrine of the soul—is made one more object of ontology. This allows him a neater correspondence between "the triple object of consciousness" (sensible facts, volitional facts, rational facts—see below) (*VBB* 1836, p. 131) and the triple object of metaphysics (the world, the soul, God). In this vein he writes, "In the first fact of consciousness, there is to be found psychological unity in its triplicity which parallels ontological unity in its triplicity" (p. 77 below).
13. On Cousin's embrace of the term "dogmatism," see p. 100 below.
14. On Cousin's definition of "liberal" philosophy as a secular metaphysics of morals, see *PM*, p. 125.
15. The significance of Cousin's commitment to the experimental method even at the heights of his metaphysics is touched on in Antoine-Mahut's essay above and, in more detail, in her "Experimental Method and the Spiritualist Soul: The Case of Victor Cousin," in *Perspectives on Science* 27.5 (2019), pp. 680–703.
16. Cousin writes, "Psychological observation is much more difficult than observation in the natural sciences.... In philosophy observation is entirely internal.... The observed object is at the same time the observing subject." He continues, "every observed fact in psychology is simultaneously 'object,' 'subject,' and 'instrument'" (*PM*, p. 127).
17. The importance of the factuality of principles is emphasized: "For a long time I concerned myself solely with the properties of truths in themselves, failing to sufficiently consider them as perceived" (*PM*, p. 232).
18. It is here (as well as in terminological choices like "principle") that Cousin most exemplifies Madden's remark that "the best way to think about [him] is not as an eclectic but as a significant member of the [Reidian] commonsense tradition." E. H. Madden, "Victor Cousin and the Commonsense Tradition," *History of Philosophy Quarterly* 1.1 (1984), p. 109.
19. See V. Cousin, *Leçons sur la philosophie de Kant* (Paris: Ladrange, 1844), pp. 126–8.
20. So too is Fichte's (*VBB* 1836, p. 42). Cousin's use of pre-reflexivity as a means to radicalize and ultimately overcome the Kantian-Fichtean legacy suggests that the scholarship on pre-reflexive self-consciousness in German philosophy by Dieter Henrich and Manfred Frank could be helpfully extended into nineteenth-century France. See e.g. M. Frank, *Präreflexives Selbstbewusstsein: Vier Vorlesungen* (Berlin: Reclam, 2015).
21. For a recent sketch of the political, ethical, and religious implications of Cousin's recourse to impersonal reason, see M. Sonenscher, *After Kant: The Romans, the Germans, and the Moderns in the History of Political Thought* (Princeton: Princeton University Press, 2023), pp. 273–6.
22. e.g. "To wish to describe inspiration reflectively is to reduce it to the impossible and condemn it to the absurd" (*PM*, p. 291).
23. Cousin, "1818 Programme," p. 279.
24. H. Poret, quoted in R. Ragghianti, "Victor Cousin et la querelle du panthéisme," in V. Cousin, *Nouvelle théodicée d'après la méthode psychologique* (Paris: L'Harmattan, 2001), pp. 12–13.
25. F. W. J. Schelling, *Werke*, vol. 10, ed. K. F. A. Schelling (Stuttgart: Cotta, 1853), p. 209.
26. F. W. J. Schelling, *The Grounding of Positive Philosophy: The Berlin Lectures*, trans. B. Matthews (Albany, NY: SUNY, 2007), p. 160. Cousin will himself speak of this aspect of his project as "making use of thought in order to escape it" (*PM*, p. 161). On the above, see further D. Whistler, "'True Empiricism': The Stakes of the Cousin–Schelling Controversy," in *Perspectives on Science* 27.2 (2019), pp. 739–65.
27. The later Cousin does not locate this argument within Descartes' texts alone but uses it more broadly as the basis of an entire "Right Cartesian" tradition he constructs (Bossuet, Fénelon, Malebranche). Ultimately, its roots are, as Cousin himself stresses, Augustinian: he follows *De Trinitate* in describing a trinity in human consciousness that reflects a metaphysical trinity. See *VBB* 1856, pp. 71–109.
28. Cousin will repeatedly formulate the above in the language of revelation: "Yes, I admit, I proclaim a revelation," he exclaims. "Reason is a faculty of revelation" and its "genuine revelation" is the absolute, i.e. that something mind-independent (such as God) exists. In other words, through revelation "we do manage to pass outside ourselves" (*PM*, pp. 293–5). One of the ways Cousin diagnoses Kant's failure "to access the domain of existences" is precisely in terms of his acknowledgement of solely "a subjective degree of reason"—reason as reasoning, as logical, as relative, rather than reason as revelation. From inside this logical reason Kant can only conceive a "logical God," not the "true God" of rational revelation (*PM*, pp. 297–9).
29. W. Hamilton, "M. Cousin's Course of Philosophy," in *Edinburgh Review* 50.99 (1829), p. 196.
30. In his 1828 lectures on the history of philosophy, for example, Cousin frames his historical method as "the alliance of the ideal and the real," the "abstract a priori" and the "a posteriori" in "a realized system." V. Cousin, *Cours de philosophie. Introduction à l'histoire de la philosophie*, ed. Patrice Vermeren (Paris: Fayard, 1991), p. 103.

II
THE THREE PREFACES

Preface to the 1826 Edition of *Philosophical Fragments*[1]

These *Fragments* consist of articles which were for the most part included in the *Journal des savans* and in the *Archives philosophiques* from 1816 to 1819.[2] Borrowed from my lectures of the period, I cannot hope to impose any unity upon them without speaking of the teaching to which they are related[3] and which they represent, as isolated pieces can represent a whole. Called upon to speak of myself, I will do so without any of those precautions of modesty which denigrate simplicity and uprightness of intention, and I will speak faithfully of all that I have done or wanted to do from the day when, named *maître de conférences* in philosophy at the École Normale, and *suppléant* professor of the history of modern philosophy at the Faculty of Letters [at the University of Paris],[4] I devoted—unreservedly and irrevocably—my whole life to the pursuit of the philosophical reform begun so honourably by Royer-Collard.[5]

In this position, my first concern[6] was method. A system is little more than a method applied to certain objects. Nothing is more important than immediately recognizing and determining the method one wishes to follow,[7] making an account to ourselves of our good and bad instincts, and of the direction in which they lead us and to which we[8] should either consent or not. For our own philosophy should be like our own destiny: it must belong to us. Of course, one must borrow it from the truth and from the necessity of things, but one should also receive it freely, knowing well what is being taken and what received. Speculative or practical philosophy is the alliance of necessity and freedom in the mind of a man who spontaneously puts himself in harmony with the laws of universal existence. The goal is in the infinite, but the starting point is in ourselves.[9] Open the history books: every philosopher who has respected his fellow men and who has wished to not only offer them the indefinite result of some dream has started out by returning to method. Every doctrine that has exercised some influence has done so, and could have done so, only by the new direction it imprinted on minds, by the new perspective by which it has considered things—that is, by its method.[10] Every philosophical reform[11] has its avowed or secret principle in a change to or in the progress of method. My first effort had then to be to consciously examine the point from which I was to depart, the direction I was to take,[12] the method I was going to employ, which contained in it the results of all kinds, unknown to myself but which its repeated application would finally lead me.[13] Moreover, as a public teacher and *maître de conférences* at a school of teachers[14] who had been called by their teaching or by their writings to influence the philosophical future of France, it was a sacred duty for me to, first of all, inculcate in them the spirit of examination and criticism with which they could, sooner or later, recognize my own errors, modify my teachings or separate themselves from them. The more a conviction is sincere and profound, the more it can be dangerous; and so an honest man who feels its perilous authority in his heart has an obligation to absolve himself in advance from the plague of errors he is letting slip by arming his listeners against himself, by forming them for independence, by provisionally and continuously discussing the general spirit of his lectures—that is, by insisting on method.

This was my first concern. But to what method was I to adhere? To that [method] which accorded with the spirit[15] of the age, studied seriously and willingly accepted, [imprinted] on national habits and my own habits. I will explain.

It is an incontestable fact that, in England and in France in the eighteenth century, Locke and Condillac replaced the older principal schools and reigned without opposition up to the present day. Instead of becoming upset by this fact, we must try to understand it; for, after all, the facts did not create themselves: they have their own laws which form part of the general laws of the human species. If the philosophy of sensation was really assented to in England and France, this phenomenon must have its reason.[16] And as soon as one thinks about it, this reason does honour, rather than injury, to the human mind. It is not its fault that it was unable to remain bound by the shackles of Cartesianism, for it was up to Cartesianism to remain vigilant and to satisfy all the conditions for making a system eternal. In the general movement of things and the progress of time, the spirit of[17] analysis and observation had to also have its place, and it took up this place in the eighteenth century. The spirit of the eighteenth century needs no apology. The apology for a century is its existence, for its existence is the decision and judgement of God himself, or else history is but an insignificant phantasmagoria. This new spirit[18] is often accused of incredulity and scepticism, but it is sceptical solely about what it did not understand, incredulous about what it could not believe—that is, the conditions of understanding and believing had, as in many earlier epochs, changed for the human race.[19] On pain of abdicating its independence, it had to impose these new conditions on all that aspired to govern its intellect and faith.[20] Faith is neither exhausted nor diminished. Like the individual, the human race lives by faith alone; but it is just that the conditions of faith are [continually] renewed. In the eighteenth century, the general condition for understanding and believing [something] was to have observed [it], and, owing to this, all philosophy which aspired to authority needed to be grounded on observation. But Cartesianism, especially its development by Malebranche, Spinoza, Leibniz, and Wolff[21]—Cartesianism which, in its second stage, abandoned observation and was lost to ontological hypotheses and scholastic formulae[22]—could not claim the title of experimental philosophy. Another system presented itself with this title and was accepted as such. This is the explanation for the fall of Cartesianism and the extraordinary success of Locke's and Condillac's philosophy. If one thinks about it, the success of this sorry philosophy is still testament to the dignity and independence of the human mind, which successively abandons the systems that abandon it, and will pursue its path through the most deplorable errors, rather than not advance at all. It did not take up the philosophy of sensation as materialist, but as experimental—and it was, up to a certain point. The success of this philosophy did not come from its dogmas, but from its method, which did not belong to it, but to its century.[23] And such is the truth of the claim that the experimental method was the necessary fruit[24] of the age, rather than the ephemeral work of some sect in England and France, that, if one impartially examines those contemporary schools most opposed to [the school] of sensation, one discovers the very same claims to observation and experience. Reid and Kant, in Scotland and in Germany, fought hard against Locke's doctrine and reversed it from top to bottom—but with what weapons? With those of Locke himself, with the experimental method applied differently. Reid begins from the human mind and its faculties which he analyses into their real act and then records their laws. Kant separates reason from all its objects and considers it from within, so to speak, providing a subtle and profound enumeration of it. His philosophy is a *critique*, which is always a matter of observation and experience. Across Europe and the world, everywhere it was the same spirit, everywhere the same method—this is the real unity of the [eighteenth] century, since this unity is to be found within such major differences.[25]

Let us examine further our own [century's] very different thinkers and especially our French thinkers of the nineteenth century. The spirit of analysis has destroyed much that lies around us. Born amidst ruins of all kinds, we now feel the need to reconstruct; this need is intimate, present, imperious. There is danger for us in our condition, and yet, even if we are to be more just than our fathers towards the past, we cannot rest [in the past] any more than they did: we offer amnesty to our fathers and their epoch and have faith solely in observation and experience. This is what we are, and we must resign ourselves to it.

And is there anything wrong with that? Let us reflect further on it. To limit [something] to observation and to experience is to limit [it] to human nature; for we observe only with ourselves, to the extent of the measure, scope, and limits[26] of our faculties and their laws. We are thus led back to human nature. But do we need anything else? If observation, which proceeds just as far as human nature can, is not enough to attain all truths and all beliefs and to constitute the entire circle of science, the problem is not in the method, which limits us to our natural means of knowing, but in the impotence of these means and of our nature, from which we cannot escape. In fact, whatever method we borrow, we are the ones doing so and using it: it is always with ourselves that we act; it is always human nature, which, under the appearance of forgetting itself, is ever present and undertakes all that it does or attempts to undertake, even when this seems to be beyond its power. Either one must despair of science or else human nature is sufficient to attain it. Observation, i.e. human nature[27] accepted as the unique instrument of discovery, is sufficient when it is employed well—or else nothing is sufficient; for we have nothing else and our precursors had nothing more. Let us study the system that time has consigned to the past: what has [time] destroyed and what might it have destroyed? The hypothetical part of these systems. But what gave life and consistency to these hypotheses? Precisely those truths discovered by observation, which observation today rediscovers and which today still have the same truth[28] and the same novelty as before. What was it that elevated so high and still sustains Pythagoras' *numbers*,[29] Plato's *ideas*, Aristotle's *categories*? A fact, as real today as it was in antiquity—that is, in the intellect, there are real elements inexplicable by the acquisitions of the senses alone. What produced Malebranche's vision in God and Leibniz's pre-established harmony? Again facts—that there is no single piece of knowledge which does not imply the concept of existence and so of God to the mind; [the fact] that intellect and sensibility are distinct in us, but inseparable; that each has its independent laws which govern it, although these laws exist in secret relations and harmony. If we were to thus examine the most famous hypotheses, we would see that, even when they get lost in the clouds,[30] their root remains here below in some fact that is real in itself; and it is for this reason that they have been established and accredited among men. Error, by itself, is incomprehensible and inadmissible; it is in its relation to the true that it is sustained. Not even the most extravagant systems can fail to have some reasonable aspects; and it is always unperceived common sense that bestows success on the hypotheses[31] with which it is combined. At the bottom of everything, what is true and durable in systems scattered across the ages is the work of observation: it works for philosophy often without the philosopher knowing anything about it; and—a remarkable thing—what is immortal in the passing of human doctrines comes solely from this experimental method, which appears to grasp merely what is happening [at the present moment].

The method of observation is good in itself. It is given to us by the spirit of the age, which is itself the work of the general spirit of the world. We have faith in it alone, we can do nothing without it, and yet, in England and in France, it has until now been merely destructive without founding anything. Among us, its one philosophical work is the system of transformed sensation.[32] Who is wrong? Men, not method. The method is irreproachable and is always sufficient, but it must be applied in accordance with its spirit. We must merely observe, but still observe everything. Human nature is not impotent, but one should not take any of its strength away. We can arrive at a system that lasts, but only as long as we are not first blocked by some systematic prejudice.[33] Eighteenth-century philosophy did not act in this way and could not act in this way. Born from a struggle against the past and itself an instrument of that struggle, it was experimental against the past, systematic in the experiments it undertook, and, for fear of being led astray by ancient shadows, it found real[34] facts close at hand, tarried with them, initially due to weakness (since every method in its infancy is weak), then due to the almost irresistible seduction that resulted from the success of the physical sciences distracting its attention from every other order of phenomena, and finally due to the blindness of the spirit of revolution which was only illuminated by its very excess and whose destiny was to keep going until some absolute triumph was obtained. Its cradle had been England and its battlefield became France. Bacon has been much celebrated as the father of the experimental method;[35] however, the truth is that Bacon traced the rules and operations of the experimental method within the framework of the physical sciences, but not beyond them, and he was also the first to lead this method astray—onto a systematic path—by limiting it to the external world and to sensibility. From Bacon comes this claim: "Mens humana si agat in materiam, naturam rerum et opera Dei contemplando, pro modo materiae operatur atque ab eadem determinatur; si ipsa in se vertatur, tanquam aranea texens telam, tunc demum indeterminata est; et parit telas quasdam doctrinae tenuitate fili operisque mirabiles, sed quoad usum frivolas et inanes." ["The wit and mind of man, if it work upon matter, which is the contemplation of the creatures of God, worketh according to the stuff and is limited thereby; but if it work upon itself, as the spider worketh his web, then it is endless, and brings forth indeed cobwebs of learning, admirable for the fineness of thread and work, but of no substance or profit."][36] Bacon's[37] [power of] observation is addressed solely to sensible phenomena; and his inductions, which rest on this basis alone, do not carry him far. Any positive[38] philosophy that begins from such an incomplete application of method could only be incomplete itself—sadly incomplete.[39] The system of transformed sensation was the result of this kind of counsel, and so Bacon necessarily produced Condillac.[40] Such is the significance of aberrations in method: the most minor [errors] trail in their wake the most serious errors that can only be destroyed by turning back to their principle. The initial aberration in true philosophical method is due to Bacon; its consequences reach fulfilment only with Condillac—and beyond him there is no longer any room for new aberrations, either in a fact of method or in a fact of system.[41] Do we accept Bacon's incomplete method? If so, we accept all the lacunas[42] of Condillac's system; only weakness and inconsistency would allow us to stop halfway. Does Condillac's system, in all its rigour, shock human nature and inattentive observation?[43] We must turn back to Bacon and[44] try to rectify the evil at its source; we must borrow experimental method from Bacon, without immediately corrupting observation by imposing a system upon it. We must employ the method of observation alone, but apply it to all the facts, whatever they may be, as long as they exist. The exactness [of such a method] is in its impartiality, and its impartiality is found solely in its extensity.[45] In this way, the sought-after alliance of the metaphysical and physical sciences may well be achieved, not through the systematic sacrifice of one to the other, but through[46] the unity of their method applied to diverse phenomena related by their coexistence and the possibility of being observed.[47] We would therefore satisfy the conditions of the spirit of the age, as well as what was legitimate and necessary in the revolution of the eighteenth century; and we might also satisfy the most elevated needs of our human nature, which are themselves facts—facts as incontestable and imperious as any other.

Such were the reflections manifest to my friends and[48] me at the beginning of our philosophical career. Out of historical conscientiousness I have reproduced them in all their imperfection roughly as they were recorded in my lectures of the period. Methods are perfected only by being applied and, if, after eleven years of teaching and study, I remain faithful to the method which oriented my first essays, it is perhaps for deeper motives closer to the nature of things than those I have just set out. But in 1815, these motives were enough for me to adopt the method of observation and induction as philosophical method,[49] along with the law of all [forms of] observation[50]—that is, [the law] that it must be complete, exhaust its object[51] and stop only when it lacks facts, where, therefore, induction no longer has any basis and man's mind no hold.[52] The facts—these are the starting point, if not the limit of philosophy. Moreover, the facts, whatever they may be, exist for us only insofar as they occur to consciousness. It is there alone that observation obtains them and describes them before delivering them over to induction, which reveals the consequences contained within them. The field of philosophical observation is consciousness; there is no other; but within it nothing should be neglected; everything is important, since everything forms a whole and the total unity is ungraspable if even one part is lacking. To return into consciousness and scrupulously study all its phenomena, their differences and their relations—this is the first study of philosophy; its scientific name is *psychology*. Psychology is therefore the condition and vestibule of philosophy. Psychological method consists in relinquishing everything but the contents of consciousness to establish and orient itself there where everything possesses reality, but where reality is so diverse and so delicate. Psychological talent consists in placing oneself voluntarily into this completely internal world, to give oneself a view of oneself, and to reproduce freely and distinctly all the facts that the circumstances of life have fortuitously and confusedly brought us.[53] I repeat: the passing of time and the exercise [of this method] have fully revealed to me the diverse degrees of depth in this psychological method; but ultimately, at whatever degree one considers it, it constitutes the fundamental unity of my lectures and all these fragments. This is the first perspective by which they may still merit the attention of friends of philosophy.

I now turn to an account of the results to which the ever more rigorous application of the psychological method led me over time.

The year 1816[54] was entirely spent testing my strength and the philosophical method on very particular questions, in which I often found many traces of Royer-Collard and the Scottish philosophers, who were such excellent guides at the beginning of my career. We should not forget—neither my friends nor I—this exacting year of 1816, which were marked by our initial efforts and during which time the philosophical reform in the École Normale was definitively established on foundations which did not collapse with the school.[55] That year gave us the method which still presides over all our works. Their positive results scarcely went beyond the sphere of Scottish philosophy and do not merit the public's attention.[56] [The results] of 1817[57] have a little more importance.

As soon as we enter back into consciousness, free from any systematic perspective, we observe such varied phenomena manifest there with their real characteristics that[58] we are immediately struck by the presence of a mass of phenomena that are impossible to confuse with those of sensibility. Sensation—as well as the concepts it furnishes or with which it is combined—constitutes a real order of phenomena in consciousness; but there we encounter other equally incontestable[59] facts which can be grouped into two large classes: volitional facts and rational facts. The will is not sensation, since, often, it struggles against it, and it is precisely in this opposition that it manifests itself eminently. Reason is equally not identical to sensation,[60] since, among the concepts with which reason furnishes us, there are some whose characteristics are irreconcilable with those of sensible phenomena—for example, the concepts of cause, substance, time, space, unity, etc. Fashion sensation however you like and submit it to the most subtle metamorphoses[61] and you will never draw from it the characteristics of universality and necessity by which these concepts and many others are incontestably marked. The concepts of the good and the beautiful are the same, and they thereby remove the origin and limits imposed on art and morality by the exclusive philosophy of sensation and place them within metaphysics, in a higher and independent sphere. However, this sphere itself, in all its sublimity, forms part of consciousness, and so falls under observation. Observation draws back the clouds that ordinarily envelop it, establishes it on the unshakeable foundation of consciousness[62] and bestows on all the phenomena it comprises the same authority as all the other phenomena for which consciousness is the theatre. Hence, the method of observation, in the limits within which it initially retains its modesty and[63] its circumspection, already opens up quite attractive perspectives. They must be pursued and extended.

The first task of the psychological method is to withdraw into the field of consciousness where there are only phenomena, all of which are perceptible and measurable[64] by observation. Moreover, as no substantial existence falls under consciousness's gaze, it follows that the first effect of such a severe application of method is to adjourn ontology. It is adjourned,[65] not destroyed. Indeed, it is a fact attested by observation that,[66] within this same consciousness where there are only phenomena, there are also concepts whose further development transcends the limits of consciousness and reaches existences.[67] Do you hinder the development of these concepts?[68] If so, you arbitrarily limit the scope of a fact, you attack this very fact and thereby destroy the authority of all other facts. One must either revoke the authority of consciousness in itself or else admit this authority as a whole[69] for all facts attested by consciousness. Reason is neither more nor less certain[70] than the will and sensibility; its certainty, once admitted, must be followed everywhere it rigorously leads, even across into ontology. For example, it is a rational fact attested by consciousness[71] that, for the intellect, all phenomena that are manifest presuppose a cause. It is again a fact[72] that this principle of causality[73] is marked by the characteristics of universality and necessity. If it is universal and necessary, to limit it is to destroy it. Moreover, for the phenomenon of sensation the principle of causality intervenes universally and necessarily and relates this phenomenon to a cause; and consciousness attests that this cause is not the personal cause that the will represents.[74] Hence, it follows that the principle of causality, in its irresistible application, leads to an[75] impersonal cause—that is, to an external cause, and that, later and always irresistibly, the principle of causality enriches those features and laws[76] which together comprise the universe. Here is an existence, but an existence revealed[77] by a principle which is itself attested by consciousness. This is a first step into ontology, but via psychology—that is, via observation.[78] Similar operations lead to the cause of all causes, to the substantial cause, to God, and not only to a powerful God but to a moral God, to a holy God. The result is that this experimental method—which, when applied to one incomplete and exclusive order of phenomena alone, destroys ontology and the higher elements of consciousness—when applied faithfully and firmly and extended to all phenomena, raises up what it had[79] overturned and itself furnishes ontology with a sure instrument and a large and[80] legitimate basis. Therefore, after having begun modestly, we can end up with results whose importance are the equal of their certainty.

This scarcely gives an indication of them, but the reader will find all the methodological procedures that gave rise to them and justify them fully explained in the programme of my 1817 lectures, printed among these fragments.[81]

In 1818,[82] my works advanced further along the same path and began to take on more extensity and depth.[83] Having reduced the facts of consciousness the previous year to three principal classes (sensible facts, volitional facts, and rational facts), the time had come to analyse each of them more closely, as well as the relations which united them in the indivisible unity of consciousness. It was primarily voluntary facts and rational facts which occupied my attention, because they had been most neglected in French philosophy.

Sensible facts are necessary; we do not impute them to ourselves; rational facts are necessary as well and reason is no less independent of the will than sensibility is.[84] Voluntary facts are the only ones marked, under consciousness's gaze,[85] with the characteristics of imputability and personality. The will alone is the person or the I.[86] The I stands at the centre of the intellectual sphere.[87] Without it, the conditions of existence of all other phenomena would still be valid, but, without any relation to the I, they would not appear in consciousness, and, for [consciousness], it would be as if they were not. The will creates no rational or sensible phenomena;

it[88] presupposes them, since it grasps itself only in distinction from them. We would [otherwise] find ourselves merely in an alien world, between two orders of phenomena that do not belong to us, which we perceive only under the condition of separating ourselves from them.[89] Furthermore, we perceive[90] solely by means of a light which does not come from us, since our personality is will and nothing more:[91] all light comes from reason, and it is reason which perceives itself, [perceives] the sensibility that envelops it and [perceives] the will, which [reason] obligates without constraining. The element of knowledge is rational in its essence, and,[92] although composed of three integral and inseparable elements, consciousness borrows its most immediate ground from reason, without which no science would be possible and therefore no consciousness either. Sensibility is the external condition of consciousness; the will stands at its centre, and reason is its light.[93] A deepened analysis of reason is one of the most delicate undertakings of psychology.

Reason is impersonal by its nature. We do not make it, and[94] it possesses so little that is individual that its character is precisely the contrary of individuality—that is, universality and necessity, since it is to [reason] that we owe knowledge of necessary and universal truths, principles which we all obey and which we cannot not obey. The existence of these principles is therefore a preliminary given which[95] must have been posited at the beginning in full self-evidence.[96] This is a victory for the method of observation and it must become its uncontested foundation.[97] Let us come next to the question of precisely how many of these regulatory principles of reason—which for us comprise reason itself—there are. After recording the existence of such principles, the method must attempt to provide an enumeration and a complete classification of them.[98] Plato, who, after Pythagoras,[99] rested his philosophy on them, neglected to count them; it seems that he refused to let his divine wings—by which he flew through the world of ideas—touch them in profane analysis. The methodical Aristotle was faithful to his master, but more faithful still to analysis, and so, after transforming ideas into categories, he submitted them to a severe examination and dared to supply a list of them. This list, which has been ridiculed by frivolous minds as arid nomenclature, is the most daring and most perilous undertaking of method. Is Aristotle's enumeration complete? I think so; it exhausts the subject—this is its immortal glory. However, if his enumeration is complete, does the classification and coordination of these categories leave anything to be desired? It is here that error enters into Aristotle's list. In my opinion, its order is arbitrary and does not correspond to the progressive[100] development of the intellect. What is more, does this list contain any repetitions and would it be possible to reduce it? Once more, I think so. Among the moderns, Cartesianism[101] recognized necessary truths, but did not undertake anything of such a comprehensive and precise nature. In the eighteenth century, in France,[102] necessary truths were downgraded from an initial [philosophical] question: they were not even accorded the honour of examination and were erroneously included in the old system. Instead, [necessary truths] were to be sacrificed to sensation, the unique foundation[103] and measure of all possible truth. The Scottish school restored their dignity and enumerated some of them, but did not think to give a full account of them.[104] It was reserved to Kant to renew Aristotle's enterprise and to be the first among the moderns to attempt a complete[105] list of the laws of thought. Kant undertook an exact and profound review of them, and his work is superior to Aristotle's. However, I think one might still make the same reproaches against him, and a long, detailed examination was able to demonstrate, to those who followed my 1818 lecture course,[106] that, if Kant's list is complete, it is still arbitrary in its classification and can be legitimately reduced. If in my teaching I have achieved anything useful, it is perhaps on this point. I have at least renewed an important question, I have interrogated the two most famous solutions, and I have tried to produce one myself—one which neither time nor further discussion has yet undermined. I contended that all the laws of thought can be reduced to just two: the law of causality and that of substance.[107] These are the two essential and fundamental laws from which all the others derive and develop in a non-arbitrary order. I believe I have demonstrated that, if one synthetically examines[108] these two laws according to the order of the nature of things, the first is that of substance and the second that of causality, whereas, analytically and[109] according to the order of the acquisition of our knowledge, the law of causality precedes that of substance—or rather both are given together and are contemporaneous in consciousness.

It is not enough to have enumerated, categorized, reduced, and systematized the laws of reason; one must prove that they are absolute, so as to prove that their consequences, whatever they may be, are also absolute.[110] What is at stake here is Kant's discussion[111] of the objective and the subjective in human knowledge.[112] After discerning so perceptively all the laws which preside over thought, this great man was struck by these laws' character of necessity—that is, the impossibility for us not to recognize and follow them—and he believed he saw precisely in this character a dependence on and relativity to[113] the I, the real and distinctive nature of which he was far from grasping. Moreover, once the laws of reason had thus been diminished into laws that were nothing more than relative to the human condition, their whole scope was circumscribed by the sphere of our personal nature,[114] and their most extensive implications, which remained forever marked by the indelible character of subjectivity, engendered only irresistible beliefs, if one wished, but certainly no independent truths.[115] This is how, after describing all the laws of thought so well, this incomparable analyst rendered them impotent, and, [despite passing] through every certainty,[116] ends up in ontological scepticism, against which he found no other refuge except the sublime inconsistency of lending to the laws of practical reason more objectivity than those of speculative reason. After providing an inventory of the laws of reason, all my efforts in the 1818 lecture course were[117] to eliminate this character of subjectivity which [the character] of necessity had seemingly[118] imposed on them and to re-establish them in their independence, thereby saving philosophy from the reef it had hit at the very moment it reached port. Many months of public debate were devoted to demonstrating that the laws of human reason are nothing less than the laws of reason in itself.[119] Ever faithful to the psychological method, I kept on insisting more on observation, instead of moving away from it, and it is by observation that—in the depths of consciousness and to a degree to which Kant had not penetrated—underneath the apparent relativity and subjectivity of necessary principles, I reached and untangled the momentary, but real fact of the spontaneous perception of the truth.[120] This perception does not immediately[121] come to reflection and so passes unperceived in the depths of consciousness, but which is there the veritable foundation of what, later—under a logical form and in the hands of reflection—becomes a necessary conception. All subjectivity, along with all reflection,[122] expires in the spontaneity of perception. But the primitive light[123] is so pure that it is insensible;[124] it is just its reflected light which strikes us, but often by obscuring in its unfaithful brightness the purity of the primitive light. Reason becomes subjective in relation to the voluntary and free I, the seat and archetype of all subjectivity; however, in itself, [reason] is impersonal; it does not belong to one I or another among humanity; it does not even belong to humanity, and its laws therefore reveal only themselves.[125] They preside over and govern humankind who perceives them, as well as nature which represents[126] them, but they do not belong to [humanity or nature]. One can even truthfully[127] say that nature and humanity belong to them, since both have beauty and reality[128] only in their relation to the intellect. Without laws to rule it or principles to direct it, nature and humanity would soon fall into a void from which they could never escape.[129] The laws of the intellect thus constitute a world apart, which subjects the visible world, presides over its movements, sustains it and bears it, but does not depend on it. It is this intelligible world, this sphere of *ideas* distinct from and independent of their internal and external subjects[130] that Plato glimpsed and which modern analysis and psychology rediscover today within the depths of consciousness.

Once the laws of thinking have been demonstrated to be absolute, induction can be employed without fear; and the absolute principles obtained by observation can legitimately lead us where observation itself no longer has immediate hold. Moreover, among these laws of thinking that psychology provides, the two fundamental ones which contain all the others—the law of causality and the law of substance—are irresistibly applied to themselves, raising us up directly to their cause and substance; and, since they are absolute, they raise us up to an absolute cause and an absolute substance. However, an absolute cause is identical in essence to an absolute substance, for every absolute cause must be substance insofar as it is absolute, and every absolute substance must be a cause in order to be able to manifest itself. What is more, in order to be absolute, an absolute substance must be unique: two absolutes are contradictory, and so absolute substance is one or it is nothing. Ultimately,[131] all substance is absolute as substance, and therefore one;

for relative substances destroy the very idea of substance, and finite substances, which assume another substance beyond them to which they are attached, strongly resemble phenomena.[132] The unity of substance thus derives from the very idea of substance[133]—a result incontestable by psychological observation—with the result that, when applied to consciousness, experience gives, at a certain degree of profundity, what is most opposed to it in appearance: ontology. Substantial causality is being in itself, and so the laws of reason are laws of being and reason is true existence. It follows that, just as analysis, when applied to consciousness, first separated reason from personality, so too now, from the point to which analysis has led us, we see that reason and its laws pertaining to substance can be neither a modification nor an effect of the I, since they are the immediate effect of the manifestation of absolute substance. Ontology thus returns to psychology the illumination it had borrowed from it, bringing about the identity of the two extremes of science.[134]

Such is the complete[135] analysis of reason; [the analysis] of activity is no less important.

Of all active phenomena the most salient is, without a doubt, the will. It is a fact that, in the midst of the movement which external agents bring about in us despite ourselves, we still have the power to initiate a different movement, that is, to first conceive it, then to deliberate on whether we will execute it and finally to come to a resolution and move on to its execution, to commence it, pursue it or suspend it, accomplish it or stop it, and always to be master of it. The fact is certain, and what is no less certain is that the movement executed in these conditions takes on a new character for us: we impute it to ourselves, we treat it as an effect of ourselves, who we then consider as its cause. This, for us, is the origin of the concept of cause—not an abstract cause, but a personal cause, which pertains to us. The characteristic proper to the I is that of causality, or will, since we relate to ourselves and impute to ourselves only what we cause, and we cause only what we will. To will, to cause, to be for ourselves—these are all synonymous expressions of the same fact which simultaneously comprises the will, causality and the I. The relation of the will to the person is no mere relation of coexistence; it is a genuine relation of identity.[136] It is not that being for the I is one thing and willing another, since then[137] there could be either impersonal volitions, which is contrary to the facts, or else a personality, an I which could know itself without willing, which is impossible, for to know oneself as an I is to distinguish oneself from a not-I; and one can only so distinguish by separating the two, by going beyond impersonal movement to produce [a movement] that is imputed to oneself—that is, by willing. The will is therefore the being of the person. Far from constituting personality, the movements of sensibility, desires, and passions destroy it. Personality and passion essentially subsist in an inverse relation, in a contradiction, and this is life. Just as we cannot discover the element of[138] personality elsewhere than in the will, so too we cannot discover the element of causality[139] anywhere else. The will or that internal causality which immediately produces effects—primarily as their cause from within—must not be confused with the external and really passive instruments of this causality which, as instruments, have the appearance of also producing effects, but without being their first cause, that is,[140] their true cause.[141] When I push one marble against another, it is not the marble which truly causes the subsequent movement, since this movement was imprinted on [the first marble] by my hand, by the muscles which, in accordance with the mystery of our organism, are at the service of the will. Properly speaking, these actions are just a chain of effects, one following from the other, each in turn simulating a cause without containing the genuine one, and all relating to each other as relatively distant effects of the will, as their first cause. Seek the notion of cause in the action of marble against marble, as was done prior to Hume, or [in the action] of hand on marble, and [in the action] of the first locomotor muscles on their extremities, or even in the action of the will on the muscle, as [Maine] de Biran did,[142] and you will not find it in any of these cases, not even the last, since it is possible a paralysis of muscles might render the will impotent, non-productive, incapable of being a cause and therefore [incapable] of suggesting such a concept. However, what no paralysis can prevent is the action of the will on itself, the production of a resolution—that is, an entirely spiritual causation, the primitive archetype of causality, of which all external actions, from the muscular effort to the movement of marble against marble, are merely more or less unrepresentative symbols. Therefore, for us, the first cause is the will, and its first effect is a volition. This is the source of the highest and the purest concept of cause, which is merged with that of personality. And it is this ownership, so to speak, of the cause by the will and personality which is for us the condition of conceiving further impersonal external causes, whether they are subsequent to it or simultaneous with it.

The phenomenon of the will includes the following moments: (1) predetermining an act to be done; (2) deliberating; (3) choosing or[143] reaching a resolution. If we [look] carefully, it is reason which entirely constitutes the first [moment], and even the second, since it is [reason] which deliberates, but it is not [reason] which resolves and determines itself. Moreover, reason, here mixed with the will, is mixed with it in a reflective form: conceiving a goal and deliberating involves the idea of reflection. Reflection is therefore the condition of every voluntary act, if every voluntary acts presupposes a predetermination of its object and deliberation. Moreover, to act voluntarily is indeed to act in this way, as we have seen; and it is because the will is indeed reflective that it presents so striking a phenomenon.[144] But can a reflective operation be a primitive operation? To will is—[in addition to] knowing one can reach a resolution and act—to deliberate over whether one can reach a particular resolution, whether one can act in a particular way, and choosing in favour of one or the other [particular resolution]. The result of this choice, of this decision preceded by deliberation and predetermination is a volition, the immediate effect of personal activity. However, to reach a resolution and to act thus, one had to know that one could so reach a resolution and act, and so one must have previously reached a resolution and acted otherwise, without deliberation or predetermination, that is, without reflection. The operation prior to reflection is spontaneity. It is a fact that, even today, we often act without having deliberated, and that, when rational perception[145] encounters in us spontaneously the act to be performed, personal activity also enters spontaneously into action and immediately comes to a resolution, not by means of a foreign impulse, but by means of a kind of immediate inspiration, higher than reflection and often better than it. The *I would have him die!* of the elder Horatius,[146] the *To me, Auvergne!* of the brave d'Assas[147] are resolutions that are neither blind nor reflective;[148] their heroism is no longer imposed on them by an external fatality, nor is it[149] borrowed from reasoning and reflection. The phenomenon of spontaneous activity is therefore just as real as that of voluntary activity. Yet, since everything reflective is deeply determinate and therefore clear,[150] the phenomenon of voluntary and reflective activity is more visible than that of spontaneous activity, which is less determinate and more obscure. What is more, every voluntary act properly consists in its ability to be repeated at will, [its ability] to be summoned, so to speak, before consciousness, so that [consciousness] can examine it and describe it at leisure, whereas the proper character of a spontaneous act (as involuntary) is that it cannot be repeated at will and passes by [consciousness] either unperceived or irrevocable;[151] it can only later be recalled on the condition of being reflected, that is, of being destroyed as a spontaneous fact. Spontaneity is thus necessarily obscure, exhibiting that obscurity which surrounds everything that is primitive, fugitive, and instantaneous.[152]

Let us seek further and we will find no other modes of action. Reflection and spontaneity comprise all the real forms of activity.

Reflection—both in principle and in fact—presupposes and follows spontaneity. However, since nothing more can exist in the reflective than in the spontaneous [act], all that we have said of one applies to the other, and, although spontaneity is accompanied by neither predetermination nor deliberation, it is no less than the will a real power of action and, therefore, a productive and so personal cause. Hence, spontaneity contains all that the will contains, and it contains it prior to the latter, in a less determinate, but purer form—and this raises even higher the immediate source of causality and of the I.[153] The I already exists with its productive power in the flash of spontaneity, and it is in this instantaneous[154] flash that it grasps itself instantaneously. We might say that [the I] discovers itself in spontaneity, but constitutes itself in reflection. The I, says Fichte,[155] posits itself in a voluntary determination. This perspective is that of reflection. In order for the I to posit itself, as Fichte puts it, it must explicitly distinguish itself from the not-I. To distinguish is to negate; to distinguish one thing from another is to again affirm, but by negating—it is to affirm after having negated. Moreover, it is not true that intellectual life begins with a negation, and, prior to reflection and the fact (the description of which Fichte has forever attached his name to), there exists an operation by which the I is found without being sought, posits itself, if you like, but without having willed to posit itself—and does so by the virtue and energy that is proper to the activity alone, an activity that [the I] itself recognizes by bringing it about, but without having known of it in advance. This is because this activity only reveals itself by its acts, and the first [act] must have been the effect of a power of which it had been ignorant until that moment.

What, therefore, is this power which reveals itself only by its acts, which is discovered and perceived in spontaneity and then is rediscovered and reflected in the will?

Whether spontaneous or voluntary, all personal acts have this in common: they are immediately related to a cause which has its point of departure uniquely in itself—that is, they are free. This is the proper notion of freedom. Freedom cannot be solely located in the will, since then spontaneity would not be free; and, on the other hand, freedom cannot be reduced to spontaneity alone, since the will would in turn not be free. If, then, the two phenomena are equally free, they can be so solely on the condition that anything that belongs exclusively to one or other of these two phenomena is removed from the notion of freedom and only what is common to them remains. Moreover, what do they have in common if not their starting point in themselves and their immediate relation to a cause, which is their own cause and acts by their own energy alone? As freedom is the common characteristic of spontaneity and the will, it encompasses both of them, and so must possess and does possess something more general than they do, which is not exclusively absorbed by either one or the other, and this constitutes their identity.[156] This theory of freedom is the only one which accords with the diverse facts that humanity's consciousness proclaims free and which, in their diversity, have given rise to contradictory theories formed exclusively for a specific order of phenomena. Hence, for example, the theory which limits freedom to the will must admit no other freedom than reflective freedom—freedom preceded by predetermination, accompanied by deliberation and marked by characteristics which singularly reduce the number of free acts [in existence] and removes all freedom from anything that is not reflective, [such as] from the poet's and artist's enthusiasm in moments of creation,[157] from those without knowledge who reflect little and scarcely act but spontaneously—that is, from three-quarters of the human race. Because the expression of arbitrary freedom implies the idea of choice, of comparison and of reflection, these conditions have [in turn] been imposed on freedom, of which arbitrary freedom is but one form. Arbitrary freedom is free will,[158] that is, the will. However, the will is so little representative of freedom [as such] that language itself adds the epithet free to it and, in so doing, relates it to something more general than itself. The same should be said of spontaneity. Abstracted from the apparatus of reflection, comparison, and deliberation—which all comes relatively later—spontaneity manifests freedom in a purer form, but it is only one form of freedom and not freedom in its entirety: the fundamental idea of freedom is that of a power which, in whatever form it acts, acts solely by its own energy.

If freedom is distinct from free phenomena and as the characteristic of all phenomena is to be more or less determinate, but nevertheless always [determinate], then it follows that the proper characteristic of freedom, in its contrast with free phenomena, is indetermination. Freedom is, therefore, not a form of activity, but activity in itself, indeterminate activity which, precisely as such, is determined into one form or another. From this it further follows that the I or personal activity—whether spontaneous or reflective—represents merely the determinateness of activity, rather than its essence. Freedom is the ideal of the I; the I should continually tend towards it without ever attaining it; it partakes of it, but is not it. [The I] is freedom in act, not freedom as potential; it is a cause, but a phenomenal, not a substantial cause, relative and not absolute. Fichte's absolute I is a contradiction. It implies that something of the absolute and the substantial is encountered in what is determinate, that is, in what is phenomenal. In the fact of activity, substance can be found only outside and above all phenomenal activity, in a potentiality that has not yet passed into action, in the indeterminacy capable of determining itself, in the freedom abstracted from its forms which, by determining it, limit it and phenomenalize it. Here is the ontological perspective on freedom.[159] This is, therefore, my analysis of *the I*, moving once again from psychology to a new aspect of ontology, to a substantial activity, prior to and superior to all phenomenal activity—[an activity] which produces all the phenomena of activity, outlasts them all and renews them all, immortal and inexhaustible when exhausting its temporary modes. And yet—something admirable!—since it is simultaneously cause and substance, and since [it is] the very basis of the substance of active phenomena, this absolute substance in its essential development takes on, as rational substance does,[160] two forms that are parallel to those of reason—that is, spontaneity and reflection. These two moments meet each other in a circle both here and in the other [case of reason], and the principle of one, like that of the other, is always a substantial causality. Activity and reason, freedom and intellect thereby penetrate each other intimately in the unity of substance.[161]

The final phenomenon of consciousness yet to be analysed, sensation, would demand an analogous exposition that time prevents, and I must content myself here with a few words that our thinkers will understand and which will at least serve as a prelude to my further works on the philosophy of nature.

Sensation is a phenomenon of consciousness just as incontestable as the other two; and if this phenomenon is real—since no phenomenon is able to be sufficient onto itself—reason, which acts according to the law of causality and substance, compels us to relate the phenomenon of sensation to an existent cause, and, since this cause is evidently not *the I*, it must be that reason relates sensation to another cause, for the action of reason is irresistible. [Reason] thus relates [sensation] to a cause foreign to *the I*, placed outside of the dominion of the I—that is, to an external cause.[162] This forms for us the concept of the outside as opposed to the inside which *the I* constitutes and comprises,[163] the concept of an external object as opposed to the subject (which is personality itself), the concept of passivity as opposed to freedom. However, do not let this expression "passivity" deceive us, for *the I* is not passive and can never be so, since it is free activity; nor is the object passive, since it is given to us uniquely on the basis of cause, of active force. Passivity[164] is therefore solely a relation between two forces which act on each other. Vary and multiply the phenomena of sensation, as soon as reason perceives them, it will relate[165] them to a cause that it attributes—to the extent that experience allows—not to the internal modifications of the subject, but to objective properties capable of exciting them—that is, it expresses the concept of cause without departing from it, since [external] properties are always causes and can be known only as such.[166] The external world is, therefore, merely an assemblage of causes corresponding to our real or possible[167] sensations; the relation[168] of these causes among themselves is the order of the world. Hence, this world is composed of the same material as us, and nature is the sister of man; it is active, living, animated like we are; and its history is a drama just as much as our own.

Moreover, just as personal or human force is developed and formed in consciousness, as it were, under the auspices of reason, which we recognize as our law even when we violate it, so too external forces are necessarily[169] conceived in terms of developing laws; or, better put, the laws of external forces are nothing but their mode of development and the constancy of this development constitutes for us their regularity.[170] Force in nature is distinct from its law, just as personality in us is [distinct] from reason. I say distinct, and not separate, for all force bears its law along with it and manifests it in its action and by its action. Moreover, every law presupposes a reason,[171] and the laws of the world are nothing but reason considered in the world. Hence, this is a new relation of man to nature: nature is composed, like humanity, of laws and forces, of reason and activity, and from this perspective the two worlds return closer together.

Is there nothing else?[172] Just as we reduced the laws of reason to two and the modes of free force [to two], could we not attempt a similar reduction of the forces of nature and their laws? Could we not reduce all of nature's regular modes of action to two modes which, in their relation to the spontaneous and reflective action of the I and of reason, would manifest a still more intimate harmony than that just indicated between the internal world and the external world? We glimpse here the sort of thing I wish to say about expansion and contraction. However, until methodical labour has converted these conjectures into certitudes, I will merely live in hope and remain quiet. I will content myself with remarking that the philosophical considerations which reduce the concept of the external world to that of force have already made some progress and govern modern physics without [physics] knowing it. What physicist, since Euler, seeks anything in nature but forces and laws? Who speaks today of atoms? And who now takes molecules, derivative of atoms, as anything but a hypothesis? If the fact is incontestable,[173] if modern physics is now solely occupied with forces and laws, then I can conclude rigorously that physics, whether it knows it or not, is no longer materialist and that it became spiritualist the day it rejected all methods other than observation and induction—[methods] which can only ever lead to forces and laws. For is there anything material in forces and laws? It is for this reason that the physical sciences have themselves started down the great path of spiritualism properly understood, and they have now only to walk with firm step and to increase their knowledge of these forces and laws to generalize them better. Let us go further. It is a law already acknowledged by reason itself, which governs humanity and nature, to unify all finite causes and manifold laws—that is, every phenomenal cause and law—into something absolute which no longer leaves anything discoverable beyond its own existence, that is, into a substance. Likewise, this law unifies the external world composed of forces and laws into a substance, which must also be a cause (to be the subject of the causes of this world),[174] which must, in turn, be an intellect (to be the subject of its laws), a substance which must ultimately consist in the identity of activity and intellect. By observation and induction, we therefore arrive once again within the external sphere at precisely the same point where observation and induction had led us within the sphere of personality and within that of reason. Consciousness in its triplicity is therefore one: the physical world and the moral [world] is one; science is one—that is, in other words, God is one.[175]

Let me summarize these ideas and develop them by the act of summarizing them.

In turning back into[176] consciousness, we have seen that the relation[177] of reason, activity and sensation is so intimate that, given one of these elements, the other two begin to function—and that the element [which is given] is free activity. Without free activity or the I, there would be no consciousness; that is, the two other phenomena—whether they occurred or not—would be as if they were not for the I, which, in turn, would not yet exist. Moreover, the I exists for itself, perceives itself and can perceive itself only by distinguishing itself from sensation which, in so doing, it likewise perceives, and which thus takes up its place in consciousness. However, just as the I can perceive itself and perceive sensation only in perception, that is, by the intervention of reason (the necessary principle of all perception),[178] it follows that the exercise of reason is contemporaneous with the exercise of personal activity and sensible impressions.[179] The triplicity of consciousness, whose elements are distinct and irreducible to each other, is thus resolved in a unique fact, just as the unity of consciousness only exists on condition of this triplicity.[180] What is more, if the three elementary phenomena of consciousness are contemporaneous, if reason immediately illuminates activity which then distinguishes itself from sensation—since reason is nothing other than the action of the two great laws of causality and substance—then reason must immediately relate action[181] to an internal cause and substance, the I, and [relate] sensation to an external cause and substance, the not-I. However, one cannot stop at the ideas of the I and not-I as truly substantial causes, as much because their manifest phenomenality and their manifest contingency divests them of all absolute and substantial character as because, as two, they limit each other and are thus excluded from the status of substance. Hence, reason must relate them to a unique substantial cause,[182] beyond which there is no longer any existence to seek—that is, [to the categories] of cause and substance, for the existence of [this substantial cause] is the identity of the two.[183] Therefore, what exists as both substantive and causative—along with the two finite causes or substances in which [this substantial cause] is expressed—comes to be known at the same time as these two causes [the I and the not-I], as well as the differences which separate them and the bond of nature which unites them. In other words, ontology is given to us in its entirety at one and the same moment and given to us at the very same time as psychology. Hence, in the first fact of consciousness, there is to be found psychological unity in its triplicity which parallels ontological unity in its triplicity. The fact of consciousness which encompasses three internal elements simultaneously also reveals to us three external elements immediately and simultaneously:[184] every fact of consciousness is psychological and ontological all at once, and already contains the three principal ideas which science will later divide or bring together, but which it cannot get beyond: man, nature, and God. However, the man, nature, and God of consciousness are not vain formulae, but facts and realities.[185] For consciousness, man does not exist without nature, nor nature without man, but both of them encounter each other[186] [within consciousness] in their opposition and their reciprocity, as causes, specifically relative causes, whose nature is to always be developed by means of each other.[187] The God of consciousness is not an abstract God, a solitary king sitting behind creation on a deserted throne in silent eternity and with an absolute existence which resembles the very nothingness of existence; he is a God, both true and real, both substance and cause, always substance and always cause—substance only insofar as he is cause and cause only insofar as he is substance. That is, as absolute cause,[188] [he is] one and many, eternity and time, space and number, essence and life, indivisibility and totality, beginning, end, and middle, at the summit of being and at its lowliest degree, infinite and finite all together, and ultimately triple—that is, God, nature, and humanity all at once.[189] Indeed, if God is not everything, he is nothing; if he is absolutely indivisible in himself, he is inaccessible and therefore he is incomprehensible, and his incomprehensibility is for us his destruction.[190] [But] incomprehensible as a formula and in the schools, God becomes clear within the world which manifests him, possesses him and feels him.[191] Present everywhere, he turns back, as it were, into himself in man's consciousness, and he constitutes indirectly the mechanism and the phenomenal triplicity [of this consciousness] by reflecting his own movement and substantial triplicity, whose absolute identity he is.[192]

Having attained such heights, philosophy illuminates itself by enlarging itself; universal harmony enters human thinking, extends it, and pacifies it. The divorce of ontology and psychology, of speculation and observation, of science and common sense, is overcome by a method which attains speculation via observation, ontology via psychology, so as to then strengthen observation by speculation and psychology by ontology. From the immediate givens of consciousness, out of which is composed the common sense of the human race, is drawn the science which contains nothing more than this common sense, but raises it to a severer and purer form, and gives an account of it. However, here I am touching on a fundamental point.

If every fact of consciousness contains all the human faculties, sensibility, free activity, and reason, the I, the not-I and their absolute identity,[193] and if every fact of consciousness is equal to itself, then it results that every man who has consciousness of himself possesses and cannot not possess[194] all the ideas necessarily contained[195] in consciousness. Hence, every man, whether he is aware of it or not, knows everything else: nature and God at the same time as himself. Every man believes in his own existence, therefore every man believes in the world and in God; every man thinks, therefore every man thinks God;[196] every human proposition, by reflecting consciousness, reflects the ideas of unity and of being essential to consciousness; therefore, every human proposition encompasses God; every man who speaks speaks of God and all speech is an act of faith and a hymn. Atheism is an empty formula,[197] a negation without reality, an abstraction of mind which destroys itself in its own affirmation; since all affirmation, even negative [judgement], is a judgement which encompasses the idea of being and therefore of God in his entirety.[198] Atheism is the illusion of a few sophists who oppose their freedom to their reason and do not even know how to account for what they necessarily[199] think. However, the human race, which does not disown its own consciousness and does not put itself into contradiction with its own laws, knows God, believes in him and proclaims him without cease.[200] Indeed, the human race believes in reason and cannot but believe in it, in that reason which appears in consciousness in a momentary relation to the I, a pure, if somewhat faded reflection of that primitive light which flows out of the very breast of eternal substance, which is substance, cause and intellect all at once. Without the apparition of reason in consciousness, there is no psychological knowledge and certainly no ontological knowledge. Reason is, as it were, the bridge thrown between psychology and ontology, between consciousness and being; it touches down on both [sides]; it descends from God towards man; it appears in consciousness as a guest who brings news of an unknown world and gives both the idea of [that world] and the need for it. If reason were[201] personal, it would possess no worth and no authority outside of the subject and the individual I. If it remained in a state of unmanifested substance, it would be, as it were, not for the I, which would not exist.[202] Intelligent substance must therefore manifest itself; and this manifestation is the apparition of reason in consciousness.[203] Reason is thus literally a revelation, a necessary and universal revelation, which no man lacks and which has enlightened every man on entering this world: *illuminat omnem hominem venientem in hunc mundum* ["[the true light that] shines on everyone was coming into the world"].²⁰⁴ Reason is the necessary mediator between God and man, the λόγος of Pythagoras and Plato, the *Word* made flesh which serves as interpreter to God and preceptor to man, simultaneously both man and God together. It is certainly not the absolute²⁰⁵ God in his majestic indivisibility; rather, it is his manifestation in spirit and in truth; it is not the being of beings, but it is the God of the human race. Just as the human race never lacks God and he never abandons it, the human race believes in God with an irresistible and inalterable belief, and this unity of belief is itself its highest unity.

If this sum of beliefs exists in every fact of consciousness, and if consciousness is one across the whole human race, from where then comes the prodigious diversity which seems to exist between men and in what does this diversity consist? In truth, when at first glance we believe we perceive so many differences between individuals, between countries, between different epochs of humanity, we experience a profound sensation of melancholy, and we are tempted to see in such capricious intellectual development across humanity as a whole merely an irregular phenomenon without grandeur or interest. However, when the facts are more attentively observed, they demonstrate that no human being is stranger to any of the three principal ideas which constitute consciousness: personality or the freedom of man, impersonality or the fatality of nature and the providence of God. Every man immediately understands these three ideas, because he has immediately found them and continually rediscovers them in himself. The exceptions—by their small number, by the absurdities they engender, by the disturbances they give rise to— serve merely as further examples of the universality of faith in the human species, the treasure of good sense deposited in the truth, and the peace and happiness for a human soul which does not separate itself from the beliefs of others. Leave aside the exceptions which appear every now and then in some critical era of history and you will see that always and everywhere the masses who alone exist live in the same faith, and its forms alone vary. Yet, the masses do not possess the secret of their beliefs. Truth is not science; truth is for all, science is for the few: all truth is in the human race, but the human race is not a philosopher. At bottom, philosophy is the aristocracy of the human race. Its glory and its strength, like that of every true aristocracy, is to be found in not separating itself from the people, in sympathizing and identifying with them, working for them by supporting them. Philosophical science is the rigorous [sévère] account that reflection makes for itself of ideas which it has not produced. We have demonstrated this above: reflection presupposes a preliminary operation to which it is applied, since reflection functions as a return. If no prior operation had occurred, then there would be no place for the voluntary repetition of this operation, that is, for reflection—since reflection is nothing else [than such a repetition].²⁰⁶ It does not create; it records and it explains.²⁰⁷ Hence, nothing exists in reflection more integrally²⁰⁸ than it had in the operation which precedes it, in spontaneity; reflection merely exists at a degree of intellect more rarefied and more elevated than spontaneity, but only on the condition that it accurately resumes it and develops it without destroying it. Moreover, I believe humanity as a whole is spontaneous and not reflective:[209] humanity is inspired. The divine breath within [humanity] reveals to it—always and everywhere—all truths in one form or another, depending on time and place. The soul of humanity is a poetic soul which discovers in itself the secrets of beings and expresses them in prophetic songs passed down through the ages. And beside humanity stands philosophy which listens to it attentively, gathers up its words, records them, so to speak; and when the moment of inspiration has passed, it presents them respectfully back to the admirable artist who was not conscious of his own genius and who often does not recognize his own work.[210] Spontaneity is the genius of human nature; reflection is the genius of a few human beings. The difference between reflection and spontaneity is the only difference possible in the identity of the intellect.[211] I believe I have proven that it is the only real difference in the forms of reason, in [the forms] of activity, perhaps even in [the forms] of life. In history too,[212] it is the only [difference] which separates one human from another—and it follows from this that we are all penetrated with the same spirit, all from the same family, children of the same father, and that our fraternity admits solely those dissimilarities necessary for individuality. Considered in this way, individual dissimilarities possess nobility and interest, because they testify to our independence from each other and separate man from nature.[213] We are men, not stars: we have movements that are our own, but all our movements—even the most irregular in appearance—take place along the ellipse of our nature, whose two extremities are two essentially similar points.[214] Spontaneity is the starting point, reflection the point of return, the entire circumference is our intellectual life, and the centre is the absolute intellect which presides over and explains everything.[215] These principles have an inexhaustible fruitfulness. Proceed from human nature to external nature and you will rediscover spontaneity under the form of expansion and reflection under that of contraction. Carry your gaze to universal existence: external nature there plays the role of spontaneity and humanity that of reflection. Finally, in the history of the human species, the Eastern world represents this first movement for which potent spontaneity supplied the human race's indestructible foundation, whereas the pagan world and, above all, the Christian [world] represents reflection, which gradually develops, is added onto spontaneity, breaks it apart and puts it back together with the freedom proper to it. The spirit of the world glides over all these forms and remains at the centre; but in all these forms, in all these worlds, at all degrees of physical, intellectual, or historical existence, the same integral elements can be uncovered in their variety and in their harmony.

Such is the kind of system in which all the work of the preceding years had resulted by the end of 1818—a very imperfect system, I am sure, and one which has since been enlarged and modified in my mind, but whose principal foundations[216] I would still defend today, and which had, at the very least and despite all its faults, the advantage at the time it was conceived and elaborated of realizing in part the dominant thought of my life—that of reconstructing eternal beliefs in line with the spirit of the age, and to reach their unity via the experimental method. This is the perspective from which [this system] must be considered and evaluated.

This system formed the basis of my teaching in 1818, and to it are united—directly or indirectly—all the fragments that compose this volume.[217] It constitutes their unity and can serve as the thread for recognizing [such unity] in the midst of articles with very different dates and subject matter. It formed the limit of my research until 1819 and is the foundation for all the dogmatic and historical developments of my subsequent teaching. If one is sufficiently attentive, the system I have just hastily sketched looks like nothing other than an impartial eclecticism applied to facts of consciousness.[218] It was subsequently applied to the diverse doctrines which compose the history of philosophy, and many traces of this can be seen in these fragments. However, ever since [1819] it has taken on, in my mind and my works, an importance of which it is impossible for me to give the slightest idea here. I will content myself with saying that, since, from 1819 onwards, my systematic and dogmatic viewpoint became a little stronger and more elevated, I quit speculation for some time, or rather I pursued it and realized it by applying it more particularly than I had yet done to the history of philosophy.[219] Always faithful to the psychological method, I transposed it onto history,[220] and confronting[221] systems with the facts of consciousness and interrogating each system for a complete representation of consciousness without being able to obtain it, I soon attained the result that my subsequent studies developed—that is: each system expresses an order of phenomena and ideas, which is very real in truth,[222] but which is not the only one in consciousness and, nevertheless, plays in the system an almost exclusive role. It follows from this that each system is not false, but incomplete; and it further follows from this that by reuniting all incomplete systems, one would form a complete philosophy, adequate to the totality of consciousness. Of course, the gap is large between this [idea] and a genuine system that is simultaneously historical, universal, and precise,[223] but the first step had been taken and the task begun. I will try to pursue it; despite all the obstacles, I will try to undertake the reform of philosophical studies in France by clarifying the history of philosophy by means of a system,[224] and by demonstrating this system via the entire history of philosophy. It is this goal which informs my series of historical publications[225]— my friends alone can understand their scope. Moreover, this is the plan on which I had already embarked in my teaching from 1819 and 1820 on the history of eighteenth-century philosophy in France, England, and Germany. Perhaps I will publish these lectures;[226] but my earlier lectures from 1815 to 1818 will not appear.[227] These are studies I composed in the public eye and which, I hope, will not have proven useless in reviving the taste for philosophical subjects in my country, as well as[228] imprinting a salutary direction on the students of the École Normale and the young people who followed my lecture courses at the Faculty of Letters. However, I consign them to oblivion myself;[229] they stand too far behind the point all of us have now reached. I would have had to plead for mercy on behalf of these fragments which relate to [the lectures] and are even inferior to them, if it were not the case that they are already in print,[230] and if [it were not the case that] to reproduce them is to bury them definitively. Moreover, it occurs to me that, without having enough of that generality to speak to the needs of the moment and the controversies that party quarrels have given rise to,[231] they could still prove useful in drawing attention to psychological details, arid no doubt and lacking all apparent grandeur, but which one must never forget, since they are the legitimate starting point for all developments which philosophy can and should take. It also occurs to me that, at this moment when industrialism and theocracy[232] are working so hard to divert all minds from the broad and impartial ways of science, it is almost a duty for me to once more raise my banner of independence, which has perhaps not been forgotten, and to recall friends of the truth to the only philosophical method which, in my opinion, can drive forward progress—the method of observation and induction which has raised all of the physical sciences so high and carried them so far and which imprints on thinking a movement both vast and regular,[233] which depends solely on human nature and comprehends it entirely, and, with it, attains infinity. It imposes no system on reality, but is charged with demonstrating that, if such reality is complete, it is a system, a living, finished system, both inside and outside of consciousness, in the universe and in history.[234] It is a method which, proposing no other task that that of understanding things, accepts, explains, and respects everything, and destroys[235] solely artificial arrangements of exclusive hypotheses. It is a severe method whose circumspection both veils and justifies its audacity, and outside of which all movements of the mind are but fruitless torments for oneself and for others, for science, for one's country and for the future.

Finally, I would like to officially take leave of these three years of my life which were dear to me because of the memory of the obscure and painful labours which constitute them. I here salute them for the last time and say goodbye to them forever. From now on it is from 1819 that my publications will be dated.[236]

V. Cousin
1 April 1826

Notes

1. *Fr. phil. 1826*, pp. i-l (subsequently: *Fr. phil. 1833*, pp. 1-50; *Fr. phil. 1838*, vol. 1, pp. 45-84; *Fr. phil. 1847*, vol. 4, pp. 1-44; *Fr. phil. 1855*, vol. 5, pp. 1-44; *Fr. phil. 1865*, vol. 5, pp. i-xxxv). We take the 1826 publication as our base text for this translation and note the significant modifications to later versions in the endnotes. A translation of the 1833 version of the text exists, under the title, "Exposition of Eclecticism Continued," in George Ripley's *Philosophical Miscellanies* (Boston: Hilliard and Gray, 1838), pp. 108-57. This text is the manifesto of eclectic psychology that proved so influential on a generation of young philosophers—see the Editors' Preface above (p. xvii).
2. *Fr. phil. 1847* and subsequent editions: "1819" replaced with "1820" (considering the fact that most of the "fragments" after 1838 were from a later period, there seems little reason for this

change other than to align with Cousin's collected works—see next note). The *Journal des savants*, founded in 1665, was the establishment journal of choice, particularly for philological notes and displays of erudition; the *Archives philosophiques, politiques et littéraires* was founded in 1817 and edited by P. P. Royer-Collard and F. Guizot (Cousin co-edited the philosophy section with Royer-Collard).
3. *Fr. phil. 1847* and subsequent edition: Cousin inserts a footnote which notes that "since then, this teaching has been published in all its truth and its appropriate breadth," before citing the series of early lecture extracts and revisions published as the five volumes of series 1 of his *Œuvres* from 1846. *Fr. phil. 1865*: "in all its truth and its appropriate breadth" is omitted from this footnote.
4. From 1812, Cousin began teaching at the École Normale while still a student there, as was expected, and continued to teach there after graduating; from 1813, he also became Royer-Collard's "*suppléant*," giving classes in his stead at the Sorbonne.
5. On Royer-Collard and Cousin's relation to him, see Antoine-Mahut's essay.
6. *Fr. phil. 1865*: "In this position, my first concern" replaced with "The first problem which had to concern me."
7. *Fr. phil. 1865*: "immediately recognizing and determining the method one wishes to follow" is omitted.
8. *Fr. phil. 1865*: "we" replaced with "our reason."
9. *Fr. phil. 1865*: the passage from "... like our destiny ..." to "is in ourselves" is replaced with "be the work of our free choice and belongs to us as our destiny."
10. *Fr. phil. 1865*: this sentence is omitted.
11. *Fr. phil. 1865*: "reform" replaced with "enterprise and reform."
12. *Fr. phil. 1865*: The passage from "My first effort ..." to "... to take" replaced with "One must then above all consciously examine."
13. *Fr. phil. 1865*: "lead me" replaced with "produce."
14. The École Normale, then (as now), was primarily concerned with training students for the *agrégation* by which they qualified as a *lycée*-teacher.
15. *Fr. phil. 1865*: "spirit" replaced with "genius."
16. *Fr. phil. 1865*: "they have laws which form part of the general laws of the human species. If" replaced with "and there must be a reason why."
17. *Fr. phil. 1865*: "the spirit of" is omitted.
18. *Fr. phil. 1865*: "spirit" replaced with "century."
19. *Fr. phil. 1865*: "for the human race" is omitted.
20. *Fr. phil. 1865*: "its intellect and faith" replaced with "it."
21. *Fr. phil. 1847* and subsequent editions: "Spinoza, Leibniz and Wolff" is omitted. *Fr. phil. 1865*: Cousin inserts a footnote on Malebranche, citing texts collected in volumes 3 and 4 of *Phil. frag.* 1855, and lecture 8 of the *Histoire générale de la philosophie*.
22. *Fr. phil. 1847* and subsequent editions: "to ontological hypotheses and scholastic formulae" replaced with "in hypotheses."
23. *Fr. phil. 1865*: this sentence is omitted.
24. *Fr. phil. 1865*: "the necessary fruit" replaced by "the wish and necessary fruit."
25. *Fr. phil. 1847* and subsequent editions: Cousin inserts a footnote that cites the conclusion to "Attempt at a Classification of Philosophical Questions and Schools" (pp. 150–8 below), the opening lecture to *Du Vrai, du Beau et du Bien*, as well as the third lecture of the 1829 course on eighteenth-century philosophy. *Fr. phil. 1865*: the final citation is omitted.
26. *Fr. phil. 1833* and subsequent editions: "scope and limits" is omitted.
27. *Fr. phil. 1865*: the passage from "And is there anything wrong?" to "i.e. human nature..." is omitted.
28. *Fr. phil. 1865*: "truth" is replaced with "force."
29. *Fr. phil. 1847* and subsequent editions: "Pythagoras's *numbers*" is omitted.
30. *Fr. phil. 1865*: the passage from "What was it that elevated..." to "... lost in the clouds" replaced with "Seen from up close, all famous chimeras which have seduced and led humanity astray, by getting very lost in the clouds...."
31. *Fr. phil. 1865*: "hypotheses" replaced with "reveries."
32. i.e. Condillac's philosophy of "transformed sensation," which charts the transformations sensation undergoes to become memory, attention, abstract thought, etc.
33. *Fr. phil. 1865*: this sentence is omitted.
34. *Fr. phil. 1833* and subsequent editions: "real" is replaced with "evident."
35. e.g. Voltaire's presentation of Bacon as the "father" of experimental science.
36. *Fr. phil. 1847* and subsequent editions: Cousin inserts the following footnote, "*De Augmentis*, 1."; *Fr. phil. 1865*: he adds a reference to his *Histoire générale de la philosophie*, lecture 7. The English

is taken from Francis Bacon, *The Advancement of Learning*, I.iv.5 (New York: Modern Library, pp. 183–4).
37. *Fr. phil. 1833* and subsequent editions: "In general," added before "Bacon's."
38. *Fr. phil. 1833* and subsequent editions: "positive" is omitted.
39. *Fr. phil. 1865*: "sadly incomplete" is omitted.
40. *Fr. phil. 1865*: "give rise to Condillac" replaced with "give rise to Hobbes first and finally to Condillac."
41. *Fr. phil. 1865*: the passage from "… that can only be destroyed …" to "… fact of system" is omitted.
42. *Fr. phil. 1865*: "lacunas" replaced with "errors."
43. *Fr. phil. 1865*: "human nature and inattentive observation" replaced with "the best instincts of human nature."
44. *Fr. phil. 1865*: "We must turn back to Bacon and …" is omitted.
45. *Fr. phil. 1865*: this sentence is omitted.
46. *Fr. phil. 1865*: "through" is replaced with "thanks to."
47. *Fr. phil. 1833* and subsequent editions: "related by their coexistence and possibility of being observed" is omitted.
48. *Fr. phil. 1833* and subsequent editions: "my friends and" is omitted.
49. *Fr. phil. 1865*: "and induction as philosophical method" is omitted.
50. *Fr. phil. 1865*: "legitimate" added before "observation."
51. *Fr. phil. 1865*: "exhaust its object" is omitted.
52. *Fr. phil. 1865*: "where, therefore, induction no longer has any basis and man's mind no hold" is omitted.
53. *Fr. phil. 1865*: "the circumstances of life fortuitously and confusedly brought us" replaced with "ordinary life fortuitously and confusedly shown us."
54. *Fr. phil. 1847* and subsequent editions: Cousin adds a footnote citing the lecture extracts first collected in *Fr. phil. 1826* and then moved to *Premiers essais de philosophie*.
55. *Fr. phil. 1847* and subsequent editions: Cousin adds a footnote, "In 1822, the École Normale had been destroyed. It was reestablished in 1830"; *Fr. phil. 1865*: Cousin replaces this footnote with a citation to the appendix to the *Premiers essais de philosophie* on "The Teaching of Philosophy at the École Normale." The École Normale was temporarily closed in 1822 owing to its close association with liberal radicalism; it was reopened in 1830 under Cousin's own stewardship.
56. *Fr. phil. 1847* and subsequent editions: "and do not merit the public's attention" is omitted.
57. *Fr. phil. 1847* and subsequent editions: Cousin adds another footnote citing the new edition of his early lecture extracts.
58. *Fr. phil. 1865*: "As soon as we enter back into consciousness, free from any systematic perspective, we observe such varied phenomena manifest there with their real characteristics that" replaced with "When we enter back into consciousness and observe what occurs there without bringing to this study any systematic perspective."
59. *Fr. phil. 1865*: "incontestable" replaced with "certain."
60. *Fr. phil. 1865*: "is equally not identical to sensation" replaced with "equally does not come from sensation alone."
61. *Fr. phil. 1833* and subsequent editions: "and submit it to the most subtle metamorphoses" is omitted.
62. *Fr. phil. 1865*: "establishes it on the unshakeable foundation of consciousness" is omitted, and the two uses of "all" in the clause that follows are omitted.
63. *Fr. phil. 1833* and subsequent editions: "its modesty and" is omitted.
64. *Fr. phil. 1833* and subsequent editions: "measurable" replaced with "appreciable."
65. *Fr. phil. 1833* and subsequent editions: "I say" added after "adjourned."
66. *Fr. phil. 1865*: "Indeed, it is a fact attested by observation that" is omitted.
67. *Fr. phil. 1865*: "concepts whose further development transcends the limits of consciousness and reaches existences" replaced with "concepts which transcend the limits of consciousness and presuppose existences."
68. *Fr. phil. 1865*: "hinder the development of" replaced with "neglect," and "limit" similarly replaced with "neglect" in the following sentence.
69. *Fr. phil. 1865*: "as a whole" is omitted.
70. *Fr. phil. 1833* and subsequent editions: "certain" replaced with "real and certain."
71. *Fr. phil. 1865*: "It is a rational fact attested by consciousness" replaced with "It is a certain fact."
72. *Fr. phil. 1865*: "and just as certain" added after "fact."
73. *Fr. phil. 1865*: "to speak with the schools" added after "principle of causality."

74. *Fr. phil. 1865*: "the will represents" replaced with "resides in the will."
75. *Fr. phil. 1865*: "an" replaced with "another."
76. *Fr. phil. 1865*: "and that, later and always irresistibly, the principle of causality enriches those features and laws" replaced with "and successively to others of the same kind."
77. *Fr. phil. 1865*: "an existence, but an existence revealed" replaced with "existences revealed."
78. *Fr. phil. 1847* and subsequent editions: "that is, via observation" is omitted.
79. *Fr. phil. 1865*: "had" replaced with "seemed to have."
80. *Fr. phil. 1833* and subsequent editions: "large and" is omitted.
81. *Fr. phil. 1847* and subsequent editions: Cousin inserts a footnote citing *Premiers essais* to which the material from these lectures had been moved; *Fr. phil. 1865*: Cousin adds a reference particularly to the programmes of the 1817 and 1818 lecture courses included in *Premiers essais*.
82. *Fr. phil. 1847* and subsequent editions: Cousin inserts a footnote citing *Du Vrai, du Beau et du Bien* as a whole.
83. *Fr. phil. 1865*: "and began to take on more extensity and depth" is omitted.
84. *Fr. phil. 1865*: "rational facts are necessary as well and reason is no less independent of will than sensibility is" is omitted.
85. *Fr. phil. 1865*: "under consciousness's gaze" is omitted.
86. *Fr. phil. 1865*: "the I" replaced with "eminent sign of the I."
87. *Fr. phil. 1865*: this sentence is omitted.
88. *Fr. phil. 1865*: "Far from it" added to beginning of clause.
89. *Fr. phil. 1865*: this sentence is omitted.
90. *Fr. phil. 1865*: "we perceive" replaced with "we perceive and know."
91. *Fr. phil. 1847* and subsequent editions: "our personality is will and nothing more" is omitted.
92. *Fr. phil. 1865*: "The element of knowledge is rational in its essence, and" replaced with "such that."
93. *Fr. phil. 1865*: this sentence is omitted.
94. *Fr. phil. 1865*: "We do not make it, and" is omitted.
95. *Fr. phil. 1865*: "is therefore a preliminary given which" is omitted.
96. *Fr. phil. 1847* and subsequent editions: Cousin inserts a footnote citing the early lectures of *Du Vrai, du Beau et du Bien*.
97. *Fr. phil. 1865*: this sentence is omitted.
98. *Fr. phil. 1847* and subsequent editions: this sentence is replaced with "Let us come next to the question of their complete enumeration and rigorous classification." Cousin inserts a footnote citing *Du Vrai, du Beau et du Bien*.
99. *Fr. phil. 1865*: "after Pythagoras" is omitted.
100. *Fr. phil. 1865*: "progressive" is omitted.
101. *Fr. phil. 1865*: "Cartesianism" replaced with "The Cartesianism of Arnauld, of Bossuet, of Fénelon, of Malebranche."
102. *Fr. phil. 1865*: "in France" is omitted.
103. *Fr. phil. 1865*: "foundation" replaced with "source."
104. *Fr. phil. 1847* and subsequent edition: Cousin adds a footnote citing his early lectures on Scottish philosophy; *Fr. phil. 1865*: this footnote is omitted.
105. *Fr. phil. 1865*: "complete" is omitted.
106. *Fr. phil. 1847* and subsequent editions: "was able to demonstrate, to those who followed my 1818 lecture course" replaced with "has demonstrated." Cousin also adds a footnote citing his early lectures; *Fr. phil. 1865*: this footnote is omitted.
107. *Fr. phil. 1847* and subsequent edition: Cousin adds a footnote citing *Du Vrai, du Beau et du Bien*; *Fr. phil. 1865*: this footnote is omitted.
108. *Fr. phil. 1833*: "synthetically" is omitted; *Fr. phil. 1847* and subsequent editions: "I believe I have demonstrated that, if one synthetically examines" replaced with "If one examines."
109. *Fr. phil. 1833* and subsequent editions: "analytically and" is omitted.
110. *Fr. phil. 1847* and subsequent edition: Cousin inserts a footnote citing *Du Vrai, du Beau et du Bien*; *Fr. phil. 1865*: this footnote is omitted.
111. *Fr. phil. 1833* and subsequent editions: "discussion" replaced with "famous discussion."
112. *Fr. phil. 1847* and subsequent edition: Cousin inserts a footnote citing his lectures from 1818 to 1820; *Fr. phil. 1865*: this footnote is omitted.
113. *Fr. phil. 1865*: "and relativity to" is omitted.
114. *Fr. phil. 1865*: "circumscribed by the sphere of our personal nature" replaced with "limited to our condition."
115. *Fr. phil. 1865*: "but certainly not independent truths" replaced with "but not certain with an intrinsic and absolute certainty."

116. *Fr. phil. 1865*: "after describing all the laws of thought so well, this incomparable analyst rendered them impotent, and, despite all certain evidence" is omitted.
117. *Fr. phil. 1847* and subsequent editions: "After providing an inventory of the laws of reason, all my efforts in the 1818 lecture course were" replaced with "I attempted to eliminate from the laws of reason."
118. *Fr. phil. 1833* and subsequent editions: "seemingly" is omitted.
119. *Fr. phil. 1847* and subsequent editions: this sentence is omitted.
120. At this point, it should be remembered that "perception" here translates the French "apperception" which has stronger Leibnizio-Kantian connotations. See further the note on translations, p. xxvi above.
121. *Fr. phil. 1847* and subsequent editions: "immediately" is omitted.
122. *Fr. phil. 1865*: "along with all reflection" is omitted.
123. *Fr. phil. 1833* and subsequent editions: "the primitive light" replaced with "spontaneous perception."
124. *Fr. phil. 1833* and subsequent editions: "is insensible" replaced with "escapes us."
125. *Fr. phil. 1847* and subsequent editions: "and its laws therefore reveal only themselves" is omitted (and rest of this passage has singular verb forms as a result).
126. *Fr. phil. 1847* and subsequent editions: "represents" replaced with "expresses."
127. *Fr. phil. 1865*: "One can even truthfully" replaced with "It is more accurate to."
128. *Fr. phil. 1833* and subsequent editions: "reality" replaced with "truth."
129. *Fr. phil. 1865*: "from which it could never escape" is omitted.
130. *Fr. phil. 1865*: "distinct from and independent of their internal and external subjects" replaced with "distinct from their subjects and objects."
131. *Fr. phil. 1833* and subsequent editions: "Ultimately" replaced with "One can even say that."
132. This is one of the passages that goes on to constitute a key piece of evidence in accusations of pantheism against Cousin, a his is one of the reasons it is omitted from later editions (see n. 134 below).
133. *Fr. phil. 1833* and subsequent editions: "which derives from the law of substance" is added.
134. *Fr. phil. 1847* and subsequent editions: this paragraph is omitted.
135. *Fr. phil. 1833* and subsequent editions: "complete" is omitted.
136. *Fr. phil. 1865*: this sentence is omitted.
137. *Fr. phil. 1865*: "It is not that being for the I is one thing and willing another, since then" replaced with "For the I, being and willing are not two things; otherwise."
138. *Fr. phil. 1865*: "the element of" is omitted.
139. *Fr. phil. 1865*: "causality" replaced with "causative power."
140. *Fr. phil. 1847* and subsequent editions: "their first cause, that is" is omitted.
141. *Fr. phil. 1865*: this sentence is omitted.
142. *Fr. phil. 1847* and subsequent editions: Cousin inserts a footnote that cites Maine de Biran's works "passim" and his own 1829 lecture course on eighteenth-century philosophy.
143. *Fr. phil. 1833* and subsequent editions: "choosing or" is omitted.
144. *Fr. phil. 1865*: the passage from "…if all voluntary acts…" to "…striking a phenomenon" is omitted.
145. *Fr. phil. 1865*: "rational perception" replaced with "reason."
146. Exclaimed by the character "the old Horatius" in Corneille's 1641 play, *Horace*, Act 3, sc. 6, who, with these words, chooses honour over love.
147. Nicolas-Louis d'Assas (1733–60): a French soldier who famously, on the night before a battle, was surprised by enemy soldiers and, on the point of capture, shouted out, "It's the enemy!": his fellow soldiers were saved, but he was killed.
148. *Fr. phil. 1833* and subsequent editions: "nor reflective" replaced with "nor, for that reason, lacking morality."
149. *Fr. phil. 1833* and subsequent editions: "no longer imposed on them by an external fatality, nor is it" replaced with "not."
150. *Fr. phil. 1833* and subsequent editions: "clear" replaced with "even distinct."
151. *Fr. phil. 1865*: "passes by [consciousness] either unperceived or irrevocable" is omitted.
152. *Fr. phil. 1833* and subsequent edition: "fugitive" is omitted; *Fr. phil. 1847* and subsequent editions: "fugitive and instantaneous" is omitted. Cousin also inserts a footnote referring the reader to other early discussions of spontaneity and reflection including "On Spontaneity and Reflection," pp. 166–71 below.
153. *Fr. phil. 1865*: this sentence is omitted.
154. *Fr. phil. 1865*: "instantaneous" is omitted.

155. *Fr. phil. 1847* and subsequent edition: Cousin inserts a footnote directing the reader to his 1819 lectures; *Fr. phil. 1865*: this footnote is omitted.
156. *Fr. phil. 1833* and subsequent edition: "which is not exclusively absorbed by either one or the other" is omitted; *Fr. phil. 1847* and subsequent editions: the passage from "... and so must possess ..." to "... or the other" is omitted; *Fr. phil. 1865*: "and constitutes their identity" is also omitted.
157. *Fr. phil. 1865*: "heroism in its sudden inspirations" is added after "creation."
158. *Fr. phil. 1865*: "Arbitrary freedom is free will" is omitted ("that is, the will" is moved to the end of the previous sentence).
159. *Fr. phil. 1833* and subsequent editions: "and phenomenalize it. Here is the ontological perspective on freedom" is omitted.
160. *Fr. phil. 1833* and subsequent editions: "since it is simultaneously cause and substance, and since [it is] the very basis of the substance of active phenomena, this absolute substance which in its essential development, as it is simultaneously cause and substance, and the very ground of the substance of active phenomena; this absolute substance, like rational substance" replaced with "this absolute activity takes on."
161. *Fr. phil. 1847* and subsequent editions: this paragraph is omitted.
162. *Fr. phil. 1865*: the passage from "... for the action or reason ..." to "... an external cause" replaced with "to a cause foreign to *the I*."
163. *Fr. phil. 1847* and subsequent editions: Cousin inserts a footnote citing many of his early lectures from 1817 to 1819; *Fr. phil. 1865*: "which *the I* constitutes and comprises" is omitted.
164. *Fr. phil. 1865*: "since it is free activity; nor is the object passive, since it is given to us uniquely according to the ground of cause, of active force. Passivity" replaced with "since, on the foundation of the necessary *substratum* of extension, it is essentially given to us as deprived of forces, of causative energies, such that passivity." Cousin also inserts a footnote citing his 1817 lecture extracts, as well as lecture eight of his early course on Scottish philosophy.
165. *Fr. phil. 1833* and subsequent editions: "it will relate" replaced by "reason will always and necessarily relate."
166. *Fr. phil. 1865*: the passage from "that is, it expresses" to "only as such" is omitted.
167. *Fr. phil. 1833* and subsequent editions: "real or possible" is omitted.
168. *Fr. phil. 1865*: "relation" replaced by "harmony."
169. *Fr. phil. 1865*: "necessarily" replaced with "also."
170. *Fr. phil. 1865*: the passage from "... in terms of developing laws" to "... the regularity" replaced with "in terms of laws." This passage draws on the dual meaning of 'to develop' and 'to express' in Cousin's use of the verb 'développer'.
171. *Fr. phil. 1865*: "every law presupposes a reason" replaced with "whoever speaks of laws speaks of reasons."
172. *Fr. phil. 1865*: "Is there nothing else?" is omitted.
173. *Fr. phil. 1865*: the passage from "I will content myself ..." to "... is incontestable" replaced with "I will content myself with remarking that today, without claiming to create, like Leibniz, a pure dynamism from the world and without negating the existence of matter, no physician considers in [the world] anything but the attributes which it manifests, the forces which animate, the laws which regulate the action of these forces." Cousin adds a footnote to this passage that cites his *Historie générale de la philosophie*, lecture 9 and a footnote in *Premiers essais*, which reads in part, "At the end of the seventeenth century, when interrogating the concept of substance, Leibniz reduced it to that of force. This reduction was for Leibniz the very task of the reform of philosophy in its entirety, and he entitled a small work devoted to this large subject: *De prima philosophiae emendation et notione substantiae*. This writing is from 1684. In his last works, Leibniz reproduced the same principle, particularly in the *Principia philosophiae* [...] with the result of [achieving the same] reduction I attempted in 1817 from all the categories, all the principles of common sense, all the universal and necessary truths, to two of them—this reduction, which seemed to us then and which was indeed a considerable innovation with respect to Reid and Kant, was, without my knowing it—and like eclecticism itself—merely a return to Leibniz's thought. But, in returning the concept of substance to that of cause, did Leibniz keep the perfect balance? Certainly, substance is revealed to us only through cause; for example, take away all operations of the cause and the force which is in us, and we are not for ourselves; it is thus the idea of cause which introduces the idea of substance into the mind; but is substance merely the cause which manifests it? We must distinguish between the cause in act and the cause which has not yet passed into act, to speak the language of Aristotle, accepted by Leibniz. But a cause which is not in act is not really a cause, and a cause in act is not self-sufficient, it presupposes a ground, a subject, a substance.

Causative power is the essential attribute of substance; it is not substance itself. In a word, it appeared to us more certain to take these two primitive concepts which are distinct, though inseparably united in terms of [substance] as the sign and manifestation of [cause], the root and the ground of [cause].... To speak of substance independently of the cause which manifests it is to render substance an abstract being; but to speak of cause and the phenomena it produces without relating them back to their common ground is an error of no less importance. Likewise, when the question of psychology is transposed into theodicy, the infinite and eternal substance is inaccessible in itself and is attained only in its manifestations, in the world and in the soul; but, at the same time, these manifestations—however great they are—do not exhaust [divine] power, because this power resides in its infinite essence" (p. 311).

174. In this passage, Cousin intends "subject" to mean the subject of a proposition, a logical antecedent.
175. Fr. phil. 1847 and subsequent editions: passage from "Let us go further" to "God is one" is omitted.
176. Fr. phil. 1865: "turning back into" replaced with "interrogating."
177. Fr. phil. 1865: "relation" replaced with "harmony."
178. Fr. phil. 1865: the passage from "However, just as ..." to "... all perception" replaced with "However, to perceive oneself and to perceive in general is to know, is to make use of reason, the necessary principle of all perception."
179. Fr. phil. 1865: "sensible impressions" replaced with "sensibility."
180. Fr. phil. 1865: this sentence replaced with "Consciousness thus encompasses three distinct and, at the same time, inseparable elements, and the unity of consciousness is achieved only on the condition of this triplicity."
181. Fr. phil. 1865: "since reason is nothing other than the action of the two great laws of causality and substance—then reason must immediately relate action" replaced with "Since reason always acts under the dominion of the two great laws of causality and substance, then it relates the acts attested by consciousness."
182. Fr. phil. 1847 and subsequent editions: the passage from "However, one cannot ..." to "... substantial cause" replaced with "Moreover, since it can [only] stop at those causes and substances which possess their existence in themselves, reason is invincibly led to relate them to an absolute and therefore unique cause and substance."
183. Fr. phil. 1847 and subsequent editions: "that is, [to the categories] of cause and substance, for the existence of [this substantial cause] is the identity of the two" is omitted.
184. Fr. phil. 1833 and subsequent editions: "immediately and simultaneously" is omitted.
185. Fr. phil. 1847 and subsequent editions: the passage from "Therefore what exists as ..." to "facts and realities" replaced with "Hence, absolute substance and cause are known at the same time as the two contingent and finite causes and substances by the power of this very same reason which simultaneously extends itself out of consciousness and roots itself in consciousness by the side of free activity and sensibility. With the result that, in the last analysis, every well-developed fact of consciousness is psychological and ontological at the same time and already contains the three principal ideas which later science cannot surpass: man, nature, and God. And these are not rarefied abstractions, the laborious work of analysis. Rather, we are always here on the solid ground of facts and experience."
186. Fr. phil. 1865: "effectively" added after "each other."
187. Fr. phil. 1865: "as causes, specifically relative causes, whose nature is to always be developed by means of each other" replaced with "which constitute their common reality."
188. Fr. phil. 1847 and subsequent editions: the passage from "both substance and cause ..." to "as absolute cause" is omitted.
189. Fr. phil. 1847 and subsequent editions: Cousin inserts a footnote citing lecture 5 of the 1828 *Introduction à l'histoire de la philosophie* and a note to the appendix on pantheism he later added to the lecture course.
190. Fr. phil. 1847 and subsequent editions: Cousin inserts a footnote "on the comprehensibility and incomprehensibility of God," citing, for example, his lectures on Scottish philosophy.
191. Fr. phil. 1833 and subsequent editions: "possesses him and feels him" replaced with "and for the soul which possesses him and feels him."
192. Fr. phil. 1847 and subsequent editions: the passage from "and he constitutes ..." to "identity he is" replaced with "which express his most sublime attributes, insofar as the finite is able to express the infinite."
193. Fr. phil. 1847 and subsequent editions: "their absolute identity" replaced with "God."
194. Fr. phil. 1865: "and cannot not possess" is omitted.
195. Fr. phil. 1865: "necessarily" is omitted.
196. Fr. phil. 1833 and subsequent editions: "if I can express it thus" added after "thinks God."

197. *Fr. phil. 1865*: "an empty formula" is omitted.
198. *Fr. phil. 1865*: "in his entirety" is omitted.
199. *Fr. phil. 1833* and subsequent editions: "necessarily" is omitted.
200. *Fr. phil. 1847* and subsequent editions: Cousin inserts a footnote citing *Du Vrai, du Beau et du Bien*.
201. *Fr. phil. 1847* and subsequent editions: "entirely" added after "were."
202. *Fr. phil. 1833* and subsequent editions: "exist" replaced with "know itself."
203. *Fr. phil. 1847* and subsequent editions: the previous two sentences are omitted.
204. John 1:9. Cousin uses the Vulgate text.
205. *Fr. phil. 1865*: "absolute" replaced with "abstract."
206. *Fr. phil. 1847* and subsequent editions: "since reflection is nothing else" is omitted.
207. *Fr. phil. 1865*: "it records and explains" is omitted.
208. *Fr. phil. 1865*: "integrally" is omitted.
209. *Fr. phil. 1865*: "Moreover, I believe humanity as a whole is spontaneous and not reflective" replaced with "It is not reflection which governs humanity."
210. *Fr. phil. 1847* and subsequent edition: Cousin adds a footnote citing *Du Vrai, du Beau et du Bien*; *Fr. phil. 1865*: this footnote is omitted.
211. *Fr. phil. 1865*: "the intellect" replaced with "the human intellect."
212. *Fr. phil. 1865*: the passage from "I believe..." to "in history too..." is omitted.
213. *Fr. phil. 1865*: "nature" replaced with "the universe."
214. *Fr. phil. 1865*: "whose two extremes are two essentially similar points" replaced with "The two most opposed points one can imagine are always two essentially similar points."
215. *Fr. phil. 1865*: "and the centre is the absolute intellect which presides over and explains everything" is omitted.
216. *Fr. phil. 1865*: "principal foundations" replaced with "general design and fundamentals."
217. *Fr. phil. 1847* and subsequent edition: Cousin adds a footnote specifying that "most of these Fragments have been reconstituted as part of the teaching to which they were related," followed by a reference to his newly published edition of his early works; *Fr. phil. 1865*: this footnote is omitted.
218. *Fr. phil. 1847* and subsequent editions: Cousin inserts a footnote citing his "Attempt at a Classification" (see pp. 150–8 above) and the opening lecture to *Du Vrai, du Beau et du Bien*.
219. *Fr. phil. 1865*: the passage from "it was subsequently applied..." to "... the history of philosophy" replaced with "I gradually introduced it into history."
220. *Fr. phil. 1865*: "I transposed it onto history" is omitted.
221. *Fr. phil. 1865*: "continually" added before "confronting."
222. *Fr. phil. 1865*: "an order of phenomena and ideas which is very real in truth" replaced with "an order of very real phenomena in truth."
223. *Fr. phil. 1865*: "a genuine system that is simultaneously historical, universal and precise" replaced with "a general history of philosophy, conceived, undertaken and executed in this spirit."
224. *Fr. phil. 1865*: "which would be the faithful tableau of consciousness" added after "system."
225. *Fr. phil. 1865*: Cousin inserts the following footnote, "Plato, Proclus, Abelard, Descartes," referring to the editions of their works he edited and published.
226. *Fr. phil. 1865*: "with those of 1818, which at least form a regular lecture course of philosophy" added after "lectures." Cousin also adds two footnotes: the first which is present from *Fr. phil. 1847* cites his editions of the 1819–20 lectures on sensualist philosophy, Scottish philosophy and Kant's philosophy; the second introduced in *Fr. phil. 1865* reads, "Having allowed to appear a kind of very unsatisfying summary of my 1818 lectures, I was condemned to return to them and correct them to make them less unworthy of the reader's benevolence, under this title: *On the True, the Beautiful and the Good.*"
227. *Fr. phil. 1847* and subsequent edition: Cousin inserts the following footnote, "We have published them and this very much condemned me to revisiting them and correcting them to make them a little less unworthy of the reader"; *Fr. phil. 1865*: this footnote is omitted.
228. *Fr. phil. 1865*: "reviving the taste for philosophical subjects in my country, as well as" is omitted.
229. *Fr. phil. 1865*: Cousin inserts the following footnote, "The *First Essays* contain the debris of them."
230. *Fr. phil. 1865*: the passage from "I would have to plead" to "in print" replaced with "I would even have suppressed those fragments which relate to them, if they were not already printed in part." Cousin also inserts the following footnote, "Since then and above all in this definitive edition, the primitive fragments have gradually disappeared for more extended and more recent fragments."
231. *Fr. phil. 1865*: "without having enough of that generality to speak to the needs of the moment and the controversies that party quarrels have given rise to" is omitted.

232. *Fr. phil. 1865*: Cousin inserts the following footnote, "Saint-Simon and the Abbé de Lamennais. See below the Preface to the second edition, p. lii and p. lxvii [pp. 100–1, 109–11 below]."
233. *Fr. phil. 1865*: the passage from "the only philosophical method" to "vast and regular" replaced with "the only proven method, this method of observation and induction already so happily applied to all the physical sciences."
234. *Fr. phil. 1865*: this sentence is omitted.
235. *Fr. phil. 1865* and subsequent editions: "understanding things, accepts, explains and respects everything, and destroys" replaced with "understanding things as they are, battling…."
236. *Fr. phil. 1847* and subsequent editions: the final paragraph is omitted.

Preface to the 1833 Edition of *Philosophical Fragments*[1]

I am reprinting these *Fragments* just as they appeared in 1826, with some corrections that are not worth the trouble to enumerate. It seemed appropriate to me to retain the initial character of this work—if a collection of detached pieces can so be named—as well as the faults and qualities with which it was first presented to the public.

The preface to these *Fragments* was all that merited any comment. What occurred went well beyond my expectations. Welcomed in Germany with indulgence, it there found a skilful interpreter.[*] A translation of such precision that it betrayed a mind familiar with these matters was disseminated in the North of Italy.[†] It even excited some interest in England, and I was very astonished to see it attract the attention of transatlantic critics.[‡] In France, it has been the subject of a controversy which has not proven useless for philosophy. After six years, I am not going to exhume and, on the hoof, take up this controversy once more, the details of which are forgotten and should stay so. I merely want to say here some words about it which might not be out of place considering the current state of things.

The preface to these *Fragments* aimed to give an idea of the general system to which they are related; it could only indicate this system, but it at least marked out all its elements in their interconnection and harmony. Rapidly sketched, here are the four points to which all the others can be reduced:

1. Method;
2. The application of method to that part of philosophy which this very method places above all others—that is, psychology;
3. The transition from psychology to ontology and to higher metaphysics;
4. General views on the history of philosophy.[5]

---

[*] F. W. Carové, *Religion und Philosophie in Frankreich*, Göttingen, 1827. See also the *Globe*, 9 March 1830, for the review of this translation and its notes.[2]

[†] A. Mathiae, *Manuale di Filosofia*, translated from the German with a summary of Cousin's new philosophy (Lugano, 1829).[3]

[‡] *North American Review*, no. LXIV (July 1829). This article is by Mr Everett, former minister of the United States in Spain.[4]

I. Here as elsewhere, as everywhere, as always, I pronounce myself for that method which places the starting point of all sound philosophy in the study of human nature and therefore in observation, and which is subsequently directed to induction and to reasoning to draw out of observation all its implications. One is deceived if one states that true philosophy is a science of facts, unless one adds that it is also a science of reasoning. It rests on observation; but has no limits other than those of reason itself; just as physics begins from observation, but does not stop there and, through calculation, raises itself to general laws of nature and to the system of the world. Reasoning is in philosophy what calculation is in physics; for, after all, calculation is only reasoning in its simplest form. Calculation is no mysterious power, it is the very power of human reason and all of its peculiarity lies in its language.[6] Philosophy abdicates, it renounces its end—which is the understanding and explanation of all things by the legitimate use of our faculties—when it renounces the unlimited use of reason; and, what is more, it is led astray and it leads reason itself astray when it employs [reason] haphazardly, instead of putting it at the service of scrupulously observed and rigorously catalogued facts. Hence, two dangers [become clear]: a badly regulated flight, which, disdaining observation or passing by it too rapidly, is thrown into risky inductions; and a feint-hearted wisdom, which, despite the most intimate of our needs and the most imperious of our instincts, restricts itself to the poverty of[7] sterile observation. To limit philosophy to observation is, whether one does so intentionally or not, to put it on the path to scepticism; to neglect observation is to throw it onto the paths of hypothesis. Scepticism and hypothesis: here are the two pitfalls of philosophy. The true method avoids them both. It does not begin at the end and does not end at the beginning. It recognizes no limits to reasoning, but supports it with sufficient observation; for, the more observation becomes valid, the more, then, will all our science be valid. Therefore, whenever it has reservations about the covert use of intellectual forces,[8] philosophy cannot attach itself too strongly to observation, and, like true physics, cannot[9] proclaim observation too highly as its necessary point of departure. It is thus distinguished from physics only by the nature of the phenomena it observes. The phenomena proper to physics are those of external nature, that vast world of which man is such a small part. The phenomena proper to philosophy belong to that other world which each man carries within himself and which he perceives thanks to that internal light called[10] consciousness, as he perceives the other world by his senses. The phenomena of the internal world appear and disappear so rapidly that consciousness perceives them and loses them from view almost at the same time. Thus, it is not enough to observe them fugitively and so, while they pass across this moving theatre, one must retain them by means of the most focused attention possible. And furthermore, one can [in fact] evoke a phenomenon at the dead of night after it has evaporated, recalling it to memory and reproducing it so as to consider it at one's ease: one can recall one part rather than another, leave [that part] in shadow in order to make another appear, vary the aspects so as to pursue them all and comprehend the entire object—this is the office of reflection. Reflection is to consciousness what artificial instruments are to our senses. It is not enough to listen to nature, one must interrogate it; it is not enough to observe, one must experiment.[11] Experiment has the same conditions and the same rules, whatever object it pertains to; and it is in following these rules that one arrives, in the science of man as in that of nature, at exact classifications. These classifications contain the entirety of the first part of philosophy, that which stands at the head of all the others, and which because of its proper object—humanity, the human soul—is called in the schools, psychology. The science of man, psychology, is not of course the whole of philosophy, but it is its ground. This point is of the highest importance, since it decides everything else, including the character of the entire system. It is to the task of establishing this that I devoted, not I hope without some fruit, the first years of my teaching; on all occasions since, I have recalled it and treated it as something already demonstrated and[12] as a truth that is now beyond debate. Those who believed that it should carry on being insisted on after me are right; for, in philosophy, one cannot insist too much on true method, as long as one does not, over time, turn it into a commonplace in which some find rest but confine others. I thus repeat: if psychology is not the limit of philosophy, it is its basis; and it is by this principle, which contains all others, that my philosophical enterprise in its most general character has been profoundly imprinted with the spirit of modern philosophy, which, since Descartes and Locke, admits no other method but experience and places the science of human nature at the head of philosophical science. It is even closely related to eighteenth-century philosophy, which it perpetuates by modifying it, and is, on the contrary, thereby separated from the new German philosophy.[13] The latter, aspiring to reproduce in its concepts the very order of things, begins with the being of beings, so as to descend by each degree of existence to man and to the various faculties with which he is equipped. It arrives at psychology by ontology, by metaphysics and physics reunited. Certainly, I am also convinced that, in the universal order, man is only a result,[14] the summary of all that preceded him, and that the root of psychology is at bottom in ontology; but how do I know this? How did I learn of it? Because, having studied man and having discerned certain elements in him, I rediscovered—with qualification and in different forms—these same elements in external nature and so, from induction to induction, from reasoning to reasoning, I had to connect these elements, those of humanity and those of nature, to the invisible principle of them both. But I did not begin with this principle, and I did not immediately posit certain powers and attributes in it;[15] for what would have enabled me to do so? It could not have been an induction, since I did not yet know man or nature; it must then have been what in Germany is called a *construction*[16] and among us is a hypothesis. Whether or not this hypothesis is true, as I believe it to be, it is nevertheless scientifically void. The first thing I necessarily stumble upon in trying to know anything is myself; it is I who am the instrument by which I know everything; I must then assess this instrument before employing it, for otherwise I would know neither what I am doing nor with what right I do so. Without doubt, I now know that the small world of humanity is only a reflection of a greater world; but it is by this small world that I have arrived at the large one, and I understand the latter only thanks to the former. I stand here today on top of a mountain from which an immense horizon is revealed to my eyes, but I came from a dark valley, and I can still perceive and show to others the paths which led me to where I now am, so as to help them and encourage them to climb up like me, instead of letting them believe and persuading myself that I fell straight from the sky. In a word, in my exposition of ideas, I wish for the same path to be followed in the exposition of ideas as in their discovery. I prefer analysis to synthesis, because it reproduces the order of discovery, which is true, whereas synthesis, by claiming to reproduce the necessary order of things, runs the risk of engendering only hypothetical abstractions. Where would we be, I ask you, if the author had not more or less practised that humble method which he afterwards conceals or disdains; if, when listening to him or reading him, we did not tacitly verify his assertions by means of knowledge acquired by a different route; and if, finally, we did not arrive at a part of the system—psychology—whose light was reflected onto all the other parts and[17] whose truth became for us the measure of the truth of the entire system? Can we take synthesis for a method of presentation solely suitable for the author and some adepts? Perhaps, but this is nothing but a question of art. However, if one makes it a question of philosophy, if one establishes synthesis as a philosophical method, and if at the height of this method one takes pity on psychological method as incapable of attaining such grand results, the affair is then more serious and I abandon genius for fear of going astray on its tracks.

II.—But if, in terms of method, I distance myself from the new German philosophy and am close to the old French philosophy of the eighteenth century, I am quick to separate myself from the latter when it comes to the first applications of that shared method. This philosophy observes, it is true, but it observes only the facts that agree with it, and it immediately corrupts the experimental method with systematic views.[18]

When first glancing at consciousness, one certainly perceives a succession of[19] phenomena which, analysed into their elements, boil down to sensation. These phenomena are incontestable and they are numerous; their interplay, although quite complex, is easily untangled and they have the advantage of resting on a primitive fact which, by linking the science of man to the physical sciences, has the air of certainty; this fact is that of the impression produced on the organs and reproduced by the brain in[20] consciousness. It is thus a very natural illusion to believe that this order of phenomena encompasses all that are possible in consciousness.[21] Moreover, if there really were only one sole order of phenomena in consciousness, we could relate these phenomena merely to one faculty alone, which by means of its transformations would produce all the others. This faculty is sensibility. But if sensibility is the root of all our intellectual faculties, it cannot not be the root of our moral faculties.[22] If everything in man were reduced to sensing, everything would be reduced to pleasure and pain: the avoidance of suffering and the seeking of pleasure would be the unique rule for our actions; from there, in a word, follows the entire system whose consequences were implemented and which are perfectly well known today. This system is that of the sensualist school, so named on account of the unique principle that it recognizes. A single impartial observation destroys both this principle and the entire system by making visible that there is, within consciousness, phenomena[23] that no effort can legitimately reduce to that of sensation[24]—numerous, very real ideas which play a huge role in both life and language and which sensation does not explain. After being struck by the relations among human faculties, one is also struck by their differences, and a severe method expands the domain of psychology.

I have catalogued[25] all phenomena in consciousness into three classes that are in turn re-ascribed to three major elementary faculties, which, in their combinations, encompass and explain all the others: these faculties are sensibility, activity, and reason. Here is not the place to give an account of this classification; it is enough to remark that it has proven a successful one, since I see it reproduced[26] in almost all the psychology books that have appeared for some time past. It is superfluous to show how such a psychology overthrows the philosophy of sensation and leads to a philosophy opposed to it in each of its parts: metaphysics, morals, theodicy, politics, history. This philosophy is represented on the stage of nineteenth-century philosophy by the Scottish school[27] and, above all, by the school of Kant, which, professing the same method, applied it very differently, although still rigorously and extensively, thereby enriching psychology with many ingenious and profound observations, and on account of the grandeur and beauty of its morality, above all, will always be one of the most admirable schools[28] of philosophy which can do honour to the human mind.[29]

Judge the importance of psychology! One sole psychological error is enough to throw Kant onto a path that leads into the abyss.[30] Kant completed an admirable analysis of human reason. It is impossible to describe with more accuracy and precision the conditions and laws of its development; but having failed to analyse with the same care voluntary and free activity, this great man did not see that it was specifically to that class of phenomena that personality pertained, and so, reason, although united to personality, is profoundly distinct from it.[31] Moreover, if reason were to be personal like attention and will, it would follow that every concept suggested by it to us would also be personal, all truths discovered by it for us would be purely relative to[32] our manner of conceiving them, and that objects which are apparently real (things, beings, substances whose existence reason reveals to us) would rest solely on this equivocal testimony and could have only subjective value[33](relative to the subject who perceives them) and no objective value—that is, real and independent of the subject. One could, of course, still believe in the reality of these objects, if our reason is so made that it cannot not believe this and because it has been made thus;[34] but there would still exist an abyss between belief and knowledge; and all our knowledge would consist merely in recognizing the internal and psychological conditions of the necessity of believing, empty of all real and absolute knowledge.[35] Out of this emerges a new and original[36] scepticism which, while recognizing in us the existence of reason as a faculty distinct from sensibility, still does not deny that, in its regular development, reason suggests to us the ideas of the soul, God, and the world. This is a scepticism entirely distinct from that of the sensualist school: it avoids all dogmatism in psychology, and only starts doubting when it comes to ontology to there contest the legitimacy of[37] every transition from psychology to ontology, owing to the principle that reason, being a faculty proper to the subject, can have no value[38] beyond the limits of the subject, and thus all objective and ontological truths that it reveals[39] to us are only the subject itself transported out of itself by a force that belongs to it and which is itself subjective.[40]

Do you want the final word on this system? Look from the principle to the consequence, from the circumspect master to the audacious student—look from Kant to Fichte. You will see reason already become subjective in Kant,[*] and, in Fichte,[†] it is confounded with the I itself, whence the formula:[43] the I posits itself, posits the world, posits God; it posits itself as primitive and permanent cause from which everything proceeds and to which everything is led back, as both circle and circumference; it posits the world as a simple negation of itself; it posits God as [the I] itself taken absolutely. The absolute I—this is the ultimate degree of all subjectivity, the extreme and necessary[44] completion of Kant's system—and at the same time its refutation. Good sense does justice to this extravagant consequence; but it is philosophy's job to destroy it at its principle, and its principle is the subjectivity and personality of reason. This is the radical error, the psychological error, that a severe psychology should get rid of. All my effort has thus been to demonstrate that personality, the I, is eminently voluntary and free activity, that this is the true subject and that reason is as completely distinct from this subject as it is from sensation and organic impressions.[45]

Assuredly, reason only develops on condition that the I is already there, just as the I appears in consciousness only under the condition of sensation and preliminary organic movements. [Reason] pertains closely to both personality and sensibility, but is neither one nor the other. And it is because it is neither one nor the other, it is because it is in us without being us, that it reveals to us[46] what is not us— objects other than the subject itself, placed outside of its sphere. Indeed, has the human race ever doubted for an instant, I do not say only the existence of objects that reason reveals to it, such as the existence of the external world, but the very

---

[*] *Tennemann's Manual*, vol. 2, pp. 230–72.[41]
[†] *Tennemann*, vol. 2, pp. 272–94.[42]

truth in itself of this existence. No abuse of language has ever been able to reach the point of relating and attributing the revelations of reason to ourselves. We say: my action and therefore my virtue, my crime; we impute them to ourselves; we are them and[47] we feel ourselves responsible for them.[48] We say: my reason, but only to explain the relation of reason to the I in consciousness. We say: my error, with good reason; for there is often something of our doing in our errors, and this is why we sometimes reproach ourselves for them. But I ask, who has ever dared say: my truth? Each of us feels, each of us knows that the truth is neither his nor anyone's.[49] Strange inconsistency! When it transports us outside of consciousness, the independence of reason is contested;[50] but within consciousness itself it is not contested. For example, who doubts the truth of the immediate perceptions of consciousness, perceptions on which knowledge of our own personal existence is founded?[51] Not one sceptic doubts this; for, at the very least, no sceptic doubts that he doubts; yet, to not doubt that one doubts is to know[52] that one doubts—that is, to know something, and this is to know. But who knows that it is the case, who perceives it, who knows of it to such a degree, I ask you, if not reason itself? Thus, if the knowledge that reason gives within these limits and to this degree is uncontested, why would this other knowledge that the same reason gives be more uncertain? Why admit the independence of reason in one case and not admit it in the other? Reason is one across all its degrees. No one has the right to arbitrarily restrict or extend its authority, and to say of it when one pleases: you will reach this point but go no further.

III.—With reason again restored to its true nature and independence, it is easy to recognize the legitimacy of its applications, even when, after having been enclosed in the field of consciousness, they are consistently extended into the beyond. Reason attains beings as well as phenomena; it reveals to us the world and God with the same authority as our own existence and the least of its modifications, and ontology is just as legitimate as psychology, since it is psychology that itself leads us to ontology by illuminating the nature of reason for us.

Ontology is the science of being; it is the knowledge of our personal existence, of the external world, of God. This triple knowledge is given by reason in the same way as any knowledge—reason, unique faculty of all knowledge, unique principle of all certainty, unique rule of the true and the false, of good and evil, which alone can perceive its own failings, which alone can correct itself when deceived, which alone can rectify itself when it is led astray, accuse itself, absolve itself, or condemn itself. One must not imagine that reason passes through a long development to bring man to this triple knowledge of himself, the world and God; no, this triple knowledge is given to us entirely in each of its parts, and even in every fact of consciousness, in the first as in the last. It is still psychology which here illuminates ontology, but a psychology which only profound reflection can attain.

Can there be one fact of consciousness without the intervention of some attention? Weaken or completely take away attention and our thoughts become confused and dissipate little by little into indistinct dreams, which soon themselves evaporate and are for us as if they never were. Even the perceptions of the senses are disturbed without attention and degenerate into pure organic impressions. The organ is often struck with force, but the mind—being elsewhere—fails to perceive the impression; there is no sensation; there is no consciousness. Attention is thus the condition of all consciousness.

Now, is not every act of attention a more or less voluntary act? And is not every voluntary act marked by the fact that we conceive ourselves as its cause? And is not this cause, whose effects vary but which remains the same, that power which its acts alone reveal to us, but which is distinguished from its acts and that its acts do not exhaust? Is not, I say, this cause, this force that we call I [*je*], me [*moi*], our individuality, our personality, this personality which we never doubt and that we never confound with any other, because we never relate to any other voluntary acts which give us such intimate sensation and unbreakable conviction?

The I is thus given to us by the concept of cause, of force. But can this force, this cause that we are, do all that it wants to, does it not encounter obstacles? It encounters them at all times and in all forms, and onto the feeling of our power is continually added that of our weakness. Thousands of impressions assail us without cease; withdraw your attention and they do not attain consciousness; apply your attention to them and the phenomenon of sensation begins. Hence, at the same time as I relate the act of attention to myself as cause, I cannot, in the same way, relate sensation—that to which attention is applied—to myself; I cannot do it, but I can no more fail to relate it to some cause, to a cause necessarily different from me—that is, to an external cause, and to an external cause whose existence is as certain to me as my own existence, since the phenomenon which suggests it to me is as certain to me as the phenomenon that had suggested[53] my own [existence] to me, and both are given to me together.

Here, then, are two kinds of cause distinct from each other: one, personal and placed at the very centre of consciousness, the other outside of consciousness and external. The cause that we are is evidently limited, imperfect, finite, since at every moment it encounters obstacles and limits among this variety of causes to which we necessarily relate the phenomena that we do not produce, the purely affective and involuntary phenomena. On the other side, these causes themselves are limited and finite, since we resist them to a certain degree as they resist us, and we limit their action as they limit ours and also limit each other reciprocally. It is reason which discovers for us these two kinds of cause; it is [reason] which, by developing itself in consciousness and perceiving both attention and sensation, makes us immediately conceive two kinds of distinct causes that are correlative and reciprocally finite. But does reason stop there? No, it is a fact once more that, once the concept of finite and limited causes is given, we cannot but conceive a superior, absolute, and infinite cause, which is itself the first and last cause of all others. The internal, personal cause and the external causes are incontestably causes relative to their own effects: but the same reason, which gives them to us as causes and which gives them to us also as limited and relative causes, prevents us from stopping there as though [they were] self-sufficient causes, but instead forces us to relate them to a supreme cause which brings them into being and maintains them, which is relative to them what they are relative to their phenomena, and which, being the cause of all causes and the being of all beings, suffices in itself and suffices for reason, since reason looks for nothing and finds nothing beyond it.

Let us note this fundamental point which has significant implications. Just as the concept of the I is that of a cause to which we relate the phenomena of volition, so too the concept of the not-I lies completely within that of a cause of sensible and involuntary phenomena. Moreover, since the being that we are and the external world are nothing but causes, it follows that the being of beings to which we relate them is equally given to us[54] under the concept of cause. God is for us only as cause; if he were not, reason would relate neither humanity nor the world to him. [This first cause] is absolute substance only insofar as [it is] absolute cause and its essence is precisely in its creative power. I would need a volume to properly describe and fully illuminate the manner by which reason raises us to the absolute cause,[55] after giving us the duality of personal and external causes.[56] I am just summarizing in a few lines the long[57] investigations discernible in the debris of these *Fragments* and[58] the reasoning of its Preface. It is merely this reasoning that I wanted to recall.

There is no hypothesis here: it is enough to turn back to consciousness, but at a certain depth, to rediscover there all that has just been presented: for, to summarize this summary again, no fact of consciousness is possible without the I; moreover, the I cannot know itself without knowing the not-I; neither one nor the other can be known—alongside the reciprocal limitation which characterizes them—without a more or less distinct conception of something infinite and absolute to which they relate. These three ideas of the I or free person, of the not-I or nature, of their absolute cause, their substance[59] or God, are held closely together and compose one and the same fact of consciousness whose elements are inseparable. There is no man who does not carry this fact entirely within him in his consciousness. And from this [follows] the natural and permanent faith of the human race. But not all men give an account of what they know. Knowing without giving an account of it and knowing by giving an account of it—this is the entire difference possible between man and man, between the people and the philosopher. In the former, reason is entirely spontaneous and obtains all its objects, but without returning into itself and asking for an account of its own operations; in the latter, reflection is added to reason, but this reflection, in its most profound investigations, can add to natural reason not one single element that it did not already possess: it can add nothing but knowledge of itself. Again, I add: well-directed reflection; for if it were badly directed, it would not comprehend the whole of natural reason; it would cut off some element and repair its mutilations only by arbitrary inventions. To first omit, then invent—this is a common vice of nearly all systems of philosophy. The ambition of [well-directed reflection] is to reproduce in its scientific formulae the pure belief of the human race—nothing less than this belief, nothing more than this belief, this belief alone, but this belief entirely. Its singular character is to ground ontology on psychology and to pass from one to the other thanks to a faculty that is both psychological and ontological together, subjective and objective at once, which appears in us without properly belonging to us, enlightens the shepherd as much as the philosopher, is lacking in no one and suffices for all—that is, reason, which from the heart of consciousness extends into the infinite and attains the being of beings.

A system so simple in its operations and results which, beginning with the method of the age, rediscovers through it all of the principal elements of the human race's eternal belief, and reconstructs dogmatism without any instrument except reason, could not but shock the two schools that divide philosophy between them in France—I mean the sensualist school and the theological school: the former which enchains reason within the limits of sensible phenomena, the latter which proscribes it absolutely and declares it incapable of reaching the truth.

From the sensualist school's polemic against the *Fragments*,* I will extract two or three arguments, because they have since been much repeated and have become, with respect to me, a commonplace of sensualism.

1° There is a contradiction between the method of observation and induction proclaimed in the Preface and its systematic applications, for, when we begin with consciousness, we cannot legitimately attain ontology.[61]

I respond to this that, if, within consciousness, we find a faculty whose character is to be universal and absolute, then the authority of this faculty is not confined to consciousness's limits,[62] despite falling under consciousness's gaze—and without [this faculty] neither could sensualism get beyond consciousness, for it too begins from a given of consciousness (sensation), and it is with this given as known by consciousness that, with reasoning whose use is again attested by consciousness, it attains knowledge of external existence, that is, ontology. So, the objection fails both against [sensualism] and against myself. In fact, consciousness is a pure witness, and thus the faculties it witnesses do not cease to have their own [independent] value and their own legitimate scope which it measures and evaluates. Moreover, sensation by itself is deprived of all illumination and does not even know itself, whereas reason knows itself and knows everything else, and goes beyond the sphere of the I, because it does not belong to the I.[63]

2° This system which claims to establish a spiritualism by grounding it on experience, is in the end and in its final conclusions nothing but the famous system of

---

* See particularly some articles in the *Producteur*, journal of the disciples of Saint-Simon, whose philosophical and industrial materialism, which generated numerous partisans, led to a mystical materialism which has lost them again. These articles (vol. 3, p. 325 / vol. 4, p. 19) are by Laurent, author of a *Summary of the History of Philosophy*, cribbed from Degérando.[60]

Spinoza and the Eleatics, a pantheism which precisely destroys the received concept of God and Providence.[64]

It is to respond to this accusation, which has found so many echoes even outside the sensualist school, that I wrote a special dissertation on the Eleatic school where I categorically explained myself on pantheism, on its philosophical and historical origin, on the principle of its errors, and also on what is good and even useful in it.[65],*

Pantheism is strictly the divinization of the whole, the great whole given as God, the universe-God of most of my adversaries, for example, of Saint-Simon. It is at bottom a genuine atheism, but into which one can mix—as has been done, if not by Saint-Simon himself, then at least by his school[67]—a certain religious taint, by applying very illegitimately to the world the ideas of the good and the beautiful, of the infinite and of unity, which belong solely to the supreme cause and are to be encountered in the world only insofar as [the world] is, like every effect, the manifestation of all the powers contained in its cause. The system opposed to pantheism is that of an absolute unity that is so superior and prior to the world that it is foreign to it and it thus becomes impossible to understand how this unity was able to emerge from itself, and how from out of such a principle one can draw this vast universe with its manifold forces and phenomena. This second system is the abuse of metaphysical abstraction, just as the first is the abuse of an exalted contemplation of nature, constrained, sometimes without knowing it, within the chains of the senses and the imagination. These two systems are more natural than is assumed by those who do not know the history of philosophy, or who have not themselves passed through the various states of the soul and the intellect out of which they arise. In general, every naturalist must guard against the first [system] and every metaphysician the second.[68] The goal, but also the difficulty is, when meditating and in the schools, to not lose the feeling for nature, and, in the presence of nature, to ascend back in spirit and in truth to the invisible principle which both manifests to us and veils from us the delightful harmony of the world. Is it conceivable that the sensualist school raises accusations of pantheism against anyone else and particularly against me? To accuse me of pantheism is to accuse me of confounding the first, absolute, infinite cause with the universe, that is, with the two relative and finite causes, the I and the not-I, whose limits and evident insufficiency are the ground on which I ascend to God. In truth, I did not believe I would ever need to defend myself from such a reproach. However, if I have not confounded God and the world, if my God is not the universe-God of pantheism, neither is it, I avow, the abstraction of absolute unity, the dead God of scholasticism.[69] Moreover, since God is given only as absolute cause, I contend for this reason that he cannot not produce, such that creation ceases to be unintelligible[70]

---

* *Nouveaux fragmens philosophiques*, Xenophon and Zeno of Elea, pp. 9–160.[66]

and that God [exists] without the world just as little as the world without God. This final point appeared to me of such importance that I was not scared to express it with all the force within me: "The God of consciousness is not an abstract God, a solitary king sitting behind creation on a deserted throne in silent eternity and with an absolute existence which resembles the very nothingness of existence; he is a God, both true and real, both substance and cause, always substance and always cause—substance only insofar as he is cause and cause only insofar as he is substance. That is, as absolute cause, [he is] one and many, eternity and time, space and number, essence and life, indivisibility and totality, beginning, end, and middle, at the summit of being and at its lowest degree, infinite and finite all together infinite and finite at once."* How admirable that from this passage it was concluded that my system is merely that of Spinoza and the Eleatics. There is but one small difficulty with this: it is precisely that this passage is directed against all metaphysical speculation in the spirit of Spinoza and the Eleatics. I beg the pardon of my adversaries for saying so, but the God of Spinoza and the Eleatics is a pure substance and not a cause.[72] Spinoza's substance has attributes rather than effects. In Spinoza's system, creation is impossible; in mine, it is necessary.[73] As for the Eleatics, they admit neither the testimony of the senses nor the existence of the manifold or any phenomenon, and they absorb the whole universe into the abyss of absolute unity. No matter: my adversaries have repeated that I am a pantheist and an Eleatic so frequently that for some time a quite large section of the public has been persuaded of it and I have had to write a history of the Eleatic school just to prove I did not belong to that school.

3° However, here is the biggest, the devastating objection [made by the sensualist school]:[74] all this is just an importation of German philosophy—and this alone is enough to stir up as much patriotism as if I had introduced a foreigner into the heart of my country. I will respond curtly that in philosophy there is no other country except truth, and it is not a matter of knowing whether the philosophy I teach is German, English, or French, but whether it is true. Does one ever speak of a French geometry or physics? And does not philosophy, by the very nature of its objects, possess or at least work towards this character of universality in which all distinctions of nationality evaporate? Moreover, have we not borrowed from Italy in the arts and do we not borrow every day still from England when it comes to the understanding and practice of representative government, political economy, and everything that relates to external life? Why not also borrow from Germany when it comes to the internal life, the art of education and philosophy? Finally, have our adversaries forgotten where their own philosophy came from? Is this philosophy not an importation of Locke—that is, an English philosophy, a foreign philosophy? And yet it reigned in France during all the later years of the eighteenth

---

* *Preface* [p. 77][71]

century with an almost unlimited authority; it has been as national as a philosophy could be. That of Descartes had reigned in France during the seventeenth century; it had been profoundly national then, since the whole life of the nation, from Pascal to Madame de Sevigny, submitted[75] to its ascendency. And yet these two philosophies, at half a century's distance, are diametrically opposed. From where does their common nationality arise amongst the marked differences that separate them? In my opinion, the secret of a common nationality between these two contrary philosophies is to be found entirely in the common spirit which presides over them and subordinates all their differences: that spirit of method and analysis, that need for perfect clarity, precision, and connections, which is the French spirit par excellence. Here is our true nationality in philosophy; here is what we must establish and not abandon at any price. If I have sinned against this, I condemn myself as guilty, but guilty despite myself. And yet, in order to remain faithful to itself, this French spirit is not compelled to neglect everything else; there is nothing to fear from contact with philosophical schools which flourish in other parts of our great European family; and it would be worthwhile, by means of [France's] typical wisdom and firmness, to discern there the good from the bad, to throw to the wind what is vapour and chimera, and to profit from what is solid and true. It was thus no bad idea to engage with the fairly sombre depths of German philosophy, to rediscover there hidden treasures of meditation, and to make them known in France. If there is some wrong in that, then, yes, I admit it, I first gave the fatal example; I opened the gates: from everywhere others have followed in my footsteps and I dare to believe that it is a genuine service that I have done for my country and that sooner or later it will be recognized. Otherwise, it is just a question of originality. But where, good sirs, have you seen me make any claim to originality? In the *Republic*, when the sophist Thrasymachus makes a similar reproach to Socrates, Socrates responds to him, "You are right, Thrasymachus, to say that on all sides I learn from others; but you are wrong to add that I am not grateful to them; on the contrary, I bear witness to my gratitude to them as much as I can."* So says Socrates—and so says Plato himself, Aristotle, Leibniz, anyone who has had the happiness to be born with a slightly elevated soul, an extensive mind, and a love of truth in an enlightened century, rich in grand exemplars and beautiful geniuses. And me too, I have always thanked Providence for being born in a time when I met with such sources of instruction, so many books and so many men whose commerce was useful to me. Far from claiming that I have had no masters, I confess that I have had many, both in the past and in the present, both in France and outside France. To be brief, I will speak here only of contemporaries.

The day has remained and will always remain in my memory, with an emotion of gratitude, on which, for the first time in 1811 as a student of the École Normale

---

* *Republic*, vol. 9 of my translation, p. 27.[76]

destined for the teaching of letters, I heard Laromiguière.[77] This day decided the whole course of my life: it took me away from my first studies which had promised me peaceful success to throw me into a career not lacking in controversies and storms. I am not Malebranche, but, when listening to Laromiguière, I experienced what Malebranche is said to have experienced when opening by chance a treatise by Descartes.[78] Laromiguière taught the philosophy of Locke and Condillac, happily modified on some points, with a clarity and grace which seemed to rid it of any appearance of difficulties, and with a charm of intellectual bonhomie which penetrated and subjugated [his listeners].[79] The École Normale belonged entirely to him. The following year, a new teaching came among us to dispute the first, and Royer-Collard—by the rigour of his logic, by the gravity and weight of his words—turned us little by little, but not without resistance, from the path forged by Condillac, and, instead, onto the track that has since become so accessible, but was then painful and unfrequented, of Scottish philosophy.[80] Alongside these two eminent teachers, I had the good fortune to encounter a man without equal in France for his talent for internal observation, for the finesse and depth of his psychological sense—I speak of [Maine] de Biran.[81] These were my three masters in France; I will never exhaust all that I owe them. Laromiguière initiated me into the art of analysing thought; he gave me practice in descending from the most abstract and most general ideas that we today possess to the most crude sensations from which they first originated, and he demonstrated to me the play of the faculties, both elementary and composite, which in turn intervene in the formation of these ideas. Royer-Collard taught me that, if these faculties have need of sensation to develop and bear any idea, then they are also in their action subjected to certain internal conditions, to certain laws, to certain principles which sensation does not explain, which resist all analysis, and which are, as it were, the natural patrimony of the human mind. With Biran, I studied, above all, the phenomena of the will. This admirable observer taught me to[82] untangle, in all our knowledge and even in the simplest facts of consciousness, the part that pertains to voluntary activity, that activity in which our personality bursts forth and reveals[83] itself.

It is under this triple discipline that I was educated; and, thus prepared, in 1815 I entered into the public teaching of philosophy at the École Normale and the Faculty of Letters.

Soon I had—or believed I had—exhausted the teachings of my first masters, and I looked for new ones: after France and Scotland, my eyes were naturally carried towards Germany. I thus learnt German and began to decipher with infinite pains the principal monuments of Kant's philosophy, without any other help than Born's barbarous Latin translation.[84] I lived two whole years as if buried within the subterranean passages of Kantian psychology, and was occupied solely with the transition from psychology to ontology. I have already said how psychology itself presented me with the solution and how I went beyond Kant's philosophy.[85] Fichte's could not detain me for long, and, by the end of 1817, I had left behind me the first German school.⁸⁶ It is then that I took a trip around Germany. I can say that, at this epoch of my life, I stood precisely in the state in which Germany found itself at the beginning of the nineteenth century, after Kant and Fichte,⁸⁷ and at the appearance of the *philosophy of nature*.⁸⁸ My method, my direction, my psychology, my general views had been fixed, and so led me to the *philosophy of nature*. I saw nothing besides it in Germany. Undoubtedly, I there met men of incontestable merit, in possession of just renown, usefully applying themselves to fill the lacunas of Kant's philosophy, to repair its imperfections and to build it up to resist the new philosophy. I did justice to their talents without espousing their cause. I also came across Jacobi's school, almost reunited with Kant's against a common enemy, working together to raise faith above reason and place faith in enthusiasm. And enthusiasm is indeed one of the most legitimate sources of faith; for enthusiasm is nothing but the spontaneous intuition of truth—spontaneous intuition that is more natural, more general and more certain than reflection, and which is no less real and does not fall any less under consciousness's gaze.⁸⁹ However, the error of Jacobi's school is to not see that this veridical enthusiasm, this illumination which resembles a prophecy, belongs to reason itself and is only a purer and higher application of it, such that faith still has its roots in reason. On the contrary, Jacobi⁹⁰ separates reason from faith, and thus, depriving faith of its basis and rule, abandons it to all the vagaries of the heart and the imagination, and does not leave philosophy any other refuge but a restless and dazzling mysticism, without true light or true repose.* A philosophy which begins precisely from the divorce of faith and reason was too opposed to the results to which I had been led to give me pause, even interest me, and I was vividly struck only by the new philosophy. It was still active and spread over Germany as in the days of its novelty. The great name of Schelling rang out in all the schools; here celebrated, there almost damned, everywhere exciting that passionate interest, that concert of ardent elegies and violent attacks that we call glory. I did not see Schelling on this occasion; but in his place I met—without looking for him and quite by chance—Hegel in Heidelberg. I began with him and it is with him too that I finished up in Germany.⁹²

Hegel was then far from being the famous man that I have since rediscovered in Berlin, fixing all eyes upon him and at the head of a numerous and ardent school. Hegel did not yet have a reputation except as a distinguished disciple of Schelling. He had published books that had been little read; his teaching had scarcely begun to make him better known. The *Encyclopedia of Philosophical Sciences* appeared at this moment⁹³ and I had one of the first copies of it. It was a book entirely riven with formulae of a quite scholastic appearance and written in a very recondite language, above all for me. Hegel did not know much more French than I knew German, and, buried in his studies, still unsure of himself and his renown, he scarcely saw

---

* *Tennemann*, vol. 2, p. 330.⁹¹

anyone and, to be frank, was not extremely amiable.[94] I cannot comprehend how an obscure young man came to interest him, but at the end of an hour he was to me as I was to him and, until the last moment, our friendship, tested more than once, was not diminished. From the first conversation, I got [*devinai*] him, I understood his immense reach,[95] I felt myself in the presence of a superior man. And when from Heidelberg I continued my travels in Germany, I announced him everywhere, I prophesied him to some extent; and on my return to France, I said to my friends: gentlemen, I have seen a man of genius. The impression that Hegel had left on me was deep but confused. The following year I went to Munich to look for the author of the system himself. The disciple and the master could not resemble each other less. Hegel let fall very few rare and profound words, some a little enigmatic; his diction was strong but embarrassed; his face immobile, his brow covered with clouds—he seemed the very image of thought turning back on itself. Schelling is thinking in development; his language is, like his face, full of vividness and life: he is naturally eloquent. I passed an entire month with him and Jacobi in Munich in 1818 and it is there I began to see a little more clearly into the *philosophy of nature*.

What then is this philosophy?[96] Can I speak of it in a few words? Is it possible to give even the least intelligible idea to those who have not passed through all the antecedents to this philosophy, through all the stages of the Kantian school? The final word on Kant's philosophy had been Fichte's system, and the final word on Fichte's system was *the I* posited or rather positing itself as unique principle. Arrived at this extreme, German philosophy had either to perish or to take flight: Schelling is the man who drew it out from the labyrinth of a psychology that was both idealist and sceptical, so as to give it back reality and life. Above all, he revendicated the rights of the external world, of nature, and it is from this that his philosophy drew its name. In Kant and Fichte's system, every absolute and substantial existence[97] is but a hypothesis, without any other ground than the need of the subject and the I which admits of [this existence] just to satisfy itself. To leave behind the relative and the subjective, Schelling placed himself immediately in the absolute. According to him, if philosophy desires solid terrain, it must abandon psychology and dialectic, the I just as much as the not-I, and, without being burdened by the objections of scepticism, raise itself straightaway to absolute being, a substance and ideal common to the I and the not-I, which relates exclusively to neither the one nor the other, but which encompasses both and is their identity. This absolute identity of the I and the not-I, of man and nature, is God. It follows from this that God is in nature as well as in man. It follows then that this nature has in itself as much value as man, that it has its own truth like [man] since it exists in the same way, and that it must resemble [man] since it derives from the same principle—their only difference is that of consciousness to non-consciousness. Moreover, God cannot be less in humanity than in nature; if nature is in some sense as rational as the human mind,[98] the human mind must have laws as necessary as those of nature; and the world of humanity is as regularly made as the external world. What is more, the world of humanity is manifest in history; history then has its laws; it thus forms in its diverse epochs and in its apparent aberrations a harmonious system, just as the external world is [such a system] in the diversity of its phenomena. From these two consequences and their common principle derives the high importance of historical studies and the physical sciences. At this moment and for the first time, idealism was introduced into the physical sciences and realism into history; the two spheres of philosophy,[99] enemies until then— psychology and physics—are finally reconciled; an admirable sentiment for both reason and life, a sublime poetry extending into all philosophy; and, above all of this, the idea of God present everywhere and serving the whole system as principle and light.

The first years of the nineteenth century saw appear this great system. Europe owes it to Germany and Germany to Schelling. This system is the true one; for it is the most complete expression of the entirety of reality, of universal existence.[100] Schelling initiated this system; but he left it filled with lacunas and imperfections of all kinds. Coming after Schelling, Hegel belongs to his school: he has made of it a place apart, not only by developing and enriching the system, but by giving it, in many respects, a new face. Hegel's admirers consider him the Aristotle to another Plato; Schelling's exclusive partisans wish to see in him merely the Wolff to another Leibniz. Whatever one thinks of these slightly haughty comparisons, no one can deny that a powerful [faculty of] invention was given to the master, and profound reflection to the disciple. Hegel borrowed much from Schelling; and me, far weaker than both, I borrowed from them both. There is folly in reproaching me for it, and I certainly show no great humility in acknowledging it. More than twelve years ago, when dedicating my edition of Proclus' commentary on the *Parmenides* to Schelling and Hegel, I publicly called them both *my friends and my masters, and the leaders of the philosophy of our age.*[*] Today, it is sweet to renew this homage; I will never repeat enough my sincere admiration and my tender friendship. Thank God, I do not have a soul that would ever be embarrassed by gratitude. But while being pleased to proclaim the resemblances which link the philosophy I profess to those of these two great masters, I must also in truth confess that some fundamental differences separate me from them, despite myself. A Scottish critic whose erudition is equal to his sagacity and who certainly cannot be accused of flattering me, Hamilton, has pointed out these differences.[†] I blush to insist on them,[103] but I cannot but recall the first and most fruitful of all—that of method. As I have already said, my two illustrious friends place themselves straightaway at the pinnacle of speculation; me, I begin from experience. To escape the subjective character of inductions from an imperfect psychology, they begin with ontology, which is

---

[*] *Amicis et magistris, philosophie praesentis ducibus. Procli Opera*, vol. 4 (1821). See also my translation of Plato, vol. III (1826), the dedication to the *Gorgias*.[101]
[†] *Edinburgh Review*, no. 99.[102]

then nothing but a hypothesis; I begin with psychology, and it is psychology itself which leads me to ontology and saves me from both scepticism and hypothesis. Confident that the truth carries with it its own self-evidence, and that it is, moreover, for the whole to justify all its parts, Hegel begins by[104] abstractions which are for him the ground and[105] pattern of all reality; but nowhere does he indicate or describe the procedure which furnishes him with these abstractions. Schelling speaks sometimes of intellectual intuition as the procedure which grasps being itself; but for fear of imprinting a subjective character on this intellectual intuition, he claims that it does not fall within consciousness, and this makes it absolutely incomprehensible to me. On the contrary, in my theory, intellectual intuition, without being personal or subjective, attains being from within consciousness; it is a fact of consciousness just as real as that of reflective conceptions, but only more difficult to grasp, without yet being ungraspable; for it would then be as if it were not. Finally, to what faculty does Schelling's intellectual intuition belong? Is it a special faculty? Or rather is it not, as in my theory, only a higher and purer degree of reason? I do not believe that one can quickly pass over all these points, as well as others that I cannot even mention here. Far from it, I am profoundly convinced that the transition from psychology to ontology cannot be explained with too much care, so as to show that the latter is not, or at least does not appear to be, a tissue of hypotheses more or less cleverly linked together. Here as everywhere is manifest the general difference which separates me from the new German school—that is, the psychological character fully imprinted on all my views and to which I am scrupulously bound as a crutch for my weakness and a guarantee for my inductions.*

I ought perhaps to ask pardon for this apology, which perhaps resembles more a chapter of my memoirs than a discussion of philosophy.[107] At present, at least, the reader knows as much as me about all those who have influenced[108] my mind and my ideas. Regarding my originality, I have struck a very good bargain. I have always sought and still seek one thing, truth—first to nourish myself and fill myself with it, then to communicate it to my fellow man. I have already had[109] many masters, and I hope until my last breath to always be the disciple of someone who will have some new truth to teach me.

I now pass on to other adversaries, to accusations from the theological school[110] that are serious in a very different way.

What can be at issue between the theological school and me? Am I indeed an enemy of Christianity and the Church? I have given many lectures and [written]

---

* On the character of Schelling's philosophy, see Tennemann's excellent summary, *Manual of the History of Philosophy*, French translation, vol. 2, pp. 294–312. For Hegel, it is enough for me to cite the division of his *Encyclopedia of the Philosophical Sciences*, 3rd edn (Berlin, 1830). First part: *Science of Logic*, taken in Plato's sense as the science of ideas in themselves, that is, of the necessary essences of things. Second part: *Philosophy of Nature*. Third part: *Philosophy of Spirit*. It is in this third part of philosophical science that psychology is found. Likewise, in the *Logic*, 1° *Being*; 2° *Essence*; 3° *Concept*, and within "Being" the following three moments in this order *Seyn, Daseyn, Fürsichseyn*.[106]

far too many books; can one find in them one sole word that departs from the respect due to sacred things? Let them cite to me one sole dubious or thoughtless word and I will withdraw it and disavow it as unworthy of a philosopher.

But perhaps, without wanting to and without knowing it, the philosophy I teach weakens the Christian faith? This would be more dangerous and at the same time less criminal; for those who wish to be orthodox are not always so. Let us see. What is the dogma that my theory places in peril? Is it the dogma of the Word and the Trinity? If it is this or something else, let them tell me, let them prove it, let them try to prove it, and this will at least lead to a serious and genuinely theological discussion. I accept it in advance; I solicit it.

No, this is not at all what is at issue. They do not accuse me of either speaking badly or thinking badly of Christianity. It is not because of a specific passage that my philosophy is impious; its impiety runs deep in a very different way, since it concerns [my philosophy's] very existence: its entire crime is to be a philosophy, and not only—as in the twelfth century—a mere commentary on ecclesiastical decisions and Holy Scripture.[111]

Let me speak clearly: so as better to defend religion, the theological school undertakes the destruction of philosophy, all philosophy, the good and the bad, and perhaps the good more than the bad. This is why it becomes sceptical when faced with philosophy. However, it is a pure game, since all this scepticism tends to an enormous dogmatism. The major argument of the theological school and its battle cry is the impotence of human reason.

The following is the familiar argument made by this school:

Reason is a completely personal faculty. Hence, when we affirm something in the name of reason, it is in the name of our reason that we affirm it; certainty has no other basis, no other *criterium*, than our individual sense—and this is absurd. Thus, reason cannot give us genuine certainty. And, when convinced of its own impotence, reason must seek another authority. This authority is that of common sense as opposed to individual sense—a common sense preserved by tradition, made visible by the Church and promulgated by the Holy See.

A hundred times has the elaborate[112] scaffolding [of this argument] been brought down. First of all, we maintain—we philosophers[113]—that what it pleases the theological school to call individual reason is general, universal reason, which, in each human, is an instance of the common sense of the human race. We maintain that if this common sense does exist in the human race, it cannot be composed of fragments of manifold individual reasons, compared between each other, then combined together. This is because there cannot be more in the composite whole than in each of its elements, and a thousand individual, impotent reasons cannot be attributed infallibility from their union. Moreover, who would bring about this union? In short, we maintain that the common sense of the human race exists, because there is, within each human, a non-individual but general reason which, being the same in everyone because it is individual in no one, constitutes the true fraternity of men and the common patrimony of the human species. Otherwise, common sense is a mere hypothesis. Let us suppose that this hypothesis were a truth, so that each person submits his individual sense to the common sense of the species, then each person must, at the very least, be able to recognize this common sense; but how would they recognize it? Would it be with their individual sense? It must be so in the system in question,[114] since there would no longer be anything better in man. But then how, with this individual sense, would one infallibly recognize common sense?[115] One could not, on pain of passing from the particular to the general and of making oneself the measure of certainty. Thus, within the I, there must immediately be a measure for certainty to recognize [the certainty] of what is proposed to us. [The self] must possess another [measure of certainty] to recognize that the Church does represent the common sense of the human species; for it is this relation of conformity [between Church and common sense] which alone generates the entire authority of the Church.[116] In appearance,[117] it is reasonable to ask us to submit to [the Church's dogma]; but, for it to be so, the employment of reason is already[118] necessary.

All of the eloquence and all the sophisms[119] in the world cannot mask this continual paralogism.[120] And yet, this is the argument that has won out. Endlessly beaten, they still endlessly reproduce it. It has risen from sectarian journals into bishop's mandates;* it forms the basis of teaching in seminaries; it occupies the principal Chair of Christendom;† and so that nothing is missing from all this inconsistency, the Protestants have found it so wonderful that they have been quick to borrow it from the Catholics—open any Methodist publication‡ and, except for talent, you could easily believe you are reading the Abbé Lamennais.[124] The same principles, the same manner of reasoning, the same hatred of reason and philosophy; the only difference is that in place of common sense [the Protestants] substitute in the word of God and in place of the Church the Holy Scriptures. In every philosophy, they say, it is always a human who speaks; it is a human alone who addresses our reason with his; but we desire no human [to stand] between us and the truth; we desire [instead] to give ourselves solely to God himself and his Word. Assuredly, our adversaries are not being fiendish; but who teaches them this Word? Who tells them that it is the Word of God? What reason is there to believe them? Who tells them that God has spoken? And by what sign do they recognize it? In order to prove it to us, some of them propose erudite, critical-historical inquiries, others appeal to a kind of immediate illumination in the reading of Holy Scripture. But it is very strange to direct us to criticism out of fear of philosophy and to history so as to avoid humans putting themselves between us and the truth.

---

* See, among pieces of the same type, the general instruction of the Bishop of Chartres, against my lecture course on philosophy, *Quotidienne*, 16 February 1828.[121]

† *De Methodo Philosophandi*, 1st part (Rome, 1828), by Father Ventura, Theatine, Professor of the College of Sapienza.[122]

‡ See *Le Semeur*, organ of the Methodist party.[123]

As for immediate illumination, the intervention of reason is less obvious there, but it is just as real. Which of our faculties is to receive this sudden light when reading Holy Scripture? It is presumably not sensibility; it is not the imagination; it is not the understanding either, etc.; search for it and you will see that it must be reason. As long as reason is able to recognize the true, the good, the beautiful, the great, the holy, the divine, wherever they may be, it is reason that will recognize them in Holy Scripture, as it recognizes them in nature, as it recognizes them in consciousness and the soul, which is also a Bible in its own way. You wish to reduce philosophy to a commentary on Holy Scripture; you must therefore trust those writing this commentary. Holy Scripture has its obscurities and its veils; its language is that of the symbolic East: to understand it and interpret it, a very well-practised and very well-developed reason is necessary. In the final analysis, it is thus to reason that one must return; its testimony is the measure of all other testimonies; on its authority all other authorities rest. If this authority is purely individual, as they claim it to be, there is no longer certainty in the world, no longer universal truth. But if there is certainty, if there are universal truths, it is because reason, which teaches them to us, contains within itself a sovereign and universal authority. In truth, one cannot hold back a smile on seeing a Protestant sect, after separating from the Church in the name of the right to free examination, end up repudiating the authority of the very faculty which does the examining. Let [this sect] return to the Church[125] then: it will at least find there a uniform rule, a general discipline, acting as a support and a refuge against the extravagances of mysticism.

Is there any need to caution that all of this has nothing to do with Christianity, or the Church, or the Holy Scriptures, but just the imprudent war on reason and on philosophy which a misguided zealot declares in their name? To separate faith from reason is to badly serve the faith of the nineteenth century. To reduce philosophy to theology is an intolerable anachronism. Philosophy is forever emancipated. It is almost ridiculous to today reproach it for no longer being the handmaiden of theology. Leave each of them to their happy independence. They can very well subsist together. Their domains are distinct, and [they are] vast enough for them to have no need to meddle in the other's. Religion, which is addressed to all men, would fail at its aim if it presented itself in a form that the intellect alone can attain, for then its teachings would be lost to three quarters of the human species. It does not speak solely to the intellect, but it speaks also to the heart, to the senses, to the imagination, to the entire human being. This is what makes it infinitely more useful than philosophy for the multitude of human creatures on which it acts.[126] But this immense advantage also[127] brings with it disadvantages which gradually appear as time and civilization progress. Literally, religions are the instructors and nourishers of the human race. To them belongs the temples, the public squares, all the great influences, the popularity, and the power. None of them belong to philosophy. It speaks only to the intellect and therefore to a very small number of men; but this small number is the elite and the vanguard of humanity. Since the functions of philosophy and religion are quite different, why then do they fight against each other? They both serve the human species in their own way and according to forms that are their own. Philosophy would be insane and criminal to wish to destroy religion, for it cannot hope to replace it among the masses, who cannot follow a course on metaphysics. On the other hand, religion cannot destroy philosophy, since philosophy represents the sacred right and invincible need of human reason to give an account of all things. A profound theology which understood its genuine domain would never be hostile to philosophy, which it cannot possibly do without; and at the same time a philosophy, which well understood the nature of philosophy, its genuine object, its range and its limits, would never be tempted to impose its methods on theology. It is always bad philosophy and bad theology that quarrel amongst themselves. Christianity is the cradle of modern philosophy, and I have myself pointed out more than one deep truth hidden under the veil of Christian images.[128] Let these holy and sublime images enter early on into the souls of our children, and there deposit the seeds of all truths: our nation, humanity, even philosophy itself will draw the most precious benefits from it.[129] Nevertheless, it cannot be claimed that reason ever tries to give an account of the truth in any other form than [philosophy]. This would be to misunderstand the diversity and richness of the human faculties, their distinct needs and the legitimate scope of these needs; it would be to oppose oneself to the necessary progress of things. However, in the middle of these distractions, it is for philosophy, denigrated and under attack, to draw good from the bad and, while maintaining its independence with unshakeable sureness, to also maintain, as much as it can, the natural alliance which unites it with religion. Besides, only a very thoughtless philosophy would be embarrassed by Christianity. In so doing, it would show itself already convicted by something manifestly insufficient, since it would not understand and could not explain the greatest event of the past and the greatest institution of the present.[130] This leads me to the last point on the application of philosophy to history, and in particular to the history of philosophy which I will say a few words, so as to not roam too far from these *Fragments* and in order to not extend even further an already very long preface.[131]

IV. The views of every system on the history of its science are the surest way of judging this system, the exact measure of its principles.[132] Is it incomplete? Does it contain solely one element from consciousness and from things? Is it grounded solely on one unique principle, however alluring or imposing that might be? [If so,] then so as not to refute itself, [this system] is reduced to perceiving no truth in any systems grounded on a contrary principle,[133] and to finding a little bit of reason solely in those [past systems] which rely on the same principle. Such a historical conception is a judgement on the system, for[134] it is a sorry wisdom which has universal folly as its condition; and to defend oneself only by accusing everyone else is to accuse and condemn oneself. However, suppose a system which, by patient and profound observation, as well as by wide-ranging and scrupulous induction, is led to embrace all elements of consciousness and reality. When it casts its gaze on history—wherever it turns—it will not encounter any single system of any importance in which it does not rediscover some element of itself and with which it does not agree at least on some point. Indeed, one can scarcely separate oneself so far from the common sense accorded to all humankind to fall into and remain within errors destitute of all truth:[135] error enters into the intellect only under the mask of a truth that it disfigures.[136] A genuinely complete system is thus to be applied to history with marvellous ease. [This system] need not justify itself by proscribing all systems; it need only separate out the inevitable portion of error mixed in with the portion of truth, which forms the strength and the life of each [system]. Moreover, by operating in the same way on all of them, out of old enemies with opposed errors [this new system] creates friends and brothers through the truths they contain. Thus purified and reconciled, it composes out of them a vast assemblage, adequate to the entire truth. Moreover, the method—philosophical and historical at the same time—which, in possession of the truth, is able to rediscover its fragments here and there within all systems[137]—this is eclecticism. Three things must be distinguished in eclecticism: its starting point, its methods, and its end; its principle, its instruments, and its results.[138] Eclecticism presupposes a system which it uses as a point of departure and principle to orient itself in history; as an instrument, it has need of rigorous criticism dependent on extensive and robust erudition; its preliminary result is the dismantling of all systems by the steel and fire of criticism, and its definitive result is their re-composition into a unique system which is the complete representation of consciousness in history. Eclecticism starts from a philosophy and it tends, by way of history, to the living demonstration of this philosophy. This is why I wrote at the end of the preface to *Fragments*, after laying out the system I have recalled here: "I will try to undertake the reform of philosophical studies in France by clarifying the history of philosophy by means of a system, and by demonstrating this system via the entire history of philosophy."[139] After all this, is it conceivable to have seen in eclecticism nothing but a blind syncretism, which mixes together all systems, approves everything, confounds the true and the false, the good and the bad; a new fatalism; the dream of a sick spirit who demands a system from history, instead of being able to produce one themselves?[140] All these objections evaporate before the briefest of examinations.

First Objection.—Eclecticism is a syncretism which mixes together all systems.

Response.—Eclecticism does not mix together all systems, for it leaves no system intact; it dismantles each of them into two parts—one false and the other true; it destroys the first and admits solely the second into the work of re-composition. The true part of each system is added to the true part of another system, passing from truth to truth to form a true whole. It never mixes one entire system with another entire system; in no way, therefore, does it mix together all systems. Eclecticism is therefore not syncretism—the former is even opposed to the latter, philosophically and etymologically, as choice is to mixture, discernment is to confusion.

Second Objection.—Eclecticism approves everything, confounds the true and the false, the good and the bad.[141]

Response.—Eclecticism does not approve everything, for it professes that, within every system, there is a considerable portion of error. It does not confound the true and the false; on the contrary, it distinguishes them: it separates out one from the other, puts aside the false and employs the true alone.

Third Objection.—Eclecticism is fatalism.[142]

Response.—It is no fatalism to say that man is so made that, with his admirable intellect, he always grasps something of the truth, and that—within the limits of his intellect, above all, with its indolence, thoughtlessness, presumption—he believes he has attained the complete truth when he solely possesses part of it. From this results the fact that there is always something true and something false, something good and something bad in the works of man, and particularly in philosophical systems. It is even less fatalism to [say] that eclecticism maintains that, with much work on oneself and by redoubling one's vigilance, attention, and circumspection, one can end up diminishing the chances of error—and it is to this very result that [eclecticism] aspires.

Fourth Objection.—Eclecticism is the absence of all system.

Response.—Eclecticism is not the absence of all system; for it is the application of a system:[143] it presupposes a system, it begins from a system.[144] Indeed, to gather up and reunite scattered truths in different systems, it must first separate them from the errors with which they are mixed. And, to do so, one must be able to discern [these truths] and recognize them; however, in order to recognize whether an opinion is true or false, one must oneself know where error is and where truth is; therefore, one must be (or believe oneself to be) already in possession of[145] the truth; and one must have a system to judge all systems. Eclecticism presupposes an already formed[146] system, which it enriches and on which it sheds further light. It is therefore not the absence of all system.[147]

Now, is eclecticism a theory which is exclusively my own? Of course not; and I would strongly distrust any idea which seemed to be entirely new in the world and of which no one had [previously] thought. No, thank God, eclecticism was not born yesterday; it is [instead] born each day a well-formed mind in an accommodating soul takes it into its head to try make two passionate opponents agree by showing them that the opinions they are fighting over are not themselves irreconcilable and that, with some mutual sacrifices, it would be possible to bring them together. Eclecticism already existed in Plato's thinking;[148] it was the declared ambition—whether legitimate or not—of the Alexandrian school. Among the moderns, it was not only the ambition, but the constant practice of Leibniz,[149] and it appears everywhere among those rich historical perspectives of the new German philosophy.[150] The time has come to finally raise it to the rigour and[151] dignity of a principle; and this is what I have tried to do. This term, so long fallen into deep oblivion, scarcely uttered in a weak voice, now rings out from one end of Europe to the other, and the spirit of the nineteenth century has come to recognize itself in eclecticism: the two of them can now undertake their journey together over all obstacles.

At [the moment of] such success, when eclecticism has already made so many unsought conquests, it would be an excessive weakness both of mind and of character to be surprised or wounded by violent attacks against it. It was inevitable that all exclusive systems would rise up against a system which undertook to put an end to their quarrels by undermining their opposed claims and by bending them to a common discipline.[152] All the extreme parties thus conspired against eclecticism, under the honourable banner of continual discord. God knows what war they have waged on it and with what arms! I have had the pleasure of uniting against me over a period of some years both the sensualist school and the theological school. In 1830, both schools entered into the political arena. The sensualist school very naturally gave rise to the demagogic party, and the theological school became, very naturally again, [the party] of absolutism, except it also occasionally put on the mask of demagoguery to better attain its ends, just as, in philosophy, it is by means of scepticism that it tries to bring about theocracy. As a result, anyone who fought against all exclusive principles in science had to equally repel every exclusive principle in the state and to defend representative government. In 1828, I provided a theory I still stand by of representative[153] government and the Charter.* [These were] convictions founded, not on transitory circumstances, but on a deepened study of humanity and history, and so they were not swept away by the wind of the first storm. Three days[155] do not change the nature of things and the state of French society. Yes, just as the human soul in its natural development comprehends many elements which attain their harmonious expression in true philosophy,[156] so too all civilized society has many utterly distinct elements that a true government must recognize and represent, and the triumph of but one of these elements in a simple government can—whatever it calls itself—be nothing but tyranny.

---

* 1828 Lectures, last lecture.[154]

A mixed government is the only one appropriate to a great nation like France. The July Revolution is nothing other than the English revolution of 1688,[157] but in French—that is, with much less aristocracy and a little more democracy and monarchy. The proportions of these elements may vary according to circumstances, but these three elements are necessary. Let us leave republics to the young socialists of America, and absolute monarchies to old Asia. Placed between the old world and the new one, at an equal distance from decrepitude and childhood, our Europe in its powerful maturity contains all the elements of social life at the fulfilment of their complete development. For this reason, [Europe] is condemned, as it were, to representative[158] government. This admirable form of government is a happy necessity for our age; and, with no need for unbridled proselytism, it will travel across Europe. For France, the question—I am not afraid to say it—is whether to exist in this way or to cease to exist at all. With representative government[159] I see public liberty, concord and strength internally, and therefore the almost certain opportunity for grandeur and glory externally. Let representative government[160] fall: I predict nothing but sterile convulsions, civil war and foreign wars, an impotent imitation of a great era that has passed by without return; as well as—and this is something new—perhaps the dismemberment of France, the fate of both Poland and Italy.[161] I avert my eyes from such a conclusion, and desire nothing that might lead to it. My political faith is therefore completely in accordance with my philosophical faith, and both of them stand above party insults.

V. Cousin
Paris, 30 June 1833

Notes

1. *Fr. phil. 1833*, pp. v–lx (subsequently: *Fr. phil. 1838*, vol. 1, pp. 1–44; *Fr. phil. 1847*, vol. 4, pp. 45–94; *Fr. phil. 1855*, vol. 5, pp. 45–94; *Fr. phil. 1865*, vol. 5, pp. xxxvi–lxxix). We take the 1833 publication as our base text for this translation and note the significant modifications to later versions in the endnotes. A translation of the text exists, under the title, "Exposition of Eclecticism," in George Ripley's *Philosophical Miscellanies* (Boston: Hilliard and Gray, 1838), pp. 55–107. This is Cousin's extensive response to many of the initial criticisms of his project in France that arose in the wake of eclecticism's transformation in 1830 from the philosophy of liberal opposition to that of institutional power. It includes, in particular, further reflections on the transition from psychology to ontology, his fullest explanation of his relationship to German Idealism and a first attempt at defining his philosophy against the growing attacks of the Catholic Right and accusations of pantheism—see the Editors' Preface above.
2. Friedrich Wilhelm Carové (1789–1852): while Hegel's student in Heidelberg, he had met Cousin and they read Hegel's *Encyclopedia* together, remaining in correspondence afterwards. *Religion und Philosophie in Frankreich* includes translated extracts from Cousin's Descartes-edition, as well as his 1826 Preface. The review in *Le Globe* (no. 23, pp. 91–2) undertakes a defence of Cousin, as well as welcoming "the recommencement of philosophical communication across the Rhine."
3. An Italian translation of August Heinrich Matthiae's (1769–1835) *Lehrbuch für den ersten Unterricht in der Philosophie* (Brockhaus, 1823).
4. Alexander Hill Everett (1792–1847): his translations and reviews, including this one of Cousin's *Fragments*, came to influence the Transcendentalist movement.

5. This structure broadly reproduces the structure of the 1826 preface, which had been roughly as follows: on experimental method (pp. 59–64); on psychology as first philosophy and on the transition from psychology to ontology (pp. 65–80); and final remarks on Cousin's turn to history (pp. 80–2).
6. *Fr. phil. 1865*: the passage from "One is deceived ..." to "... in its language" is omitted.
7. *Fr. phil. 1865*: "the poverty of" is omitted.
8. *Fr. phil. 1865*: "whenever it has reservations about the covert use of intellectual forces" is omitted.
9. *Fr. phil. 1865*: "and, like true physics, cannot" is replaced with "like true physics in its beginnings cannot."
10. *Fr. phil. 1865*: "that internal light called" is omitted.
11. Throughout this section, and much of the first half of the Preface, Cousin seems to have in mind two of the more influential critiques of his work from the perspective of what Cousin calls "the sensualist school" (even if he never mentions them): F. J. V. Broussais's *On Irritation and Madness* (Paris: Baillière, 1828), as well as A. Comte's commentary on it in *Examination of Broussais's Treatise on Irritation*. Broussais vehemently attacks the "obscurantism" of the revival of Kantianism and Platonism in eclectic philosophy which "turns us away from genuine observation" and "replunges us into the illusions and chimeras of ontology" (p. 13). Comte is even more explicit: he contrasts "the physiologists who have brought about a salutary revolution in abandoning metaphysics and theology" with the eclectics who "misunderstanding in this respect the current and irrevocable direction of the human mind, have for ten years been trying to transplant German metaphysics among us, and to constitute under the name of psychology a pseudo-science independent of physiology, superior to it, and to which alone would belong the study of the phenomena specially called moral. Though these retrograde attempts are not capable of checking the development of real knowledge, since the ephemeral enthusiasm they still excite essentially stems only from strange and accidental circumstances, it is certain that they exercise a baneful influence, retarding in many minds the development of the true philosophical spirit, and wastefully consuming a great deal of intellectual activity." Hence, Comte adds, Broussais' purpose has been "to oppose the vague and chimerical direction in which people are today seeking to lead French youth" through a dismantling of psychology into physiology. A. Comte, *Early Political Writings*, ed. and trans. H. S. Jones (Cambridge: Cambridge University Press, 1998), pp. 228–9.
12. *Fr. phil. 1865*: "as something already demonstrated and" is omitted.
13. *Fr. phil. 1847* and subsequent edition: Cousin inserts a footnote "on the new German philosophy" directing readers to the 1838 Prefatory note; *Fr. phil. 1865*: the passage from "... profoundly imprinted by ..." to "... the new German philosophy" replaced with "profoundly imprinted with the spirit of modern philosophy and in particular that of French philosophy which it continues by modifying it, and, on the contrary, is separated from the new German philosophy"; Cousin also adds references in the footnote to the later discussion in the present preface and *Souvenirs d'Allemagne*.
14. *Fr. phil. 1847* and subsequent editions: "only a result" is omitted.
15. *Fr. phil. 1865*: "But I did not begin with this principle, and I did not immediately posit certain powers and attributes in it" replaced with "But I did not begin there."
16. In e.g. F. W. J. Schelling's 1803 *Über die Construction in der Philosophie*.
17. *Fr. phil. 1865*: "whose light was reflected onto all the other parts and" is omitted.
18. *Fr. phil. 1847* and subsequent editions: Cousin adds a footnote citing his discussions of eighteenth-century philosophy in 1819 and 1829; *Fr. phil. 1865*: this footnote is omitted.
19. *Fr. phil. 1865*: "a succession of" is omitted.
20. *Fr. phil. 1865*: "in" replaced with "and from there it passes into."
21. *Fr. phil. 1865*: this sentence is omitted.
22. *Fr. phil. 1865*: this sentence is omitted.
23. *Fr. phil. 1865*: "phenomena" replaced with "other phenomena."
24. *Fr. phil. 1865*: "that of sensation" replaced with "those of sensibility."
25. *Fr. phil. 1865*: "catalogued" replaced with "arranged."
26. *Fr. phil. 1865*: "see it reproduced" replaced with "encounter it."
27. *Fr. phil. 1847* and subsequent editions: Cousin adds a footnote citing his early lectures on Scottish philosophy.
28. *Fr. phil. 1865*: "admirable schools" replaced with "noble schools."
29. *Fr. phil. 1847* and subsequent editions: Cousin adds a footnote citing his early lectures on Kant.
30. *Fr. phil. 1865*: "onto a path that leads into the abyss" replaced with "into a deplorable error."
31. *Fr. phil. 1865*: "profoundly distinct from it" replaced with "yet very distinct from it."
32. *Fr. phil. 1865*: "be purely relative to" replaced with "rest solely on."
33. *Fr. phil. 1865*: "would rest solely on this equivocal testimony and could have only subjective value" replaced with "are, after all, solely our own ideas whose worth is purely subjective."

34. *Fr. phil. 1847* and subsequent edition: "and because it is made thus" is omitted.
35. *Fr. phil. 1865*: passage from "One could, of course …" to "… absolute knowledge" is omitted.
36. *Fr. phil. 1847* and subsequent edition: Cousin cites his Kant lectures once more; *Fr. phil. 1865*: "and original" is omitted, so is the footnote.
37. *Fr. phil. 1865*: passage from "This is a scepticism …" to "… the legitimacy of …" replaced with "contests the certainty of these ideas, and in general that of."
38. *Fr. phil. 1865*: "have value" replaced with "be legitimately employed."
39. *Fr. phil. 1865*: "reveals" replaced with "suggests."
40. *Fr. phil. 1865*: "which is itself subjective" replaced with "represents only it."
41. *Fr. phil. 1847* and subsequent editions: this footnote is omitted. The full citation is to: W. G. Tennemann, *Manuel de l'histoire de la philosophie*, 2 vols, trans. V. Cousin (Paris: Sautelet, 1829).
42. *Fr. phil. 1847* and subsequent edition: this footnote is replaced by a selection of citations to Cousin's lectures and his "Introduction to the Posthumous Works of Main de Biran" (see pp. 215–36 below); *Fr. phil. 1865*: this footnote is omitted. For "*Tennemann*," see previous note.
43. *Fr. phil. 1865*: "formula" replaced with "strange words."
44. *Fr. phil. 1865*: "and necessary" is omitted.
45. *Fr. phil. 1865*: "and organic impressions" is omitted.
46. *Fr. phil. 1865*: "wonderfully" is added after "reveals."
47. *Fr. phil. 1865*: "we are them and" is omitted.
48. *Fr. phil. 1865*: "them" replaced with "objects other than the subject itself."
49. *Fr. phil. 1865*: Cousin adds the following footnote, "See above, *On the True, the Beautiful and the Good*, lecture 4, where my opinions are shown to conform to St Augustine, Malebranche, Bossuet, and Fénelon. The latter uses almost the same expressions as me." The citation is to: *Du Vrai, du Beau et du Bien*, 5th ed. (Paris: Didier, 1853), pp. 71–109, which consists in a series of extracts from Malebranche, Bossuet (who cites Augustine), and Fénelon (as well as Plato and Leibniz) on this point.
50. *Fr. phil. 1865*: "contested" replaced with "attacked."
51. As discussed in the Note on the Translation above (p. xxvi), "perception" translates the French "l'aperception," and the Leibnizo-Kantian resonance of the term should be borne in mind here.
52. *Fr. phil. 1847* and subsequent editions: Cousin adds a footnote referring the reader "on this major principle of Cartesian philosophy" to his *Histoire générale de la philosophie*, lecture 8, and (what will become) vols 3 and 4 of *Fr. phil. 1855*.
53. *Fr. phil. 1865*: "suggested" replaced with "revealed."
54. *Fr. phil. 1865*: "equally given to us" replaced with "equally and necessarily known."
55. *Fr. phil. 1865*: "and therefore to the absolute, that is, unique substance" added after "cause."
56. *Fr. phil. 1865*: "of two substances, the I and the not-I" added after "external causes."
57. *Fr. phil. 1865*: "long" is omitted.
58. *Fr. phil. 1865*: "The debris of these *Fragments* and" is omitted.
59. *Fr. phil. 1847* and subsequent editions: "their absolute cause, their substance" replaced with "their cause, their absolute substance."
60. *Fr. phil. 1865*: the specific citation to Laurent's articles is omitted. *Le Producteur: Journal philosophique de l'industrie, des sciences et des beaux-arts* was founded by Olinde Rodrigues et Prosper Enfantin in 1825 and ceased publishing in 1826; Paul-Mathieu Laurent (1793–1877) was a Saint-Simonian lawyer and journalist, whose *Résumé de l'histoire de la philosophie* had appeared in 1826; on Joseph-Marie Degérando (1772–1842), see Antoine-Mahut's essay. As mentioned above, Cousin does not cite but equally has in mind Broussais' and Comte's attacks on him, and, indeed, Laurent proclaims himself an adherent of Broussais' physiology on the very first page of his review (vol. 3, p. 325)—see n. 11 above. Equally, Cousin might have had two other broadly "sensualist" reviews of his work in mind by Jean-François Thurot (1768–1832) and Aristide Valette (1794–1857).
61. For example, Laurent writes (following Broussais), "Physiology stops where the facts are lacking, whereas psychology abandons them to ascend, by the path of induction, to *causality*, that is to ontology" (*Le Producteur*, vol. 3, p. 330). He continues in the next instalment, "We asked whether Cousin's book … after claiming the method of observation for psychology, did not fall foul of the very reproach he makes to Descartes's successors—to Malebranche, to Spinoza, to Leibniz, and to Wolff—of abandoning too soon the experimental path and getting lost in ontological hypotheses" (vol. 4, pp. 19–20).
62. *Fr. phil. 1865*: the passage from "I respond to this …" to "… consciousness's limits" replaced with "I respond that, in order to fall under consciousness's gaze, reason is not thereby alone condemned to be enclosed within the limits of consciousness."

63. *Fr. phil. 1865*: this sentence is omitted.
64. Laurent writes, "Does not all this high speculation inevitably result in the doctrine of absolute identity which ascends, via Spinoza, Giordano Bruno, and the Neo-Platonists, to those first Eleatics we have just cited—a doctrine which approximates in many respects to the modern idealists of Germany?" (*Le Producteur*, vol. 3, p. 338) He later continues that Cousin's doctrine "recalls that system of pantheism which identifies substance and cause" (vol. 4, p. 36). It is noticeable that the charge of pantheism is here identified with "the sensualist school," rather than the "theological school," and, as a result, the section proceeds very differently from Cousin's later defences against this charge.
65. *Fr. phil. 1865*: "if it is permitted to say so" added after "useful in it."
66. *Fr. phil. 1847* and subsequent editions: the citation is updated to Cousin's *Frag. phil. anc.*
67. As well as Laurent himself (see n. 60 above), Cousin is presumably thinking of Prosper Enfantin (Saint-Simon's successor), as well as Eugène Lerminier (see n. 74 below) and perhaps even Comte himself, who had been a follower of Saint-Simon early in his career. The identification of Saint-Simonianism with pantheism became a staple of French philosophy during the 1830s, based in part on Saint-Simon's own postulation of the unity of spirit and matter in *Le nouveau christianisme*.
68. *Fr. phil. 1865*: this sentence is omitted.
69. *Fr. phil. 1865*: "scholasticism" replaced with "certain scholasticisms."
70. *Fr. phil. 1865*: the passage from "Moreover, God is …" to "… be unintelligible …" replaced with "Far from it, since God is given, as we have seen, not only as absolute substance but as absolute cause, for this reason he cannot not produce, such that creation is so little impossible that it is necessary."
71. *Fr. phil. 1865*: this footnote replaced with: "For this phrase we have already cited the 2nd series, 1st vol., lecture 5, note 3 of the Appendix. On the true meaning by which the necessity of creation must be understood, see again 2nd series, 1st vol., note 2 of the Appendix, but first of all the Prefatory Note to the third edition of these *Fragments*.—On the Eleatics, as well as the already cited dissertation, one could consult *Histoire de la Philosophie*, lecture 3; and on Spinoza, lecture 8 of the same work, as well as the *Fragments of Modern Philosophy*, both vols, *passim*." The citations are to the later appendix to Cousin's 1828 *Introduction to the History of Philosophy*, the *Histoire générale de la philosophie*, and vols 3 and 4 of *Fr. phil. 1865*.
72. *Fr. phil. 1847* and subsequent editions: Cousin adds a footnote citing various passages in his lectures on the Eleatics and Spinoza; *Fr. phil. 1865*: this footnote is omitted.
73. *Fr. phil. 1847* and subsequent editions: Cousin adds a footnote directing readers to a selection of passages "on the true meaning by which one must understand the necessity of creation," including the 1838 Preface; *Fr. phil. 1865*: this sentence is omitted. Alongside the passage from the 1826 preface on the uniqueness of substance, this became a considerably controversial remark in Cousin's ongoing battles with the Catholic Right over the charge of pantheism.
74. While Laurent had alluded to Cousin's closeness to the idealist doctrine of absolute identity in his review (see n. 64 above), Cousin's phrasing here recalls more than anything else Comte's attack on him for "transplant[ing] German metaphysics among us" (see n. 11 above). As becomes clear, Cousin also has in mind the criticisms made by Eugène Lerminier (1803-57) in his 1832 *Lettres philosophiques adressées à un Berlinois*, one of the most influential anti-eclectic manifestos of the period. Speaking to an unnamed liberal-Hegelian correspondent in Berlin, Lerminier calls out Cousin very directly for plagiarizing Hegel: "Reappointed to his chair in 1828, Cousin took pleasure in exciting surprise and admiration.... I know, sir, that in Berlin you do not share the enthusiasm with which we welcomed these lectures; you could not understand how we could import a doctrine without naming its author. Hegel joked about this with a fairly satirical indulgence and you, sir, you uttered on this topic a harsh word that I can scarcely write—the word *plagiarism*" (Paris: Paulin, 1832), pp. 84-5.
75. *Fr. phil. 1847* and subsequent editions: "Pascal" replaced with "Bossuet"; Cousin also adds a footnote citing *Fr. phil. cart.*; *Fr. phil. 1865*: "from Pascal to Madame de Sevigny, submitted" replaced with "the clergy, the magistrates, high literature, almost everyone in the end except the Jesuits, submitted more or less"; the footnote is omitted.
76. The quotation is from *Republic*, 338b (our translation); the citation is to *Œuvres de Platon*, vol. 9, trans. V. Cousin (Paris: Rey and Gravier, 1833).
77. P. Laromiguière (1756-1837)—see Antoine-Mahut's essay above.
78. According to Yves André (whose work Cousin edited), on opening Descartes's *Traité de l'homme* by chance, Malebranche underwent an "ecstatic" reading experience of "such violent palpitations of the heart that he was obliged to leave his book at frequent intervals, and to interrupt his reading of it in order to breathe more easily." *La vie du R. P. Malebranche* (Paris: Ingold, 1886), pp. 11-12.

79. *Fr. phil. 1847* and subsequent editions: Cousin adds a footnote directing readers to his "fragment" on Laromiguière's lectures ("Leçons de M. Laromiguière sur les facultés de l'âme," *Fr. phil. 1826*, pp. 1-51), as well as to Cousin's eulogy on Laromiguière's death.
80. *Fr. phil. 1847* and subsequent editions: Cousin adds the following footnote, "See the fragments of Royer-Collard's lectures in vols 3 and 4 of the *Œuvres de Reid*, trans. Jouffroy. The first series of my lecture course contains perpetual allusions to these admirable lectures." On Royer-Collard, see Antoine-Mahut's essay.
81. *Fr. phil. 1847* and subsequent editions: Cousin adds the following footnote, "I have published his works and endeavour to conserve his memory. See below the article devoted to this great metaphysician." This article is translated below on pp. 215-36.
82. *Fr. phil. 1865*: "taught me to" replaced with "made me."
83. *Fr. phil. 1865*: "and reveals" is omitted.
84. Friedrich Gottlob Born (1743-1807) had translated Kant's *Critique of Pure Reason* into four volumes of Latin between 1796 and 1798, long before any French translation appeared.
85. See pp. 95-7 above (as well as pp. 68-70 of the 1826 Preface).
86. *Fr. phil. 1847* and subsequent editions: this sentence is omitted.
87. *Fr. phil. 1847* and subsequent editions: "after Kant and Fichte" is omitted.
88. In the French reception of Schelling and Hegel of the time, references to "the philosophy of nature" were primarily to Schelling's 1800 *System of Transcendental Idealism*, although many of his contemporaneous works had also been mentioned in a French context by 1833.
89. *Fr. phil. 1865*: "spontaneous intuition that is more natural, more general and more certain than reflection, and which is no less real and does not fall any less under consciousness's gaze" replaced with "a more secure intuition but one that is no less real than reflection."
90. *Fr. phil. 1865*: "insofar as I could judge" added before "Jacobi."
91. *Fr. phil. 1847* and subsequent edition: this footnote is replaced with a citation "on enthusiasm and sentiment" to his 1818-19 lectures; *Fr. phil. 1865*: the footnote is omitted. On "Tennemann," see n. 41 above.
92. *Fr. phil. 1847* and subsequent editions: this sentence is omitted.
93. The first edition of Hegel's *Encyclopedia* was published in 1817.
94. *Fr. phil. 1847* and subsequent editions: "he scarcely saw anyone and, to be frank, was not extremely amiable" is omitted.
95. *Fr. phil. 1847* and subsequent editions: "I understood his immense reach" is omitted.
96. The following two paragraphs are a close paraphrase of an unfinished and unpublished obituary on Hegel's death that Cousin had begun dictating in 1832. J. Barthélemy-Saint-Hilaire (ed.), *M. Victor Cousin, sa vie et sa correspondance*, vol. 3 (Paris: Hachette, 1895), pp. 48-54. Indeed, Cousin's different approaches to Hegel and to Schelling in this preface are due in part to Hegel's recent death.
97. *Fr. phil. 1865*: "absolute and substantial existence" replaced with "real object."
98. *Fr. phil. 1865*: "if nature is in some sense as rational as the human mind" is omitted.
99. *Fr. phil. 1865*: "the two spheres of philosophy" is omitted.
100. *Fr. phil. 1847* and subsequent editions: this sentence is omitted. This is one of the more famous of Cousin's later edits of his texts.
101. *Fr. phil. 1865*: in the main text, "leaders of the philosophy of our age" is omitted, and in the corresponding footnote the reference to the *Gorgias* dedication is also omitted. The *Gorgias* dedication to Hegel from 1826 is a message of thanks to Hegel for his assistance in arranging Cousin's release from the custody of the Berlin police—see the Editors' Preface above.
102. William Hamilton, "M. Cousin's Course of Philosophy," *Edinburgh Review* 50/99 (1829), pp. 194-221—see further n. 17 to the 1838 Preface below. This is a review of Cousin's 1828 lecture course, rather than the *Fragments* themselves.
103. *Fr. phil. 1847* and subsequent editions: Cousin inserts the following footnote, "A sentiment of delicacy and pride carried me away here to depict the *philosophy of nature* with a flourish and to exaggerate a little what I owed it. To the extent that the new German philosophy was developed and has come into appearance with its principles and its consequences, I have visibly separated myself from it and French spiritualism is today, in terms of the basis of its ideas and its method, the most decided adversary of the school which is taken, even in Germany, as Hegel's heir, in terms of its ground and in terms of its form, in terms of its principles as well as in terms of its method." *Fr. phil. 1865*: the final words after "as Hegel's heir" are omitted.
104. *Fr. phil. 1865*: "begins by" replaced with "grounds himself."
105. *Fr. phil. 1865*: "the ground and" is omitted.
106. *Fr. phil. 1865*: this footnote is omitted. On the Tenneman citation, see n. 41 above.

PREFACE TO THE 1833 EDITION   121

107. *Fr. phil.* 1865: Cousin inserts the following footnote, "This is indeed a chapter of philosophical memoirs—that is, notes penned by myself in Germany during a journey I made in 1817 and during which I had the good fortune to meet Hegel in Heidelberg. The following year I paid a visit to Jacobi and Schelling in Munich. I have decided to let these notes appear—see below *Souvenirs d'Allemagne, notes d'un journal de voyage en l'annee 1817*. One will there find to an extent what I here say of Hegel, almost in the same terms, and so will recognize, at least, that the portrait of the illustrious philosophers traced in 1833 is only a faithful summary of my impressions of 1817." The *Souvenirs d'Allemagne* were included in *Fr. phil.* 1865, vol. 5, pp. 1–220—they provide a fuller description of the biographical material contained in the above, particularly the first meeting with Hegel, as well as Cousin's initial struggles to understand Hegelianism.
108. *Fr. phil.* 1865: "influenced" replaced with "exercised some influence on."
109. *Fr. phil.* 1865: "already had" replaced with "previously had more than one."
110. On Cousin's characterization of "the theological school," see n. 121 below.
111. *Fr. phil.* 1865: "and not only—as in the twelfth century—a mere commentary on ecclesiastical decisions and Holy Scripture" is omitted.
112. *Fr. phil.* 1865: "elaborate" is omitted.
113. *Fr. phil.* 1865: "and we maintain with Bossuet, Fénelon, and Malebranche" added after "philosophers."
114. *Fr. phil.* 1847 and subsequent editions: "It must be so in the system in question" replaced with "Evidently."
115. *Fr. phil.* 1865: the passage from "... but how would they ..." to "... recognize common sense" replaced with "But who makes it if one possesses only an individual reason?."
116. *Fr. phil.* 1865: the passage from "Thus, within the I ..." to "... authority of the Church" is omitted.
117. *Fr. phil.* 1865: "finally" added before "in appearance."
118. *Fr. phil.* 1865: "already" replaced with "it seems."
119. *Fr. phil.* 1865: "and all of the sophisms" is omitted.
120. *Fr. phil.* 1847 and subsequent editions: Cousin adds a footnote directing readers to the opening to his Preface to Tennemann, p. 200 below; *Fr. phil.* 1865: this footnote is omitted.
121. *Fr. phil.* 1847 and subsequent editions: this footnote is omitted. *La Quotidienne* was a conservative daily newspaper of the era and the current Bishop of Chartres was Claude-Hippolyte Clausel de Montals (1769–1857), an outspoken opponent of Cousin and his students. Other Catholic critiques of Cousin's writings were beginning to appear by 1833, mainly owing to Cousin's political role in removing oversight of primary-level education in France from the Church (see Barancy's and Bernard-Granger's introductory essay above). For example, 1833 marked the moment when the Abbé Bautain's criticisms began appearing (see n. 39 to the 1838 Preface below) as well as the Abbé de Riambourg's "Théorie nouvelle sur l'histoire," *Annales de la philosophie chretienne* 39/40 (1833). Nevertheless, as he will always do, Cousin ultimately understands all the arguments of "the theological school" according to the model given in the 1817–23 *Essai sur l'indifférence en matière de religion* of Félicité de Lamennais (1782–1854).
122. Gioacchino Ventura (1792–1861): Superior General of the Theatines and early supporter of Lamennais.
123. *Le Semeur: journal religieux, politique, philosophique et littéraire* was founded in 1831 and ran until 1850.
124. On Lamennais, see n. 121 above. Lamennais did in fact contribute to *Le Semeur* on a very few occasions, despite its Protestant leanings.
125. *Fr. phil.* 1865: "Church" replaced with "Catholic Church."
126. *Fr. phil.* 1865: "for the multitude of human creatures on which it acts" is omitted.
127. *Fr. phil.* 1865: "also" replaced with "has its price and."
128. *Fr. phil.* 1847 and subsequent editions: Cousin inserts a footnote to his *Introduction à l'histoire de la philosophie*, lecture 5.
129. This allusion to the education of children is not incidental—see n. 121 above.
130. *Fr. phil.* 1865: Cousin inserts the following footnote, "Yes, the most necessary: I do not hesitate to say it, I who am not a spoilt child of the Church. This is why in the controversies of our age I am always and definitively in favour of the Church, by imploring it to come to an understanding with philosophy in their common interest."
131. *Fr. phil.* 1865: "so as to not roam too far from these Fragments and in order to not extend even further an already very long preface" is omitted.
132. *Fr. phil.* 1865: "the exact measure of its principles" is omitted.
133. *Fr. phil.* 1865: "to perceiving no truth in any systems grounded on a contrary principle" is omitted.

134. *Fr. phil. 1865*: "Such a historical conception is a judgment on the system, for" is omitted.
135. *Fr. phil. 1865*: "destitute of all truth" replaced with "without mixing in some truth."
136. *Fr. phil. 1865*: "that it disfigures" replaced with "that uses it as a kind of passport." Cousin also inserts the following footnote, "See this consoling theory of error, above p. v [p. 94 above]."
137. *Fr. phil. 1865*: "here and there within all systems" replaced with "everywhere."
138. *Fr. phil. 1865*: "its principles, its instruments, and its results" is omitted.
139. See p. 81 above.
140. Here and elsewhere in this section on the history of philosophy, Cousin seems to have Lerminier in mind, who in his attack on Cousin in the *Lettres philosophiques* (see n. 74 above) had written, "As a literary spirit, [Cousin] turned towards the literature of philosophy; his is a mobile imagination and so he easily quit one beautiful theory for another he found more beautiful still; he is an ardent speaker and so he made flow in other souls an understanding and enthusiasm for science. Such has been Cousin: it is his character to never be able to find and feel philosophical reality himself; he must do so translated, discovered, systematized; then he understands it, borrows it, and presents it. I sense, sir, that we are together reaching an inevitable conclusion; we are obliged to infer that Cousin is not, properly speaking, a philosopher; and I know that this has been your view for a long time" (p. 75).
141. Cousin's critics tended to focus on a claim he had made in his 1828 lecture course that eclecticism "excludes nothing, accepts everything, comprehends everything." *Cours de philosophie: Introduction à l'histoire de la philosophie*, ed. P. Vermeren (Paris: Fayard, 1991), p. 38. In his *Lettres philosophiques* (see n. 74 above), for instance, Lerminier speaks of Cousin learning in Germany of a philosophy that "boasted of its ability to explain all, comprehend all and accept all" (p. 81).
142. The charge of "fatalism" had been brought by Armand Marrast (1801-52) in his review of the 1828 lectures, which accuses Cousin of making individuals into "nothing but the instruments of the idea of time, who submit to a fatality." *Examen critique des leçons de M. Cousin* (Paris, Corréard 1829), p. 45. A similar charge was also beginning to be made by Pierre Leroux in his early criticisms of Cousin—and would culminate in the discussion of "eclectic fatalism" in the 1839 *Réfutation de l'éclectisme*.
143. *Fr. phil. 1865*: "it is the application of a system" replaced with "up to a certain point."
144. *Fr. phil. 1865*: "it begins from a system" is omitted.
145. *Fr. phil. 1865*: "in possession of" replaced with "on the path to."
146. *Fr. phil. 1865*: "an already formed" replaced with "a more or less formed."
147. *Fr. phil. 1847* and subsequent editions: Cousin inserts the following footnote: "See below, on this essential point, the article, *De la philosophie en Belgique* [p. 209-11 below]."
148. *Fr. phil. 1847* and subsequent editions: "and Aristotle's" added after "Plato's thinking." Cousin also inserts a footnote, "For Plato, see many of our Arguments; for Aristotle, our translation of the first book of the *Metaphysics*, with preface and notes, *Fragments de philosophie ancienne*, 'Aristotle's Metaphysics.'" Before becoming part of the late *Fragments* volumes (e.g. *Fr. phil. 1865*, vol. 1, pp. 191-235), Cousin's translation was originally part of a separate 1835 volume, *De la métaphysique d'Aristote*; the Plato reference is to the various "arguments" by which Cousin prefaced his translation of each dialogue.
149. *Fr. phil. 1847* and subsequent editions: Cousin inserts a footnote referring the reader to material from his 1829 lecture course on eighteenth-century philosophy.
150. *Fr. phil. 1865*: "and it appears everywhere among those rich historical perspectives of the new German philosophy" is omitted.
151. *Fr. phil. 1865*: "rigour and" is omitted.
152. *Fr. phil. 1865*: "and by bending them to a common discipline" is omitted.
153. *Fr. phil. 1865*: "representative" replaced with "constitutional."
154. *Fr. phil. 1847* and subsequent editions: Cousin adds an additional citation to lectures 6-8 of his 1829 course on sensualist philosophy, along with its appendix included in the 1847 edition. The original citation is to Lecture 13 of the *Introduction à l'histoire de la philosophie*.
155. The 1830 Revolution was equally known as the "Trois Glorieuses," since it occurred over three days: July 26, 28, and 29, 1830.
156. *Fr. phil. 1865*: "attain their harmonious expression in true philosophy" replaced with "true philosophy gathers up and expresses."
157. The overthrow of James II and ascension of Mary II and William III which was traditionally understood as the triumph of individual freedoms and constitutional rule over despotism.
158. *Fr. phil. 1865*: "representative" replaced with "constitutional."
159. *Fr. phil. 1865*: "representative government" replaced with "constitutional monarchy."

160. *Fr. phil. 1865*: "representative government" replaced with "constitutional monarchy."
161. *Fr. phil. 1865*: Cousin inserts the following footnote, "In 1848 and in 1851 [there arose] new circumstances, but the same principles; I defended these principles then and I defend them still today, as in 1833. See *Discours Politiques*, "Introduction, Des principes de la révolution française" from 1851; and the foreword to *La société française au dix-septième siècle*, 2nd edn, 1866." As a symbol of the moderate liberal tradition (and the July Revolution in particular), Cousin found himself on the side of opposition to the more radical 1848 Revolution and, equally, to Louis Napoleon's Second Empire from December 1851.

Prefatory Note to the 1838 Edition of *Philosophical Fragments*[1]

Philosophical Fragments reappears here, not perfected but considerably augmented, and, since it includes a new volume, composed of diverse pieces, written according to the same method and using the same principles as those of the previous volume, everything seems capable of being used to fortify the philosophical and historical system that is spread through the entire work and summarized in the two prefaces to the first and second editions.

I dare not brave the ridicule of a third preface to a third edition. However, I hope to be permitted, in a few words, to recall—as I did for the 1826 edition [in the second edition]—the lively controversy aroused by the 1833 [edition]. This second controversy far exceeded the first one and got to the very ground of things, and it had the benefit of, among other things, sketching more precisely the character of the new French philosophy and its place among contemporary schools.

Of course, I will sift out the elegies and the satires to mention only the serious writings.

In Germany, Amadeus Wendt, recently lost to the History of Philosophy,[2] the successor of Tennemann and Professor of Philosophy at the University of Göttingen,[3] produced a long review* of the second edition of the *Fragments*. Beckers, Professor of Philosophy at the Lyzeum Dillingen in Bavaria,[4] did me the honour of translating the Preface, and Schelling wished to use it to introduce me to the German public, by prefacing to Becker's translation a few pages in which he explains himself in relation to all the points I touch on, with the clarity and vigour which characterize him. In breaking the silence that the author of the *philosophy of nature* had imposed on himself for so many years, this little piece† was a genuine philosophical event; and, if my work had done nothing more for philosophy than having provoked it, I would still have congratulated myself on publishing it.

---

* *Göttingsche gelehrte Anzeigen*, 22 September 1834. The *Revue germanique* translated this article in their issue from September 1834.[2]

† *Victor Cousin über französische und deutsche Philosophie*, by Dr Hubert Beckers; preface by Schelling, Stuttgart and Tübingen (1834). There are two French translations of Schelling's preface— one by Ravaisson, inserted into the *Revue germanique* (October 1835); the other entitled, *Schelling's Judgment on Cousin's Philosophy*, translated from the German and preceded by an *Essay on the Nationality of Philosophies*, by J. Willm (Strasbourg and Paris, 1835).[5]

Moreover, no one should believe that Wendt's or Schelling's articles are hymns to my glory—far from it. While doing justice to my intentions and efforts and while approving—even if within strict limits—the systematic conclusions I reached, Schelling, like Wendt, does not hesitate to condemn the path I followed to arrive there, the psychological method. He summarily declares that, if psychology can be a relatively useful preparation for philosophy, it is not its basis, and that observation applied to consciousness can in the end perceive—even from its highest pinnacle—only facts of consciousness, concepts, universal and necessary principles, from which it is impossible to derive anything objective and real.[6] For Schelling, metaphysics is no chimera; it is very much given to man[7]—this privileged creature illuminated by divine rays—to know the truth and the real system of beings, and my illustrious friend knows of my desire to find this system, to aspire to this noble end.[8] However, he insists that psychology is entirely unable to lead me there. In a word, he approves of the end, but disapproves of the means.

At the other end of the civilized world—on the other side of the Atlantic—the *Fragments* found an even more hospitable welcome than in Germany. At the same time as my writings on education were circulated across much of the United States of America, thanks to the beautiful translation by [Sarah] Austin, and sometimes even under the auspices of state authority,[*] the *Fragments*—along with my *Lectures*—founded, without me knowing, a philosophical school in the homeland of Jonathan Edwards and Franklin. In 1832 and in 1834, [H. G.] Linberg[†] and [C. S.] Henry[‡] translated my *Lectures* and, at the very moment I am writing these lines, [George] Ripley has just placed the second preface of the *Fragments*, alongside many other of my writings, at the head of his *Philosophical Miscellanies*[§] devoted to French writers. In 1836 and 1837, [Orestes] Brownson[§§] published an apology for my principles: the talent for thought and style which burns brightly there, if developed properly, promises a philosophical writer of the first order for America.[14] But do you know what recommended the new French philosophy to New York and Boston? Along with its moral and religious character, it is its method—that psychological method which almost makes the President of the Munich Royal Academy[15] smirk. There is more. From the moment this method overcame previous limitations and raised itself up to new heights, the most energetic minds [in America]

---

[*] *Report on the State of Public Instruction in Prussia*, translated by S. Austin, London, 1834. This translation, superior to the [original] text thanks to the grace of its language, has often been reprinted in the United States, as a whole or in part. The legislatures of New Jersey and Massachusetts have decided to distribute it to schools at the State's expense and of all the literary distinctions I have received, none has touched me as much as the title of foreign member of the *American Institute of Instruction*.[9]

[†] *Introduction to the History of Philosophy*, translated by H. G. Lindberg (Boston, 1832).[10]

[‡] *Elements of Psychology, included in a critical Examination of Locke's Essay on the Human Understanding*, translated by C. S. Henry, with an introduction, notes and additions (Hartford, 1834).[11]

[§] *Philosophical Miscellanies*, translated from the French with introductory and critical notices, by G. Ripley, 2 vols (Boston, 1838).[12]

[§§] *The Christian Examiner* (September 1836): *Cousin's Philosophy*; ibid. (May 1837): *Recent Contributions to Philosophy*.[13]

have taken the trouble to follow it* and drawn back from [other] dogmatic conclusions which, in Germany, pass undisturbed and are admitted just as they are. Philosophy in America still feels the weight of the 1829 article in the *Edinburgh Review*,† an admirable article which displays the high worth of its author, but its slightly dissimulated conclusion is that psychology and logic are the only certain parts of philosophy and that, beyond them, doubt and ignorance reign.[17]

I would be ungracious towards Italy, if I did not here publicly thank the most famous of its philosophers, [Pasquale] Galluppi, Professor of Philosophy at the University of Naples, who, after introducing Kant into the country of Vico and Genovesi, was kind enough to translate the *Fragments* himself.‡ Another excellent mind, [Salvatore] Mancino, Professor of Philosophy at the University of Palermo, has, as it were, naturalized eclecticism into Sicily;§ while at the other end of the Italian peninsula, [Baldassarre] Poli, Professor of Philosophy at the University of Padua,§§ and the ingenious and often profound Abbé Rosmini§§§ have called attention to the new philosophy—the former to affirm it almost completely, the latter to undertake a severe, but always hospitable critique of it.

This is not argument; it is just exposition. I am recalling the most remarkable writings that the previous edition of the *Fragments* provoked but abstaining from judging them. Controversy over the nature and value of philosophical method will not cease tomorrow; it has now become part of the very movement of the philosophy of our age; every system of any importance will necessarily reproduce [this controversy] and, one day or other, an occasion will arise for me to intervene and explain myself comfortably in response to the objections addressed to me from diverse philosophical horizons. At the very least, I can declare that these objections have not shaken my conviction, and, in time, we shall see how difficult it might be to refute one [set of them] by another. To [some of] my adversaries I need only oppose the others and, if they would all allow themselves for a moment to be

---

* See in the *Boston Quarterly Review*, no. 1 (January, 1838), an article by Brownson: *Philosophy and Common Sense*, in response to an article in the *Christian Examiner* (November 1837), entitled: *Locke and the Transcendentalists*.

† I have already cited this article in the preface to the second edition of *Fragments*. I recall it with great pleasure as a masterpiece of criticism. A French writer, Peisse, reproduced, with a talent which is his own, the objections of the *Edinburgh Review*, in various articles in the *National*, particularly in the nos. of 25 September and 29 October 1833.[16]

‡ *La filosofia di Vittorio Cousin*, translated from the French and analysed by Baron Pasquale Galluppi, of Tropea, 2 vols in 8° (Naples, 1831-2). See also another work by the same author, in which critical observations, attached to the translation of the *Fragments*, are developed with much clarity and strength: *Filosofia della volontá*, 2 vols in 8° (Naples, 1833-4).[18]

§ *Elementi di filosofia*, Palermo, 2 vols in 8° (1835-6). See above all vol. 1, p. 9, in the chapter *Stato attuale della filosofia*. It is said that this volume forms the basis of teaching in all Sicilian colleges.[19]

§§ *Manuele della Storia della filosofia di G. Tennemann*, supplemented by B. Poli, 3 vols (Milan, 1832-6).[20]

§§§ *Nuovo Saggio sull'Origine delle Idee*, 4 vols (Rome, 1830), vol. 2, p. 540: *Sul Punto di Partenze della filosofia del sig. prof. Cousin*. An Italian translation of the first preface of the *Fragments* in 1829 and of the second in 1834 was also printed by the publishers Ruggia in Lugano.[21]

represented by Schelling and Hamilton*—that is, by the greatest thinker and the greatest critic of our century—I will, with some confidence, give them a foretaste [of this refutation] through this brief and very simple response.

To Germany and to Schelling I will say: With respect to your haughty disdain for psychological method, permit me to oppose the authority of Hamilton and all my other adversaries. If this authority does not suffice for you, I will join to it that of these persons who may well hold some weight for you: they are Socrates, Descartes, and Kant, the father of German philosophy—not to mention Fichte and Jacobi; since—let me note in passing—before the *philosophy of nature*, the excellence of psychological method was as uncontested in Germany as it is today in other countries.

And what have you put in place of this method? Before there was at least *intellectual intuition*.[23] However, one of two things [is true of it]: either intellectual intuition falls under consciousness's gaze, or it does not. If it does not fall under it, from where do you come to know it? What reveals its marvellous existence to us? With what right, on what grounds do you speak of it? If it does fall under consciousness's gaze, we are thereby brought back to psychology and I refer you back to your own objections.

They are reduced to this argument: psychology cannot lead to metaphysics, to real objects, to existences; for it does not get out of consciousness and all that is in consciousness is purely subjective.[24] Here is their formidable principle. However, this principle is only an assertion; where is its proof? According to us, it is reason which directly knows the truth, and not only abstract truths, universal and necessary principles, but real objects, existences. The question is whether this power of reason is less legitimate because it falls under consciousness's gaze. But who has demonstrated that consciousness does not just contemplate what it sees, but also has the astonishing property of metamorphosing [what it sees] under its magic gaze and imposing its own nature upon it? If that were the case, all truth would forever be subjective; for all truth can only be known by a mind which has consciousness of it. If, for this reason alone, it is subjective, then the objectivity of knowledge is a chimera; it is even an extravagance, for it forms a problem whose conditions, equally necessary, are contradictory—[that is,] this problem requires a mind that knows the truth and also requires, at the same time, that this mind does not know that it knows [the truth]. And this implies a contradiction. God himself knows things only when he knows that he knows them; feeling for his science would [otherwise] become an insuperable barrier separating him forever from real knowledge. All this cannot be serious. Either reason must be incapable by itself of knowing beings, or if one does not claim this, then—so as to not destroy all

---

* The author of the article mentioned above from the *Edinburgh Review*, no. 99 (October 1829): *M. Cousin's Course of Philosophy*, as well as many other articles as remarkable for their erudition as their dialectic.[22]

philosophy at its root—one must avow that reason is not struck impotent whenever it acts under our consciousness's gaze. [Reason] does not change; it does not lose its divine, indwelling force and the wings it has been given to reach beings and raise itself to that [source] from which it emanates. Consciousness attests to this magnificent development of reason; it does not construct it, nor does it alter [reason's] character.

Furthermore, to what God does Schelling aspire today? Is it to the abstraction of being which I have taken the liberty of mocking a little, notwithstanding all the respect I bear for the memory of Hegel?* No assuredly. Is it the absolute identity of subject and object, of the *philosophy of nature*?[26] It does not appear so. Schelling's God is[27] the spiritual and free God of Christianity. I applaud this with all my heart; but what can better guide us on this new route than the deepened study of the intelligent and free being which God made in his image and in which [God] has placed features which it is impossible not to recognize in man and, in so doing, to recognize them in their first cause, increased and amplified to all the grandeur of infinite being? If Spinoza had known that man is essentially endowed with activity and freedom, he would not have stripped God of all similar attributes, and his God would not be a mere substance, but a cause—a cause worthy of this name. Knowledge of God completes knowledge of man, but knowledge of man inaugurates true knowledge of God. Do not disdain a method that leads to such results.

A word now to Hamilton and my Scottish and American adversaries.

You admit that the psychological method is the true philosophical method, and you pay it homage; but you are not certain that this method leads legitimately to ontology; and so, instead of sacrificing psychology for ontology like Germany and Schelling, it is the latter that you sacrifice for the former. Out of scientific virtue, you resign yourself to doing without ontology, and you exhort me to do the same and remain ignorant of what is not given to man to know. What does this mean? Let us have no fear of words. Ontology is nothing less[28] than the science of being, or, actually, of beings—that is, of God, the world and the human being. So, this is what you ask me to exclude on the basis of methodological scruples! But if your science does not get at God, nor nature, nor the I, what does it matter to me what it teaches?

To those who despise the psychological method I have just opposed the great names of Socrates, Descartes, and Kant. To its exclusive partisans I now oppose the equally significant names of Plato, Aristotle, Leibniz, and even that German philosophy which has already endured and progressed for almost half a century, and which is incontestably the most prominent of modern philosophies since Cartesianism.[29] All great philosophies have been dogmatic. What would the immortal authors [of these philosophies] say if they were to be taught that their

---

* Second preface, p. 31 [pp. 105–6 above].[25]

sublime works concerning the world and God were idle speculations and that philosophy must limit itself to the analysis of memory or of attention? To the authority of genius, I add a further, even greater one: [the authority] of common sense and the human race. Even without constraining its immense needs and powerful instincts by way of artificial hindrances, has not the human race come to know of[30] its own existence, [the existence] of the world it inhabits, and ultimately that of the supreme, invisible and omnipresent intellect which everywhere penetrates beneath the veil of the universe? In this the human race has faith. I will endlessly repeat that the mission of philosophy is to explain [such faith], not destroy it. All philosophy which remains aloof from the natural faith of the human race condemns itself and proclaims that its own wisdom is not wise; for there is no true wisdom in separating oneself from one's kindred and remaining on the other side, as it were, in order to take oneself beyond the unanimous convictions of the human family.

I could go further still; I could demonstrate that not daring to advance into the world of existences, stopping at the surface of consciousness is to deceive oneself, if one believes such constraint would furnish limited, but firm and solid ground. No: a healthy logic does not abandon this refuge to the exclusive partisans of psychology. Indeed, if, as they claim, reason does not have the power to give us certain knowledge of beings, how does it discover certainty, and, when it is applied to phenomena, such as [the phenomena] of consciousness,[31] [from where comes] that absolute value of which they suppose [reason] is deprived? It is always a matter of knowing,[32] and it is the same faculty which knows; but, then, from where comes that privilege accorded to [psychological] phenomena in grounding certain knowledge? On what grounds would one legitimately believe that these phenomena have a real existence, while everything else is but a dream?[33] To speak rigorously,[34] we ought to also doubt the reality of phenomena of consciousness,[35] that is, of the reality of our own thought, of the very reality of our doubt. Reason—certain of itself[36]—can give doubt a role at those moments when [reason] affirms that it is not appropriate to affirm itself. But who is responsible for assigning doubt a role, when it bears on the very ground of intellectual and moral life, on the authority and veracity of reason, the unique principle of all certainty, all truth, all illumination, both outside and within consciousness? It is in this sense that one must understand Royer-Collard's persuasive maxim: "One should not assign scepticism any role [in thought], for as soon as it enters the understanding, it will invade it entirely."[37]

Hence, to summarize: I am renewing the challenge I laid down to my various adversaries. To those who dogmatize in metaphysics without having traversed psychology, [my challenge is] to avoid hypothesis while still encountering truth; to those who begin from psychology but stop there too, [my challenge is] to avoid scepticism, the most absolute scepticism.[38] Hypothesis and scepticism—here are the two consequences that argumentation in turn imposes on my various opponents and of which I leave them the choice. For me, I accept neither one nor the other. I explicitly aspire to a philosophical dogmatism as extensive as the natural faith of the human race, and I think that, to get there, one must proceed by the very same route the human race has followed: the great route of internal and external experience—these serve as authority and illumination for reason, such as it manifests itself in consciousness.

I do not wish to put down my pen without briefly responding, once more, to attacks of a very different nature, whose persistence,[39] despite all my explanations, prove to me that something might need altering in the way I express my thought, at the very least. I am speaking of the vague accusation of pantheism in which I am often implicated* and with which I wish to conclude.

This accusation is grounded on the following two propositions attributed to me:

1. There is one, unique substance, of which the I and the not-I are merely modifications;
2. The creation of the world is necessary.

Now, I declare that I reject absolutely and without reserve these two propositions, in the false and dangerous sense they can be understood.

1. In the rare places I have spoken of a unique substance,[41] the term substance must be understood, not in its ordinary acceptation, but as it was understood by Plato, the most illustrious doctors of the Church and the Holy Scripture's great claim: *I am who I am*.[42] Evidently, this is a question of the substance which exists with an absolute and eternal existence, and it is very certain that there is and can be solely one substance with this nature.

2. Never have I said, nor could have said, that the I and the not-I are merely modifications of one unique substance, and I have said the opposite a hundred times. If I have often[43] designated the I and the not-I by the term phenomena,[44] it is in opposition to [the term] substance understood in its Platonic sense and reserved for God; and I do not understand why, on the basis of this uncontested opposition, others wish to conclude that these phenomena do not really exist in the manner I believe they do and with the limited independence that pertains to them? How could I have been able to make the I and the not-I mere modifications of another being, when I everywhere established that they are causes—forces, in Leibniz's sense—and[45] when all of my moral and political philosophy rests on the concept of the I considered as a force essentially endowed with freedom?[46] Finally, after so often demonstrating, with Leibniz and Maine de Biran, that the concept of cause is the ground of [the concept] of substance,[47] should I really have found it necessary to add that the I and the not-I, as already causes and forces, are also substances, as long as one is happy to speak of finite substances, ceasing to take the

---

* See *Nouveaux fragments*, Xenophon and Zeno of Elea; *Lectures on Philosophy*, 1829, vol. 1, p. 465; second preface to the *Philosophical Fragments*, p. 18 [p. 101 above].[40]

words being and substance according to the high acceptation mentioned above?[48] For the rest, if the expression finite substances might see off some honest scruples, I willingly agree to add it to [the expressions] phenomena and forces, as applied to nature and to man. It is a hundred times better to clarify or reform a word—even unnecessarily—than to run the risk of scandalizing one of our contemporaries.

3. There[49] remains the necessity of creation. On reflection, I also find this expression[50] to be insufficiently reverential towards God, whose freedom it appears to compromise, and I have no scruples in withdrawing it. However, in withdrawing it I should explain myself. There is no mysterious fatalism behind it: it expresses an idea which is found everywhere, in the holiest [Church] doctors as in the greatest philosophers. God, like man, acts and can act solely in conformity with his nature, and even his freedom is relative to his essence. Moreover, in God above all, force is adequate to substance, and[51] divine force is always active; so, God is essentially active and creator. It follows from this that, unless one strips God of his nature and his essential perfections, one must admit that an essentially creative power is unable to not create, just as an essentially intelligent power can only create intelligently, just as an essentially wise and good power can only create with wisdom and benevolence. The word necessity does not express anything else. It is inconceivable that from this word anyone could have drawn and impute to me a universal fatalism. Because I relate God's action to his very substance, do I really consider this action blind and determined by fate? Is there really impiety in placing one of God's attributes, freedom, in harmony with all of his other attributes and with the divine nature itself! Do piety and orthodoxy really consist in subordinating every attribute of God to one alone, such that whenever the great masters [of the Church] have written: the eternal laws of divine justice, one should replace it with: the arbitrary decrees of God; and wherever they have written: it is appropriate to the nature of God, to his wisdom, to his benevolence, etc., to act in a certain way, one should replace it with: it is neither appropriate nor inappropriate to his nature, but rather has pleased him to arbitrarily make it so? This is Hobbes' doctrine of human legislation transposed into divine legislation. Over two thousand years ago, Plato already struck down such a doctrine, dubbing it in the *Euthyphro* the most impious absurdity. St Thomas fought against it as soon as it began to resurface in Christian Europe, and it seemed to have perished from the consequences that were drawn from Ockham's intrepid logic. However, let us get to the root of the evil: an incomplete and vicious theory of freedom. And this is where the power of psychology comes to the fore. All psychological error brings with it the gravest of errors: if one is deceived about human freedom, then one will almost necessarily be deceived about God's freedom too. I believe I have proven elsewhere,* without vain subtleties, that there is a real distinction between

---

* Everywhere in my writings. See, above all, *Fragments*, preface to the first edition, and a thesis *on the diverse forms of freedom*. See also the *Lectures on Philosophy* vol. 2 (1829), p. 497.[52]

arbitrary freedom and freedom [as such]. Arbitrary freedom is [freedom] of the will based on the apparatus of deliberating between diverse parties, on the condition that—as a result of the deliberation—we have the resolution to will something specific, such that we possess the immediate consciousness of having been able and of still being able to will the opposite.[53] Freedom [as such] too appears in the will and those phenomena which surround [the will], even if [they appear there] more energetically; but [freedom as such] is not exhausted there. It exists in those rare and sublime moment when freedom is so much greater than it appears to the eyes of the superficial observer. I have often cited the example of d'Assas:[54] d'Assas did not deliberate; and, because of this, was d'Assas any less free? Did he not act with complete freedom? Of the saint who, after a long and painful practice of virtue, ends up practising—as if by nature itself—acts of renunciation out of disgust at human weakness, we must ask whether, in order to leave behind the contradictions and anguish of the form of freedom called the will, the saint has fallen lower, rather than being raised higher? And is he no more than a mere passive and blind instrument of grace, as both Luther and Calvin inopportunely claimed through an excessive interpretation of the Augustinian doctrine?[55] No: he remains free; and, far from being annihilated, his freedom, in so purifying itself, is raised up and increased. From the human form of the will, he has passed to an almost divine form of spontaneity.[56] Spontaneity is essentially free, although it is not accompanied by any deliberation and although, often in the rapid burst of its inspired action, it escapes [our attention] and leaves scarcely a trace in the depths of consciousness. Let us import this precise psychology into theodicy, and we will see, without hypothesis, that spontaneity is also the eminent form of God's freedom. Yes, certainly God is free: among other proofs of this, it would be absurd for there to be less in the first cause than in one of its effects, humanity. God is free, but not from the freedom which pertains to our double nature, which is made for the struggle against passion and error, and which painfully gives birth to virtue and our imperfect science. [God] is free with a freedom that pertains to his own divine nature—that is, unlimited, infinite, knowing no obstacle. The purest spontaneity in man—what Christianity calls the freedom of the children of God[57]—is still but a shadow of the freedom of their father. Between the just and the unjust, between the good and the bad, between reason and its opposite, God cannot deliberate, nor can he therefore will as we do. Is it even possible for him to take what we call the worse path? This supposition alone is impious. Therefore, it should be avowed that, when [God] takes the contrary path, he has done so freely, of course, but not arbitrarily and without the consciousness of being able to choose the other path. His omnipotent, entirely just, entirely wise nature expresses itself with this spontaneity which contains freedom in its entirety and excludes both the troubles and the woes of willing and the mechanical operation of necessity. Such[58] is the principle and the true character of divine action. Remove the principle, consider the action in itself, so to speak, from an external perspective[59] and you have what are called acts of nature in their potent regularity—that is, fatality. Nature is the image of God; *Fatum* is Providence itself made visible; and before [Providence] one must bow; but by relating it back in spirit and in truth to its principle, to that ineffable source where divine perfections are mixed together in that wondrous unity which human science can treat in no way except by breaking it down for its own ends, and by subordinating it to a number of perspectives, including to the contradictions of the theologians and the philosophers. *O altitudo!*[60]

I have perhaps insisted too much on this point, which I have still scarcely touched upon, and what remains is just to say one word on eclecticism.

Let us proceed straight to the argument that hides behind the polemics of all kinds directed against eclecticism: the principles of diverse systems are often contradictory; and contradictions exclude each other; therefore, one cannot propose to reunite them in one and the same system. Here is my response: this argument rests on a confusion between two very distinct things—the state in which eclecticism encounters the principles of diverse systems and that to which it reduces them before making use of them. [Eclecticism] does indeed often find [these principles] at war with each other and in contradiction, and, in this state, it cannot use them. Let us suppose, for example, that one system professes the principle: All ideas come from the senses; and another system the principle: No idea comes from the senses. There is certainly no means of combining these two principles. What, then, does eclecticism do? It begins by destroying them both: it first proves that they are both false as exclusive[61] claims; then, by means of investigating what they can contain that is true, it draws the two following principles from them: Many ideas come from the senses; Many ideas do not come from the senses. And these two new principles are no longer contradictory; they are now just different, and so are no longer irreconcilable. It is then and only then that the final work of eclecticism occurs.

I have already said it[62] and will repeat it here: when after long revolutions [political] parties appear before the legislative power, they each make extreme, contradictory claims which cannot ground a system of laws that would be applicable to all. The legislator must remove all that is exclusive and[63] unjust in these claims, reduce them to what they legitimately contain, and, through such a salutary transformation, these discordant and warring elements turn into diverse, energetic, and living principles of a great and powerful constitution.

Hence, the legislator of philosophy can and must work in spite of the clamour of opposed systems; for such clamour is inevitable—it is the cry torn from [the warring parties] by the painful operation to which eclecticism forces them to submit, so as to put them in that state in which it can employ them and make them contribute, in a just manner, to the beautiful and subtle harmony of contraries which is genuine unity.

Moreover, I must be hard to please not to be satisfied with eclecticism's success. Thank God, it has travelled a fortunate route across the world; and, instead of needing to undertake its defence, it should rather be tasked with mine. Eclecticism is not perhaps the primary principle of the new philosophy, but it is its most visible banner. When I flew it previously, at the start of my career, within the humble walls of the École Normale and the Faculty of Letters, whatever my personal conviction, I did not expect its fortunes to improve so rapidly or for it to so quickly assemble so many enlightened and independent minds among the most advanced countries of the old and new world. Eclecticism is moderation and extensity in all things. Therefore, it is not vain self-love,[64] but something else elevated within me which finds sweet satisfaction in noting its progress and following its fate.

V. Cousin
Paris, 20 July 1838

Notes

1. *Fr. phil. 1838*, vol. 1, pp. i–xxxi (subsequently: *Fr. phil. 1847*, vol. 4, pp. 95–114; *Fr. phil. 1855*, vol. 5, pp. 95–114; *Fr. phil. 1865*, vol. 5, pp. lxxx–xcviii). We take the 1838 publication as our base text for this translation and note the significant modifications to later versions in the endnotes. The first half of this third preface takes up the international reception of Cousin's philosophy (in comparison to the national context addressed in the second preface), before Cousin provides his first of many attempts at a response to the burgeoning pantheism controversy, continued, for example, in the "Foreword" to *On Pascal's Pensées*, pp. 242–9 below.
2. *Fr. phil. 1865*: "recently lost to the History of Philosophy" is omitted.
3. On Wendt, see also p. 206 below and accompanying note. Wendt's relatively positive review appeared in *Göttingische gelehrte Anzeigen* 153 (1834), pp. 1522–8. The translation in the *Nouvelle revue germanique* was undertaken by J. Willm at Cousin's own instigation.
4. Hubert Beckers (1806–89)—a student and follower of Schelling.
5. *Fr. phil. 1865*: Cousin adds to the end of the note, "Finally, a third by Grimblot follows his translation of Schelling's *System of Transcendental Idealism*, Paris, 1842." Earlier in the note, "two translations" is accordingly altered to "three." Schelling's "beurtheilende Vortheile" was later published in his *Werke*, ed. K. F. A. Schelling (Stuttgart: Cotta, 1856–61), vol. 10. Cousin had himself commissioned the Willm translation, and then the Ravaisson translation when Willm began taking too long.
6. Schelling writes, "We willingly agree that psychology can be a useful preparation for philosophy in general (though it can never serve as its ground).... However, this preparation itself is necessary only subjectively, for he who is yet to raise himself towards this philosophy; it is necessary only to understand this proposition by which it can begin: *I do not want mere being; I want being which is or exists*." *Werke*, vol. 10, p. 214.
7. *Fr. phil. 1865*: "For Schelling, metaphysics is no chimera; it is very much given to man" is replaced with "Certainly, Schelling does not doubt that it is very much given to man."
8. Cousin had met Schelling in Munich in 1818 and they had remained in contact since, exchanging correspondence regularly, particularly in the mid-1830s. As well as rehearsing his criticisms of Cousin, Schelling had indeed praised his objectives—writing in 1826, for example: "Keep going! You have followed entirely the idea of the true system" (V. Cousin and F. W. J. Schelling, "Correspondance, 1818–1845," ed. C. Mauve and P. Vermeren, *Corpus* 18/19 (1991), p. 204). Likewise in his Preface, Schelling writes, "Cousin reunites to an eminent degree and has shown in all his work persevering investigations, penetration, calm and impartiality, all the qualities—in a word—which form the historian of philosophy, the philosopher himself" (*Werke*, vol. 10, p. 221).
9. Sarah Austin (1793–1867): a British translator of primarily German literature, who penned a substantive translator's preface to Cousin's text. The American Institute of Instruction was founded in 1830 by social reformers in Boston.

10. Henning Gottfried Lindberg (1784–1836): a Swedenborgian intellectual.
11. *Fr. phil. 1865*: Cousin adds to the end of the note details of further editions. Caleb Sprague Henry (1804–84): translator, author, and from 1839 Professor of History and Philosophy at New York University.
12. George Ripley (1802–80): Unitarian minister and founding member of the Transcendental Club.
13. Orestes Brownson (1803–76): founding member of the Transcendental Club, who from the early 1840s increasingly renounced his earlier enthusiasm for Cousin and transcendentalism and was radicalized towards a form of Catholic socialism.
14. *Fr. phil. 1847* and subsequent editions: "if developed properly, promises a philosophical writer of the first order for America" is omitted.
15. i.e. Schelling, President of the Bayerischen Akademie der Wissenschaften from 1827 to 1842.
16. *Fr. phil. 1865*: adds to this note after the second sentence, "The author has collected it with other articles of the highest worth in his *Discussions of Philosophy and Literature*, etc. London, 1852." To the end of the note, Cousin also adds, "See *Fragments of Philosophy*, by Sir William Hamilton, translated from the English by. L. Peisse, Paris, 1840." On Hamilton's article, see the next note. Louis Peisse (1803–80): French art critic and journalist.
17. Hamilton's argument is framed as a defence, against Cousin, of the claim that "the unconditioned is incognisable and inconceivable; its notion being only negative of the conditioned, which last can alone be positively known or conceived." He concludes, "After the tenor of our previous observations, it is needless to say that we regard M. Cousin's attempt to establish a general peace among philosophers, by the promulgation of his Eclectic Theory, as a signal failure. But ... we cannot disown a strong feeling of interest and admiration for those qualities, even in their excess, which have betrayed him, with so many other aspiring philosophers, into a pursuit which could end only in disappointment—we mean his love of truth, and his reliance on the powers of man.... Loath to admit that our science is at best the reflection of a reality we cannot know, we strive to penetrate to existence in itself; and what we have laboured intensely to attain, we at last fondly believe we have accomplished. But, like Ixion, we embrace a cloud for a divinity. Conscious only of limitation, we think to comprehend the infinite, and dream of establishing our human science on an identity with the omniscient God. It is this powerful tendency of the most vigorous minds to transcend the sphere of our faculties, that makes a 'learned ignorance' the most difficult acquirement of knowledge." "M. Cousin's Course of Philosophy," *Edinburgh Review* 99 (Oct. 1829), pp. 214, 220–1.
18. Pasquale Galluppi (1770–1846): a philosopher with a general viewpoint similar to Cousin's in its critical engagement with Kant, Reid, and Descartes.
19. Salvatore Mancino (1802–66): Italian disciple and translator of Cousin, who would go on to translate this third edition preface in 1840 as well.
20. Baldassarre Poli (1795–1883): Eclectic philosopher with a background in jurisprudence.
21. Antonio Rosmini (1797–1855): liberal Catholic philosopher and founder of the Rosminian movement. The Ruggia editions are, more fully: *Prefazione del Signor V. Cousin premessa a' suoi Frammenti filosofici* (Lugano, 1829); *Due prefazioni poste innanzi alla prima e seconda edizione dei Frammenti filosofici del Signor V. Cousin* (Lugano, 1834).
22. *Fr. phil. 1865*: this note is omitted.
23. Cousin is referring to the fact that it was widely held that Schelling's philosophy had changed radically since he stopped publishing in 1809, but that, apart from hints in the 1834 Preface and other rumours, little was known about exactly what this change consisted in.
24. *Fr. phil. 1847* and subsequent editions: Cousin adds the following note, "See the detailed refutation of this principle which we cannot allow to be repeated across the Rhine, *Philosophy of Kant*, lecture 8."
25. *Fr. phil. 1865*: Cousin adds a citation to his *Souvenirs d'Allemagne*.
26. *Fr. phil. 1865*: the passage from, "Is it to the abstraction ..." to "... the *philosophy of nature*?" is replaced with 'Is it to the abstraction of being in itself, to the absolute identity of subject and object of the *philosophy of nature*?"
27. *Fr. phil. 1865*: "is" is replaced with "seems to now."
28. *Fr. phil. 1865*: "nothing less" is replaced with "nothing other."
29. *Fr. phil. 1865*: the passage from "and even that ..." to "since Cartesianism" is omitted.
30. *Fr. phil. 1865*: "know of" is replaced with "avow."
31. *Fr. phil. 1865*: "such as [the phenomena] of consciousness" is omitted.
32. That is, it is a matter of knowing whether we are talking about knowledge of phenomena in nature or in consciousness.
33. *Fr. phil. 1865*: this second question is omitted.
34. *Fr. phil. 1865*: "No:" is added before "to speak rigorously."

35. *Fr. phil. 1865*: "of consciousness" is omitted.
36. *Fr. phil. 1865*: "certain of itself" is omitted.
37. The closing words of Pierre Paul Royer-Collard's opening lecture to his course on philosophy at the Sorbonne. *La Vie politique de M. Royer-Collard: ses discours et ses écrits*, vol. 1, ed. Barante (Paris: Didier, 1861), p. 134.
38. *Fr. phil. 1865*: This sentence is simplified to: "I am dealing with two kinds of adversary who are faced with two kinds of pitfall: hypothesis, if they dogmatize in metaphysics without having traversed psychology; scepticism, if they both begin from and stop with psychology."
39. The "vague accusations of pantheism" to which Cousin is referring stem in particular from Louis Bautain's *La philosophie du christianisme*, 2 vols (Paris: Derivaux, 1835). Bautain had briefly been a student of Cousin's in the mid-1810s before moving to Strasbourg as Professor of Philosophy; in 1835, he explicitly attacks eclecticism as pantheism: "Eclecticism, envisaged in a large and profound manner, as the leader of this current school wishes it to be, is merely a pantheism more intellectual than Spinoza's. It is the conclusion of German philosophy and the so-called philosophy of nature; it is the idealism of the ancients renewed, where everything is united, mixed together and disappears into a *je ne sais quoi*, which is neither God or man, nor spirit or matter, nor objective or subjective, nor truth or illusion, nor good or evil, but the pure and absolute indifference of all things.... His *I* is the universal I which opposes itself to itself in order to contemplate itself: all *non-Is* emanate from it and return to it; they perpetually arise from the abyss of Being to plunge back into it endlessly; and this is the confusion of God and man: there is no man, nor God, but the absolute alone. How can Christian piety not reject such a doctrine?" (vol. 2, pp. 41–2). See Barancy's and Bernard-Granger's essay above.
40. The Xenophon and Zeno fragments are in *Nov. fr. phil.*, pp. 14–146. The passage cited from the 1829 lectures concerns Cousin's discussion of Spinoza, in which he shows that, far from being an atheist, Spinoza's expands the concept of God to leave no space for the I or for nature. Tellingly, Cousin sees this position as a result of a radicalization of the Cartesian notion of substance as being in itself with the result that "man and nature are pure phenomena, mere attributes of unique and absolute substance." *Cours de l'histoire de la philosophie*, vol. 1 (Paris: Pichon and Didier, 1829), pp. 465–7.
41. See e.g. pp. 69–70 above.
42. Exodus 3:14.
43. *Fr. phil. 1847* and subsequent editions: "often" replaced with "sometimes."
44. See e.g. p. 74 above.
45. *Fr. phil. 1865*: "when I everywhere established that they are causes—forces, in Leibniz's sense—and" is omitted.
46. See e.g. pp. 141–3 below.
47. See p. 68 above.
48. *Fr. phil. 1865*: Cousin adds the following note, "In very similar circumstances, the father of French philosophy gave an example which his most recent disciple did not hesitate to follow. In the *Meditations*, Descartes seemed to recognize no other substance than that which 'by itself is capable of subsisting' (3rd Meditation). But, if there are only substances which exist and subsist by themselves, one can conclude that there is only one substance—and this leads straight to Spinozism before Spinoza. Descartes responded in the *Principles of Philosophy*, 1st part, §51: 'Some obscurity may concern this phrase, *to have need of solely itself*, for, properly speaking, only for God is this so and there is no created thing which can exist one sole moment without being sustained and conserved by his power. This is why it is right to say with the schools that the term substance is not univocal with respect to God and his creatures, that is, that there is no signification which we distinctly conceive that appropriately refers with the same sense to him and to them.'" On the Descartes quotation from the *Principles*, see the version of the text translated in *The Philosophical Writings of Descartes*, trans. J. Cottingham et al. (Cambridge: Cambridge University Press, 1991), vol. 1, p. 210; and the phrase in the *Meditations* is to be found at *The Philosophical Writings of Descartes*, vol. 2, p. 31. Cousin goes on to cite other defences of Descartes' definition of substance along similar lines in *Fr. phil. cart.* and lecture 8 of the *Histoire générale de la philosophie*.
49. *Fr. phil. 1847* and subsequent editions: paragraph renumbered to "2" in line with the two accusations above.
50. See pp. 101–2 above.
51. *Fr. phil. 1865*: "in God above all, force is adequate to substance, and" is omitted.
52. *Fr. phil. 1847*: solely the Preface to the first edition is cited; *Fr. phil. 1865*: this footnote and the accompanying phrase in the main text, "I believe I have proven elsewhere" is omitted. Cousin is here citing pp. 73–4 above; "On Freedom and its Different Modes", *Fr. phil. 1826*, pp. 389–405;

and *Cours de l'histoire de la philosophie* (Paris: Pichon and Didier, 1829)—where the passage on freedom in fact occurs on pp. 502–15.
53. *Fr. phil. 1865*: Cousin adds a note, "See *On the True, the Beautiful and the Good*, lecture 14; *Scottish Philosophy*, lecture 10; *Locke's Philosophy*, lecture 13."
54. On Nicolas-Louis d'Assas, see n. 147 to the 1826 Preface.
55. Augustine's view on the freedom of the will is notoriously complex, but presumably Cousin is claiming that Luther and Calvin made excessive use of Augustinian claims like the following, "God works in the hearts of human beings to incline their wills to whatever he wills, whether to good actions in accord with his mercy or to evil ones in accord with their merits." *Grace and Free Choice*, 21.43.
56. *Fr. phil. 1865*: Cousin adds the following note, "On spontaneity as distinct from the will, see the Preface to the first edition, pp. xix–xxiii [pp. 71–3 above], and *passim* in my writings."
57. John 1:12–13. *Fr. phil. 1847* and subsequent editions: this clause is omitted (and "father" later in the sentence changed to "God" as a result).
58. *Fr. phil. 1847* and subsequent editions: Cousin here adds a note citing a passage from the "Foreword" to *On Pascal's Pensées*, from which he quotes at length in *Fr. phil. 1865*, as well as a citation to the appendix of his *Introduction à l'histoire de la philosophie*—a collection of passages from Cousin's works on the three topics of "the comprehensibility and incomprehensibility of God," "the true sense in which one must understand the necessity of creation," and "God present in the world and distinct from the world." 4th ed. (Paris: Didier, 1861), pp. 319–39.
59. *Fr. phil. 1865*: "Remove the principle, consider the action in itself, so to speak, from an external perspective" replaced with "Consider the action from an external perspective."
60. *Fr. phil. 1847* and subsequent editions Cousin adds a footnote citing the "Foreword" to Pascal's *Pensées* and the material on Vanini in *Fr. phil. cart*; *Fr. phil. 1865*: this footnote is omitted. *O altitude!* is from the Vulgate translation of Romans 11 (which in the Authorized English reads, "O [the heights] of the riches both of the wisdom and knowledge of God! how unsearchable are his judgments, and his ways past finding out!").
61. *Fr. phil. 1865*: "exclusive" replaced with "extreme."
62. See e.g. pp. 115–16 above.
63. *Fr. phil. 1865*: "exclusive and" is omitted.
64. The term Cousin uses is "amour-propre."

III
1816–1818

On the Moral Law and Freedom[1]

The moral law can command a free will alone. The moral world is that of freedom. Wherever there is a free determination, a willed and deliberated act, there is the spiritual world. Moreover, we live on the earth and subsist only by continual acts of will and freedom. The spiritual world is thus already present for us on this earth. We live between two worlds,[2] on the border of two separate kingdoms of which we form the mysterious union. To penetrate Heaven, there is no need to pierce the shadows of the tomb; Heaven already exists within the heart of the free man: *et caelum et virtus*, Lucan writes.[3] I am a citizen of the invisible kingdom of active and free intellects. But what is the determination of my will that illuminates this invisible world to me? Ask this of consciousness.[4] Examine yourself when you do your duty, and Heaven will appear to you at the bottom of your heart. It is not by argumentation that one acquires conviction of the spiritual world; it is by a free act of virtue, which is always followed by an act of faith in moral beauty and an internal vision of God and Heaven.

The sensible world acts on me and the impression I receive is an occasion for me to exercise my will. My will in turn determines an alteration in the sensible world. This is ordinary human life, where the will is manifest solely as a consequence of sensible movements and by way of sensible movements. But determine for yourself, so that your will has its ground solely in itself: already you escape slavery, your life is purified and elevated.[5] Do it again: contain your willing in itself, so that it acts without manifesting itself externally, so that its free determinations do not breach the internal sanctuary. Do not seek to imprint your will on sensible effects—and you completely transcend the material world, your life becomes wholly spiritual, you have attained the source of genuine activity, you are in possession of the holy, of the pure, of the divine, you have an internal vision of the divine life which is revealed in yours. To place oneself outside of all sensible conditions; to will without regard for the consequences of one's willing, independently of every antecedent and every consequent; to fold its determinations back on themselves—this is true freedom, the commencement of eternity. We may speak of freedom, of holiness, of purity but we do nothing but combine words until we have freed ourselves. Christianity says, we obtain the meaning of eternal life only when renouncing the world and its ends.[6] At this moment, faith in the Eternal enters the soul. Ultimately, according to the images of Christian doctrine, one must die and be born anew to enter into the kingdom of Heaven.[7]

Philosophy is nothing but the soul's vision rendered general. If the will were attached to the sensible world, how could one believe in holiness and another life? One would treat eternity as a fable, or believe in it out of prejudice. Reform your life to reform philosophy. The powers of the mind would merely be shadows without the power of virtue. Oh! If the soul of the last of the Brutuses,[8] if the soul of St Louis[9] could tell their own story, what a beautiful moral psychology we would have! But the base act has [merely] been analysed and criticized in its principle.[10]

The infinite and eternal will is revealed in us in moral conscience, in the supreme commandment, *Will what is good*; and the individual human will merges with the infinite will by freely obeying its voice. God lowers himself to man in the law of duty; man raises himself to God in internal submission to this law.[11] Here is the great mystery of eternity discovering itself in humanity and of humanity freely taking on eternity. Man is entirely within this mystery; hence, morality is the source of all truth, and true enlightenment resides in the depths of voluntary and free activity.

This is an incontestable fact of consciousness—simple and unable to be broken down: "Do what is good without regard to the consequences—that is, will what is good."

Since this commandment has no earthly, visible, material object applicable to the needs of this life and of this sensible world, it follows that either it has no end or goal; or it has an invisible end or goal, and that it concerns a world that is different from ours, where the movements[12] which result from volitions count for nothing and where the volitions themselves are everything.

If there is no invisible world, where all our good acts of will count for us, what is then the goal of virtue on earth?

1. Does [virtue] serve the mechanism of the universe?
2. Does it have as its end the civilisation of the globe?
3. Or the amelioration of human destiny in relation to local and physical benefits?
4. Or world peace?
5. Or the greatest moral development of the human species, which would result in its greatest perfection in general along with its greatest happiness?

There is no need of virtue for any of this. God had only to construct machines without freedom and he would have made a spectacle just as beautiful, if he desired solely the spectacle of happiness. Yet, it might be said, he willed for us to produce it. [But] it is not so, for universal happiness on earth is a chimera. Moreover, to arrive at the above goal, God could have dispensed with giving us the moral law and conscience; egoism would have been enough. Notice that in the sensible world it does not much matter why a fact occurs, so long as it occurs. Enlighten my egoism or strengthen the power of my natural sympathy and I will do as much or even more good to others as by the sentiment of duty alone.

One should always bear in mind the following maxims:

1. The consequences of an action, whatever they may be, do not render it morally good or bad; intention is everything. Strictly speaking, there is no moral action, only moral intentions.
2. For an intention to be morally good, it must be disinterested.
3. All intentions can be considered interested which have a personal return. Hence, to make a thing for the sake of honours, glory, praise, pleasure, either sensual or intellectual, external or internal, for the sake of hearing oneself called generous or to be able to say it to oneself, for the sake of earthly recompense or even heavenly recompense—all of this is equally external to morality.
4. Actions which arise from the impulse of the organism are considered indifferent. Hence, the man who, pulled by an irresistible movement of pity and sympathy, sacrifices his life for the sake of his fellow man is not yet a moral being.
5. An action is considered moral when, after weighing it and finding it just, someone does it solely because he believes he ought to do it and solely for the reason that it is just.

Notes

1. *Fr. phil. 1826*, pp. 173–8 (subsequently: *Fr. phil. 1833*, pp. 209–13; *Fr. phil. 1838*, vol. 1, pp. 216–20). We take the 1826 publication as our base text for this translation and note the significant modifications to later versions in the endnotes. A translation of the 1833 version of the text exists in George Ripley's *Philosophical Miscellanies* (Boston: Hilliard and Gray, 1838), pp. 158–62. As a piece of juvenilia, it is very different from the work Cousin was producing even a few months later—not only in subject matter, but also in tone and style. Nevertheless, it does provide a clear, if crude statement of the early Cousin's "spiritualism", i.e. a metaphysical dualism that guarantees the freedom of the individual will, as well as insisting on the importance of moral philosophy to his vision of the philosophical project which would culminate in the 1820 lecture course on moral philosophy.
2. *Fr. phil. 1833* and subsequent editions: "in the middle of two worlds" replaced with "in some sense."
3. Lucan, *The Civil War*, l. 579: "both heaven and the virtuous heart."
4. "Conscience" is an equally plausible translation.
5. *Fr. phil. 1833* and subsequent editions: this sentence is omitted.
6. e.g. Luke 14:33.
7. e.g. John 3:3.
8. Marcus Junius Brutus (85–42 BCE): politician and assassin of Julius Caesar, who was regularly cited as a model of virtue, despite his actions: as Plutarch put it, he "slayed Caesar because he was driven by the splendour and nobility of the deed" (*Life of Brutus* 29.7).
9. Louis IX of France (1214–70): king of France often cited as the model Christian ruler.
10. *Fr. phil. 1833* and subsequent editions: this sentence is omitted.
11. *Fr. phil. 1833* and subsequent editions: this sentence is omitted.
12. *Fr. phil. 1833* and subsequent editions: "movements" replaced with "external movements."

On the True Meaning of the *cogito, ergo sum*[1]

Next to the peripatetic axiom, *nihil est in intellectu quod non prius fuerit in sensu*,[2] I know of no philosophical claim which has given rise to so much noise in the intellectual world as Descartes' famous *cogito, ergo sum*. It reigned uncontested over all schools for nearly a century, then underwent regrettable revivals, and ended up being lavished with as much contempt as it had initially elicited praise. After being [previously] celebrated as an indubitable demonstration of personal existence, it has come to appear ridiculous, demonstrating nothing and containing a *petitio principii*. It would be curious to prove that this argument—in turn so lauded and so decried [precisely] as an argument—is not in fact [an argument] at all, and that Descartes inserted no logical link between thought and existence.

I owe it to Dugald Stewart to here name him the only philosopher since Gassendi to have dared raise some doubt over the nature of the Cartesian enthymeme. "The celebrated enthymeme of Descartes," Stewart writes,* "does not deserve *all* the ridicule bestowed on it by those writers who have represented the author as attempting to demonstrate his own existence by a process of reasoning. To me it seems more probable, that he meant chiefly to direct the attention of his readers to a circumstance which must be allowed to be not unworthy of notice in the history of the human mind;—the impossibility of our ever having learned the fact of our own existence, without some sensation being excited in the mind, to awaken the faculty of thinking." And he adds in a note: "After looking again into the *Meditations* of Descartes, I am doubtful if I have not carried my apology for him a little further than his own words will justify. I am still of the opinion, however, that it was the remark which I have ascribed to him that first led him into this train of thought."

I too have often reread the *Meditations*, but without finding either Descartes' justification [for the *cogito, ergo sum*] or [the justification] for Stewart's suspicion. First of all, does not the *ergo sum* itself express such a logical link? Secondly, since Descartes always employs this word [*ergo*] when he reasons, is it not natural to believe that it here possesses the same meaning as it does everywhere else, and, what is more, does not such a relation of two terms mark a relation of intellectual operations? And, if the *ergo* does not possess a logical meaning [in this specific

---

*Essays philosophic (Edinburgh, 1810).[3]

instance], why did Descartes not say so? Moreover, if Descartes did not want to demonstrate existence through argumentation, what method revealed it to him instead? where does Descartes speak of this other method? where does he describe it? Leaf through the entire book of the *Meditations* and try to locate one single relevant passage. In fact, in the *Principles of Philosophy*—a perfectly composed work to be recommended for its admirable clarity and rigour of expression—I read these precious lines on the question which concerns us: *Facile substantiam agnoscimus ex quolibet eius attributo per communem illam notionem quod nihili nulla sunt attributa: nullaeve proprietates aut qualitates. Ex hoc etiam quod aliquod attributum adesse percipimus, concludimus aliquam rem existentem sive substantiam, cui illud tribui possit necessario etiam adesse.* ["We can easily come to know a substance by one of its attributes, in virtue of the common notion that nothingness possesses no attributes, that is to say, no properties or qualities. Thus, if we perceive the presence of some attribute, we can infer that there must also be present an existing thing or substance to which it may be attributed."]* Does not *concludimus*[6] belong to the language of argumentation? It therefore seems that there are more problems than are needed to destroy the authority of Stewart's simple doubt.

However, Stewart is right: Descartes does not argue with the *ergo*; he knows that he doesn't reason, and he declares it explicitly. He knows of an [alternative] intellectual method by which personal existence is revealed to us, and he describes it with as much and even more precision than any of his adversaries did. According to Descartes, this method is not argumentation, but reason, one of those pure, immediate, absolute concepts[7] that, a century after Descartes, Reid and Kant obscured with the apparent clarity of their *constitutive principles* and their *intellectual forms*.[8]

Where then is to be located this theory that escapes every inquiring gaze? Neither in the *Meditations* where Dugald-Stewart seeks it in vain, nor in the *Principles*; but in Descartes' correspondence,[9] where it is, as it were, buried. It is there one must seek it out. On rereading this long collection of objections and replies, I have extracted a number of decisive passages in which Descartes prohibits argumentation when obtaining the idea of personal existence, and in which he clearly establishes the true method which leads us there. I will cite solely the most important passages.

Before Spinoza and Reid, Gassendi had attacked Descartes' enthymeme. This proposition, *I think, therefore I am*, presupposes, Gassendi writes, a major premise: what thinks exists, and therefore implies a *petitio principii*. To which Descartes responds: This is not a *petitio principii*, for I do not presuppose the major [premise]. I maintain that this proposition, I think, therefore I exist, is a

---

* *Princip. Philosophiae*, 1st part, ch. 52.—French edition (Paris, 1824): vol. 3, p. 96.[4]

particular truth which is introduced into the mind without the aid of another, more general [truth], and independently of all logical deduction. This is not a prejudice, but a natural truth which immediately and irresistibly strikes intelligence. As for you, Descartes adds, you think that all particular truths rest on a general truth from which one must deduce it by syllogisms, according to the rules of dialectic. In possession of this error, you gratuitously attribute it to me; your method is to constantly assume false major [premises], to form paralogisms and then to impute them to me.*

If this passage does not appear clear enough, the following will leave no doubt as to Descartes' opinion: The notion of existence, he says in his response to other objections, is a primitive notion which is not obtained by any syllogism; it is self-evident, and our mind discovers it by intuition.[10] If it were the fruit of a syllogism, it would presuppose the major [premise], all that thinks, exists; whereas it is by means of [the primitive notion alone] that we arrive at this principle.†

Everywhere in the collection of his letters[12] Descartes expresses himself with the same precision: *the natural light makes us see that nothing does not have attributes, that every quality presupposes a subject.*‡

---

* Here is the passage in full which is curious for more than one reason: "The author of the *Counter-Objections* [Gassendi] claims that when I say 'I am thinking, therefore I exist', I presuppose the major premiss 'Whatever thinks exists', and hence I have already adopted a preconceived opinion. Here he once more misuses the term 'preconceived opinion'. For although we can apply the term to the proposition in question when it is put forward without attention and believed to be true only because we remember that we judged it to be true previously, we cannot say that it is always a preconceived opinion. For when we examine it, it appears so evident to the understanding that we cannot but believe it, even though this may be the first time in our life that we have thought of it—in which case we would have no preconceived opinion about it. But the most important mistake our critic makes here is the supposition that knowledge of particular propositions must always be deduced from universal ones, following the same order as that of a syllogism in Dialectic. Here he shows how little he knows of the way in which we should search for the truth. It is certain that if we are to discover the truth we must always begin with particular notions in order to arrive at general ones later on (though we may also reverse the order and deduce other particular truths once we have discovered general ones). Thus when we teach a child the elements of geometry we will not be able to get him to understand the general proposition 'When equal quantities are taken from equal amounts the remaining amounts will be equal', or 'The whole is greater than its parts', unless we show him examples in particular cases. It is by failing to take heed of this that our author has gone astray and produced all the invalid arguments with which he has stuffed his book. He has simply made up false major premisses whenever the mood takes him, as though I had used them to deduce the truths which I expounded."—*Letter which serves as a response to a selection of counter-objections by Pierre Gassendi.*[5]

† "When we become aware that we are thinking things, this is a primary notion which is not derived by means of any syllogism. When someone says 'I am thinking, therefore I am, or I exist,' he does not deduce existence from thought by means of a syllogism, but recognizes it as something self-evident by a simple intuition of the mind. This is clear from the fact that if he were deducing it by means of a syllogism, he would have to have had previous knowledge of the major premiss 'Everything which thinks is, or exists'; yet in fact he learns it from experiencing in his own case that it is impossible that he should think without existing. It is in the nature of our mind to construct general propositions on the basis of our knowledge of particular ones."—*Reply to the Second Set of Objections.*[11]

‡ "We call substance every thing in which there is some property, quality or attribute of which we have a real idea. The only idea we have of a substance itself, in the strict sense, is that it is the thing in which whatever we perceive (or whatever has objective being in one of our ideas) exists, either formally or eminently. For we know by the natural light that a real attribute cannot belong to nothing."—*Arguments proving the existence of God and the distinction between the soul and the body arranged in geometrical fashion.*[13]

It might be said that he is afraid of not being understood, so much so that he scrupulously expresses himself with clarity, and so what he had said [on this topic] before [the above replies] no longer seems enough: he fears that the fact he admits the idea of substance as a first idea is not yet convincing enough. So, after showing that it cannot be the work of argumentation, he adds that it should also not be attributed to reflection, but, rather, to an operation prior to reflection, an operation whose result one could well deny with one's lips, but without being able to do the same from one's understanding or one's faith.*

It remains to know why, in his *Meditations*, Descartes did not set out this interesting theory, and whether it stands in harmony with the totality of Cartesian philosophy. A deeper knowledge of the genuine subject matter of the *Meditations* and Descartes' philosophy easily resolves this question.

The true goal of Descartes' efforts is to give philosophy a scientific starting point by resting it on a firm and unshakeable principle (*aliquid certum et inconcussum*);[15] and since personal existence had alone escaped the hypothesis of universal doubt, in which Descartes first positioned himself, personal existence was for Descartes this indubitable principle on which he established his philosophy. This philosophy is an immense chain whose first ring is founded on the existence of the soul, and which, from there, attains the Being of beings, and in its ample scope comprehends the universality of phenomena and the laws of matter. From personal existence, or humanity, Descartes ascends to God and descends to the universe. Personal existence is for him the basis of all other certainties: once this initial certainty had been obtained, argumentation deduces everything from it, but it does not ground [the principle] on which [argumentation] rests. This is the [foundation] stone of the edifice: everything rests on it, but it does not rest on anything but itself. The soul demonstrates God and, as a consequence, the universe; but no prior principle demonstrates the soul: its certainty is primitive; it is revealed to us in the relation between thought and the thinking being. If the soul did not think, it could not know itself; but since its nature is to think, it necessarily knows itself. Argumentation does not identify a logical point of departure in the existence of thought; rather, the soul cannot think without knowing itself, because being is given to us through thought: *cogito, ergo sum*. The certainty of thought does not

---

* "It is true that no one can be certain that he is thinking or that he exists unless he knows what thought is and what existence is. But this does not require reflective knowledge, or the kind of knowledge that is acquired by means of demonstrations; still less does it require knowledge of reflective knowledge, i.e. knowing that we know, and knowing that we know that we know, and so on *ad infinitum*. This kind of knowledge cannot possibly be obtained about anything. It is quite sufficient that we should know it by that internal awareness which always precedes reflective knowledge. This inner awareness of one's thought and existence is so innate in all men that, although we may pretend that we do not have it if we are overwhelmed by preconceived opinions and pay more attention to words than to their meanings, we cannot in fact fail to have it. Thus when anyone notices that he is thinking and that it follows from this that he exists, even though he may never before have asked what thought is or what existence is, he still cannot fail to have sufficient knowledge of them both to satisfy himself in this regard."—*Replies to the Sixth Set of Objections*.[14]

precede the certainty of existence; it contains it, it envelops it; these are two contemporaneous certainties which are mixed into one—the fundamental certainty. This composite fundamental certainty is the unique principle of Cartesian philosophy. This powerful doctrine is to be found in the *Meditations*, one of the most beautiful and most robust monuments to philosophical genius. Descartes claims to demonstrate by argumentation, with the rigour of geometry, *more geometrico*,[16] that the existence of nature and the existence of God are incontestable truths, since they rest on our personal existence, which sits above every effort by scepticism. Such was Descartes' design; it was not to establish a personal existence which no one could deny in good faith. Nevertheless, he still establishes [the latter] in the first and second Meditations, and in a very robust manner, by showing the simultaneity of the concept of existence and the perception of thought. And he indicates this relation of simultaneity by *ergo*; but he does not pause to warn us that knowledge of this relation is not the work of argumentation, for this was not his concern at this juncture. He is content with establishing the certainty of personal existence, and he makes use of it to establish all the principal truths. He did not need to have any specific discussion [on this topic] to prove that we do not draw existence from thought; he needed solely to establish the certainty of personal existence, and he does so. He affirms, with the utmost certainty, that we exist, since we think; hence, the reader is not deceived on the nature of the link with unites thought and existence. Descartes does not say it occurred by way of argumentation; he even implicitly says that it does not function by way of argumentation, since he goes immediately and necessarily from one to the other. But once again, he does not pause, and need not pause there. The *Meditations* is therefore irreproachable: it presents what it needs to present—the Cartesian doctrine in all its extensity, but also within its limits. If one wished to insert there a detailed theory of personal existence, this would in no way upset the general system, for [such a theory] does not form part of it. It stands outside this system, and this is why Descartes did not develop it in a work dedicated uniquely to the exposition of his philosophy, that is, to the demonstration of the existence of God and of the existence of the body. Whenever his contemporaries did not understand him and accused him of wrongly deducing existence from thought, Descartes would explain himself; but he would not change the proportions of that immortal monument in which his thoughts and his method are deposited; he would explain himself, but in his letters,[17] in his responses (*responsiones*), in which he demonstrated that all the reproaches addressed to him were mistaken, since they focus on the principle of his system which is accused of being established by argumentation; as if, he says, the principle of a system could be a logical principle, and as if knowledge of principles in general were within the scope of dialectic: *notitia principiorum non fit dialectice*.[18]

Notes

1. First published in *Archives Philosophiques, Politiques et Littéraires* 3 (1818), pp. 316–25 (subsequently: *Fr. phil. 1826*, pp. 312–22, *Fr. phil. 1833*, pp. 329–38; *Fr. phil. 1838*, vol. 1, pp. 45–84). We take the 1818 publication as our base text for this translation and note the significant modifications to later versions in the endnotes. According to the *Cours d'histoire de la philosophie moderne pendant les années 1816 et 1817* (Paris: Ladrange, 1841), where this text was later published, it is a fragment from Cousin's sixth lecture of his 1815–16 lecture course on personal existence. This is Cousin's earliest attempt to construct a spiritualist Descartes for the nineteenth century on the basis of his own distinction between spontaneity (primitive intuition) and reflection (argumentation). It also becomes clear in later work (see p. 253 below) that Cousin is here responding to Reid's critique of the *cogito* as circular and using Stewart as a provocation to overcome Reid in favour of Descartes. This essay then is indirect evidence for the extent to which the Cousin of this period saw Scottish philosophy as his primary dialogue partner.
2. The maxim of Aristotelian (and subsequently empiricist) epistemology: "Nothing is in the mind that is not first in the senses."
3. Dugald Stewart, *Philosophical Essays* (1810), p. 8. Dugald Stewart (1753–1828) was one of Cousin's main international interlocuters of the 1810s (see the review of Stewart's *Sketches of Moral Philosophy* in *Fr. phil. 1826*, pp. 73–131). Cousin does not reproduce Stewart's italics and, indeed, his own translation into the French is loose, particularly the closing phrase.
4. Cousin reproduces the original Latin in his text; our translation is taken from *The Philosophical Writings of Descartes*, trans. J. Cottingham et al. (Cambridge: Cambridge University Press, 1991), vol. 1, p. 210. The French edition to which Cousin here refers is his own; we omit further citations of this edition in what follows.
5. This passage is extracted from Descartes' 1646 Letter to Clerselier on Gassendi's further objections to the *Meditations* in his *Disquisitio Metaphysica sive Dubitationes et Instantiae*. Cousin reproduces the original Latin; the translation is taken from *The Philosophical Writings of Descartes*, vol. 2, p. 271.
6. Translated above as "we can infer."
7. *Fr. phil.* 1833 and subsequent editions: "pure, immediate, absolute" replaced with "necessary."
8. *Fr. phil.* 1826 and subsequent editions: "Reid and Kant obscured with the apparent clarity of their *constitutive principles* and their *intellectual categories*" replaced with "Reid and Kant made famous with the names, *constitutive principles* of the human mind and *intellectual categories*."
9. *Fr. phil.* 1826 and subsequent editions: "Descartes' correspondence" replaced with "the objections and replies to the *Meditations*."
10. The 1818 version of the text mistakenly prints "intention" rather than "intuition" here.
11. Cousin reproduces the original Latin; the translation is taken from *The Philosophical Writings of Descartes*, vol. 2, p. 100.
12. *Fr. phil.* 1826 and subsequent editions: "letters" replaced with "responses."
13. This is Descartes' definition of substance within the second set of replies. Cousin reproduces the original Latin; the translation is taken in modified form from *The Philosophical Writings of Descartes*, vol. 2, p. 114. Cousin doesn't indicate that he has missed out a line from the beginning of the definition which reads in full: "Every thing in which whatever we perceive immediately resides, as in a subject, or to every thing by means of which whatever we perceive exists. By 'whatever we perceive' is meant any property...."
14. Cousin reproduces the original Latin; the translation is taken from *The Philosophical Writings of Descartes*, vol. 2, p. 285.
15. The meaning here is identical to the preceding phrase. The Latin phrase is omitted from the 1833 and subsequent versions of the text.
16. i.e. "in a geometrical manner." *Fr. phil. 1833* and subsequent editions: "*more geometrico*" is omitted.
17. *Fr. phil.* 1833 and subsequent editions: "in his letters" is omitted.
18. i.e. "knowledge of principles does not occur dialectically." The maxim is typically attributed to Leibniz.

Attempt at a Classification of Philosophical Questions and Schools[1]

Instead of hurrying blindly and exhausting oneself in the obscure maze of those thousands of particular questions whose infinite variety dazzle and disconcert the firmest and most stubborn attention, it might be best to try—through an initial and powerful[2] effort—to bring together all these scattered, disparate questions into a determinate number of eminent problems which the reunited powers of the intellect can approach. The preliminary question of all philosophy is [the question] of the classification of philosophical questions.

The first law of any classification is to be complete, to encompass all general and particular questions—both those which are [immediately] manifest and those which must be sought in the depths of science, both all known and all possible questions.

The second law of any classification is to establish the relation between all the questions it enumerates and to precisely chart, in large, clear categories,[3] the order in which each question must be treated.

Now, when I think of all the questions which have occupied my mind, when I compare them to those which have occupied every philosopher, when I interrogate both books and myself, and, above all, when I consult the nature of the human mind, my reason and my experience reduces all philosophical problems to a very small number of general problems, whose character is determined by the general aspect under which I have come to know philosophy and, above all, by metaphysics which is here particularly in question.

I contend that philosophy is just the science of human nature considered in terms of the facts it furnishes for our observation. Among these facts, there are some which are related more particularly to the intellect and which, for this reason, are commonly called *metaphysical*. Metaphysical facts—the phenomena by which human intellect is produced—when gathered into general formulae, constitute intellectual principles. Therefore, metaphysics is nothing but the study of the intellect, in [the study] of our intellectual principles.

Intellectual principles are manifest in two ways—either in relation to the intellect in which they exist, to the subject which possesses them, to the consciousness and reflection which considers them; or in relation to their objects, that is, no longer in themselves and in ourselves, but in their external consequences and applications. However one conceives them, every intellectual principle is related to the human mind; and, at the same time as it is related to the human mind, to the subject of all knowledge and all consciousness, it concerns objects placed outside of the conceiving mind. To make use of famous expressions—useful and even necessary[4] for their concision and vividness—every intellectual principle is either *subjective*, or *objective*, or *subjective* and *objective* at the same time. There is no principle, no knowledge, no idea, no perception, no sensation which disturbs this general division that immediately divides all philosophical problems into two large classes: problems relative to the *subject* and problems relative to the *object*—or, more concisely, problems of the *subject* and problems of the *object*.[5]

Let us open up this general division and draw from it the particular divisions it contains. First, let us examine intellectual principles independently of the external consequences that can be deduced from them. Let us develop the science of the *subject*.

This is the science of the internal world; it is the science of the *I*, a science entirely distinct from that of the *object*, which is, properly speaking, the science of the *not-I*. And this science of the I is no novel on the nature of the soul, on its origin and its end; it is the genuine history of the soul, written by reflection, dictated by consciousness and memory. It is thought folding back on itself and making a spectacle of itself; it is occupied uniquely with internal facts, phenomena that can be perceived and evaluated by consciousness. I call it *psychology*, or further, *phenomenology*, to indicate the nature of its objects.[*] Moreover, despite the difficulties posed to a wavering reflection of a being immediately thrown and then constantly detained outside of itself by the needs of its sensibility and its reason—this completely subjective science is not out of man's reach. It is certain, for it is immediate. The I and that with which it is occupied are enclosed within the same sphere, within the unity of consciousness. The object of science is here entirely internal; it is perceived intuitively by the subject; subject and object merge into one another. All facts of consciousness are self-evident, as soon as consciousness attains them. However, they often slip from its grasp owing to their extreme delicacy or the foreign covering in which they are enclosed. Psychology gives the most complete certainty; but we find this certainty only in depths which not all eyes are able to penetrate. To attain [such depths], [the mind] must separate itself from the extended and determinate world in which we have lived for so long, whose colours at present taint all our thoughts and all our languages and without which we scarcely

---

[*] *Phenomena* names all facts which occur in the soul and which it immediately perceives; all modifications to which the soul is subjected and which it knows with the help of consciousness. Hence, *psychology*, or the science of the soul, can also be called *phenomenology*, or the science of phenomena, of internal facts which occur in the soul and to which consciousness bears witness for it. Consciousness is that inherent faculty in the human soul of observing itself and seeing the modifications to which it submits.—*Editor's note.*[6]

think at all; it must separate itself from that external world, a world which is difficult to discard in a completely different way than [the world] which precedes it, a world which constitutes all notions of being and the absolute. That is, it must separate itself from an integral part of thought, for within every thought there is being and the absolute.* And what is more, it must separate out thought without mutilating it, and abstract the phenomena of consciousness from the ontological notions which naturally envelop them and the logical forms which currently suffocate them, without falling into abstractions. Finally, after establishing itself in this world of consciousness, so delicate and so slippery, [the mind] is required to undertake a vast and profound review of all the phenomena that it understands, for such phenomena are the elements of science. It must assure itself that no element has been omitted, otherwise science is incomplete; it must assure itself that it has assumed no fact, that it has not taken phantoms of the imagination for phenomena of consciousness; it must assure itself that it has not only omitted no real element and not only that it has introduced no foreign element, but also that it has viewed the real elements, and all the real elements, according to their true aspect, and according to all their possible aspects. When this preliminary work has put us in possession of all the elements of science, there remains the task of constructing this science by bringing together all its elements and combining them in a way that makes them all visible in the different classes to which their different characteristics are assigned, just as the naturalist perceives his plants or his minerals within a certain number of divisions which account for them all.

After doing this, still more is to be done. The science of the *subject* is far from being exhausted; the greatest difficulties are not yet overcome. We have examined the internal world, the phenomena of consciousness, as consciousness currently presents them to us. We know the man of today; we do not yet know primitive man. It is not enough for man to contemplate the analytic inventory of his knowledge, arrange it according to categories and, so to speak, methodological labels. Indefatigable human curiosity cannot find rest in these circumspect classifications, for [the mind] aspires to higher problems which terrify and attract it, charm and overwhelm it. It seems as though we do not legitimately grasp present reality as long as we have not obtained the primitive truth, and so we endlessly try to return to the origin of our knowledge, as to the source of all light. Moreover, the question

---

* The soul can be considered and considers itself from two perspectives: 1° As *substance*, as a really existing *being*, independent of all modifications; 2° as *subject* of certain modifications, as a theatre of internal facts, of phenomena perceived by consciousness. The difficulty of which the author here speaks consists in distinctly separating these two perspectives and ensuring that there enters into *psychology*, which is the science of internal phenomena, of modifications of the soul, nothing that relates to *ontology*, which is the science of being, of the absolute—that is, of the soul considered as *substance* and independently of all modification. Consciousness sees and witnesses solely internal phenomena; it does not attain, it does not see the *soul-substance, thinking being* itself. *Thinking being*, the *soul-substance* is thus external to consciousness, and it is this second world—not extended, not figured and yet also external, from the perspective of consciousness—of which the author speaks and which is very difficult to disclose, when one wants to remain rigorously within the limits of *psychology.—Editor's note.*[7]

of the origin of knowledge gives birth to a new [question], just as difficult, perhaps even more so—that of the relation of the primitive to the actual. It is not enough, in fact, to know where we are and from where we came; we must know all the paths by which we arrived at the point where we now stand. This third piece of knowledge completes the other two. Here ends all questioning: the science of the subject is truly exhausted, for when one possesses the two extreme points and their intermediaries, there is nothing left to ask.

Let us now consider intellectual principles in relation to their external objects.

What a strange thing! a being who is able to know outside of his own sphere; he is only himself, yet knows something other than himself; his existence is for him just his own individuality and, from the midst of this individual world he inhabits and he constitutes, he reaches a world foreign to his own; and he does so by means of forces which—entirely internal and personal owing to their inherent relation to their subject—extend themselves beyond his limits, and illuminate for him things placed well beyond his own reflection and his own consciousness. That the human mind is equipped with these marvellous forces cannot be in doubt; but is their scope legitimate and does what they reveal really exist? Are those intellectual principles which have an incontestable authority in their *subject's* internal world equally valid in relation to their external *objects*?

This is the *objective* problem par excellence; and, since everything placed beyond consciousness is objective, and since all real and substantial existences are external to consciousness, which operates solely on internal phenomena, then it follows that every problem which is related to some particular being, or which, in general, implies the question of existence, is an objective problem. Ultimately, just as the problem of the legitimacy of the instruments by which we know anything objective, whatever it may be, is the problem of the legitimacy of the instruments by which we know in an *absolute* manner (the *absolute* is what is not relative to the *I*, but to *being*), it follows that the problem of the legitimacy of external, objective, ontological knowledge is the problem of absolute knowledge. The problem of the *absolute* constitutes higher logic.

When we have assured ourselves of the legitimacy of our instruments of knowing in an absolute manner, we apply these legitimate instruments to some object, that is, to some particular being; and we concern ourselves with the reality of the existence of the substantial *I*, of the *soul* which conceives itself and does not perceive itself; [the existence] of that extended and determinate being that we call *matter*; and [the existence] of that supreme Being, the ultimate ground of all beings, of all external objects and of the subject itself which ascends to it—*God*.

Finally, after these problems of the existence of diverse particular objects, there arise [problems] concerning the modes and attributes of this existence—problems higher than all the others, since, if it is strange that the personal intellect knows that there are existences outside its sphere, it is strange in a very different way that it knows what occurs in these spheres external to its own.

These special investigations constitute higher metaphysics, the science of the objective, of being, of the invisible; for every being, everything objective is invisible to consciousness.

Let me recap: objective problems are divided in two: one is logic and the other is metaphysics—that is: (1) the problem of the absolute, the question of the reality of the existence of everything objective; (2) the question of the reality of the existence of various particular objects. Add to these two objective questions the three sub-questions corresponding to the general question of the subject and you have all metaphysical questions. There are none that do not sit within these general frameworks. We have therefore satisfied the first law of any classification. Let us try to satisfy the second, and understand the order in which it is appropriate to examine each question.

Let us first examine the two problems which contain all the others—that of the subject and that of the object.

Whether the object exists or does not exist, it is evident that it exists for us only insofar as it is manifest to us via the subject; and, when it is claimed that subject and object are actually and primitively given to us together, it should always be admitted that, in this natural relation, the term which knows must be considered—as well as truly being—the fundamental element of this relation. It is therefore with the subject that one must begin; it is first of all ourselves that we must know, for we know nothing except in ourselves and by ourselves. It is not we who rotate around the external world; it is rather the external world which turns around us; or, if these two spheres each have their own individual—and merely correlative—movements, we know this only because one of them teaches it to us: it is always from [the subject] that we must learn everything, even the existence of the other and its independent existence.

Therefore, one must begin from the subject—from the I, from consciousness.

However, the question of the subject contains within it three others—with which of them should one begin? First, there is the [question] which determines the relation of the two others, the relation of the primitive to the actual. It is clear that we can only treat this [question] after treating the other two. It remains to determine the order of these other two. Now, a severe method will not hesitate in placing the actual before the primitive; for, by beginning from the primitive, one could well obtain merely a false primitive, which, in its deduction, would generate nothing but a hypothetical actual, whose relation to the primitive would be nothing more than the relation between two fairly consistent hypotheses. If one errs when beginning from the primitive, then all is lost; the science of the subject is false and so what becomes of the object? Moreover, to start off with the primitive is to begin with one of the most awkward and obscure of problems, without any guide or insight. Instead, when beginning with the actual, one begins with the easiest question, with that which serves as an introduction to all the others. Everywhere, experience and the experimental method are celebrated as the triumph of the century and the genius of our epoch; the experimental method in psychology begins with the actual, exhausts it, if that is possible, and offers a severe account of all the principles which currently govern the intellect, admitting solely those which are manifest and rejecting none of them. [In psychology] we ask none [of these principle] where it came from or where it is going to; it is—and this is enough; it ought to have a place in science, since it has one in nature; we will impose on facts neither arbitrary censure nor systematic decree; we will be content to catalogue them one by one. Nor will we be too quick to disturb them, in order to lift them up into some premature theory; we will wait patiently for their number to increase, their relations to disentangle and for the theory to present itself.

If we now pass from the subject to the object, and if we seek the order of the two questions of which it is composed, it is easy to see that logic must be treated before metaphysics, the problem of the absolute and of existence in general before that of particular existences; for the solution to the first problem, whatever it may be, is the principle of the second one.

Hence, both laws of any classification have been satisfied; the philosophical frameworks divided and ordered—now who has been able to implement them?

Indeed, has any philosopher ever been able to implement them? If they had, there would now be a metaphysical science, just as there is a geometry and a chemistry. Have philosophers at least distinguished between these different frameworks, even if they could not implement them? Have they sketched the contours and proportions of the edifice, even if they could not yet realize it? If they had done so, there would be a beginning to science, an opening up of the path, a judgement on method. However, if philosophers have been able to neither implement the philosophical frameworks, nor even perceive them and distinguish between them, then what have they accomplished? In short, this is the answer.

The first philosophers discussed everything and resolved everything, but in a confused manner; they treated everything, but without method or with arbitrary and artificial methods. There is no metaphysical problem which was not considered from every [possible] viewpoint and analysed in a thousand ways by the Greek schools and by those of Alexandria;[8] and by the Italian metaphysicians of the sixteenth century. However, neither the former with their vast genius nor the latter with all their wisdom could either discover or circumscribe the true limits of each problem, the relations between them and their scope. No philosopher before Descartes had precisely posed the first philosophical problem, the distinction between subject and object; this distinction had been nothing but a scholastic and grammatical distinction which Aristotle's successors vainly raised without being able to draw from it anything but implications of the same nature as their principle—grammatical implications which, passing from grammar into logic, and from there into metaphysics, corrupted the science of the mind and filled it with vain verbal arguments. Despite all the vigour of his mind, Descartes himself did not recognize the entire scope of this distinction; his glory is to have made [the distinction] and placed the true starting point of philosophical inquiry in thought or in the I. However, he was not struck, as he should have been, by the abyss which separates subject and object; and, after posing the problem, this great man resolved it too easily. It was reserved to the eighteenth century to apply and to disseminate the spirit of Cartesian philosophy, and to produce three schools which, instead of losing themselves in external and objective investigations, began from a relatively severe and profound examination of the human mind and its faculties.[9] It belonged to the greatest philosopher of the previous century to indicate the character of modern philosophy in the very title of his own work: Kant's system is called a *critique*. The two other European schools—one prior to and one contemporaneous with [Kant]—Locke's school and Reid's school, both sit decisively below Kant's school: because of their leaders' inferior genius and their inferior doctrines. Both of them—although in very different ways—approximate[10] to Kant's [school] in both their principles and their consequences, and relate to each other through their spirit of critique and analysis, for which they are to be praised. Even if Reid's analysis is stronger and more extensive than Locke's, it should not be forgotten that it was able to be so illuminating and rich on the basis of the insights which the works and writings in Locke's system provided, and one must guard against being unjust to Locke, who will always be regarded as one of the most reasonable philosophers there has been, and[11] to Descartes, the founder of modern philosophy.[12]

However, as much as these three major European schools are linked together by the general spirit which animates them, so too they differ in their positive principles; and the reason for this difference is the particular viewpoint by which each of them considered philosophy. Having reduced all philosophical questions to three major questions—for the object, the question of the absolute and of the reality of existences; for the subject, that of the actual and the primitive—the weakness of the human mind, from which not even the strongest minds are exempt, did not permit Locke, Reid or Kant to give their attention equally to these three questions, but to concentrate on one alone. Locke, Reid, and Kant all took up a different question, such that, by a quite strange destiny, each of the three major questions which divides up metaphysics became the special object and exclusive possession of each of the three major schools of the eighteenth century. Locke's school aspired to the origins of knowledge; the Scottish school investigated the current characteristics of human knowledge in a developed intellect; and Kant's school was occupied above all with the legitimacy of the transition from subject to object. I do not mean that each of these schools was concerned with one problem alone; I mean that each of them occupied themselves more particularly with a specific problem and that the manner in which they resolved this problem eminently characterizes [their philosophy]. Everyone agrees that Locke was profoundly ignorant of[13] the current characteristics of human knowledge; Reid does not conceal that the question of their origin has very[14] little importance for him; and Kant is content to indicate generally the source of human knowledge without investigating the specific origin of each intellectual principle—that is, each of the famous categories he establishes.[15] Moreover, it seems to me that by following this parallel division of questions and philosophical schools, we could envisage the history of philosophy under a new aspect: within the three major modern schools one could study and develop the three major philosophical questions—each of these three schools, limited and incomplete in itself, could be expanded and enlarged by its proximity to the two others. Opposed, they reveal to us their relative imperfections; brought together, they would each supply to the others what they lack.

I propose to provide the reader with such an interesting and instructive spectacle; I will show the vices of these modern schools by putting them into battle against each other; I will collect their different merits in the centre of a vast eclecticism which will contain and complete all three of them: we will see them pass before our eyes in turn and regulate each other reciprocally. The Scottish school will demonstrate to us the vices of Locke's school; I will use the spirit of Locke's school to interrogate the Scottish school on the questions it neglected; and examination of Kant's system will introduce us into the depths of a problem which escaped the other two—such that, at the conclusion of these articles, we will perhaps know quite profoundly: 1° the genuine philosophical problems; 2° the manner in which Locke, Reid, and Kant treated them; 3° the relative imperfections of each of their systems; 4° the vices and merits of Buhle's[16] analyses.[17]

Notes

1. First published in *Archives philosophiques, politiques et littéraires*, vol. 1 (1817), pp. 200–12 in the guise of a continuation of Cousin's review of the Göttingen Professor, J. G. Buhle's, *History of Modern Philosophy*—see note 9 below (subsequently with the above title: *Fr. phil. 1826*, pp. 295–311: *Fr. phil. 1833*, pp. 313–28; *Fr. phil. 1838*, vol. 1, pp. 319–33). We take the 1817 publication as our base text for this translation and note the significant modifications to later versions in the endnotes. The text is a schematic summary of the inaugural lecture of Cousin's 1817 course given on 5 December 1816. A translation of the 1833 version of the text exists in George Ripley's *Philosophical Miscellanies* (Boston: Hilliard and Gray, 1838), pp. 171–85.
2. *Fr. phil. 1826* and subsequent editions: "and powerful" is omitted.
3. *Fr. phil. 1826* and subsequent editions: "in large, clear categories" is omitted.
4. *Fr. phil. 1826* and subsequent editions: "and even necessary" is omitted.
5. *Fr. phil. 1833* and subsequent editions: "or, more concisely, problems of the *subject* and problems of the *object*" is omitted.
6. *Fr. phil. 1826* and subsequent editions: this footnote is omitted. The note is almost certainly Cousin's own: he co-edited the philosophy material in the journal with P. P. Royer Collard and this (and the subsequent notes) could well be explanations to passages that Royer Collard himself found obscure while preparing the text for publication. Cousin's use of "phenomenology" should be placed in the context of Cousin's first meeting with Hegel in 1817, when he began reading the recently published *Encyclopedia of Philosophical Sciences*, although this passage could precede Cousin's familiarity with Hegel.
7. *Fr. phil. 1826* and subsequent editions: this footnote is omitted. See previous note—again, this note is almost certainly Cousin's own.
8. *Fr. phil. 1826* and subsequent editions: "schools and by those of Alexandria" replaced with "philosophers."
9. This is a very different picture of the relation between Descartes and the eighteenth century than what emerges in Cousin's later work—see e.g. pp. 251–2 below.

10. *Fr. phil. 1833* and subsequent editions: "approximate" is replaced with "are to be linked to."
11. *Fr. phil. 1826* and subsequent editions: "and" replaced with "nor above all."
12. *Fr. phil. 1833* and subsequent editions: the passage from "Even if Reid's analysis…" to the end of the paragraph is omitted.
13. *Fr. phil. 1826* and subsequent editions: "was profoundly ignorant of" replaced with "misrecognized many of."
14. *Fr. phil. 1826* and subsequent editions: "very" replaced with "somewhat."
15. *Fr. phil. 1833* and subsequent editions: "and whose scope he measures" is added to the end of the sentence.
16. The original 1817 article is framed in its title as a continuation of Cousin's review of the 6-vol. *Geschichte der neuern Philosophie seit der Epoche der Wiederherstellung der Wissenschaften* by Johann Gottlieb Buhle (1763–1821), which had been partially translated into French. The final sentence makes a gesture back to this original framing. The first part of the review is separately republished in *Fr. phil. 1826*, pp. 62–72. The reference to "these articles" (and the use of the future tense) is to the further lecture-extracts Cousin planned to publish (and for the most part did publish) in the subsequent issues of *Archives philosophiques, politiques et littéraires*.
17. *Fr. phil. 1826*: the concluding paragraph replaced with the following: "It would be an interesting and instructive spectacle to ascertain the vices of the modern schools by putting them into battle against each other, and to collect their different merits within a vast eclecticism which would contain and complete all three of them. Scottish philosophy would demonstrate to us the vices of Locke's philosophy; Locke would be used to interrogate Reid on the questions he neglected; and the examination of Kant's system would introduce us into the depths of a problem which escaped both the other schools." *Fr. phil. 1833* and subsequent editions: "spectacle" replaced with "study."

On the Fact of Consciousness[1]

Philosophy exists ready-made, for man's thinking is [already] present.

There is not and cannot be an absolutely false philosophy; for the author of such a philosophy would need to place themselves outside of their own thinking—that is, outside of humanity. This ability has not been given to any human being.

What then can error in philosophy be? It is to consider just one side of thought, and to see it completely from this perspective. There are no false systems, just many incomplete systems, true in themselves but wrong in each of their claims to possess the absolute truth, which is [instead] only to be found in all of them.

The incomplete and therefore the exclusive—this is philosophy's unique vice;[2] in fact, it would be better to speak here of philosophers; for philosophy is what overcomes all [incomplete] systems.[3] A friend to reality, [philosophy] constitutes the total description of traits borrowed from each system. Each system contains reality within itself;[4] but unfortunately, it reflects it from one angle alone.

To grasp reality as a whole, one must remain at its centre. To establish the intellectual life that has been mutilated by each system, one must return into consciousness without an exclusive and systematic mind, analyse thinking into its elements and into all of its elements, and there investigate the characteristics—and all of the characteristics—by which it now manifests itself to consciousness's gaze.

Moreover, when I descend into consciousness and there peaceably contemplate my intellectual life, I am irresistibly struck by the immediate perception[5] of three elements—three elements I say, no more, no less—which are encountered always and in every [mind]. They are simultaneous, but still distinct; they constitute thought in its necessary complexity, but destroy it whenever one of them becomes faulty. Thought is an intellectual fact in three parts, which all perish together at the slightest neglect of one of them. The three parts of this fact are the object of thought, the subject of thought and the form of thought. But let us leave behind these logical expressions, even if they are able to precisely capture the triplicity of consciousness; and let us [instead] discover them by analysis.[6]

The one [element] I know best—that is, most immediately—is myself, my personality, my individuality.[7] In every intellectual fact, in every thought, in all knowledge, I perceive myself as the subject of this fact, as the subject of thought or knowledge, as the constitutive and fundamental element of consciousness; for without me, everything becomes for me as if it were not; without the I, the I knows nothing, senses nothing, recalls nothing, abstracts nothing, combines nothing, reasons about nothing. There could still exist the material of a thought, of a sensation, of a judgement, of a memory, of reasoning; but, if the I did not exist, then it would know nothing of them and could know nothing of them. The I is therefore the necessary element of all thinking.

It will be said that the I is thinking itself, that is, sensation, judgement, etc., reunited in a collective unity dubbed the self. But I sense and I know—*certissima scientia et clamante conscientia*[8]—that, although thought, memory, sensation do not exist without the I,[9] the I is not solely a logical and verbal link invented to express the unity of my thoughts, but something real which unites them and out of them forms an interconnected chain, insofar as it exists within each of them. Even more so, I sense and I know that the I is not some circumstance, some degree of a particular thought, that it is not the verbal link between many thoughts. I know it to be false that sensation or memory, or desire—at any degree of vividness—constitutes the I, for it is I who constitute sensation or desire by means of adding myself onto a specific movement, onto a specific sensible affection which would [otherwise] be solely intellectual, as it were, and which becomes sensation or desire for me solely insofar as I am conscious of it.

I further know that there are two notable circumstances in which the I is manifest: spontaneity or reflection.[10] In order for it to appear before me, it must act; its action is the necessary condition of its being perceived, but this action is either spontaneous, that is,[11] accomplished straightaway without the I anticipating its outcome or consenting to it; or it is reflective, that is,[12] accomplished because the I does consent to it and know of its consequences.[13] Spontaneous action and reflective or voluntary action are the two internal actions which consciousness makes known to me; we cannot neglect either one of these actions, without mutilating one of the two parts of this internal force which is the I. The I is the appearance of mind to itself by way of its redoubled activity within itself and its return into itself—that is, into consciousness. Consciousness is not a special[14] faculty which stands on one side perceiving what is occurring on the other; there is no separate stage on which the events of our intellectual life pass by, and, when it comes to someone sitting in the stalls watching on, the stalls are in fact on the stage: consciousness of life is life itself, for there is genuine life only insofar as it manifests and perceives itself. Hence, as consciousness is the I itself and as this I is the very activity of the mind and this activity operates either spontaneously or reflectively, consciousness is either spontaneous or reflective.[15] The latter is eminently free; every free act is a reflective act.[16] Spontaneity is not blind, nor fatal—it is just not preceded by reflection. In practice, the I is a continuous force, one which tends to [undergo] the most significant developments,[17] sometimes proceeding directly outwards and sometimes returning into itself, and this [return] constitutes a new starting point, a fulcrum for its further development. Life is an action, and life is really ours only insofar as such an action belongs to us and we appropriate it for ourselves through freedom. Freedom is the highest degree of life, and freedom belongs solely to reflection, for there is no freedom without choice, without comparison and deliberation—that is, without reflection.[18] As mother of freedom and daughter of freedom, reflection is a free act which produces free acts. In the midst of the spontaneous activity of the I and of the other activity I have yet to describe which does not come from the I but which attempts, on the contrary, to act upon it and envelop it in its determined activity—in the midst of this world of forces which struggle against it and which always go ahead of it,[19] reflection stops itself and, according to a famous expression, posits itself. Reflection or the free I is a point of inhibition within the infinite. Fichte calls it a check[20] within infinite activity. The I, this great man says, posits itself in a free determination—this perspective is one of reflection: the I posits itself because it desires to, and so it owes its own existence entirely to itself, to its free determination. The determination which accompanies and characterizes reflection is a determination preceded by or mixed with a negation. In order to posit the I, as Fichte puts it, I must explicitly distinguish it from the not-I; and all distinction implies a limitation, a negation.[21] But is it true that we have begun with a negation? And is there nothing prior to reflection and the fact, as in that description with which Fichte's name will forever be associated? All our investigations of ourselves are reflective, and our fate is to seek the spontaneous point of view by means of reflection, and so to destroy it in the very act of seeking it. However, by examining oneself in peace, it is not impossible to grasp spontaneity in reflective form. In the very moment of reflection, we sense under this activity which returns into itself an activity which has to first occur without reflection. This is fatal to psychology, but inevitable! all primitive judgement is positive; everything primitive in the I is spontaneous,[22] and even though the primitive action is redoubled in consciousness, it is redoubled in it weakly and obscurely; and, if we wish to cast light on these shadows, to convert obscure consciousness into clear and distinct consciousness, we can only do so by means of reflection—that is, from a distinct viewpoint and from judgements mixed with negation. In other words, to repeat, we can clarify the spontaneous point of view only by destroying it. What we need to sense [so as to perceive spontaneity] is the activity of the I without any external impulse; acting by itself without being commanded to act; not yet determining itself, but determining its acts and thoughts; finding itself without being sought after; perceiving itself without positing itself—in a word, as spontaneous, but not voluntary and free. Spontaneity redoubled in itself is natural consciousness; positive, immediate, and pure consciousness. Freedom redoubled in itself is reflection or mediate, negative, and distinct perception. Such are the two forms of the I in which it is continuously reproduced.[23]

The I is the element of all knowledge; but knowledge does not rest uniquely on the I, even if we must repeat with Fichte that it is but a development of the I. When one withdraws into one's consciousness, there is inevitably to be found an element opposed to the I, an order of phenomena[24] which the I has not made itself and which introduces into the internal world of consciousness the external manifold [these phenomena] represent. I am speaking of sensation, which would not exist without an I to perceive it, but which, no less, is no daughter of the I, but of the external world. I will explain.

It is certain that the I has knowledge of certain phenomena which belong to it, which it constitutes, which it posits itself: volitions, determinations of the I, are the object of the I in consciousness; and these are sensations which are dubbed voluntary, because they are the product of human freedom in its self-affection. Here the object is not distinct from the subject, the not-I from the I, the multiple from the individual.[25] But not only does consciousness create, it encounters. The I is distinguished from two very different phenomena: the phenomena it produces and those it does not produce and that it only perceives. The I is not to be confused with any phenomenon; it existence is its individuality, that is, its indivisibility, and this is what one must understand by its immateriality. The determinations of the I, although they are the effects of the I itself, are distinct from it; it relates itself to them by distinguishing itself from them; but there is another kind of distinction which can be confused with this—that is, the distinction that the I recognizes between itself and its involuntary affections.[26] In this instance, the not-I appears to the I not only as distinct, but as foreign; it is no longer the I which posits the not-I, nor does the not-I posit the I (since the I is only ever posited by itself); rather, the not-I posits, determinates, causes an affection of the I. The affectivity of the I consists not in being determined by the not-I, but in what it perceives as modifications of [the not-I], determined by an external cause. This difference between action and affectivity comes to light and is manifest in sensation.[27] When someone squeezes my arm, the I perceives the experienced sensation as an effect independent from it and from its determination—this alone is the passivity of the I. Properly speaking, the I is never passive,[28] for it knows itself solely to the extent that it perceives itself, and to perceive is already to act. What is more, the I continuously acts insofar as it is: we act and we will, even in sensation. Sensation is not an act of the I, but sensation is sensed and so is sensation only because, when coming to know it, the I is already constituted, is already posited:[29] it is [sensation] only through action and volition. If the I were passive, there would have to be another active I to come to know the passion of the first I; there would be two Is, and this is absurd. The I is an indivisible being, and its indivisibility is equally that of its will and its activity. However, in the midst of this continuous activity there appear external affections which the I perceives involuntarily—[affections] to which [the I] is forced to submit, it is true, but within which it still acts and wills, since it judges them, evaluates them, distinguishes itself from them, resists them or surrenders to them, and even, by surrendering to them, determines the extent to which it desires to surrender to them. Each affection does not extinguish freedom, but limits it, depending on whether [the affection] is more or less vivid. When an affection which is too violent and too vast overwhelms freedom, the I disappears; there is what is called atrophy. There is no longer perception, not even of the not-I; for there is no longer the I.[30] And yet, [in this instance] it is not the not-I which is lacking for perception [to take place], but rather the internal force by which the I constitutes itself and so is able to perceive. There is no longer any pleasure or pain, because there is no longer perception—a degradation whose beginning is already a beginning of the weakening of freedom.[31] This is the privilege and grandeur of freedom! Whenever it is missing, the intellect is extinguished, and, whenever the intellect dies, there too expires sensibility. I am not saying that knowledge is free; rather, I mean that only a free being can know. Likewise, I am not confusing intellect with sensibility; rather, I am claiming that one must be intelligent in order to sense, since—to speak rigorously—to not know that one senses is not to sense.

Let me summarize. The I is free—it is [free] in its ground; and on this ground are sketched a thousand varied scenes which freedom manifests. The I distinguishes itself from its acts; this is a not-I that is posited by the I.[32] However, there is also an order of involuntary phenomena which limit the freedom of man, struggle against it and sometimes overcome it—this is the genuine not-I, which the I does not oppose to itself, i.e. does not itself posit, as Fichte claimed,[33] but which the I discovers opposed to itself. The relation of the I and the not-I is a reciprocal relation of opposition; it is a genuine fight. Moreover, since the I fights at the same time as it is fought, and since, as soon as it ceases to fight, it ceases to be, and since this fight is the necessary condition for the I to know that it is being fought against; then it follows that passivity presupposes freedom and a state of pure passivity can never exist within consciousness. The opposition of the I and the not-I constitutes consciousness; consciousness is the theatre of this perpetual combat of the intellectual and moral life, just as physiological life is nothing but the struggle of internal force, of the vital principle, against external forces or the principles of destruction. Health is the victory of the internal force; its defeats are diseases; its flight and its destruction are death. Our physical constitution is such that the vital principle or the internal force—which stands alone against all the other forces—is soon exhausted in its resistance; and, after having survived the fight for a time that is different [for each of us] but which is always short and composed of more defeats than victories, the body succumbs and abandons itself to all the enemy forces which invade it, divide it up, decompose it, and resubmit it to the laws of universal nature of which they are the agents. If we turn from the physical world to the moral world, we will discover that here external nature attacks the I in a thousand increasingly redoubtable ways, by the self's own body, by its pains, above all by its joys, by all its passions, offspring of circumstance which encompasses us and the whole universe which overwhelms us.[34] To defend itself, the I can rely only on itself, much like Medea. However, the I is intelligent and free: because it is free, it can always fight; because it is endowed with a limited freedom, a relatively powerful freedom, it can be beaten, but can still always resist; and even when it is beaten, it knows that it is not destroyed and can fight on. Whether one is beaten or not does not depend on that [organic] vital principle, which others have wished to confuse with the I; it depends on the being's I; above all, whether one surrenders or continues the fight, when it cannot be finished off in victory, depends on [the I] too. But, in all of this, I see only the combat of two phenomena, I see only this constant and primitive duality which consciousness always perceives. Is there anything else in consciousness?*

Notes

1. *Fr. phil. 1826*, pp. 214–27 (subsequently: *Fr. phil. 1833*, pp. 242–52; *Fr. phil. 1838*, vol. 1, pp. 248–58). We take the 1826 publication as our base text for this translation and note the significant modifications to later versions in the endnotes. This text is a fragment extracted from Cousin's 1817 lecture course. It is one of Cousin's fullest discussions of the relation of the activity of the I to sensation, and, significantly, is one of the texts most edited over the course of the 1820s and 1830s, as Cousin refines his views.
2. *Fr. phil. 1838*: "unique vice" replaced with "error."
3. That is, philosophers have tended to write systems (which manifest this vice), as opposed to *genuine* philosophy (which is eclectic).
4. *Fr. phil. 1833* and subsequent editions: "contains reality within itself" replaced with "reflects reality."
5. It should be remembered that, throughout, Cousin uses the slightly more technical "l'aperception" for what is here translated 'perception'—see the note on the translation above for more details.
6. *Fr. phil. 1833* and subsequent editions: the passage from "Thought is an intellectual fact …" to the end of the paragraph replaced with "Let me separate out these three elements analytically."
7. *Fr. phil. 1833* and subsequent editions: "my personality, my individuality" is omitted.
8. i.e. "by way of sure knowledge and the cry of conscience." This is an Augustinian phrase which is later used, inter alia, by Arnauld in dispute with Descartes and by Maine de Biran.
9. *Fr. phil. 1833* and subsequent editions: this clause is omitted.
10. *Fr. phil. 1833* and subsequent editions: this sentence is altered to read: "The I is manifest in two notable instances."
11. *Fr. phil. 1833* and subsequent editions: "spontaneous, that is," is omitted.
12. *Fr. phil. 1833* and subsequent editions: "reflective, that is," is omitted.
13. The oddness and unsettling effects of the splitting of the self in Cousin's language is deliberate and anticipates what he is about to claim about the self-division of the I into two operations.
14. *Fr. phil. 1833* and subsequent editions: "special" is omitted.
15. *Fr. phil. 1833* and subsequent editions: this sentence is omitted.
16. *Fr. phil. 1833* and subsequent editions: "every free act is a reflective act" is omitted.

---

* It is here that should be added the analysis of reason as distinct from sensation and from will, which are merely external and internal conditions of perceptions, whereas reason is its direct ground. Reason constitutes knowing in itself and, since there is knowing in every act of consciousness (*conscientia seu scientia cum*), it follows that reason constitutes consciousness itself, and that it is from [reason] that consciousness borrows all illumination. Reason thus constitutes consciousness and, what is more, besides the possibility of all knowledge, particularly knowledge of the I, of the not-I and of their relation, it brings to consciousness a new, sui generis knowledge—the knowledge or conception of the infinite, of substance, of being, of absolute thought, the source and principle of all existence and all thought. On this important point, see the programme of the 1818 lectures. Moreover, when reunited, these three elements of thought compose the whole of philosophy, which cannot avoid any of them. Nonetheless, philosophers have constantly mutilated one or other element, endlessly reducing either substance and the I to the not-I—erected as a unique and fundamental fact—or substance and the not-I to the I, transformed into an absolute I (as if these two words were not incompatible) or finally the not-I and the I to substance, which thus becomes a completely abstract substance, a substance which is not a cause, but a sterile abyss within which everything is engulfed, and from which nothing can escape, eternity without time, space without dimension, the infinite without form, absolute force which cannot even pass into act, power without energy, unity without number, existence without reality.[35]

17. *Fr. phil. 1833* and subsequent editions: this clause is omitted.
18. This article (and the next extract below) proposes a noticeably different concept of freedom from what is later found in the 1826 Preface (see pp. 73–4 above).
19. *Fr. phil. 1833* and subsequent editions: "always go ahead of it" replaced with "pull it along."
20. A reference to Fichte's concept of the *Anstoß*, the point of inhibition in the activity of the I out of which a feeling of the not-I is produced.
21. See, for example, Fichte's claim: "Nothing is known regarding what something is without the thought of what it is not" (discussed in M. Frank, *The Philosophical Foundations of Early German Romanticism*, trans. E. Millán-Zaibert [Albany: SUNY Press, 2004], p. 87).
22. *Fr. phil. 1833* and subsequent editions: "all primitive judgement is positive; everything primitive in the I is spontaneous" is omitted.
23. *Fr. phil. 1833* and subsequent editions: this final sentence of the paragraph is omitted and replaced by "*Hic labor.*" i.e. "this is the hard work to be done," from the maxim "hic opus, hic labor est" in Virgil's *Aeneid*.
24. *Fr. phil. 1833* and subsequent editions: "an element opposed to the I, an order of phenomena" replaced with "an element different from the I, and phenomena."
25. *Fr. phil. 1833* and subsequent editions: "the not-I from the I, the multiple from the individual" replaced with "since the not-I is an effect of the I."
26. *Fr. phil. 1833* and subsequent editions: the passage from "But not only does consciousness …" to "… its involuntary affections" replaced with: "In this instance, there is certainly a contrast within consciousness, but there is no opposition, for this contrast is established by the I itself, and such diversity is just a difference in the exercise of individual unity. However, in addition to the I producing these [voluntary] phenomena, it comes to recognize that it has not made its involuntary affections, for example."
27. *Fr. phil. 1833* and subsequent editions: the passage from "The affectivity of the I …" to "… manifest in sensation" is omitted.
28. *Fr. phil. 1833* and subsequent editions: "or, at least, never knowingly passive" is added.
29. *Fr. phil. 1833* and subsequent editions: "is already posited" is omitted.
30. *Fr. phil. 1833* and subsequent editions: the passage from "… the I disappears …" to "… no longer the I" replaced with: "there is no longer perception of the I, nor even of the not-I, for there is no longer an I and so no possible perception."
31. *Fr. phil. 1833* and subsequent editions: "a degradation whose beginning is already a beginning to the weakening of freedom" is omitted.
32. *Fr. phil. 1833* and subsequent editions: this sentence is omitted.
33. See e.g. Fichte, *Science of Knowledge*, "Every opposite so far as it is so, is so absolutely, by virtue of an act of the I, and for no other reason. Opposition in general is posited absolutely by the I." Ed. and trans. P. Heath and J. Lachs (Cambridge: Cambridge University, 1982), p. 103.
34. *Fr. phil. 1833* and subsequent editions: "which encompasses us and the whole universe which overwhelms us" replaced with "and this vast, encompassing universe."
35. It is not clear when this footnote was written; it is most likely, however, to be an indication of the subsequent progress of the argument in the 1817 lectures. The three errors noted here correspond to materialism, Fichtean idealism and Spinozism. The programme of the 1818 lectures to which Cousin here refers is from *Frag. ph. 1826*, pp. 263–94; this reference to the 1818 programme is omitted from the 1833 and subsequent versions of the text.

On the Clear and the Obscure in Knowledge, or On Spontaneity and Reflection[1]

Human knowledge* can be considered according to either its origin and primitive character, or its development and current character.

I claim that all primitive knowledge is spontaneous, and all developed knowledge reflective.

From this it follows that all primitive knowledge is positive, indistinct, obscure, and all developed knowledge is negative, distinct, and clear.

From this it further follows that the latter is the starting point and the former the foundation of philosophy; for, if philosophy desires to avoid abjuring itself, it should begin from reflection, so as to start off in the light; and if philosophy wishes to rest on something, it should presuppose this foundation for itself in a necessarily obscure fact—that is, one that is prior to all reflection.

What then is this primitive fact, hidden in the shadows which surround the cradle of thought?

And first of all, what is reflection and what does it contain?

Reflection is free thought: it interrupts the natural movement by which [thought] develops in a straight line, so to speak, and folds back on itself into the very interior of thought which it goes on to perceive precisely, because it considers [this interiority] in distinct fashion—that is, divided into two parts: thought as it folds back on itself and contemplates itself and thought as contemplated.

Thought which contemplates is the subject of reflection; the thought that is contemplated is its object.

Hence, [there is] no reflection without a subject or an object; and from this [follows] the axiom: no object without subject and no subject without object.

---

* The objective of this article is to combat Fichte's doctrine, which, beginning from the free *I*, or from reflection, and only ever employing the reflective element, has constructed an admirable system as a monument to his art, but one which lacks reality and foundation. To combat Fichte, the author has positioned himself on [Fichte's] terrain, borrowed his language and scientific forms; he has followed him step by step, opposing him principle by principle, consequent by consequent, result by result. However, although there is not a single line in this article which does not address one of Fichte's ideas, either directly or indirectly, the author hopes that it will be understood by all those who, without knowledge of German philosophy, have meditated on the major problems of the foundation and starting point of all philosophy. It is for them and them alone that he has written it.[2]

In reflection, subject and object are distinct from each other, because they are opposed to each other.

The subject distinguishes itself from the object only by opposing itself to it; that is, only by affirming itself and negating itself at the same time.

The subject affirms itself, posits itself, and says I or me; but, at the same time as it posits itself, it opposes itself to the object, which, in its opposition to the subject-*I*, is called the *not-I*. The subject thus posits itself only by opposing itself to something, and it opposes itself to something only by positing itself.

The *I* negates itself by affirming the *not-I*; it negates the *not-I* by affirming itself, and it is to this reciprocal negation that we owe the light which illuminates the reflective act.

The *I* and the *not-I* are given to us simultaneously and distinctly in an opposition, in a reciprocal limitation.

The two terms of this opposition are two phenomena which come to appearance and then slip out [of appearance] in turn.

Phenomenon, relative, variable, contingent, finite—all of these are synonymous expressions.

Moreover, at the same time as we perceive the phenomenon, the relative, the variable, the finite, we conceive and cannot not conceive its contrary—the infinite, the immutable, the eternal. And from this [follows] the axiom: no infinity without the finite, no finitude without the infinite.

The infinite, in relation to the finite, is absolute being, the immobile theatre of this restless phenomenon, of this struggle between the *I* and the *not-I* called life.

The *I* is individuality; the *not-I* is multiplicity or plurality; being is absolute unity.

The infinite—being *par excellence*, absolute unity—contains in its breast the *I* and the *not-I*, the primitive duality, and through its reflection in this [duality] [the infinite] communicates the unity which makes it possible: unity of consciousness which becomes unity of knowledge, which because the unity of the proposition.

Now, since, in the highest developments of human science, we never pass beyond the limits of the finite and the infinite, of the phenomenon and being, it follows that all subsequent developments of human science are already contained in the first act of reflection. However, the first reflective act is not the primitive fact.

That the reflective viewpoint presupposes a prior viewpoint is sufficiently demonstrated by the nature of reflection and logic; reflection is an essentially regressive operation; we do not begin from reflection, for to reflect is to distinguish, and to distinguish is to negate; in order to negate, one must have affirmed; hence, all negative, distinguishing, reflective judgement presupposes a prior affirmative, positive, composite, and indistinct judgement.

Reflection or freedom is without doubt the highest degree of intellectual life; free reflection constitutes our only genuine personal existence; it is only by free reflection that we belong to ourselves, for it is by it alone that we posit ourselves.

But, before positing ourselves, we discover ourselves; before willing to perceive, we perceive; before acting freely, we act spontaneously. Free action presupposes a relatively accurate knowledge of the desired result. In such a case, freedom cannot be the primitive fact.

The word *freedom* can be taken in two different senses. A free act can be attributed to [the act] which a being produces because he willed to produce it, because, when initially representing it to himself and knowing by experience that he can produce [the act], he happily exercises his will in relation to the preconceived act—that is, [exercises] the productive power with which he knows himself to be endowed. Such is freedom properly speaking or the will.

A being is also called *free*, when the principle of his acts is within himself and not in another being, when the act he produces is the expression of his own force which acts solely by its own laws. For example, when an external force pushes my arm without my knowledge or despite myself, my arm's movement does not belong to me; and even if one were to call this movement an *act*, it is certainly not a *free act*. My arm's movement here falls under the laws of external mechanics: it is not by my own individual laws that I act, it is not me who acts; it is the universe who acts by way of me. But, when on the occasion of an organic affection, the mind immediately enters into action by means of its native energy, and produces some act, I can say that the mind is free insofar as the organic affection is the external occasion and not the principle of its action, whose ground is [instead] the natural power of the mind. It is in this sense, and not in the other one, that every action of the mind can be called *free*. However, if, confounding the two senses of the word *freedom* and thus confounding two very distinct facts, it is maintained that the mind is always free with a reflective freedom, then, since reflection necessarily presupposes a prior operation, this [prior] operation must [itself] be either reflective or not reflective; if it is not [reflective], then this is the non-reflective act that one wished to avoid;[3] and if it is reflective, then it presupposes another operation, which, if assumed to be itself reflective, presupposes yet another, always reflective [operation]—and there we have an insoluble circle, passing from reflections to reflections, grounding reflection on itself—that is, leaving it afloat without any foundation.

The ground and the nature of things thus demonstrate the necessity of presupposing a prior operation for reflection that is different from it, and this operation is what I call *spontaneity*.

This is further—and very importantly—demonstrated by the fact that reflection, as a regressive operation, sheds light on what is prior to it; it develops it, but does not create it; and therefore everything that appears from the reflective viewpoint pre-exists [this reflective viewpoint] when enveloped in the *spontaneous* viewpoint.

However, these are merely logical inferences. What is this *spontaneous* viewpoint? How is it to be grasped and described? If we try to grasp it, it escapes us, for then we are reflecting—that is, we are destroying it. The trap is inevitable; all precautions are in vain, because they are intended for the will and reflection, which are precisely what are to be discarded. How express a spontaneous viewpoint in languages, when all the terms of [language] are fully determinate, that is, profoundly reflective?

As I see it, we can grasp the spontaneous viewpoint only by catching it, as it were, in the act, from the reflective point of view, at the dawn of reflection, at the almost indivisible moment when the primitive gives way to the present, when spontaneity expires in reflection. Not being able to consider spontaneity fully and just as we might like, we must grasp it with a rapid glance and, so to speak, in profile during those acts of ordinary life which are naturally redoubled in consciousness and can be perceived without seeking them out to perceive them. It is this natural consciousness which must be surprised in itself and faithfully described. Moreover, I think that primitive consciousness presents the same elements, the same facts as reflection, with the sole difference that in the latter [case] they are precise and distinct and in the former [case] they are obscure and indeterminate.

Hence, primitive consciousness perceives the *I* and the *not-I*, without being able to say that they are two phenomena and two correlative phenomena. It does not grasp them in the opposition which necessarily limits them, but it perceives them together and naturally limiting each other. As for *infinite being*, primitive consciousness does not manifest to us the action of reflective reason which posits [being] as infinite, absolute, necessary; but it does manifest to us the spontaneous action of reason which perceives [being] immediately in a pure and simple perception, without recognizing any of its limits, and which remains with [this perception] without seeking or conceiving anything beyond [it]. The primitive fact explicitly contains no idea of the *limited* and the *unlimited*, of the *relative* and the *absolute*, of the *finite* and the *infinite*, but it implicitly contains all of this in its confused perceptions which reflection later comes to clarify and convert into distinct and necessary truths. Whereas natural consciousness had vaguely perceived natural limits, reflection posits essential limits; whereas primitive reason remains in itself without perceiving any limits, developed reason affirms that there are no possible limits, and it does so with the assistance of its subsequent doubled clarity, expanded across phenomena and being, which was formed out of its distinct ideas of the finite and the infinite, the relative and the absolute, and which confusedly pre-existed [this affirmation] in the first fact [of consciousness]. The more reflection is applied to this first fact, the more the facts that it contains are clarified, the more the intellect grows, the more the limits of human knowledge recede before the freedom of man. The primitive fact, which offered only the obscure composite [perception] of the I, the non-I and being, breaks apart—and is clarified through this process of breaking up—in reflection, which then precisely distinguishes the I and the not-I, the multiple and the individual, and opposes each of them clearly within the unique being that explains and contains them both. Once more, it is reflection which, by determining with increasing precision the intrinsic properties of the I and the not-I, as well as their relative qualities or their relations, determines with increasing precision the relation between phenomena and being—that is, [it determines] the qualities of being with respect to the phenomenon. It is [reflection] which, by discovering in turn the various characteristics of the I and the not-I, of man and of nature—all captured in the general character of the finite and the contingent—reveals to us in the necessary opposition between being and phenomenon the diverse characteristics of being, and captures them in the general categories of the necessary and the infinite. This is a fruitful and profound distinction which necessarily divides up all human knowledge into two classes: knowledge relative to the finite and knowledge relative to the infinite, contingent principles and absolute principles. Aristotle and Kant, the two most methodical minds of antiquity and modernity, exhausted their genius in the inventory and classification of the elements of thought: Aristotle could scarcely subdivide them and so did not articulate the true demarcation which distinguishes them; Kant was more successful and divided all ideas into two principal classes: contingent ideas and necessary ideas; but he still often placed what belongs in the contingent [class] in the necessary [class], and could not lead either contingent principles or necessary principles back to their primitive elements. The theory I have outlined completes Kant's by reducing his voluminous categories to their elementary number—a simplification which has not been attempted until now and which had left a great lacuna in science. Contingent and necessary principles are, I contend, just principles relative to the phenomenon and those relative to being. Moreover, since the phenomenon is doubled and is grasped by us in its duality only through the opposition of the I and the not-I—manifest in the latter instance by blind action and in the former case by voluntary action, but always by some action—then it follows that the character of the phenomenon is activity, causality; and all contingent principles can be reduced to [the principle] of causality with its diverse nuances which encompass the whole of the finite world. On the other hand, since being is given to us in its opposition to the phenomenon of which it is the substance, and since all its characteristics are solely the expression of [substance], and since all necessary principles are merely different points of view on the necessary and the infinite (which itself is being), it follows that all necessary principles can be reduced to the principle of substance. The principle of causality and that of substance are therefore the two primary principles—the former of contingent principles and the latter of necessary principles. The principle of causality makes contact with the necessary principles, but it is not itself a necessary principle; it[4] reigns over phenomena; it governs contingent and finite natures, but it stops before the necessary and infinite being, before that which exists by itself.[5] It cannot attain substance, that is, that beyond which it is impossible to conceive anything existent. The ideas of substance and cause are the two fundamental ideas on which the whole of philosophy turns. Inquiries into their nature, their origin and their certainty constitute the entirety of philosophy. The principal philosophical question is knowing whether the human mind should begin with one or the other of them. I claim that the human mind should begin with both of them. In the first reflective act, the phenomenon and being, the finite and the infinite, the relative and the absolute, are already present. To posit one without the other is to abstract from one of the two integral parts of thought; to posit phenomena without substance or substance without phenomena is to separate out immediate intuition from reason. Internal and external intuition perceive the I and the not-I, the phenomenon, the finite, cause; reason reveals being, the infinite, substance—and it is their simultaneous action which constitutes the intellect. Reflection distinguishes between the various parts of what appears simultaneously, and, in so distinguishing between them, places them into opposition. Nevertheless, however distinct they might be, they are still simultaneous: they are so in that first reflective act which contains the ideas of the finite and the infinite, of cause and substance, even if it opposes them. Furthermore, there is nothing in reflection that does not already exist in spontaneity. Hence—an admirable thing—the two ideas which are the unsurpassable limits of thought are found together at its origin and, so to speak, in its cradle. Man begins with what he finishes and finishes with what he begins; he develops and he applies, he abstracts and he combines, with an insuperable inability to add one sole element to those which are given in the very first fact [of consciousness], in that obscure and composite fact which he spends his life developing and clarifying. Life is a perpetual transition, a tendency from obscurity to clarity; and human science, in all its extensity, is merely a circle whose two extremities are two basically similar points.

Notes

1. First published in *Archives Philosophiques, Politiques et Littéraires*, vol. 2 (1817), pp. 330–40 (subsequently: *Fr. phil. 1826*, pp. 337–50; *Fr. phil. 1833*, pp. 351–61; *Fr. phil. 1838*, vol. 1, pp. 354–64). From 1826 onwards, it is given a different title, "On the First and the Last Fact of Consciousness, or On Spontaneity and Reflection" (although typically referred to as "On Spontaneity and Reflection"). We take the 1817 publication as our base text for this translation and note the significant modifications to later versions in the endnotes. The text is a fragment extracted from Cousin's 1817 lecture course (and, in *Premiers essais de philosophie*, is placed immediately following "On the Fact of Consciousness"). As will become clear, it is one of the early Cousin's most intricate presentations of his psychology and a constant reference point in his later work.
2. *Fr. phil. 1826* and subsequent editions: this footnote is omitted.
3. That is, one tried to avoid it by claiming that all the mind's operations are reflective.
4. *Fr. phil. 1826* and subsequent editions: "makes contact with the necessary principles, but it is not itself a necessary principle; it" is omitted.
5. That is, which has no cause and so cannot be understood in terms of the principle of causality.

On Real Beauty and Ideal Beauty[1]

In this article, I wish to investigate the nature of the beautiful, real beauty and ideal beauty, how they resemble each other and how they differ; how we grasp each of them, and how we move from one to the other.

First of all, what should be understood by real beauty?

Real beauty should be understood just as each person understands it—that is: as all beauties which man and nature manifest; all physical, moral, intellectual beauties insofar as they are encountered in a real, determinate object.

Now, we can consider beauty in general (and so real beauty which is our concern here) either in the soul, in the internal acts by which it is grasped, or in the characteristics of the external objects which contain it—objects which are external only with respect to the subject that perceives them, and which can be ideas, the most intimate sentiments of the soul, as long as they are beautiful and, as such, become objects of admiration.

Let us successively consider real beauty under these two perspectives. First, let us consider it in the soul, in the operations which reveal [beauty] to us.

These operations can, I take it, be reduced to one unique, but complex operation, composed of a judgement and a sentiment, folded into each other.

It is indubitable that, on [perceiving] one feature of some object, you pronounce that it is beautiful; and if someone claimed the opposite, you would tell him that he is deceived, that the object you are judging beautiful is truly so, and that everyone should judge it just like you. The judgement you make is individual in its relation to you who are making it and who are an individual; but although you make [the judgement], you know that you do not constitute it, and the truth that it expresses to you appears to you universal, invariable, absolute, infinite. This judgement is an act of reason, of that wondrous faculty which contemplates[2] the infinite at the heart of the finite, attains the absolute in the individual, and participates in two worlds, whose mysterious[3] union it effectuates.

It is again indubitable that added to the judgement you make on the beauty of the object is an exquisite sentiment of pure and disinterested love, equal and similar to that which excites in us the good and the true. This sentiment is individual in its relation to you who experience it; and at the same time it is absolute—that is, you impose it on everyone, like judgement itself. It is absolute, not by virtue of its own nature, but through its relation to the judgement with which it is mixed, and which marks it with its character. Separate [the sentiment] from judgement and you will render its nature essentially individual, and therefore variable, capricious; and far from attributing to it a universal authority, you will be able to reclaim in its favour only the liberty and indulgence you accord yourself in all individual sentiments which, without pertaining intimately to reason, are not opposed to it. Hence, the sentiment of the beautiful is either merely indivisible and thus not only distinct, but separated from judgement; or individual and absolute at the same time, and in this latter case it is also distinct from the judgement which accompanies it and which it does not constitute.[4] To confuse judgement with sentiment is to reduce the beautiful to the agreeable, and to remove from it all absolute truth, if one takes the sentiment merely for what it is: individual, variable, relative. If one were to suppose in it a force of universality that it does not possess, that it cannot possess, and that a relatively severe investigation would easily take away from it, this would be to substitute for scepticism a kind of intellectual mysticism, which, like all mysticism, necessarily contains and reproduces scepticism.[5] Enlightened analysis guards against these two deficiencies by recognizing and distinguishing sentiment and judgement, reason and love, whose happy harmony constitutes what is called taste, the faculty of discerning and sensing the beautiful. Admiration and enthusiasm, which accompany taste, are also two complex phenomena, mixtures of love and reason—with this difference, perhaps, that the intellect is more involved in admiration and sentiment in enthusiasm.

Judgement, absolute by its nature, is one and excludes all nuance. Sentiment, relative by its nature, admits and presents varieties which learned analysis surveyed and recorded in the famous distinction between the beautiful and the sublime. It is possible to dispute the terms, but not the facts. It is recognized that, according to the objects which excite it and the circumstances which express it, the sentiment of the beautiful affects the soul in completely different ways—charms it and opens it out, or astonishes it and closes it up, casts it up into levity and gaiety or plunges it down into melancholy. Here a thousand details full of interest present themselves all at once. Since the limits of this article force me to leave them aside, I send the reader back to the works of Burke and Kant, who, on this point, appear to me to leave little to be desired, and I will move on to an examination of the external characteristics of beauty.

I consider the character of external beauty to be double, like the operation which is related to it. This character is composed of two elements that are always mixed together, though they are entirely distinct—the individual element and the general element.

At the same time as every human figure is composed of a certain number of detailed features which constitute its individuality or physiognomy, it presents general traits which constitute its nature, its figure as figure. The figure of some person is not [the figure] of another person; it has individual traits which distinguish it; but also this figure is a human figure because of its primordial constitution and its general lineaments. This distinction applies to every object, whatever it is, whatever it could be, for, if it exists, it must possess something constitutive which makes it exist; and something also which distinguishes it and by which it is itself and not something else.

Now, the constitutive part of an object is its absolute part; its individual part is its variable part. And the individual varies endlessly; it is destroyed and reproduced in order to be destroyed and reproduced once again, without the nature of the object—its absolute part, the principal, invariable lineaments which constitute its essence—being altered. The essence does not change; for it to change would be to perish. Remove from a natural straight line all that you like along the whole line, except for the aspect of it—visible or intellectual—which is the shortest path between two points and you will have destroyed the individual, what is variable in this line; but the absolute straight line remains in its entirety in accordance with the essential character you have conserved. However, alter this [essential] character and you are no longer modifying one straight line, you are destroying the straight line. The straight line is or it is not; it is a straight line or it ceases to be [anything at all]; its existence is in its essence. It is the same for the triangle and the circle.

General and particular, variable and absolute, essential and non-essential—by generalizing all these ideas in turn without changing their nature, they ultimately raise me to the idea which comprehends and sustains all others—that of substance and phenomenon.

In each object, there is something phenomenal, if in that object there is something individual, variable, non-essential, for all these ideas are equivalent to [the idea] of the phenomenon. And in each object there is something substantial, if there is something essential and absolute [in it] (absolute being [defined as] what is sufficient to itself—that is, equivalent to substance). I do not mean that every object has its own individual substance; for that would be absurd, since substantiality and individuality are contradictory notions. The idea of attaching a substance to each object, leading to an infinite number of substances, destroys the very idea of substance; for, since substance is that beyond which it is impossible to conceive anything with respect to its existence, a substance must be unique to be substance. It is very clear that thousands of substances that would necessarily limit one another would not be sufficient in themselves and would have nothing absolute or substantial about them. Moreover, what is true of a thousand is true of two.[6] I know that one can distinguish finite substances from infinite substance; but finite substances seem to me to strongly resemble phenomena, since phenomena are what necessarily presuppose something beyond themselves with respect to their existence. Therefore, each object is not a substance; but there is substance in each object, for everything that is can be only in relation to *that which is what it is,* [i.e. in relation] to that which is its existence, unity, absolute substance. It is in this respect that each thing finds its substance; it is in this way that each thing is substantially; it is this relation to substance which constitutes the essence of each thing. This is why the essence of each thing cannot be destroyed by any human effort, nor even supposed to be destroyed by human thought; for in order to destroy it, or to suppose it destroyed, one would have to destroy or suppose destroyed what is indestructible, the absolute being which constitutes it. However, if each thing has something absolute and eternal because of its relation to eternal and absolute substance, it is [also] perishable and changeable: it changes and perishes at every moment because of its individuality, that is, because of its phenomenal part, which is in perpetual fluctuation. From this it follows that the essence of things or their general part is what is most real and most hidden and their individual part in which their reality appears to triumph is what is in fact most apparent and least real. It is from the heights of such a theory that one should judge Plato.

If we apply all of this to beauty by translating the expressions general and particular, individual and absolute, essential and non-essential, substance and phenomenon into [the expressions] unity and variety, we will have the external characteristics of beauty, its avowed and recognized characteristics.[7] Hence, after so many detours, philosophy ends in a triviality, and what we initially admired as extraordinary speculation or disdainfully rejected as absurd is reduced with some word-changes to a few common ideas on which the good sense of the people rests: *simplex veri index*.[8]

Real beauty is therefore composed of two elements, the general and the individual, reunited into a real, determinate object. Now, if one asks for the element which appears first—the general or the individual, the variable or the absolute—I will respond just as I did for substance and phenomenon, that the general and the particular, the absolute and the variable, are given to us simultaneously in each other and with each other. There is no phenomenon without substance, no substance without phenomenon; nothing absolute without the relative, nor anything relative without the absolute; nothing general without the particular, nor the particular without the general. We start neither with one nor the other, but with both of them at once. This is what should be understood. Philosophy turns on this fundamental question reproduced everywhere in innumerable forms: do we begin from the individual or the general? Each school responds exclusively one way or the other. That is, some [schools begin from] general ideas without being able to say anything about what they are or from where they came, and so, to explain them, are obliged to make recourse to innate ideas, laws of human nature, forms of the mind;[9] and others [begin from] particular ideas without really knowing how to extract from them general ideas, which are, as a result, exiled to the understanding. This question can only be resolved by a composite solution, by positing the individual and the general as two correlative and simultaneous terms. It is not that we can immediately distinguish these two terms precisely, for reflection alone clarifies and distinguishes and we do not begin from reflection, but from spontaneity—that is, from a composite and obscure perception.* This additionally answers the

---

* See the theory of the clear and the obscure, of spontaneity and reflection, *Archives philosophiques* (January 1818).[10]

celebrated question: do we and should we begin from analysis or synthesis? Of course, philosophy must begin from what is clear and so ought to begin from reflection, and reflection breaks apart and must necessarily break things apart prior to putting them together. But prior to philosophy exists a nature which serves as its basis and which—because it does not begin by reflecting on itself—can begin neither from analysis nor, even more so, from synthesis, which presupposes analysis. Rather, [it must begin from] composite, unreflective, indistinct intuitions—that is, from a spontaneous primitive synthesis which differs as much from the other [reflective] synthesis as it does from analysis.

Therefore, in the object as in the mind, the external characteristics of beauty and the intellectual acts related to them are fundamentally composite. The intellectual acts are reason and love—acts that are initially unreflective and confused, because they are spontaneous, and spontaneous because they are primitive. Reason and love initially offer to the eyes of consciousness merely a kind of confused unity, within which it can distinguish nothing and of which it expresses only a vague and obscure reflection. Likewise, in[11] the object, the general and the particular come together primitively, but implicitly. They are already in the mind, but the mind knows nothing of them yet. Although it perceives them both, it does not distinguish them. In this case, there exists neither a distinct general nor a distinct particular, but a confused totality without apparent characteristics,[12] which does not yet manifest either variety or unity, although it contains them. This is real beauty, the primitive beauty in nature and in the mind.

Now, what is the ideal? How does it differ from and how does it resemble real beauty? How do we grasp the ideal and how do we pass from real beauty to ideal beauty? Such is the second part of the questions we proposed.

The ideal in beauty—as in everything—is the negation of the real, and the negation of the real is not a chimera, but an idea. Here the idea is the pure general, the absolute abstracted from the individual part which naturally envelops it, which realizes it.[13] The ideal is the real minus the individual—this is the difference which separates them. Their relation consists in what the ideal, without being itself real, is within the real, within that part of the real which, in order to appear in its pure generality, needs merely to be abstracted from the part which accompanies it. So, how does one undertake this kind of abstraction?

I distinguish between two kinds of abstraction. The first which I call comparative abstraction proceeds, as its name indicates, by comparison between many individuals, discarding their differences to grasp their similarities, and, from these abstracted, compared similarities, forming a general idea—what I call the general, collective, mediate idea. It is collective because all the compared individuals are involved in the result; and mediate because its formation requires many intermediary operations. The other [kind of] abstraction has the peculiarity that it is exercised, not on many individuals, but on one object, which is composite like all objects and whose individual part [this kind of abstraction] disregards, separating out the general part and elevating it gradually to its pure form. These two [kinds of] abstraction both aspire to the general idea. But the former, which considers solely the individual part of an object, is necessarily constrained to reach the desired general idea by means of examining many other objects from which it again abstracts the individual parts that it brings together and compares.[14] However, if every object is essentially composed of a general part and an individual part, in order to obtain a general idea there is no need to make recourse to an amalgam of many objects; it is enough to disregard the individual part in each object, so as to abstract the general part from it and arrive immediately at this idea—what I call the immediate, abstract, general idea. It is general because it is not individual; abstract because, to obtain it, one must abstract the general element in one object from its individual element, with which it is in actuality mixed; and immediate because we obtain it, or at least we can obtain it in our initial intuition of one object,[15] without recourse to the comparison of many objects. This is the theory of how the ideas of cause, of triangle and of circle are generated and originate; and it seems to me that within this theory the two extreme doctrines of innate general ideas and comparative general ideas shed what is false in them, while conserving what is true. Innate ideas come from the impossibility of explaining general ideas through surveying and comparing; comparative general ideas come from the impossibility of conceiving innate ideas. It is not possible to account for ideal beauty by the combination of diverse individual beauties scattered throughout nature—hence, the recourse to the desperate hypothesis of innate ideal beauty; and the absurdity of a primitive ideal by which we judge all individual objects has pushed many good minds towards incomplete and false theories of the comparative ideal and still keeps them there. The ideal is neither prior to experience nor the belated fruit of laborious comparison. In the first beautiful object that nature shows us, we discover the general and constitutive traits of beauty, whether physical, intellectual or moral, and it is through this first object that we immediately construe the general type, which we then use to appreciate all other objects, just as, with the help of the first imperfect triangle that nature supplies the geometer, he construes the ideal triangle, the rule and the model for all triangles. Ideal beauty[16] is just as absolute as the geometrical ideal, and it is formed no differently. Nature at once hides it from us and reveals it to us; it reflects eternal beauty only in forms which ceaselessly disappear; and yet, it does still reflect [such beauty], and, to see it, it is enough to just open one's eyes. There is something absolute in nature as there is in the mind of man, both outside as within, and it is in the relation—more intimate than might be imagined—between the absolute which contemplates and the absolute which is contemplated that the perception of the truth lies.

Notes

1. First published in *Archives Philosophiques, Politiques et Littéraires*, vol. 3 (1818), pp. 5–16 (subsequently: *Fr. phil. 1826*, pp. 323–36; *Fr. phil. 1833*, pp. 339–50; *Fr. phil. 1838*, vol. 1, pp. 344–53). We take the 1818 publication as our base text for this translation and note the significant modifications to later versions in the endnotes. The text is a fragment extracted from Cousin's 1817 lecture course. The French title, "Du beau idéal et du beau réel," has the peculiar feature that both "beau" and "idéal/réel" can serve as either noun or adjective in this construction—that is, very literally the title might equally read: "The ideal beautiful and the real beautiful" or "The beautiful ideal and the beautiful real." The essay is significant, first, for its subject matter of philosophical aesthetics, which was rarely treated in early nineteenth-century France; secondly, for its status as a preliminary sketch of the aesthetics section of Cousin's 1818 much-read lectures, *On the True, the Beautiful, and the Good*; and thirdly for the incipient discourse of the absolute and abstraction present here which suggests Cousin's increasing interest in Platonism and German absolute idealism.
2. *Fr. phil. 1833* and subsequent editions: "contemplates" replaced with "perceives."
3. *Fr. phil. 1826* and subsequent editions: "mysterious" is omitted.
4. *Fr. phil. 1833* and subsequent editions: the passage "This sentiment is individual…" to "… does not constitute" replaced with: "This sentiment is encountered in all men, but in all men it is different to some degree; and far from attributing it to a universal authority, you can claim for it solely the freedom and indulgence that you accord yourself in all individual sentiments."
5. *Fr. phil. 1833* and subsequent editions: the clause beginning: "which, like all mysticisms …" is omitted.
6. This is the kind of passage that Cousin returns to in the late 1830s and 1840s when defending himself from accusations of a pantheistic monism.
7. That is, "unity in variety" (*unitas in varietate*) had become since Leibniz a standard and somewhat hackneyed definition of beauty in European art theory.
8. i.e. "the simple is a sign of the true."
9. *Fr. phil. 1826* and subsequent editions: "laws of human nature, forms of the mind" is omitted.
10. See pp. 166–71 above. *Fr. phil. 1826* and subsequent editions: this footnote is omitted.
11. *Fr. phil. 1833* and subsequent editions: "in" replaced with "for."
12. *Fr. phil. 1833* and subsequent editions: "without apparent characteristics" is omitted.
13. *Fr. phil. 1833* and subsequent editions: "which naturally envelops it, which realises it," is omitted.
14. *Fr. phil. 1833* and subsequent editions: "that it brings together and compares" replaced with "under comparison."
15. *Fr. phil. 1833* and subsequent editions: "in our initial intuition of one object" is omitted.
16. Or: "the beautiful ideal" (see n. 1 above).

IV
1826–1830

On the True Beginning of the History of Philosophy[1]

It is a grave error to confuse the history of philosophy with [the history] of the human mind and of humanity. Not all thoughts are philosophical thoughts properly speaking, neither in the species nor in the individual. The individual person begins to think early on, and his faculties—even in their most imperfect state—already carry ideas and beliefs of all kinds. [Such a person] lacks nothing in his first impulse for attaining the truth, not within him, around him or above him. The world exists; God exists; man knows it, and knows himself, as long as he possesses but one idea. In contact with everything, the intellectual instinct with which he is endowed is applied to everything and immediately gets as far as it will ever go. It is true that man does not begin by posing problems and trying to solve them: he sees, he feels, he conceives, and he believes; and, from his first day onwards, his intellect develops in the richest and most fruitful manner. But its development is entirely spontaneous. Reflection comes later—and, with it, philosophy. Whereas the spontaneous activity of the intellect is mixed in with and identified with the objects to which it is applied, and is tainted, so to speak, by their colours, reflective activity separates itself from them, returns into itself and, there taking itself as the object of its own action, asks itself for an account of what it has thought, how and why it has so thought, how and why it thinks, thereby converting into a problem what was previously a fact, proceeding by way of method when previously it obeyed instinct, and substituting evolving concepts for immediate inspiration and systems for natural beliefs. In a word, reflection creates science exactly where spontaneity had produced faith. This is what differentiates the abstract from the concrete, analysis from synthesis. And one cannot deny that abstraction is necessarily preceded by an operation that is different from it, that synthesis is prior to analysis and that faith anticipates science. Philosophy, daughter of reflection, is thus a later development of the human mind, within which a first development completely distinct from this second one—at least in form—serves as its starting point and foundation. This is how things occur in the individual; they occur in the species in exactly the same way. Here also an immediate revelation divulges to the mind the secrets of beings, illuminates it as if from on high with admirable insight, and, from the very beginning, affixes upon it the stamp of eternal truths. Prior to all system, humankind thinks, and, by those forces with which it is endowed, attains—by itself and spontaneously—essential truths, without waiting for any belated assistance from reflection and philosophers. This distinction is of the highest importance: it raises up human nature and attributes to it enlightenment and grandeur from its very cradle, at the same time as indicating its progressive movement.*

For this reason, the history of philosophy is not contemporaneous with the history of the human mind. The latter is far more extensive than the former; it is no less interesting, but is necessarily more obscure, for, if the light of reflection is not always more abundant than the primitive light, it is still more precise and more distinct and furnishes a better view of the objects which it enlightens one after another in a manner predetermined for the spectator's ease. When, therefore, philosophy rises above the epoch in which it was born and gets lost in the origins of human thought, it leaves its domain, properly speaking, and runs the risk of disappearing into deep shadows. Its first effort should be to determine and circumscribe the field of its inquiry; it is otherwise overstretched.

On the basis of these considerations, we cannot approve of those historians of philosophy who, in order to place themselves at [philosophy's] origin, return to [the origin] of humankind, and deliver themselves over to arbitrary hypotheses, totally indifferent and foreign to their true subject. Forever confounding thought and philosophy, they seek the state of nature of systems, in which there are solely beliefs, and, because—thank God—no generation has existed without intellect, where they should just see men, they believe they have discovered philosophers. The historian of humanity and religions, which are [humanity's] most immediate expression, should of course pursue the least vestige of human thinking under the crudest of religious forms; but the historian of philosophy should just start with the thinking [that occurs] at the point when it manifests itself under that special form which constitutes philosophy. It is sad to see the illustrious Brucker[3] divide the history of philosophy into antediluvian and postdiluvian philosophy, and, in the latter category, distinguish between what he calls barbaric philosophy and the philosophy of the Greeks; and, in this latter category, further distinguish between many sorts of philosophy—mythological philosophy, political philosophy, and artificial philosophy, before arriving at philosophy properly speaking; and finally, in an appendix under the title of exotic philosophy, seek vestiges of philosophy in America, and, instead of finding them, recount to us myths and fables which belong rather, we repeat, to the history of the human mind than to [the history] of philosophy. Of course, no one does more justice than us to the esteemed Brucker, so indefatigable in his research, so exact in his citations, so scrupulous in his judgements, and who erected the first major monument in honour of philosophy. But this monument would be more admirable still if a stricter order had removed the

---

* See in the *Philosophical Fragments* (1826) the piece entitled: *On Spontaneity and Reflection* and the last fifteen pages of the preface.[2]

superabundant wealth of accessory constructions, and this would have led more directly to the sanctuary.

In our opinion, one must remove from the history of philosophy all hypotheses about a supposedly savage state, or about some first civilization superior to the civilizations that followed it; for this is not even history. There is more: one must perhaps remove from the history of philosophy the entirety of the first genuinely historical epoch of humanity, that is, the era of the East. In fact, if one considers it as a whole and in its most general relations to the West, the East exhibits all the characteristics of that rich and powerful spontaneity which preceded the age of reflection and philosophy in the human species. In the East, everything is illumination, an immediate perspective, dogma, symbol, mythology. Of course, we should avoid thinking that there was no reflection or philosophy in the East—for, first of all, that is impossible in itself and, secondly, facts prove the opposite.[4] But it is certain that, in general, in this first epoch of the world, it is religions more than systems and priests more than schools that are to be sought. At its dawn, the mind already glimpsed everything, but through a cloud; and, too weak yet to sustain itself in the face of these powerful intuitions, it abandoned itself to them and confounded itself with them, without the will or power to submit them to any examination or methodical judgement. Thus, in a certain way, humanity does not play much of a role in its first concepts. [Formed by] gigantic and excessive objects, they overwhelm the human soul, instead of elevating and liberating it. This great universe and the omnipresent God as yet leave too little space in man's mind for man himself. Thinking already possesses immense scope, but little freedom; and it is precisely freedom which constitutes philosophy. What is more, cast a glance over the monuments which survive from these ancient times and you will never discover in them the original movement of some particular thought, but only the imprint of an idea without name and almost without date, so mysterious in its origin, so imposing in its forms and in all its features that, even from the distance of so many centuries, the individual thought can scarcely be submitted to modern methods and examined and analysed as the result of another similar thought. Philosophy feels itself in the presence of a world which is not its own and which it can only comprehend on condition of dropping all its habits and regrasping, in the silence of reflection, that sense of inspiration which alone can reveal to us the secret of high antiquity and primitive inspirations. With its religions, its universal symbolism and its formidable priesthood, the East belongs more to the scholar of mythologies than to the philosopher. The philosopher will thus do well to scarcely pause over the East and move straight on to Greece. And it is above all with Greece that, for humanity, commences both the feeling for and the exercise of voluntary, free activity, this individual energy which dares confront reigning dogmas, this solitary reflection which abstracts from all things outside of itself and takes itself as its point of departure and its unique criterion—that is to say, philosophy. It is Greece which gave philosophy to humankind; it is thus in Greece that the history of philosophy properly speaking begins, and it is there that one must first look for it; it is [Greece] that witnessed its childhood, its errors, and its growth. Everything which precedes it is foreign to [philosophy].

Notes

1. First published in *Le Globe* (12 May 1827), pp. 85–6 (subsequently: *Nouv. fr. phil*, pp. 1–8). We take the 1827 publication as our base text for this translation and note the significant modifications to the later version in the endnotes. The text was originally a fragment extracted from Cousin's 1817 lecture course, but left unpublished for a decade. Its topic—the relationship between Greek philosophy and Eastern philosophy—is a favourite one for Cousin, common in his later lecture courses (see Moreau's essay above).
2. See pp. 86–9, 166–71 above. This fragment also markedly anticipates Cousin's flagship 1828 lecture course on the history of philosophy with its use of spontaneity and reflection as historical descriptors.
3. J. J. Brucker (1696–1770) whose *Historia Critica Philosophiae* in its 6-volume second edition (1766–7) is referred to by Cousin in what follows. Cousin is almost entirely referring to the final volume of appendices which is divided in roughly the way Cousin describes, with "antediluvian philosophy" as the initial appendix and "exotic philosophy" as the final one.
4. *Nouv. fr. phil.*: Cousin inserts the following footnote: "As well as the *Bhagavad-Gita* (ed. W. Schlegel, Bonn, 1823) and the excellent analysis given by William von Humboldt (Berlin, 1826), see Colebrooke's learned essays on the philosophy of the Hindus, in the *Transactions* of the Asiatic Society of London (1824–7), and the exact and extensive extracts that Abel-Rémusat has inserted into the *Journal des Savans* (December 1825, April 1826, March and July 1828)." In addition to Schlegel's translation, the texts to which Cousin is referring are: Humboldt's *Über die unter dem Namen Bhagavad-Gita bekannte Episode des Maha-Bharata* (1826); H. T. Colebrook's "On the Philosophy of the Hindus," which appeared in the *Transactions of the Royal Asiatic Society of Great Britain and Ireland* (1827, pp. 19–43, 92–118, 439–66, 549–79); and various reviews of works on Eastern thought by J.-P. Abel-Rémusat in his role as editor of the *Journal des savants*.

Plato

Language of the Theory of Ideas[1]

Dialectic is the instrument of Plato's philosophy, and Plato's dialectic is entirely a matter of definition. Moreover, definition proceeds in two ways—by generalization and by division. In fact, definition is double: it is formed either *per genus* or *per differentiam*.[2] What is distinctive to definition *per genus* is the process of establishing in all discussions—by leaving behind examples which are always of particulars—the general idea of the thing in question, the general idea which must subordinate all particular examples and comprehend them in terms of what they have in common. This definition therefore has generalization as its principle. Reciprocally, the division or the resolution of the general idea—not into all the indefinite particularities in which it can be encountered, but into essential elements—is the necessary principle of definition *per differentiam*. These two procedures constitute the whole of definition, that is, Platonic dialectic. The former is the foundation of the latter, and the latter is the development of the former.

But if division[3] rests on generalization, on what does generalization rest? Evidently on the theory of ideas, which is therefore the fundamental principle, the soul of all Plato's dialectic and philosophy. The language in which this famous theory is expressed thus merits particular attention.[4]

The language of the theory of ideas gradually becomes fixed, alongside the theory itself: just as the latter is still a little[5] uncertain in the *Phaedrus* (that is, in Plato's first dialogue),[6] although it is already present, so too the language used to express it has not yet attained the point it reaches from the *Meno*, the *Parmenides*, the *Phaedo*, and the *Republic*[7] onwards. Here are [presented] the different stages which—within Plato's fully constituted language and theory—represent the different degrees of the idea, with a precise meaning to be attributed to each of them.[8]

First,[9] at the apex of this theory[10] stands the idea in itself, εἶδος αὐτὸ καθ' αὐτό,[11] the idea taken absolutely, without any relation either to the world of the mind[12] or to that of nature, the idea considered as the invisible ideal, the primary and ultimate reason—eternal and absolute—of all things, which reflect it here below in this world of the relative and of appearance,[13] [this world of] the perpetual metamorphosis of phenomena constantly in a state of renewal and becoming, without ever being as substance, γένεσις, τὸ μὴ ὄν, τὰ μὴ ὄντα.[14] In opposition to phenomena, the εἶδος αὐτὸ καθ' αὑτό, the idea in itself is the true essence, ἢ οὐσία τὸ ὂν ὄντως,[15] and it resides in the λόγος θεῖος[16] or the absolute intellect, beyond man's finite intellect and the inferior region of this world.[17]

But the idea does not remain and cannot remain in this absolute state within the eternal intellect.[18] As it is both cause as well as essence and attribute of substance,[19] it passes—by its own force and the energy with which it is endowed[20]—into action and movement, and so passes into humanity and into nature. Now, it is no longer εἶδος αὐτὸ καθ' αὑτό; rather, it becomes εἶδος[21] in the human mind and ἰδέα[22] in nature; and it is here that something of the absolute mixes with the relative.[23]

In the human mind, εἶδος is the general idea, for a notion of generality is always attributed to this term. Generality is precisely that without which no genuine knowledge is possible.[24] In fact, without generality, there is no definition, for, first and foremost, every definition takes with it the idea of being, which is essentially general. Hence, all definition is necessarily formed *per genus* as well as *per differentiam*:[25] the element of difference always presupposes a general element, which alone classifies—that is, defines—the individual being to be defined. The result is that every individual and every species must be related to a genre in order to be definable, that is, to be intelligible;[26] and that, in order to count as a thought, even what appears to be the most particular thought implies some concept of generality, τι εἶδος. The εἶδος is thus the foundation of all knowledge within the human mind; it forms the governing principles of the understanding,[27] the universal and necessary concepts, the laws of all judgement and of all understanding, the universals of Peripateticism.[28] This is why the εἶδος is nearly always developed in Plato by the καθ' ὅλου[29]—for example, εἶδος τῆς ἀρετῆς or[30] ἀρετὴ καθ' ὅλου (*Meno*, Bekk., p. 339).[31] Likewise, every other passage. Κατ' εἶδος, κατ' εἴδη λέγειν [or] σκοπεῖν means to consider[32] things from a general perspective—such as, for example, the κατ' εἴδη σκοπεῖν of the *Republic*[33] which provides a perfect gloss on the analogous expression in the *Sophist*, κατὰ γένος διακρίνειν.[34] We can already find this technical expression in the following passage from the *Phaedrus*: δεῖ γὰρ ἄνθρωπον ξυνιέναι κατ' εἶδος λεγόμενον, ἐκ πολλῶν ἰὸν αἰσθήσεων εἰς ἓν λογισμῷ ξυναιρούμενον (Bekk., pp. 45–6): "What defines the human is the understanding of what is general, that is, what, from the diversity of sensations, can be comprehended under a rational unity."[35] Here, κατ' εἶδος λεγόμενον[36] (substituting τὸ following Heindorf and Schleiermacher, either by implication or by inserting it into the text)[37] is properly the category of generality.

We have seen that, in the human mind, the idea of generality comprehends and subordinates the most particular ideas, and that, therefore, the εἶδος is the very ground of the human mind, which, through it, maintains a constant relationship with the absolute intellect. Nature is the sister of humanity; it too is the daughter of eternal intellect; it reflects it, it too represents it,[38] but in a different manner, a less intellectual and so less intelligible manner—one that is clear for the senses, but obscure for thought. The εἶδος at this degree is ἰδέα; the ἰδέα is the εἶδος fallen into this world, spirit become matter, cloaked in a body and passed over into the state of image. But in this very state, the ἰδέα conserves its relationship both with the εἶδος and with the εἶδος αὐτὸ καθ' αὑτό, and therefore it always implies something general, no longer in the internal form of thought, but in the form of the object. The ἰδέα is the ideal form of each thing; through it,[39] nature too is ideal, intellectual, and possesses beauty. Of course, the generality which the ἰδέα retains is far below that of the εἶδος, just as the laws of nature are infinitely less general than those of the mind. However, we cannot deny that this word still awakens, indirectly, some concept of generality, as soon as it is applied directly to an image, to something external and visible.[40]

Such is the proper meaning of the words εἶδος αὐτὸ καθ' αὑτό, εἶδος, and ἰδέα, and it is in this sense that Plato ordinarily uses them. But we must agree that εἶδος and ἰδέα are frequently swapped, and it is not rare to find ἰδέα for εἶδος (*Phaedrus*, Bekk., pp. 23, 39, 78, 79),[41] just as we also sometimes find εἶδος used for a species and not for a genus.[42] Hence, in the *Phaedrus* (Bekk., p. 79),[43] κατ' εἴδη τέμνειν means to divide a general idea into its elements. But then we must not understand by εἴδη any possible particularity, but only the essential elements of an idea—the species, not the individuals—and this still implies some generality, just as ἰδέα, when employed for εἶδος, almost always still implies a relation to the external world.[44]

Plato's ideas persist under different names in modern philosophy. They are Leibniz's eternal truths, "whose ground is this supreme and universal mind which cannot fail to exist, whose understanding, to tell the truth, is the region of eternal truths.... These necessary truths contain the determining reason and the regulative principle of existences themselves, and, in a word, the laws of the universe. Hence, these truths, prior to the existence of contingent beings, must be grounded in the existence of a necessary substance. It is here that I find the original of ideas and truths" (Leibniz, *New Essays*, IV.xi).[45] They are also, to a lower degree, the laws of the constitution of human nature, the principles of common sense of Scottish philosophy; but Scottish philosophers used their laws and their principles without going any further into their nature, without recognizing their origin, without embracing all of their scope, without enumerating them or classifying them, without tracing the history of their appearance and their development in consciousness, without charting their implications or relating them to their first and last principle. Kant went infinitely further down the same path. His [doctrine of the] schematism recalls the ἰδέα, his categories the εἶδος, and his ideas of pure reason the εἴδη αὐτὰ καθ' αὑτά. I scarcely dare add that ten years ago I attempted, as far as I could, a complete theory of absolute truths, of which one can see an imperfect sketch under the title: *Programme of lectures delivered at the École Normale during the first semester of 1818 on absolute truths* (*Fragments philosophiques*, p. 263).[46]

Notes

1. *Nouv. fr. phil.*, pp. 155–61 (subsequently: *Fr. phil. anc.*, pp. 144–9; *Fr. phil. 1847*, vol. 1, pp. 121–5; *Fr. phil. 1855*, vol. 1, pp. 121–5; *Fr. phil. 1865*, vol. 5, pp. 88–91). We take the 1826 publication as our base text for this translation and note the significant modifications to later versions in the endnotes. This text emerged out of Cousin's reflections on his Plato-translation; its Neoplatonic resonances also show the influence of his Proclus-edition. However, no precise dating of this text is possible and, indeed, the major reference points in this short note (e.g. the *Phaedrus*) were not translated until later. It is also a good example of the extent to which Cousin rewrote some of his fragments in later editions. Cousin developed some of its claims for his 1835 lectures at the Sorbonne on Plato's theory of ideas (in which he "explains and clarifies the theory of ideas contained in Books 7 and 10 of the *Republic* by comparing these passages to analogous passages from the *Phaedrus*, *Phaedo* and *Parmenides*"): these lecture notes are reproduced in V. Cousin, *Platon*, ed. C. Mauve et al. (Paris: Vrin, 2016), pp. 364–87.
2. Terms drawn from the theory of the definition in Aristotelian logic, stemming back to Aristotle's own *Topics* and *Categories*. Definition *per genum* supplies the generic terms in a definition and definition *per differentiam* provides those terms that are distinct to a particular species.
3. *Fr. phil. 1847* and subsequent editions: the passage from "Moreover, definition proceeds…" to "… of the former" replaced with: "Moreover, to define is to generalize—that is, to reduce some particular thing to some more or less extensive genus. But if definition…."
4. *Fr. phil. 1865*: The passage from "and Plato's dialectic is entirely…" to "… thus merits particular attention" replaced with the following: "and it rests on the theory of ideas. And the Idea is unity in its diverse degrees—it is what is one in all things, it is everywhere the genus opposed to individuals. Such is the fundamental sense of the word εἶδος. But unity can be considered, either in its first and last principle, God, or in the human mind and in nature. The word εἶδος expresses unity from these three perspectives. Thus, it always has the same essential meaning, as well as very different meanings according to the different cases to which it is applied."
5. *Fr. phil. 1865*: "a little" is omitted.
6. The chronology of Plato's dialogues was not scientifically established until later in the nineteenth century.
7. *Fr. phil. 1865*: the *Timaeus* is added to this list.
8. *Fr. phil. 1865*: this sentence is omitted.
9. *Fr. phil. 1865*: "first" is omitted.
10. *Fr. phil. 1865*: "this theory" replaced with "the theory of ideas."
11. *Fr. phil. 1847* and subsequent editions: "εἶδος αὐτὸ καθ' αὐτό" replaced with "εἶδος αὐτὸ, and as the Alexandrians will later say, εἶδος αὐτὸ καθ' αὐτό." Jowett translates this phrase as "absolute idea," when it is used, for example, in *Parmenides*, 130b. The reference to "the Alexandrians" is presumably to Proclus who uses this phrase, for example, in *On the Theology of Plato*. (We have faithfully transcribed Cousin's Greek throughout, even where it diverges from contemporary philological conventions in Plato-scholarship.)
12. *Fr. phil. 1847* and subsequent editions: "the world of the mind" replaced with "mind"; *Fr. phil. 1865*: with "human mind."
13. *Fr. phil. 1847* and subsequent editions: "ideal, the primary and ultimate reason—eternal and absolute—of all things, which reflect it here below in this world of the relative and of appearance" replaced with "type and eternally subsisting in all things which reflect it here below in this world of the relative and of appearance"; *Fr. phil. 1865*: the final phrase is replaced with: "in this sensible world."
14. The three Greek phrases mean roughly "becoming" and "not-being."
15. i.e. "the essence of being."
16. i.e. "divine reason."
17. *Fr. phil. 1865*: the passage from "γένεσις, τὸ μὴ ὄν …" to "… region of this world" replaced with: "Everywhere in Plato γένεσις [becoming] is opposed to οὐσία [essence], and οὐσία is the εἶδος. The idea in itself is the absolute one in which culminates all the unities man can conceive and which comprehends nature, and this absolute unity is also the absolute good, αὐτὸ τὸ ἀγαθόν [the good in itself], from which derives and to which is related all that is good in the world. See, above all, the seventh book of the *Republic* and the *Timaeus*."
18. *Fr. phil. 1847* and subsequent editions: this sentence replaced with: "But the idea does not remain sterile and immobile in the heart of the eternal intellect"; *Fr. phil. 1865*: replaced with "At this height, the Idea resides in God and is confounded with God. But it does not remain immobile there."

19. *Fr. phil. 1865*: "and attribute of substance" is omitted.
20. *Fr. phil. 1865*: "or rather the force and energy of its eternal principle" is added.
21. Roughly translated as "that which is seen"/"image"/"form"—the standard term for Plato's Forms.
22. Transliterated and translated roughly as "idea"—the Greek is closely etymologically related to εἶδος and maintains the same sense of "what is seen."
23. *Fr. phil. 1847* and subsequent editions: this sentence is replaced with: "It is for this reason that the human mind and nature contain the one and the absolute mixed with the relative, the true, the beautiful and the good mixed with the false, the ugly and the bad."
24. *Fr. phil. 1847* and subsequent edition: "is the general idea, for a notion of generality is always attributed to this term. Generality is precisely that without which no genuine knowledge is possible" replaced with "the notion of general ideal, in opposition to sensations and particular ideas"; *Fr. phil. 1865*: replaced with "the notion, the concept, and, as the moderns say, the general idea in opposition to sensations and particular ideas."
25. *Fr. phil. 1847* and subsequent editions: the passage from "for, first and foremost ..." to "... per differentiam" replaced with "and without definition there is no knowledge worth the name. Every definition is necessarily formed by genus and by difference."
26. *Fr. phil. 1865*: "that is, to be intelligible" is omitted.
27. *Fr. phil. 1847* and subsequent editions: "is thus the foundation of all knowledge within the human mind; it forms the governing principles of the understanding" replaced with "to this degree and within the human mind represents."
28. *Fr. phil. 1865*: "and scholasticism: εἶδος γὰρ πού τι ἓν ἕκαστον εἰώθαμεν τίθεσθαι περὶ ἕκαστα τὰ πολλὰ οἷς ταὐτὸν ὄνομα ἐπιφέρομεν (*Republic*, Bekk. III.I, Bk. 10, p. 467)" is added. "Bekk." refers to the standard (although still recent) edition of Plato's Greek texts: A. I. Bekker (ed.), *Scripta Graece omnia*, published during the 1820s. The quotation from the *Republic* is taken from 596a ("a single idea or form of the various multiplicities to which we give the same name").
29. i.e. "generally"/"in terms of the whole."
30. *Fr. phil. 1865*: "for example, εἶδος τῆς ἀρετῆς or" replaced with "for example, the idea of virtue is."
31. An imprecise reference to *Meno*, 77a (which does not explicitly use the term εἶδος).
32. *Fr. phil. 1847* and subsequent editions: "consider" replaced with "set out and consider."
33. Presumably Cousin is thinking of *Republic*, 454a ("dividing according to forms"), but he misremembers the verb, which is "διαιρούμενοι."
34. *Sophist*, 253e: "to distinguish by genus."
35. *Phaedrus*, 249c—more literally translated as "a man must understand what is said with respect to form, as it is gathered from many perceptions into a unity, being assembled by reasoning." Translated by C. Emlyn-Jones and W. Preddy (Cambridge, MA: Loeb, 2022), p. 423.
36. i.e. "the understanding of what is general," according to Cousin's translation above.
37. *Fr. phil. 1865*: the material in brackets is omitted. The point of the comment is that this definite article turns εἶδος into a more abstract noun (as opposed to Emlyn-Jones's and Preddy's translation in the previous note which reads εἶδος more concretely). Cousin here refers to the two Plato-scholars, editors, and translators: Ludwig Friedrich Heindorf (1774–1816) and F. D. E. Schleiermacher (1768–1834).
38. *Fr. phil. 1847* and subsequent edition: the passage "We have seen that ..." to "... represents it" replaced with: "Alongside humanity is nature, daughter, as [humanity] is, of the eternal intellect, which reflects it, as [humanity] does"; *Fr. phil. 1865*: replaced with "Alongside humanity is nature, which reflects the eternal intellect as [humanity] does."
39. *Fr. phil. 1847* and subsequent editions: The passage from "The εἶδος at this degree ..." to "... through it ..." replaced with: "The divine Idea fallen into nature is still called εἶδος and often also ἰδέα; for the two words are often taken for each other; they thus express what is general in sensible things, the ideal form of every material object; it is because it participates in the Idea (μεθέξις) that"; *Fr. phil. 1865*: "divine" is omitted, "express" replaced with "mark" and μεθέξις omitted. "μέθεξις" is the Platonic term for participation.
40. *Fr. phil. 1847* and subsequent editions: the passage from "Of course, the generality ..." to "... external and visible" is omitted.
41. e.g. *Phaedrus* 238d, where "ἰδέα" is better translated as "principle."
42. *Fr. phil. 1847* and subsequent edition: the passage from "Such is the proper ..." to "... for a genus" replaced with: "Such, I believe, is the proper meaning of the word ἰδέα if one wishes to distinguish it from the word εἶδος. But once again, we must agree that εἶδος and ἰδέα are frequently swapped and it is not rare to find ἰδέα from the psychological or logical perspective (*Phaedrus*, Bekk., pp. 23, 39, 78, 79), just as εἶδος [is used] to express natural genus. We also sometimes find εἶδος used for a species and not for a genus." *Fr. phi. 1865*: replaced with: "Such is the proper meaning of the

word ἰδέα if one wishes to distinguish it from the word εἶδος. In fact, it seems that, in the following examples, ἰδέα is said of the form of sensible objects: ἰδέα θηρίου ποικίλου (*Republic*, Bk. IX, p. 458);—Φαντάζεσθαι ἄλλοτε ἐν ἄλλαις ἰδέαις (*Republic*, Bk. II, p. 100).—Τοιοῦτος ἰὼν τὴν ἰδέαν, which is certainly here the material form, the appearance, the aspect (*Charmides*, Bekk., I.I, p. 346)—Εἰς μίαν ἰδέαν συνορῶντα ἄγειν τὰ πολλαχῇ διεσπαρμένα (*Phaedrus*, p. 78). But once again, we must agree that εἶδος and ἰδέα are frequently swapped and it is not rare to find ἰδέα expressing all kinds of genus, intellectual as well as sensible." The reference to *Republic* Bk 9 is to 588c ("shape of a manifold beast"), to *Republic* Bk. 2 is to 380d ("manifesting his shape in one aspect or another"), to *Charmides* is to 175d ("if you had the idea"), and to *Phaedrus* 265d ("bringing together in one idea the scattered particulars").

43. *Phaedrus*, 277b, where it means, as Cousin goes on to gloss, "to divide according to form."
44. *Fr. phil. 1847* and subsequent editions: "and to sensible objects" is added.
45. G. W. Leibniz, *New Essays on the Human Understanding*, IV.xi. The above is a literal translation of Cousin's version of the text; Leibniz's original reads in translation as follows: "The ultimate foundation of truth [is] the supreme and universal mind who can't fail to exist and whose understanding is indeed the domain of eternal truths.... These necessary truths contain the determining reason and regulating principle of existent things—the laws of the universe, in short. Thus, these necessary truths are underpinnings of the existence of contingent beings and therefore can't be in any way based on such beings; so they must be based on the existence of a necessary substance. That is where I find the pattern for the ideas and truths that are engraved in our souls." Trans. P. Remnant and J. Bennett (Cambridge: Cambridge University Press, 1996), p. 447.
46. The opening page to the programme for the 1818 lectures in *Fr. phil. 1826*, pp. 263–95. *Fr. phil. 1847* and subsequent editions: the passage from "These are still …" to the end of the text is omitted; *Fr. phil. 1865*: this entire final paragraph is replaced with: "Hence, in summary, the Platonic Idea can be taken from three distinct perspectives. The most ordinary is the psychological and logical perspective, the idea of the genus in the human mind. Often also it is the natural genus in opposition to individuals from which every genus is composed. Finally, in its principle, it is the genus of genus, the supreme genus, the primordial Idea, the absolute unity, the absolute good, God."

Plato[1]

In the collection of Plato's compositions there exist three very distinct manners, just as there exist three different epochs in his life. Nourished at the breast of religion and poetry, his first philosophical essays are all penetrated by the habits of his youth. It is true that it is still possible to sense the great metaphysician beneath it all, but the form retains something of the dithyramb and tragedy: his philosophy still bears the cassock of the priest and the lyre of the poet; his ideas are dogmas and his words a song. No essential truth is missing, but all the truths exist, both in his soul and in his writings, in the form of sublime presentiments, not rigorous demonstrations. Overwhelmed by the very grandeur of his objects, the young man's thinking does not have the strength and does not yet know the secret of separating himself from them so as to consider them more calmly from a distance, of dividing them so as to envisage them in all their aspects. Rather, [his thought] presents them as it sees them, through a cloud and under the half-light of mysticism. Mysticism is indeed the fundamental characteristic of Plato's first essays. A general rule: the great individuals who are called upon to represent humankind in its entirety reproduce in their own development the [development] of humankind itself: like [humankind], they begin not by reflection but by inspiration, not by science but by religion, not by dialectic but by poetry.[2] This is the sign by which one can recognise all great natures: their cradle is religion; it is there that they are formed; it is there that they amass those holy convictions which alone can sustain them through the trials that await them; it is from there that they cast off and throw themselves into the storms of life or science, in accordance with their mission. Like all great men, on the faith of irresistible, but not reasoned convictions, Plato first believed and advanced many things that he did not know and could not demonstrate; like his thinking, his composition is at that time forceful, rich, glittering, but without method. Such is his first manner. Towards the time of Socrates' death, Plato commences a new existence and, with it, a new manner.

If the first movement of thought is to unite oneself in faith to the truth as soon as it is glimpsed, the second is to separate oneself from it and to put it into question as a way of making sense of it. Such has been the progress of humankind and such was that of Plato. The peaceable life of his first youth—the meditation and the cult of eternal truths in the shadow of the domestic hearth and under the auspices of religion—suddenly gives way to a life of adventure, of difficult and varied studies. It is at this moment he forms relationships with the representatives of the most opposed philosophical sects, with Cratylus, the disciple of Heraclitus, with Hermogenes, Parmenides's advocate; [it is at this moment he undertakes] his stay in Megara in the midst of the subtleties and refinements of the Eristic school;[3] his voyages across Greater Greece, in Sicily, in Egypt, and perhaps further afield; finally, his political projects and that life of hazard and struggle of all kinds that led him by necessity to fulfil his destiny. For one must not believe that the destiny of a great man results from the circumstances of his life; it is rather these circumstances which are formed on the basis of his destiny and for his destiny. The second part of Plato's life served unswervingly to develop his genius. Trapped within the contradictions of the world and of the schools, at war with reality, but wanting to defend his faith, the young enthusiast sensed the need to provide a strict account of and to recall both for himself and for others the laws and form of rigorous demonstration. At the very instant when reflection begins, mysticism ceases; this is the necessary fruit of the spontaneous impulse of thinking and of its identification with its object, which, to begin, is nature and the world.

Reflection is the return of thought onto itself, the separation of thought and its necessary laws from its objects and accidental forms, the removal of any external condition to its development, the sublime attempt to reduce the whole of existence to the mind. Reflection is the internal war of the mind against the senses, the imagination, feeling, and the heart itself. The instruments of reflection are not inspiration and enthusiasm, but analysis and dialectic. This revolution in the very operation of thought inevitably results in something similar in its expression. Dialectic—superseding inspiration—replaces poetry with prose, symbolism with abstraction, the glittering use of mythological forms and the supple and stirring allure of the ode and the drama with the regular, but burdensome movement of the didactic order and the uncoloured language of reasoning. Dialectic is arid in its forms and in its means, it is true, but its end is the same as that of enthusiasm and faith; their end is always the truth—in the latter, [truth] glimpsed in confusion; in the former, [truth] distinctly demonstrated. If the dialectic remains unfinished and does not go as far as faith, it is inferior to it, and the science which it engenders is merely an incomplete and insufficient science which cannot run parallel to religion. But if the dialectic regularly attains the point to which faith launches itself, if it comprehends the same movement, as much as its objects, problems, and results, then the science which it engenders—adequate to religion in terms of extensity—surpasses [religion] in clarity, and even becomes a higher degree of intellectual life. In the history of humankind—a history which is itself nothing but the manifestation and expression of the progress and development of thought up a great ladder—this higher degree [of intellectual life] is represented by Greece, which, in succeeding the East, begins and accomplishes the second epoch of universal history. In Greece, it is Plato's second manner which eminently represents the Greek spirit, as his first represented the Eastern spirit. For, afterwards, what did Aristotle do? Nothing else than seize hold of Plato's second manner and appropriate it for himself, at the same time as perfecting it. It was reserved to Plato to attain the third and final development of thought, and, in so doing, anticipate the work of the most advanced civilization.

In gaining knowledge of the external world, the intellect, in its initial impulse, immediately becomes mixed in with it, absorbed into it and coloured by it; then, returning into itself, it begins to live its own life, even to the point of negating the world to which it had previously been chained or of absorbing [this world] into itself and making external existence a mere reflection of its own. These two states are equally incomplete: to not distinguish oneself from the world or to separate oneself from it is equally false; and it is absolutely necessary that, after passing through these two exclusive, incomplete, and false states, the mind tends to arrive at one which suits it—that is, at the union of the two preceding states which have now been purified and reconciled with each other. All truth is in the harmony of contraries; but we achieve [this harmony] only after exhausting error and exclusive hypotheses; but these exclusive hypotheses are themselves necessary givens of the definitive solution: we manage to reunite the two extreme points of all thought only after having passed through them, and, to do this, they must have existed. Everything is necessary in the intellect and therefore in history, whether in the species or in individuals. It was necessary that, when the soul initially approached the world, it fell into it, so to speak, and abdicated itself; it was subsequently necessary that, after pulling itself out of the abyss of the universe in an attempt to grasp itself and be sufficient to itself, [the soul] no longer perceived anything but itself, in the solitude of thought. Without the first state, the second would be impossible; and, without both of them, without the combat of two equally necessary and equally unbearable states, the need and the presentiment of a better state would never enter into the soul. Suppose that enthusiasm had not come first and had not immediately perceived, confusedly but certainly, all principal truths, then the dialectic would have lacked any foundation and would have had nothing to clarify or demonstrate. On the other hand, remove dialectic and analysis, you have a thousand truths without any clarity. But unite reflection with enthusiasm without destroying it, develop faith by dialectic, and religion by science, then all contradiction is vanquished, all the needs of human nature are satisfied, because all of its faculties are simultaneously and equally employed. Enthusiasm without reason or reason reduced to scepticism, faith without science or a science empty of faith, mysticism, or abstraction in philosophy; so too in society the absence or abuse of freedom, the absolute omnipotence of the state without any individual liberty, or the emancipation of all particular freedoms without any fixed point of inhibition through the state's dominance; [so too] in art, the sublime and grandiose without measure or measure without grandeur; [so too] in religion, an immobile faith, fixed and incomprehensible myths, or a perpetual taking apart of ideas which dissipate into dust; [so too] in history, the East or Greece—these are all necessary, but incomplete and therefore transitory states of the soul and of the world; they are not the final stage of either history, art, religion, society, or philosophy. The genuine last stage, the stage which always eludes us but we pursue endlessly, which it is perhaps given to no civilization as to no man to achieve absolutely, this final stage is the harmony of contraries. It is the last word of all wisdom and all true philosophy. Any philosophy that does not have a place for all the elements of thought is an incomplete and false philosophy, destined to increase the number of contradictions and errors, rather than overcoming and resolving them. True philosophy consists in representing, in itself and in its particular development, all of thought and all of its development. Moreover, to represent all of thought is to represent all of humanity, whose very essence is thought; it is to represent all of history, the visible image of the internal life of humanity; finally, it is to represent all of existence, for universal existence itself is but a thought which humanity reflects more fully and which, therefore, it is possible for one man to reflect. This man would thereby represent the all in his individuality; he would be everything at the very same time as remaining an individual; he would be existence itself—more so, he would be consciousness of this existence; that is, he would have genuinely accomplished the circle of existence; he would have attained perfection, for the perfection of existence does not consist in merely being, but in knowing oneself and understanding oneself. This is the ideal of the philosopher, a sublime but not chimerical ideal, to which one scarcely dares raise one's eyes, but which we must nevertheless still attempt to realise to some extent, even if we despair at ever succeeding: for otherwise one is worthy only of pity, one consents to the incomplete and the false, one resigns oneself to regard things from only one side, to perceive existence solely through an unfaithful aspect. The general history of philosophy offers little except systems imprinted with particular views, which represent solely the epoch in which they were born or the character of their authors. Pythagoras and Heraclitus will always be great men, but their systems, completely true from one perspective, yet otherwise exclusive and false, are still only necessary, but incomplete elements, and, if I can express it thus, individual limbs from the whole body of the history of philosophy. And this does not only apply to Pythagoras and Heraclitus, but to almost every other philosopher of antiquity.

We are not afraid to affirm that, in the history of philosophy, Plato is the first who attempted to escape the spirit of the system and to subordinate all particular perspectives. Plato is the first individual in human history to complete the entire circle of possible developments of the mind. But he arrived at these heights very late, after returning from his travels, after seeing so much and travelling a lot, too firm to fall into scepticism, too enlightened to submit to any of the systems he had encountered; what remained for him was merely their reconciliation. It was then alone that [Plato] achieved the complete expression of his genius as a philosopher and even as an artist. Indeed, in the first epoch of his life and his talent, Plato's style had just one characteristic, like his ideas—its poetic character. Naïve, sublime, movement and grace dominate there as in nature; but one would seek in vain for (or, at least, would find just a very faint degree of) order, precision, and clarity. On the contrary, Plato's second manner exhibits these latter qualities to a high degree, but to the detriment of the former. The details are sacrificed to the whole; order and method are accompanied by some rigidity and aridity; the design might be perfectly precise, but colouring and life are not present. However, in Plato's third manner, the style—by the diversity of qualities which compose it—wonderfully represents the extensity and universality which Plato's thinking had finally attained. Indeed, it is very difficult to find anything missing in this style, just as in the vast system which it reproduces. Both the poetic character and the dialectical character are present, as they are in the works of the first and second manner, with the difference that here, for the first time in Plato as in the human language, they are dissolved together, employ each other as shadow and light, and create a perpetual contrast and a thousand effects of the most pleasant variety—all within a higher unity which tempers and intensifies them. And this happy mixture of poetry and dialectic is not only manifest in the composition as a whole, it is also in the smallest details: everywhere heat with light, force united with grace, the most delicate and the most profound traits, everywhere and always all genres and all tones. Plato's word, like his thought, reflects the universe; he is its interpreter and, as it were, its hierophant. Moreover, as a writer, Plato's place has since remained unoccupied, and it will always be so. Beauty is the flower of humanity; once it has bloomed and been picked, one cannot hope to see it reborn in the winter of civilization. Plato had the good fortune to live in an epoch and among a people where beauty was a feeling and universal need, as well as the natural form of all things. The centuries seem to work deliberately to bring onto the world-stage just once such a privileged people, the marvellous civilization which Plato transposed into his works and expressed like some immortal perfume. But there will be no more Greece, no Athens, no Phidias, no Socrates; there will be no more writers like Plato. At least, as a thinker he can be reproduced, equalled, and even surpassed. Of course, Plato was the first philosopher to conceive the idea of true philosophy in all its extensity. He conceived it and realized it to some extent—this is his immortal glory. But he realized it, and could only do so, on the basis of the strengths and givens of the global epoch in which he lived. Once or twice more during the subsequent centuries, there have been thinkers who renewed this enterprise, and a grateful humankind associated their names with Plato's. Without speaking of the Alexandrians[4] and Proclus, it seems that nature formed Leibniz expressly for such a role; it deliberately placed him at the end—that is, at the height—of all the religious, political, and scientific movements of the sixteenth and seventeenth centuries. Leibniz later suspected what his destiny should have been; he glimpsed it and died. Who will take his place and recover this legacy! Unfortunately, in this case good will is no substitute for strength. The course of centuries has gradually taken up all the major ideas, spread them and sowed them, so to speak, into all minds, such that the same idea which, prior to Plato, did not even exist, which subsequently frustrated Proclus' vast erudition and great intelligence, which was not even suspected by Descartes or Spinoza, and appeared for an instant before the dying eyes of Leibniz—this same idea is present today in the mind of any ordinary man who understands it and is willing to dedicate all his faculties and his entire life to it, even if he can never realize it. Today, the idea of eclecticism has come into the world. It is the idea of the century in philosophy, and it must be the case that someone will [finally] appear to realize it, for this person is necessary.

Notes

1. First published in in *Le Globe* (3 November 1827), pp. 485–7, to which was added a note informing the reader that the fragment would also appear in volume 6 of Cousin's Plato-translation, which included the *Phaedrus*, the *Meno*, and the *Symposium*. (Plato, *Oeuvres*, vol. 6, trans. V. Cousin [Paris: Pichon and Didier, 1831]). However, the essay does not appear in this volume and, in fact, no such "general introduction" is included in any of the thirteen volumes of Cousin's Plato translation. This is one of two short writings in the present volume that did not appear in any of the *Fragments* volumes. It is reprinted under the title "Argument du *Globe*" in P. Janet, *Victor Cousin et son œuvre* (Calmann-Lévy, 1885), pp. 234–46 and subsequently V. Cousin, *Platon*, ed. C. Mauve et al. (Paris: Vrin, 2016), pp. 237–42.
2. More than anything which Cousin writes about Plato himself in this essay, what follows is most significant as the fragment that most closely approximates to the approach taken in Cousin's famous 1828 lectures on the philosophy of history, which were something of an intellectual event of the period. This is true not only of their sketch of a universal history of humankind, but also—and above all—in their use of a triadic schema to make sense of historical phenomena in a way that Cousin's French contemporaries considered "Hegelian." In *Victor Cousin et son œuvre*, Janet devotes several pages to the reproduction and analysis of this "entirely forgotten and, I believe, unknown" work (p. 231), arguing that Cousin's omission of it from his Plato translations or other later works is due to the fact that "this writing is the most precise and most certain witness to Hegel's immediate influence" (p. 232), written in the weeks following Hegel's visit to Paris in 1827, and, to this extent, it anticipates the 1828 lecture course. It is for these reasons—as one of the more controversial of Cousin's shorter works—that we include it in this volume.
3. i.e. the Megarian School founded by Euclides of Megara (*c*.435–*c*.365 BCE), another student of Socrates, which later came to be associated with the practice of eristics.
4. Alexandrian philosophy, it should be remembered, included what Diogenes Laertius identified as "the eclectic sect" founded by Potamo of Alexandria—after which Cousin (in part) names his own philosophy. This relationship between ancient and modern eclecticisms resulted in the philosophy of Alexandria becoming a highly politicised field of research in early nineteenth-century France.

Prefatory Note to *New Philosophical Fragments*[1]

I have elsewhere[2] explained how it was philosophy itself which led me to the history of philosophy, including everything that has been, since 1818, the object and direction of my historical works. Among these works, a new translation of Plato[3] and a complete edition of Proclus' manuscripts[4] indicate well enough the importance I ascribe to the study of ancient philosophy. But independently of these two long and laborious undertakings, constant commerce with philosophical antiquity necessarily occupied me with more or less extensive secondary investigations—sometimes [these were investigations] into the significant, but neglected points I encountered on my path; sometimes into famous philosophers whose name alone has survived; sometimes into similar publications that had recently appeared in Germany; sometimes, finally, into unedited manuscripts in the royal library in Paris. Such are the following dissertations, of which only a few have seen the light of day and which I am advised to gather up and offer to the public today as fragments for use in the study of ancient philosophy, much like the type of fragments I published two years ago for use in the study of philosophy itself.[5] The earlier ones touched on all the particular questions that a general system must encompass; the present ones touch on all the epochs and all the schools that a complete history of ancient philosophy should encompass. Moreover, I have here placed them in chronological order to constitute, in some way, a prelude to such a history and to serve as steppingstones for a more considerable work.

All genuine science—and the history of philosophy is such—advances by way of two opposed movements which seem to exclude each other and yet which are equally useful, equally necessary. A science exists as science solely insofar as it forms a theory, and there is no theory without general laws to which particular facts are related. On the other hand, if every theory presupposes general laws to which particular facts are coordinated, it therefore presupposes well-recorded and well-described particular facts that it can legitimately relate to general laws. Hence, science lives both from the generalities and the details. Of course, both generalizations and detailed work have their own inadequacies and their own perils: generalizations can quickly turn into arbitrary hypotheses; the spirit of detail can bury itself in insignificant trifles. But it is no less true that details are the foundation of science than generalities are its soul, and [science] is equally served by each of the two paths. Everyone follows one [path] or the other, according to the instinct of his nature. There are scrupulous, patient, and penetrating natures far more made for details, just as there are bold [natures] who hurl themselves into generalizations. Over the course of centuries, some of [these centuries] will amass facts and experiments; others will construct theories. And it is the same with peoples as with individuals and centuries: talents are as diverse as climates, and all of this diversity conspires for the harmony of science, as it does for [the harmony] of the world. Diversity in itself is a good; the bad is when it is transformed into contradiction and enmity. And yet this is what happens. The different individual capacities, the geniuses of different centuries and the different peoples end up throwing accusations at each other. For example, in metaphysics, the ontologist scorns the psychologist who, in turn, mocks the ontologist; analysis wages war on synthesis, which despises analysis. The eighteenth century with its negative and critical genius and its marvellous talent for reducing all things to their basic elements denigrates the sixteenth and seventeenth centuries with their vast generalizations and their formidable [powers of] synthesis. English philosophy accuses German philosophy of an extravagant idealism, and the latter accuses English philosophy of a meagre and abject empiricism. My professed ambition is to see nineteenth-century France at the head, rather than the rear, of these other peoples, at the centre of the philosophical movement of Europe, rather than on its circumference; to see German idealism and English empiricism brought before a tribunal of French good sense, condemned there, and forced to absolve each other and contract a belated but fruitful alliance. What is more, eclecticism also begins to operate in historical works. Here too generalities do not exclude details, nor details generalities. It is faint-hearted to sacrifice generalities for details, resulting in a lack of meaning; it is extravagant to sacrifice details for generalities, resulting in nothing more than reveries. All that is good and true can and should accompany all that is true and good. But everything has its time and place. In the position that has been bestowed on me,[6] I will try to provide one day a general history of ancient philosophy, to show its unity, to make clear how connected and analogous its composite facts are, and so to render it a distinctive epoch, with basic variations [within it] which gave rise to its diverse periods. In what follows, I am anticipating—for my listeners and for those who are interested in this great era of the history of philosophy—a number of particular points of some importance, which I have attempted to establish with certainty. *Cras altera mittam.*[7]

Paris, 8th November 1828
V. C.

Notes

1. *Nouv. fr. phil.*, pp. i–iv. Unlike the other prefaces in Cousin's *Fragments* volumes, this text was not reproduced in any of the later editions (even in the various *Ancient Philosophy* volumes). This is presumably because of its particular function as a supplement to the 1826 Preface to the original *Philosophical Fragments*. As this prefatory note emphasizes, the *New Philosophical Fragments* contained Cousin's articles and notes on ancient philosophy from the early and mid-1820s. The volume comprises interventions on Xenophanes, Zeno, Socrates, Plato, Eunapius, Proclus, Olympiadorus, and tend to take the form of conjectural reconstructions on the basis of extant fragments or philological exercises in tracing the sources for various arguments and terms. We have included the short essays, "On the True Beginning of the History of Philosophy" and "Plato: Language of the Doctrine of Ideas," above as indicative of their content.
2. See pp. 81–2 above.
3. *Œuvres de Proclus*, 6 vols (Paris: Pichon and Didier, 1820–7).
4. *Œuvres de Platon*, 13 vols (Paris: Bossange, 1822–40)—by 1828, the first four volumes of the translation had appeared.
5. i.e. *Fr. phil. 1826*.
6. The teaching posts to which Cousin had been reinstated in early 1828.
7. "Tomorrow I will send others."—from Virgil, *Eclogues*, III.

Preface to the Translation of Tennemann's *Manual of the History of Philosophy*[1]

Today philosophy is able to do just one of three things:

[1] Abdicate, renounce its independence, resubmit to an ancient authority [and] return to the Middle Ages;
[2] Or continue to run through the cycle of worn-out systems which mutually destroy each other;
[3] Or, finally, abstract what is true in each of these systems and out of it compose a philosophy superior to all such systems, which governs them all by subordinating them all, which is not merely a particular philosophy, but philosophy itself in its essence and in its unity.

The first path is impossible. First, philosophy is merely an effect, and not a cause: the independence and, as it were, secularization of thought is due to the general progress of the spirit of independence and the secularization of all things, the state, science, art, industry. Posed in this way, the question is easily answered: What wind could today uproot a tree which has grown in the midst of so many storms and which has grown out of the blood and tears of so many generations? Modern civilization cannot turn back, nor, therefore, can the philosophy which represents it. This is the vanity of the theocratic school. Theocracy is the legitimate cradle of new-born societies, but it does not accompany them throughout their development, their necessary progress which derives from the nature of things. And, just as the nature of things cannot be separated from the designs of Providence, it follows that any struggle against the nature of things is directed against Providence itself, and so this attempt to put a stop to civilization and to extinguish philosophy is a challenge to God himself, which no mind in the world could win. Besides, what is the ground of theocracy's haughty polemic against philosophy?[2] Today, everyone has realized it: it is a paralogism.[3] They attack reason with reason, and so invoke the very authority that they contest and whose impotence they seek to demonstrate. A little rigour and consistency have led the theocratic school away from the admonishment of certain specific philosophical systems to that of the common spirit of all systems—that is, free reflection or philosophy itself. Even more rigour and consistency would push it into absolute scepticism or lead it back to philosophy. Of course, after the great movements which have recently disturbed society and human thought in such profound and diverse ways, without yet fulfilling the anxious hopes of those who wish to sow and harvest [their fruits] in a single day, the call of the Middle Ages and of blind faith might well seduce minds exhausted by the lure of novelty and the false semblance of perfect consistency. This has resulted in these disavowals of philosophy, born from discouragement and despair and which—to untrained eyes—seem to signal the defeat of philosophy and the resurgence of ancient authority. However, today the secret has been made public: the peace and innocence of the Middle Ages are well understood, and the call of blind faith against reason by reason itself is shown to be nothing but a fainthearted paralogism, and this sole truth, so revealed, will protect philosophy and prevent deserters.

On the other hand, to leave philosophy in the state in which it has been handed down to the nineteenth century from preceding centuries is to make use of reason in an almost unreasonable way; it is to consent to the disparagement of philosophy by itself; it is to lend the most redoubtable weapons to [philosophy's] enemies and to theocracy which watches over it; it is not to combat the spirit of the age, but to remain behind it. Indeed, the quality which distinguishes us [in the nineteenth century],[4] which we seek and of which we are most proud is our comprehensiveness [*l'étendue*]. Everywhere—in politics, in the arts, in literature—there is an aspiration for completeness; there is a refusal to let ourselves be taken in by just one aspect of things, no matter how brightly it shines; we wish to look at them all in turn, so as to form a complete and faithful idea of the thing in question. Such is the good; the bad is in the weakening or absence of enthusiasm and great originality; I say "great," for there is an abundance of lesser [originality]. Considering this general disposition of minds [in the present century], what could be the attraction of those old systems which modern philosophy produced at its birth and which it has reproduced a hundred times over the last two centuries without any of them being able to sustain themselves? It is evident none of the systems we have inherited from the seventeenth and eighteenth centuries is absolutely false, since it was able to exist; but it is also completely evident that none of these systems is absolutely true, since it stopped existing, in comparison to absolute truth, which, if it ever appeared, would enlighten, win over, and subjugate all intellects. There is not one of these systems on which a damning polemic has not been given; there is not one of them which is not brought to account, as it were, attacked and shown to contain intolerable extravagances. Let anyone be presented with one of these principles which, over the years, has seduced so many good minds, and there is no one today who, at this very moment, would not draw from this principle the long chain of consequences which follow from it and which have betrayed and condemned it. Do you propose to explain the intellect by the famous principle of sensation, which not long ago, in Locke's and Condillac's hands, possessed such irresistible charm for so many minds?[5] Today, even without much wisdom and dialectic, it is enough to do a little bit of reading to see the terrible implications that follow from this attractive principle—on Locke's[6] side, Mandeville and Collins; on Condillac's[7] side, d'Holbach and La Mettrie and all the saturnalias of materialism and atheism. Do you propose to explain all human knowledge solely by the force of the soul, by thinking and its laws—something which might appear quite natural? Such a noble spiritualism—which is so astute in its starting point—has the equivocal reputation of having led more than one illustrious school to sublime and chimerical abstractions. Will you try out doubt? The phantom of scepticism resides there. Are you tempted to seek refuge in sentiment? But who will not inform you straightaway of the slope down which you are already sliding towards mysticism? Such are the principles and their consequences—there is no longer anything else unforeseen, anything that will give rise to the illusion [of an entirely true system]. Do not be deceived: reason, like imagination, scarcely pursues anything except the unknown and the infinite. And which system today possesses this charm? It is the glory of human reason to give itself up solely to—I do not say absolute truth—but to what it believes to be absolute truth. Today, there is no vaguely educated mind who does not know for the most part that all the systems presented by modern philosophy are, in the last analysis, nothing but particular systems which might well contain some truth, but which it would be ridiculous to take for the entire truth.[8]

This, then, leaves the third path. When it comes to lack of fanaticism for a certain particular system—which a tendency to enthusiasm and an incomplete view of things might have produced and would lead us to despair of our qualities as well as our faults—I see no other resources for a philosophy that does not wish to submit to the yoke of theocracy than fairness, moderation, impartiality, wisdom. It is, I agree, a fairly desperate resource, but I see no other. It would be absurd if in the present day anything but common sense could have any effect on men's imagination. However, it is certain that every other form of prestige seems exhausted. All the fanatical positions in philosophy, all the parts of injustice and stupidity (that is, all the supporting roles) have been stolen from the nineteenth century by the preceding centuries; it is as if it had been condemned to a new role, humbler in appearance, but in reality the best and the grandest—[the role] of being just towards all systems and the dupe of none; of studying them all, instead of becoming the disciple of one of them, converting them all to its banner, and marching at their head in the discovery and conquest of truth. This ambition to reject no system nor to accept any in its entirety, to cast off one aspect and to take on another, to choose what appears true and good and therefore durable in everything—this, in a word, is eclecticism.

Eclecticism! I am not unaware that the word alone provokes every exclusive doctrine; but should one be astonished that a view that seems a little novel encounters vigorous resistance—and particularly a view like eclecticism? Would you, I ask, suggest to [political] parties that they renounce their tyrannical ambitions in the service of the common nation? Every party would accuse you of being a bad citizen. Exclusive doctrines are to philosophy what parties are to the state. Eclecticism attempts to replace their violent and irregular actions with a determinate, moderated direction which makes use of all their strengths, neglects none of them, but refuses to sacrifice order and the general interest to any of them. Suppose for a moment that, among the ideas which all aspire to exclusive domination, there was one which had, for fifty years, been in possession of universal and uncontested authority, was accustomed to unqualified praise, and treated almost like a religion. Think about contesting the sovereignty of this haughty idol; propose, in the politest way possible, that it descend from its throne, enter the throng, and make good on its reputation through hard work, so as to finally become one more idea just like any other—and, just like any other [idea], displaying the true and the false, accepted by some and rejected by others. In a word, ask this [idol] to consent to the right of examination, and you will soon see a fine tempest burst forth. For this reason, I had reckoned on an ardent polemic, but I had hoped it would be serious. Instead of objections, I have met only denunciations, calumnies.[9] In truth, I had believed the sensualist school to be more robust than this. If it were in my power, far from weakening it, I would actually like to have strengthened it; I would like to have furnished it with a serious and worthy representative, for it does contain great truths and should be placed high in the hierarchy of science. In good conscience, I hold the deplorable condition to which it has fallen among us to be a genuine misfortune. I sincerely regret that de Tracy,[10] disarmed by age, cannot enter the lists with the new philosophy. It is not from the arsenal of Jesuitism that such an adversary would take up his weapons; he would find them through a deepened study of philosophical materials, through a talent for analysis and rigorous logic (of which he has given so many proofs), and out of this, he might have established an accurate and scientific polemic. I would be the first to solicit it in the general interest of science.[11] In the meantime, neither my friends nor I have such a feeble heart as to let ourselves be hindered by the obstacles placed before us. We have not set out down this path for the sake of frivolous praise, but to serve philosophy. For me, it was a long time after having studied and passed through more than one school, trying to account for the attraction each of them in turn had for me—as well as for the good standing that systems as different as Condillac's and Reid's (for example) had for the best minds and distinguished men whose lectures I had heard, Laromiguière and Royer-Collard—I noticed that the authority of these different systems came from the fact that they all have in them something true and good.[12] I suspected that each was not as fundamentally and radically the other's enemy as it claimed to be; I gradually assured myself that all of them might very well agree with each other under certain conditions; I proposed a peace treatise between them on the basis of such mutual concessions. From that moment onwards, I spoke the word eclecticism. If it scares others off, I will willingly take it back, as long as the thing itself is ceded to me. Yet, this word—exact in itself, already employed by those who, over the course of centuries, have had roughly the same idea and generally accepted in the language of the history of philosophy—appears to me just as good as any such label can be, and I see no reason to abandon it. At the foundations of this project, I remain more than ever attached to it by reflection and erudition. The very perspective of fanaticism, to which an exclusive opinion can lead, recommends to me more than ever [the need for] moderation and wisdom; and it is my express wish, if not my hope, that eclecticism will serve as a guide for French philosophy in the nineteenth century.

If philosophy is to be eclectic, it must be supported by the history of philosophy. Indeed, it is clear that all eclectic philosophy should necessarily have as its ground a deep knowledge of all the systems whose essential and true elements it is claiming to combine. Besides, what is the history of philosophy if not a perpetual lesson in eclecticism? What does the history of philosophy teach if not that all systems are as old as it and inherent in the human mind itself, which has produced them from the beginning and endlessly reproduces them;[13] [what is it other] than wanting to show that the domination of just one [system] is a vain undertaking, which, if it were to succeed, would prove the tomb of philosophy, that, therefore, there is nothing to be done but to honour the human mind, to respect its freedom, to note the laws which govern it and the fundamental systems which emanate from these laws, to endlessly perfect these diverse systems one after another without trying to destroy any of them, by studying and abstracting the immortal portion of truth which each of them contains and by which each of them is brother to all others and the legitimate offspring of the human mind? The history of philosophy is itself sufficient to give birth to eclecticism, that is, to philosophical tolerance, and as soon as this tolerance appears after the long reign of fanaticism, it necessarily brings with it a demand and a taste for the deepened study of all systems.

Such is the reason for the extreme[14] importance I attach to the history of philosophy; it is what has engaged and sustained all the works I have undertaken in getting to know myself and making known for others specific epochs, specific systems, specific figures. It is also what determined me, last winter, before entering into the detailed exposition and discussion of all the schools of the eighteenth century, to present to my listeners, in a concise framework, an overview of all previous schools—ancient and modern, even including those of the East. And I would be happy if this short introduction* were to clarify the obscure labyrinth of systems and to furnish some useful direction for contemporary philosophy. However, I do not fool myself that this is a sufficient basis for the study of the history of philosophy. So, I decided to ask of Germany, so rich in works of this kind, for a work which could realize my ideas and satisfy the needs of my listeners; and I was not able to find one which, all things considered, enjoyed a more general and merited reputation than Tennemann's.

---

* *Lectures of 1829*, vol. 1, pp. 133–510.[15]

Brucker[16] is the father of the history of philosophy; Tennemann is Brucker's genuine successor. Like him, he dedicated his entire life to the history of philosophy, and he prepared for the composition of his great work with a mass of specialized dissertations,[17] which attest to the detailed labour through which alone can be formed the critical spirit and can ground the fruitful alliance of philology and philosophy. Like Brucker, Tennemann gave a complete history of philosophy that he carried on into his own time; like [Brucker] again, out of this long work he made a full and substantial abridged edition which reproduced its most excellent qualities, with the advantage of not overwhelming the intellect under too many details, yet still furnishing the robust data on which [the intellect] could rely with confidence.[18] It is this summary that I present to the French public.

I have already spoken of Tennemann elsewhere,† of his merits and faults. In summary, his merits are: (1) erudition, knowledge of sources, of the original monuments in which systems are deposited, and the works from all eras and in all countries to which these systems have given rise; (2) criticism, the rational employment of the materials amassed by erudition, discerning between uncorrupted sources and those which are [more corrupted], a prudence which relies solely on certain, well-examined and well-constituted texts; (3) a philosophical intellect elevated relatively highly into the science itself, so as to clearly discern its history. Tennemann is strong enough to be impartial; he desires to be so and generally is so. However, his historical impartiality could be even greater, for his philosophy could be raised higher. Tennemann is Kant's student; and Kant's school is of course a great school, but it is ultimately only one particular school, too narrow still to comprehend and subordinate all philosophical systems. It is merely, as I think I have said before, the Scottish school raised to its highest power. What characterizes Kant's philosophy is to have fully separated ontology and psychology and to have placed the ground of all philosophical speculation in the preliminary study of the faculty of knowing and its laws. Here, indeed, is the starting point of philosophy, but solely its starting point and not its end. One must get from this starting point to the end, from the critique of reason to the objects of reason, to beings. Yet, Kant is so firmly ensconced within the starting point, in psychology, that he remains always on route and can only arrive via detours and more or less legitimately at an uncertain ontology.[20] As an anti-sensualist in psychology, he is almost a sceptic in ontology, and in theodicy he is so far from mysticism that he is almost unjust to its viewpoint and does not understand it. This is also basically Tennemann. He arms himself with excessive severity every time he turns to systems to which his psychological measure applies less easily, and which present him with ontological components for which he cannot account well, such as a real mysticism or even just the appearance of mysticism. It would have been desirable for this skilful man to have

---

† *Lectures of 1828, Introduction to the History of Philosophy*, lecture 12.[19]

viewed and judged philosophical systems from a higher perspective; but he is far from always falling into partiality and injustice, and it is impossible[21] to reproduce with more faithfulness and precision the true characteristics of systems and their general tendencies. Moreover, I confess, I like it better that Tennemann sins by way of an excess of psychological severity than by the contrary fault, a too great capacity for climbing the perilous paths of ontology without criticism. Psychology is not philosophy in its entirety but is its legitimate beginning; just as Tennemann's work is not the conclusion to the history of philosophy but is an excellent foundation for it. As such, [this work] appears to me perfectly suited to the state of philosophy among us, and will be able to effectively contribute, by both its qualities and its faults which I have just described, to the regeneration of philosophical studies—a regeneration whose first condition is a strong culture of psychology, [for], in the beginning, the significance of psychology in science and in history should be exaggerated a little.

Just as the philosophical spirit of Tennemann's work is a little too reminiscent of the school to which the author belongs, so too its forms are too reminiscent of the forms, terminology, and language of Kantian philosophy. And, even if I am far from agreeing with every use of this language within philosophy itself, I agree far less with its transposition back onto history. It is not simple or general enough to translate every system. Nevertheless, it is, in the end, still precise and so sufficiently clear. We must not forget either that this book is a manual made to be studied and not to be glanced through quickly; it is substantial, concise and rigorous on every page; it resists trifling curiosity and will only be of profit placed in the hands of hard work and patience.

The success of this manual was such in Germany that, after initial publication in 1812, the author was obliged to produce a second edition in 1815, already much improved; and he had prepared a third when death interrupted his work. Fortunately, the materials he had assembled were entrusted to someone very capable of making use of them, Am[adeus] Wendt, then professor at Leipzig and today professor at Göttingen, who made the 1820 third edition better than its predecessor.[22] These[23] improvements were then considerably increased in the fourth edition which appeared in 1825. The notes left by Tennemann had already extended the exposition to further systems, such as those German systems which arose after Kant's. Wendt himself added some articles on additional living German philosophers, and I have retained the bibliographical part of these articles to give France an idea of contemporary German philosophy. However, I have omitted the exposition of their doctrines, as they were far too short to be intelligible anywhere but in Germany, and, since they are subject to error and to change, the doctrines of these philosophers have been modified and developed continuously.[24] It is through death that a man enters into the domain of history; he can be judged properly only when he has finished his oeuvre. I exempt only Schelling, whose grand renown has basically given him the rights of the dead.

It is on the fourth and final edition that this translation is based.[25] I take this occasion to publicly thank my friend and former colleague at the École Normale, Viguier,[26] who very much wished to help me in this thankless task. Only those who know the original could form an idea of the trouble which this translation cost us, as imperfect as it still is.

I end by offering up this manual to the youth who frequent my lectures. Let it nourish in them a love for the true philosophy, a taste for reflection and study, and for those laborious and virile habits which alone in every venture ensure genuine success, and alone can prepare the new generation to replace with dignity the powerful generation who preceded them on the world-stage and who have done and seen so many great things.

Paris, 1 September 1829
V. Cousin

Notes

1. First published as part of Cousin's 1829 translation of the fourth edition of W. G. Tennemann's *Grundriss der Geschichte der Philosophie für den akademischen Unterricht* as *Manuel de l'histoire de la philosophie* (Paris: Sautelet and Co., 1929), pp. v-xxvii (subsequently: *Fr. phil. 1838*, vol. 2, pp. 41-57; *Fr. phil. 1847*, vol. 4, pp. 189-202; *Fr. phil. 1855*, vol. 5, pp. 189-202; *Fr. phil. 1865*, vol. 5, pp. 220-34). *Fr. phil. 1847* and subsequent editions include the two-page preface to the second edition of the *Manuel* as well. With the exception of one passage (see n. 20 below), we take the 1829 publication as our base text for this translation and note the significant modifications to later versions in the endnotes. A partial translation of the text exists, under the title, "On the Destiny of Modern Philosophy," in George Ripley's *Philosophical Miscellanies* (Boston: Hilliard and Gray, 1838), pp. 45-55. It constitutes one of the clearest statements of Cousin's eclectic project, particularly the ways in which eclecticism is intended to correspond to the needs of the nineteenth century by superseding previous philosophical structures (i.e. the recurrent cycle of systems).
2. For more details on this theocratic attack on philosophy, see the opening to the extract from *On Pascal's Pensées*, pp. 242-9 below, where the early Lamennais is named as its principal representative.
3. *Fr. phil. 1847* and subsequent editions: Cousin inserts a footnote referring the reader to the 1833 Preface, p. 110-11 above.
4. Although he is using a form of words identical to how he typically defines eclecticism, Cousin is intending to speak here of nineteenth-century intellectual culture in general, before turning to how this resonates with his eclectic project in the next paragraph.
5. This passage presents the logic of modern philosophy in terms of the necessary sliding between four fundamental systematic archetypes—the sensualist, the idealist, the sceptical and the mystical. It is a narrative of the history of philosophy he had developed at length in his 1829 lectures, which tells the story of the whole of the history of thought in terms of this cyclic movement, and, in general, the present text is unsurprisingly very close to Cousin's position in the 1829 lectures on the history of philosophy.
6. *Fr. phi. 1847* and subsequent editions: Cousin adds a footnote referring the reader to his various discussions of Lockean philosophies in 1819 and 1829.
7. *Fr. phi.* 1847 and subsequent editions: Cousin adds a footnote referring the reader to his discussion of Condillacian philosophy in 1819.
8. *Fr. phi.* 1847 and subsequent editions: Cousin adds a footnote citing lecture 4 of his 1829 lecture course on eighteenth-century philosophy.
9. Cousin is presumably here thinking of critiques like Broussais's and Comte's—see n. 11 to 1833 Preface.
10. Antoine Destutt de Tracy (1754-1836): one of the leaders of the *Idéologues* whose work for the most part appeared during the Empire and who had stopped publishing by 1823.

11. *Fr. phil. 1838* and subsequent editions: "in the general interest of science" is omitted.
12. On Cousin's relation to Laromiguière and Royer-Collard, see Antoine-Mahut's essay above.
13. Once more, Cousin is here alluding throughout this sentence to the theory he had been justifying at length in his 1829 lectures on the history of philosophy, in which the four systematic archetypes that recur in philosophical history can be derived through psychological analysis from innate laws of the mind (and so without any reference to history).
14. *Fr. phil. 1838* and subsequent editions: "extreme" is omitted.
15. Cousin is here referring to *Cours de l'histoire de la philosophie. Histoire de la philosophie au XVIIIe siècle*, vol. 1 (Paris: Pichon and Didier, 1829), lectures 1–12.
16. J. J. Brucker (1696–1770), author of *Historia Critica Philosophiae*. For Cousin's opinion of Brucker, see p. 182 above.
17. During the 1790s, Tennemann had published monographs on Socrates, Plato, and Aristotle, as well as German translations of Hume's *Enquiry concerning Human Understanding* and Locke's *Essay on Human Understanding*.
18. Tennemann's *Grundriss*, which Cousin is translating, is an abridgement of his 12-volume *Geschichte der Philosophie*, published between 1798 and 1819.
19. *Cours de philosophie. Introduction à l'histoire de la philosophie*, ed. P. Vermeren (Paris: Pichon and Didier, [1828] 1991), pp. 332–5. Here Cousin criticizes Tennemann for having "reproduced Kant's system in the history of philosophy" and so seeing that history "with Kant's eyes." He continues this system "is not extensive enough" to capture history as a whole "without disfiguring it."
20. *Fr. phi. 1847* and subsequent editions: Cousin adds a footnote generally citing his 1820 lectures on Kant.
21. *Fr. phil. 1838* and subsequent editions: "impossible" replaced with "difficult."
22. Amadeus Wendt (1783–1836): Chair of Philosophy at the University of Göttingen and ally of Cousin—see p. 124 above.
23. *Fr. phil. 1838* and subsequent editions: this sentence is omitted—see n. 25 below.
24. This decision to cut the material on contemporary German philosophy affects, most visibly, the entry on Hegel.
25. We translate the 1838 version of the text at this point, because the 1829 version seems to be based on a factual error that is being corrected. That is, in 1829, Cousin appeared to be confused about the precise edition of the text he was translating, for, in place of this sentence, he had written, "It would be superfluous to give an account of the help from some parties and the mass of small improvements owed to Wendt which enriched the 1820 edition. These improvements are even more considerable in the fourth edition which appeared in 1823 and the fifth of 1825 which did nothing more than reproduce them. Hence, this book has almost attained the perfection of which it is capable. It is then on this fifth and final edition that this translation is based."
26. Auguste Viguier (1793–1867): Cousin's very close friend to whom the first volume of his Plato translation is dedicated. It is likely that Viguier was the genuine (or, at least, primary) translator of Tennemann's *Manual* on Cousin's request.

From Review of Reiffenberg's
On Eclecticism[1]

We can recommend the work we are reviewing in terms of the general spirit which governs it, as well as the variety of sources and readings to which it attests; but the very esteem in which we hold it permits us and at the same time compels us in duty to not hide the faults which mar it.[2] Its ideas and erudition are not sufficiently digested, and it does not bear the impression of sufficient preliminary reflection or of sufficiently hard work in its execution. We will end with some observations that we submit to the author and by which we would be happy if he were to profit in the continuation of his work. We continue to consider both useful and fruitful the opinion which begins to be disseminated today that every exclusive school is condemned to error, even if it necessarily contains some element of the truth. From this [arises], we contend, the very philosophical idea of borrowing from each school without adopting[3] any of them. This superior impartiality which studies everything, disdains nothing, and chooses from everywhere, with rigorous [*sévère*] discernment, partial truths which observation and common sense have almost always introduced into even the most defective systems—this is what has become known under a name which is as good as any other: eclecticism. The term is nothing, the thing is all. Besides, there is nothing that does not possess its bad and its good sides, its dangers and its attractions. The attraction here is in the extensity and richness of the materials which are presented in a mass as soon as we do not reject any system in its totality, and as soon as we admit something of all of them in the composition of our own edifice. Once more, such is the attraction, but there is also danger here. The materials are undoubtedly abundant, for humanity was not born yesterday. Philosophy is already counted in centuries, and geniuses no longer with us have bequeathed us a thousand truths; but these truths are buried in systems in which they are connected to specious errors. Thus, we must be able to distinguish these truths from the errors that surround them; we must be able to recognize that these truths are truths and not errors; and we cannot do so without an evaluative standard, a principle of criticism, without knowing what is true, what is false in itself;[4] and we cannot know this without having undertaken a sufficient study oneself into the philosophical problems of human nature, the basis[5] of its faculties and its laws. It is [only] when a scientific, patient and profound[6] analysis has put us in possession of the real elements and all the real elements of humanity that—addressing ourselves to the systems of philosophers and studying them with the same care we have taken with the study of philosophical questions—we can recognize what these systems possess and what they lack, and [so] discern the true and the false in them—disregard the latter, appropriating the former for ourselves and enlarging and extending our own thoughts by these skilful and judicious borrowings. Then alone comes the turn of historical analysis which ought to be pushed extremely far in order to arrive at the very entrails of the systems under investigation and to grasp their constitutive elements.[7] Were the historical analysis of systems not preceded by the scientific analysis of the materials in themselves, it would lack a guide and flame and lose itself in shadows; or rather, were it not preceded by scientific analysis, but rather by one lacking depth and stopping at the surface of systems, its proposed object would itself escape it. Hence, there are two conditions of eclecticism properly understood: 1° scientific analysis, 2° historical analysis—that is, philosophical spirit and an erudition as rigorous [*sévère*] as it is extensive[8]—this is the ideal that must be born in mind even when one despairs of attaining it; this is the goal to which one must approximate, and along this sketched-out path each of us can reach different points, in proportion to our strength, with some gain for science and not without honours for oneself. However, suppose that the scientific analysis is vague and superficial and that the historical analysis is no less so, and then judge what could come from such a slight piece of work. In place of the real combination of organic elements from diverse systems, you will have merely the arbitrary juxtaposition of some phrases extracted here and there from philosophical writers. There would undoubtedly be some impartiality, but the impartiality of weakness and impotence; no precision in the details, no insight in the whole—in a word, syncretism in place of eclecticism. However, even then one must not forget that every beginning is weak, every nascent direction necessarily a little vague, that nothing can do without time, and that philosophy, like all other sciences, is progressive and is given life by trying things out and experimenting. For some years, in France and elsewhere, more than one distinguished mind has started down that path we have just mentioned and which we believe to be a good one. In Belgium, van de Weyer[9] and Reiffenberg have translated eclecticism into their teaching and disseminated it through their writings. We can only applaud their enterprise and encourage their attempts, while, nevertheless, inviting them to redouble their efforts and to not put an end to their honourable course.

Notes

1. First published in *Journal des Savants* (April 1830), pp. 225–33 and then incorporated into the "fragment" "On Belgian Philosophy" in *Fr. phil. 1838*, vol. 2, pp. 10–40 (subsequently: *Fr. phil. 1847*, vol. 4, pp. 205–30; *Fr. phil. 1855*, vol. 5, pp. 205–30; *Fr. phil. 1865*, vol. 5, pp. 278–301). We take the 1830 publication as our base text for this translation and note the significant modifications to

later versions in the endnotes. This extract is from the concluding pages to the review (pp. 232–3) where Cousin turns from enumerating the specific flaws of Reiffenberg's work to provide some general principles for eclectic historiography. Frédéric de Reiffenberg (1795–1850) was Professor of Philosophy at the State University of Leuven from 1822 and later a corresponding member of the Institut de France; he published his *De l'éclectisme, ou premiers principes de philosophie générale* in 1827. In 1838, Cousin merged this review with two others of Belgian eclectic philosophy (Reiffenberg's 1827 *De la direction actuellement nécessaire aux études philosophies* and Sylvain van de Weyer's 1827 opening lecture—see n. 9 below) into the fragment "De la philosophie en Belgique" to which he often referred back as late as the 1850s (especially on the question of the relation of the history of philosophy to philosophy itself).

2. Earlier sections of Cousin's review had been arranged around various "confusions" he attributed to Reiffenberg's book (confusions in the selection of materials, confusions in the treatment of psychology, confusions of order, confusions of erudition, and confusions of style).
3. *Fr. phil. 1838* and subsequent editions: "adopting" replaced by "exempting."
4. *Fr. phil. 1865*: "in itself" is omitted.
5. *Fr. phil. 1838* and subsequent editions: "the basis" is omitted.
6. *Fr. phil. 1865*: "patient and profound" is omitted.
7. *Fr. phil. 1865*: "and to grasp their constitutive elements" is omitted.
8. *Fr. phil. 1847* and subsequent editions: Cousin adds a footnote referring the reader to the final pages of the 1833 preface.
9. Sylvain van de Weyer (1802–74): briefly Professor of the History of Philosophy at Brussels' Musée de sciences et des lettres on his way to a political career as a liberal Prime Minister of Belgium. Cousin's review of his 1827 opening lecture at the Musée forms part of "De la philosophie en Belgique."

V
AFTER 1833

Introduction to the Posthumous Works of Maine de Biran[1]

Since I am responsible for introducing this volume, some words seem appropriate to help readers orient themselves within it and within a doctrine that is complicated and obscure in appearance, but very simple in its principle and general character.

The first merit of [Maine de Biran's] doctrine is its incontestable originality. Of my teachers in France,* Biran is surely the most original, even if he is perhaps not the greatest. Laromiguière continued Condillac's work, even if he modified him on some points. Royer-Collard emerges out of Scottish philosophy, which—with the rigour and natural power of his reason—he would have infallibly surpassed, if he had carried on with his writings, which nevertheless remain not the least robust portion of his glory. For myself, I emerge out of both Scottish philosophy and German philosophy. It is Biran alone who emerges out of himself and his own meditations.

Disciple of the philosophy of his time, part of the famous society of Auteuil,[2] formed by it for the world and its affairs,† and after beginning in this tradition with a brilliant philosophical success, he gradually distanced himself from it without any foreign influence: every day he separated himself from it more and more until he finally arrived at a doctrine diametrically opposed to the [doctrine] to which he owed his first successes.

In year VIII (1800),[4] the moral and political sciences section of the Institut [de France] over which Condillac's school reigned[5] set a prize-essay in philosophy on the *Influence of Habit on the Faculty of Thinking*. Maine de Biran treated this subject according to the prevailing doctrine, but with characteristic finesse of observation. His entry[6] was crowned in 1802, and it is this book on habit which made the author's name at the time.

---

* See the preface to the new edition of *Philosophical Fragments*, p. xxxiv [p. 104 above].
† He was first named sub-prefect in Bergerac, in the department of the Dordogne, his home; then a member of the legislative body where he participated in the famous commission which was composed, alongside him, of Lainé, Raynouard, Gallois, and Flaugergues. Under the Restoration, he was a deputy and counsellor of state. He was a correspondent of the Institut [de France] and the Berlin Academy.[3]

This was, it seemed, a man very committed to a system both for his own self-worth and the acknowledgement of others.

In year XI (1803), the same section [of the Institut de France] proposed as its competition topic the following question: "How is the faculty of thought to be analysed and what elementary faculties are to be recognized there?"[7] Maine de Biran was crowned again. The same judges had expected the same principles from the same competitors; but, instead, Biran responded to the question in a way that betrayed a new direction.

What had gone on in the young laureate's mind? What insight had come to him and from where on the philosophical horizon had it come? It could not have come from either Scotland or Germany: he knew neither English nor German. No man nor contemporary writing could have modified his thought; it had modified itself out of its own wisdom. By dint of meditating on the doctrine of the day, Cabanis's and Tracy's disciple[8] had ended up glimpsing their inadequacy by sensing the need for and recognizing the reality of an element essentially distinct from sensation. It was a kind of defection; and what bestows much honour on the judges and bears witness to their sincere love of truth is the fact that in 1805 they crowned the new prize-essay which, in the politest possible terms, proclaimed its opposition to them. This circumstance appeared to me too honourable to philosophy to pass unmentioned.[9]

Maine de Biran spent his entire life developing the seed contained in this prize-essay.

There is one idea alone in it, and Maine de Biran never had anything but this one [idea] alone. This idea, still confused and advanced hesitantly in the 1805 prize-essay, was then reproduced more distinctly and precisely in his 1807 prize-essay crowned by the Berlin Academy[‡] on immediate internal perception, as distinct from sensation. He further reproduced it, increasingly precisely and vividly, in the prize-essay later crowned by the Copenhagen Academy on the relations of the physical and the moral.[11] Afterwards, all his writings were nothing more than the remnants of these three prize-essays. What, then, is the one idea which proved enough for his entire life, for his entire philosophical destiny?

This idea is nothing other than the reintegration of the active element with all its attendant implications.[12]

The reigning philosophy generated each of our faculties in turn—as well as each of our ideas—from sensation, which it explained in terms of the excitation of the brain produced by impressions made on the organs. Man became nothing more than a result of his organization, and the entire science of man an appendix

---

[‡] To speak strictly, Biran's prize-essay only received a merit; but the Academy expressed its regrets that, since the prize-essay had been submitted anonymously, this circumstance prevented it from according a prize to the author. The prize was awarded to Suabedissen, who has since become honourably known within philosophy. See the *Memoirs of the Berlin Academy*, 1804–11, p. 8. The year when the prize was awarded was 1807 and not 1809, as Biran writes in his preface, p. 5.[10]

to physiology.[13] Maine de Biran repeatedly demonstrated that all of this was just a mass of hypotheses, and that, on returning to observation and experience, one discovered among those real facts which ought to compose a true science of man, a fact just as real as the others—one which is no doubt mixed up with sensation, but which is not explicable by it; one which has organic conditions, but which is distinct from and even independent of the organism—that is, activity. And he discerned this activity from everything that is not it;[14] he traced it back to its source; he followed it in all its developments; he restored it to its rightful place in intellectual life; and from this sum of ideas and views emerged a fairly extensive, but profound theory—one which is very true in itself and indestructible in its foundations and which a complete philosophy must incorporate and give its due.

The following are the series of experimental truths which comprise this theory. On this occasion, I am obliged to present these truths without the observations which explain them and are abundant in Biran's writings.

1° True activity is in the will;
2° The will is personality and the whole of personality: the I itself;
3° To will is to cause, and the I is the first cause given to us.[15]

These three claims form the ground of Biran's theory; they are contained in one and the same fact repeatable by each of us at any moment: muscular effort.

In all muscular effort there is: 1° a muscular sensation, whether more or less vivid or agreeable or painful; 2° the effort which produces it. The muscular sensation does not just succeed the effort; rather, consciousness attests that it is produced by the effort and that the relation which links them is not a relation of mere succession, but a relation of cause and effect. And there is no need here for either reasoning or even language: to perceive muscular effort, it is enough to produce it. We can certainly be ignorant of how the effort produces the sensation, but we cannot doubt that it produces it; and, even if we knew how it produces it, we would not know with any more certainty that it produces it. Our conviction would not be heightened. Moreover, no one makes the effort who does not want to do so, and [so] there is no involuntary effort. The will is thus the ground of effort, and the cause is here a voluntary cause. What is more, it is we who make the effort; we impute it definitively to ourselves, and the will which is its cause is our own will. Person, will and cause are thus identical to each other. The I is given to us in the cause and the cause in the willing. Remove the willing—that is, the effort—and there is no longer anything: the entire fact would disappear.

This fact, studied deeply and brought to irresistible proof, is the principle of Biran's theory.[16] This theory illuminates both every part of philosophy and every part of the history of philosophy.

First, without going beyond the very fact of muscular effort, a vivid insight can already be drawn from it. Since the I is present there in the form of will and freedom is the very characteristic of will, the freedom of the I is identical to its existence and immediately perceived by consciousness. This [proof of the freedom of the I], therefore, overcomes all sophisms, since it escapes argumentation.

It is the same with the spirituality of the I. Instead of all the arguments which are scarcely worth more for than against, the spirituality of the I here appears to us in its unity and its identity[17]—a unity and identity which are again immediate perceptions of consciousness. In continuous effort, the I always senses willing and acting; and it senses the same will and the same cause, even when the willed effects and products vary. This identical and one I, distinct from its variable effects, falls neither under the senses nor under the imagination; it perceives itself directly over the course of its activity which constitutes for it the very continuity of its existence. [The I] thus incontestably exists for itself with an existence that escapes both the imagination and the senses—this is spiritual existence. No argument can procure this certainty, just as no argument can destroy it or shake it.

Here then is spiritualism re-established in philosophy on the very basis of experience. However, this is no extravagant spiritualism without relation to the world we inhabit; for the spirit that we are, the I, is given to us in a relation in which it forms the first term, and a sensation—in particular, a sensation localized to a specific place on the body—[forms] the second term. Hence, spirit is given to us with its opposite, the outside with the inside, nature at the same time as man.

Condillac and his disciples explain all our faculties by sensation—that is, by the passive element. For them, attention is sensation become exclusive; memory a prolonged sensation; the idea a clarified sensation.[18] But who clarifies the sensation in order to convert it into an idea? Who retains or recalls the sensation to make a memory of it? Who considers the sensation in isolation to render it exclusive? If sensibility plays some role among our faculties, so too does the will. A sensation become exclusive by its own vivacity is not the same as the attention which is applied to it and without which the more the sensation was exclusive, the less it would be perceived. Sensation often solicits the will; but far from constituting it, a predominant [sensation] stifles it. There are no doubt memories which are merely the echoes of sensation, images which return involuntarily under the eyes of the imagination—this is some kind of animal memory. However, there is another memory in which the will does intervene. Often, we go back to the past to seek a memory which eludes us, we reanimate it from its half-lost [condition], we give it precision and consistency, and so there is voluntary memory just as there is passive memory. Consciousness itself, which appears rather involuntary, this consciousness has for its condition some degree of attention; and attention is will. In the very cradle of intellectual life, we thus rediscover the will; in fact, we rediscover it everywhere we are, everywhere the human person, the I, already is.

If the will explains almost all our faculties, it must explain almost all our ideas. The most fruitful [idea] of all—the one on which metaphysics rests—is surely the idea of cause. In this case, it is no longer a hypothesis; it is the most certain idea gathered into a self-evident primitive fact: [the fact of] volition. Through it, false dogmatism is shaken to its roots, so too is scepticism—and the highest insight is discovered to be borrowed from the purest source, that of internal experience.

As soon as the will is conceived properly as personality itself, it clarifies a mass of curious and obscure questions about which there has long been dispute. The explanation of sleep and wakefulness, which often resemble each other so strongly, is once again at stake today: somnambulism has become one of the problems of our age.[19] The quarrel over the nature of animals rumbles on,[20] and many celebrated writings* are far from concluding the debate on the true character of madness. All these problems are resolved in Biran's theory. Wakefulness is that period of our lives during which the will is more or less exercised; sleep, in its various degrees, is the weakening of this voluntary state; absolute sleep would be its complete abolition. Somnambulism is a state in which the will is no longer in control and in which all our faculties, above all the imagination and the senses, are at work, but at work in a disordered fashion, without freedom, without consciousness, and therefore without memory. To conceptualize the animal, it is enough for man to abstract from his own will and reduce himself to sensibility and imagination. All that is not voluntary in us is animal, and man succumbs to a state of animality every time he abdicates dominion over himself. Just as many people sleep while they are supposed awake, so too we are animals for a very great portion of our lives. Finally, when some moral or physical cause destroys our freedom—freedom precisely being our true personality—that blow which strikes our freedom equally takes away the human and leaves behind a mere automaton who still performs organic and even intellectual functions, but without participating in them, without having either consciousness of them or responsibility for them. We become strangers to ourselves: we are outside of ourselves; this alienation (*alienus a se*), this dementia[22] (*amens, a mente*) [is] madness whose different degrees are the very degrees of our loss of freedom.

What piles of absurdities have been amassed on the question of language and signs! In order to demean the human mind, the theological school[23] claims that God alone could have invented language. However, the difficulty is not one of possessing signs, for sounds, gestures, facial expressions, and all of our body express our sentiments instinctively and often even despite ourselves—these are the primitive givens of language, the natural signs made by God only to the extent he made everything. To convert these natural signs into genuine signs and to institute language requires a further condition: it requires that, instead of repeatedly making the same gesture or emitting the same sound instinctively, we note of ourselves that ordinarily certain external movements accompany certain movements of the soul, and we repeat [the latter] voluntarily, with the intention of making

---

* See the treatises by Pinel and Broussais.[21]

them express the same sentiment. The voluntary repetition of a gesture or a sound initially produced by instinct and without intention—this is, properly speaking, the institution of the sign, of language. This voluntary repetition is the original convention without which all later conventions [instituted] with others are impossible. However, it is absurd to have recourse to God to form this first convention in our place; it is clear that we alone are able to do it. The institution of language by God is merely a postponement, deferring the difficulty without resolving it. Signs invented by God would not be signs for us, but things which we would then need to elevate to the status of signs by attaching certain meanings to them. Language is an institution of the will, working on [the results of] instinct and nature. Hence, remove the will and there is no longer a possible free repetition of any natural sign; true signs are no longer possible; and sensibility alone does not explain language any better than divine intervention does.[24] In the end, remove the will—that is, the sentiment of personality—and the root of I [Je] is taken away; there is no longer any subject, nor therefore any attribute; there is no longer any verb, expression of action and of existence. It is no more in God's power than that of the senses or the imagination to suggest the least idea of them in us.

Biran's theory changes everything, renews everything, including the history of philosophical systems—by which I mean the history of modern systems which were the only ones with which French philosophy was concerned at this period.

Biran was the first in France to rehabilitate Descartes' renown, which had been almost suppressed in the eighteenth century, and so dared to confront Bacon's [renown] head on. Bacon's fundamental precept is to abstract from causes and to remain with the investigation of facts and the induction of laws. And this is enough, or can be enough up to a certain point, in the physical sciences; but, in philosophy, to neglect causes is to neglect beings. In the study of man, for example, it is to abstract from the very ground of human nature, from the root of all reality—from the I, the proper subject of all the faculties, which must be recognized since it is the cause of all the acts of which these faculties are merely the generalization.[25] It is Bacon who, by turning philosophy away from the investigation of causes, separated it from reality and condemned it to observations without depth and to artificial classifications. In admitting two sources of ideas—sensation and reflection—Locke might have been able, if he could have remained faithful to his theory, to find in reflection the entire intellectual and moral life of man. However, he took too little from reflection as opposed to sensation. Soon, in Condillac's hands, reflection became a mere modification of sensation, and the subject of sensation deprived of genuine activity, will, his own power and personality is nothing more than a hypothetical phantom, an abstraction, a sign. From this arose Tracy's nominalism, or rather that systematic physiology which, in pursuing an arbitrary ideology through the cataloguing of half-verbal classifications, ends up just erecting hypothesis on hypothesis. Biran was the first and staunchest adversary of the entire sensualist and physiological school, laying bare its false method and chimerical claims.

For him, Descartes is the creator of the true philosophy. Indeed, *I think, therefore I am* is and always will be the starting point for any healthy philosophical investigation. *Thought*, Descartes' *cogito*, means consciousness in our modern language. Descartes saw very well that consciousness alone clarifies existence to us and reveals our personality to us. His failure is to have not investigated and to have been unable to recognize the condition of all true thought, of all consciousness, as well as to what order of phenomena sentiment and personality pertain. If[26] in place of vaguely saying, *I think, therefore I am*, Descartes had said: *I will, therefore I am*, he would have immediately posited an I, a cause of acts, in place of a soul, a substance of its modes: [this would have been] a personality which is not only distinct, as thought, from extension, but endowed with an energy capable of explaining all its operations and all its ideas, without any need to appeal to divine intervention. And he would have perhaps prevented the Cartesian school from slipping down the slope which leads all spiritualism into mysticism. However, once the real nature of the I and its causative power had been misunderstood, then it was quite natural for Malebranche to call on divine efficacy for help to explain those operations inexplicable by thought alone and for Spinoza to have recourse to a foreign substance, something extended, a thinking without will or power, without real individuality.

Biran's perspective naturally raised it[27] to the heights of Leibniz's perspective. And in so doing, he was happy to restore honour to this great name.[28] For the first time in France for a century, this figure who had seemed to belong solely to the mathematical sciences was reintroduced into philosophy with success; and the monadology, which had until then been relegated to hypotheses superseded by the most hypothetical school there ever was, was re-examined in light of the true method and was declared to contain more truths of experience than the entire philosophy of the eighteenth century. It is curious to see Biran rediscover all his ideas in some passages from Leibniz. Here, for example, is one [such passage] which Biran cited many times and which would hardly be exhausted by the longest reflection:

> To clarify the idea of substance, one must ascend to [the idea] of force or energy.... Active or acting force is not the bare power of the schools; it must not be understood, like the scholastics, as a simple faculty or possibility of acting, which, to be made active or reduced to act, would have need of an excitation from outside, and as a foreign *stimulus*. The genuine active force comprises action in itself; it is entelechy, a power mediating between the simple faculty of acting and the determinate and effectuated act—this energy contains or envelops effort (*conatum involvit*).

Such a rich and pregnant passage is hidden in a corner of a small writing in which Leibniz proposes nothing less than the reform of all philosophy by means of the reform of the concept of substance—that is, by ascribing cause as an attribute of the concept of [substance], something which, for different reasons, Descartes and Locke had almost equally failed to do or understand.*

Here is another passage with a less absolute and less elevated character which seems to come from the pen of Biran himself:[†] "Force can be conceived very distinctly (*distincte intelligi*); but it can be explained by no image (*non explicari imaginabiliter*)."

Everywhere Leibniz distinguishes between the pure organic impression, which is taken up into general physics; sensation strictly speaking which comprises our animal life; and the perception [*aperception*] of consciousness which constitutes the intellectual life. He perfectly characterizes this perception [*aperception*] of consciousness, or "the reflective knowledge of our internal state, a knowledge which is not given to all souls, nor always to the same soul."[‡] He elsewhere speaks of "reflective acts, in virtue of which we think the being which is called I.... By us thinking ourselves, we think at the same time being, substance, mind, and God himself, by conceiving as infinite what is finite in us."[§]

Hence, the perception of consciousness gives us knowledge of the I, substance, and cause all together—a simple force, a monad, which is developed in activity, an activity which is manifest by effort. This is truly Biran's theory; but it is still just the beginning of Leibniz's system; and this system is, in my opinion, far more robust than it seems at first glance. My conviction is that, by beginning from the perception [*aperception*] of consciousness, from the personal cause, from the monad self, the most severe psychology can arrive very legitimately at a not-I, whose sole concept would be that of impersonal cause, of force once more and so of the monad, in order to raise itself up to the cause of causes, the first monad, in a way that justifies not only the ground of the monadology, but the complete monadology, and perhaps also pre-established harmony when correctly understood. Indeed, according to the monadology, each monad mutually acts on and influences the others; but what is the nature of this action? It is here we must understand Leibniz. The action of one monad on another cannot go so far as to change the nature of this monad—that is, in the given system, its own activity or what it ought to do—so as to be the cause of its determinations. [The first monad] is not the cause of [the second's] determinations, but only of its perceptions, and, as we would say today, of its sensations. The determinations of one being as a genuine cause belongs to it alone. However, this [distinction] does not apply to its sensations: these come to it from outside and are the effect of the action of other beings or external causes. A sound philosophy can account for this very well. When acting on the I, the universe produces no operation within [the I], no volition within it; the whole universe affects

---

* *Opera Leibn*, ed. Dutens, vol. 2, p. 18: *De primae philosophiae emendatione et notione substantiae*.[29]
† *Opera Leibn*, vol. 2.2, p. 49. *De ipsa natura sive de vi insita*.[30]
‡ *Opera Leibn.*, vol. 2.1, p. 33. *Principles of Nature and Grace*.[31]
§ *Opera Leibn.*, vol. 2.1, p. 24. *Principia philosophiae, sive theses in gratiam principia Eugenii*.[32]

me solely as organism; it can thus give me just sensations, which limit my operations and do not constitute them. However, whenever [this act] does occur, my personal power immediately starts functioning and develops itself, without the external world ever being called the cause of this development. The great maxim is still applicable: *Nihil est in intellectu quod non prius fuerit in sensu, nisi ipse intellectus*.[33] The I, the personal and free cause, is expressed by its own virtue and obeys its own laws. Similarly, none of my acts can alter the impersonal cause, or the not-I, external nature, which also has its own forces and laws. I can, it is true, modify the action of bodies as theirs modifies mine; but these very modifications are achieved in virtue of the laws which govern bodies. Every being, every force thus acts on each other, but within certain limits. Just as all forces resemble each other, their laws are more similar than one might think, and because they resemble each other, they are in agreement. This concordance, established primarily by he who made everything with weights and measures,[34] is pre-established harmony. Thus understood, pre-established harmony is a consequence of the monadology; for if, otherwise, [pre-established harmony] excluded reciprocal influence between monads, it would stand in manifest contradiction with the monadology, whose principle is the perpetual action of monads. And this action seemingly does not dissipate and, in its effects, it necessarily forms perceptions of manifold monads, when such perceptions are [understood as] their representations which reflect back to each of them the whole universe. Therefore, there is no contradiction, as has been claimed and as Biran repeated too often;[35] on the contrary, there is an intimate link between the monadology and pre-established harmony. Perhaps this link is not very legible in Leibniz's own works, which are but fragments; but it had to exist within his immense intellect which contained the richest variety combined with the most powerful unity. His disciples were never able to perfectly explain their master's thought and ended up all but abandoning him. Today [Leibniz] returns everywhere. When Schelling describes the harmony between the laws of the human mind and the laws of nature, he has no doubt that he is doing nothing but developing an idea from Leibniz.[36] Moreover, after reading Leibniz like everyone else, the present author acknowledged he has arrived by himself at basically the same results by means of another method.* We scarcely understand anything but our own thoughts. I avow again that it is necessary for eclecticism to recognize and taste the eclectic direction spread throughout Leibniz's works. To the extent that I make any progress—or believe I am making progress—in philosophy, I seem to see more clearly into this great man's thinking, and all this progress consists in understanding him better. At the point where Biran stopped, he could not have grasped the whole of Leibniz's system, except the part which clarified his own theory for him. However, this part is the key to all the others, and

---

* See the system developed in the first and second preface to *Philosophical Fragments* and in the 1828 lecture course on philosophy.

those who one day penetrate further into its sanctuary should not forget that it was Biran who introduced them to it and who handed down the flame which illuminates the whole edifice.³⁷

However, if within Leibniz's dogmatism there are heights less accessible to Biran's psychology, [it is because this psychology] was deliberately made to measure up successfully to Hume's scepticism and to take from him his last refuge by victoriously refuting the famous *Essay on the Idea of Power*.* We know that, after Locke had affirmed in a chapter on the *Idea of Cause and Effect* that this idea [of power] is given to us by sensation, he decides upon a completely different origin for it in a different chapter, *On Power*, even if he is still concerned at bottom with the very same idea.³⁹ He finds this new origin in reflection applied to the will, and takes as his example the will to move certain parts of our body—a will which effectively produces the movement and suggests to us the idea of power. Locke's theory is the germ of Biran's theory and I have elsewhere considered their similarities and differences.† Hume was not the man to accept the first explanation, and he perfectly established that the idea of cause cannot come from sensation. On this point he is irresistible, and so, he forever condemned sensualism to scepticism. However, when Hume examines Locke's second explanation, he tries to reach the same end as the first by a series of very specious arguments, against which Reid was happy to protest in the name of common sense and the general belief of humanity.⁴¹ However, this protestation could only act as a sort of makeshift in expectation of a deeper examination. It is this examination which Biran instituted. He struggles face to face with the redoubtable sceptic, pursues him everywhere and opposes him with an analysis that is just as subtle but more robust than [Hume's]. For us, [Biran's] argument leaves nothing to be desired and no possibility of reply. The vanity of Hume's fundamental argument, which has been so successful, cannot better be described than as follows: to be certain that our will is the cause of a certain movement of the muscles, we must know *how* this movement is produced, the nature of the soul which wills and causes, the nature of the body in which the voluntary effect takes place and the relation between these two natures. Biran shows wonderfully well what absurdity there would be in so subordinating the irrecusable certainty of facts—and the most evident facts of all, those of consciousness— to a certainty of a very different order, which could probably never be attained and which, if it were [attained], could add nothing to the first kind; for, if I knew how I moved my arm, I would not be any surer that I was really moving it. However, this polemic is too dense for me to be able to detach any links from the [argumentative] chain: one must embrace it all, and so, I refer to Biran's book itself⁴² all those who might find themselves seduced by Hume's arguments and by his famous theory which claims to explain the relation of cause to effect by the principle of

---

* Hume, *Essays on the Understanding*, seventh essay.³⁸
† 1829 lecture course, vol. 2, lecture 19.⁴⁰

the association of ideas—a fantastical theory which belies universal beliefs and the facts, a theory destructive of all true metaphysics and one which the unfaithful successor of Stewart and Reid, a man of wit but a mediocre philosopher, [Thomas] Brown, has made deplorably popular in England, in Scotland itself and even in America.*

Such is Biran's doctrine. I believe I have brought out all its salient points and its fundamental character. I pride myself that, if the author were still here, he would acknowledge that I am taking nothing from him. I do myself at least this justice: of all the ideas of some importance which it is possible for me to connect, directly or even indirectly, to Biran, whether in his writings or his conversations, I cannot see any of them I have here failed to faithfully and religiously reconstruct. Moreover, I adopt this doctrine, such as I have just explained it, and I adopt it without reservation. Up to this point and within these limits, it appears to me immune from attack—as both exact and profound.

But did Biran have the wisdom to remain within these limits? After attempting to bring out the good, allow me to equally speak about the bad, in the higher interests of truth and the philosophical cause.

Biran believed he could derive all of philosophy out of the doctrine we have just set out. However, his doctrine is purely psychological, and, in order to successfully derive all of philosophy from psychology, the first condition is that this psychology is itself complete, that it reproduces every fact of consciousness. Otherwise, the gaps in these psychological premises would necessarily reappear in ontological conclusions and, subsequently, in historical perspectives.

The psychology of the sensualist school concluded, and could only conclude, in nominalism or materialism.

In place of sensation, Biran substituted in the will. The will constitutes an order of facts distinct from [the order] of sensible facts, and which, by enriching psychology, must enlarge philosophy. Not only did Biran recognize these new facts of consciousness, he also assigned them their true status. He proved that these facts that had been so neglected in eighteenth-century philosophy are precisely the condition of knowing all the other [orders of facts]. He grasped them and presented them according to their most striking type—muscular effort, in which the character of the will, its productive energy, and the relation of cause to effect irresistibly burst forth. Here, then, are two orders of facts: 1° sensible facts, which by themselves do not constitute consciousness; 2° active and voluntary facts, the direct and immediate perception of which alone makes possible the perception of other phenomena. Now, do these two orders of facts exhaust all the facts of consciousness? This is Biran's contention. However, for me, such a claim is an illusion, a

---

* *Lectures on the Philosophy of the Human Mind* (1820). A seventh edition appeared in 1833; and in America a summary has been produced which serves as the basis for the majority of the philosophy lecture courses.[43]

fundamental error which vitiates Biran's psychology and which, by introducing into it an immense gap, immediately trapped all his philosophy within a circle, out of which it could only break free through recourse to hypotheses.

As long as observation is not blinded by the spirit of system, the least sharp-sighted [observer] should recognize in consciousness—alongside sensible facts and voluntary facts—a third order of facts just as real as the other two and perfectly distinct from them: I mean rational facts in their strict sense.

I agree [with Biran] that the will is the condition of the exercise of all our faculties, just as Biran agrees [with the sensualist] that the senses are the condition of the exercise of the will. However, to deny or neglect the understanding, because the understanding has the will as its condition, is—and for saying this I beg the pardon of my ingenious and learned teacher—a vice of analysis that is just as serious as denying or neglecting the will because it is linked to sensibility.

I am saying nothing here except what is well known. All writers distinguish between the faculties of the understanding and those of the will, although it is also true that, having distinguished them verbally, most end up confounding these two orders of faculties in reality or even inverting them in the most bizarre manner. For example, I have remarked elsewhere* that Laromiguière attributes preference to the capacities of the will—even though [preference] is evidently involuntary; and he also assigns attention a primary position in the capacities of the understanding, even though it evidently belongs to the will. Up until a certain point, we are masters of our attention, but we are not masters of our preferences. When I prefer the good to the bad, or this to that, I do it because I cannot not do it; my will is here worth nothing. To prefer is thus a fact which has no relation to the will, nor does it relate to sensation: I assume this to be proven. It is nevertheless a fact, and, if it is a fact, it must be recognized as such and related to some faculty that is different from sensation or the will.

It is for judgement as for preference: when we assume that judging is only perceiving relations, following the common theory, I ask whether we perceive relations at will?

We think as we are able, not as we wish.

And beliefs possess the same necessity: we do not make our beliefs, we receive them.

In order to discern the manifoldness of our faculties, I have often used the example of a man who studies a book of mathematics.[45] Of course, if this man did not have eyes, he would not see the book—neither the pages nor the letters; he could not understand what he could not read. On the other hand, if he was not willing to pay attention to it, if he did not compel his eyes to read on and his mind to meditate on what he is reading, he would equally understand nothing of the book. But

---

* *Fragments*, p. 78.[44]

when his eyes are open and when his mind is attentive, is everything in place? No. He must still understand, grasp (or believe he is grasping) the truth. Grasping, recognizing the truth is a fact which can have very different circumstances and conditions; but, in itself, it is a simple, indecomposable fact, which cannot be reduced to the simple attentive will nor to sensation; and so, for this reason, it must have its own place apart within a legitimate classification of the facts which fall under consciousness's gaze.

I am speaking of consciousness, but consciousness itself, the perception of consciousness, this fundamental and permanent fact which almost all systems get wrong by claiming to explain it by one sole term—for example, sensualism explains it by a sensation become exclusive without enquiring into what made it so exclusive and Biran explains it by the will producing a sensation—could this fact [of consciousness] occur without the intervention of something else which is neither sensation nor the will, but perceives and knows both of them? Having consciousness is perceiving, is experiencing [*connaitre*], is knowing [*savoir*].[46] The very term makes this clear (*scientia-cum*). Not only do I sense, but I know that I sense; not only do I will, but I know that I will; and it is this knowledge which is consciousness. Either one must prove that will and sensation are themselves endowed with the faculty of perceiving themselves, of knowing themselves, or else one must admit a third term without which the other two would be as if they were not. Consciousness is a triple phenomenon, in which sensing, willing, and knowing serve as reciprocal conditions for each other, and, in their interconnections, in their simultaneity and their distinction, they constitute the whole of intellectual life. Take away sensing and there would no longer be either the occasion or the object of willing, which would then no longer function. Take away willing and there would be no more genuine action, no more self, no more subject of perception, leaving just the perceptible object. Take away knowing and this is equally the case for all perception—and so there would be no insight into what is, sensing, willing, and their relation; consciousness would lose its flame; it would cease to be.[47]

Knowing is thus an incontestable fact, distinct from all the others, *sui generis*.[48]

To what faculty does this fact relate? Call it understanding, mind, the intellect, reason, it doesn't matter so long as you recognize that it is an elementary faculty. It is typically called reason.

A strange thing! Biran does not seem to have suspected that there existed in this regard an order of facts worthy of particular attention. In his prize-essay on the analysis of thinking and the elementary faculties, he states without any proof that "the faculty of perception and that of the will are indivisible" (p. 189) and that "metaphysicians have been very wrong to divide the understanding and the will into two classes" (ibid.).[49] He admits just one intellectual and moral principle distinct from sensibility, which is the will, and he rejects reason as an original faculty. Later on, in response to my objections, he was content to ignore [reason] or, when he does occasionally belatedly recognize it, it is purely out of politesse; for he never makes any use of it and it plays no role in his theory.

Hence, this profound observer of consciousness did not see that [this order of facts] was precisely that without which it would be impossible to see anything; he who continuously reproaches the philosophy of sensation for mutilating the human mind when explaining it by sensation alone did not perceive that he himself robbed it of its highest faculty when explaining it by the will alone, and that, in so doing, he silenced at their source the most sublime ideas that neither the will nor sensation explain.

This is, firstly, to suppress the principle of every idea—that is, of all knowledge—since there is no knowledge, whether important or trivial, significant, or common, which is not by necessity taken from the faculty of knowing, from reason. However, even without speaking with such rigour, which is nevertheless the law of all sound philosophy, it is evident that to admit just one order of faculties, those which the will generates, is to admit only one order of ideas, that is, the idea of cause and those derived from it. A voluntary power, reduced to itself, can, of course, give rise to some ideas, such as the idea of cause, but it is condemned to give no more than that. Constrained within action, its range is limited by [action], and it cannot get beyond the relevant order of ideas without getting beyond the self. Yet, are all ideas reducible to that of cause? Many can be brought back to it; but there are also many that this idea does not explain.

In the beginning, Biran had been fairly badly disposed to the idea of substance and wished to substitute for it [the idea] of a more direct and clearer cause. He was only reconciled with the idea of substance quite late, when he learnt of its true character from Leibniz.[50] Substance, reduced to a cause in itself, to the virtual power which puts a cause into action, considered prior to the act even, was more easily discernible by the gaze of a psychology whose unique principle is perception of a personal cause. Nevertheless, strictly speaking, the I-will gives only an operative cause, and not the ungraspable and invisible principle of this cause which we necessarily conceive, but do not perceive directly. An operative cause is not the equivalent of the cause in itself. The will gives the operative cause; reason alone can furnish the cause in itself, substance.[51]

However, where Biran's theory entirely capitulates is before the idea of the infinite. The I, substance or cause, is finite and limited, like voluntary activity which is its sign. Remould and contort the I, the will and sensation—all taken in isolation or in combination—as much as you like, and you will never obtain from them the idea of the infinite. In the end, this is to be asked of reason which, equipped with its own power and in the presence of just the finite, conceives and reveals the infinite, the infinity of time and the infinity of space, whereas the senses only ever give bodies, but not the space which contains them, and effort, the continuity of willing, only ever gives the duration of the I, relative time, but not absolute time, infinite duration.*

---

* *1829 Lecture Course*, lecture 18.[52]

What will happen when it becomes a case of explaining via the will not only ideas, but principles—and, what is more, principles marked by the characteristics of universality and necessity, like [the principle] of causality? The principle of causality is incontestably universal and necessary; and this refutes the idea that the perception of a completely individual and contingent cause can give rise to [this principle]. However, it is the principle of causality alone—and not the mere concept of our individual cause—which compels us out of ourselves, demands that we conceive external causes, as well as those limited and finite causes which raise us to the infinite and indefectible cause. Let us suppose we were conscious of our causative force but could experience and perceive a sensation without relating it to a cause: the external world would never exist for us. Of course, the principle of causality would not itself have been developed, if a positive concept of an individual cause were not preliminarily given to us via the will; but an individual and contingent concept that precedes a necessary principle does not explain it and cannot take its place.* What then can Biran do? Above or alongside the mere idea of a voluntary and personal cause which cannot suffice for him, and in place of the principle of causality which he cannot do without, he imagines an operation that no philosopher had previously glimpsed, an operation that is not the principle of causality itself but still possesses all its virtues—a magical operation which its ingenious inventor scarcely describes and to which he attributes, without discussion, the marvellous property of transporting and explaining in some way the force of the I outside of itself—this operation he dubs induction (p. 393).[54]

With just one word I could thwart this new theory by asking who undertakes this extraordinary induction? Of course, it is the I itself; for, along with sensation, there is nothing else for Biran. But Biran's I is uniquely the personal subject of the will; it has no other functions than volition and action. For this reason, it can give the idea of cause, but has no power whatsoever to make any induction from it, whether legitimate or illegitimate: to induct is a completely rational procedure which does not belong to the will.

This radical objection would, it seems, be enough. However, since for Biran this theory is key to the transition from psychology to ontology; and since someone else whose judgement most influenced me in other respects, Royer-Collard, put Biran's works and conversations to good use like I am, and, in so doing, both adapted and strengthened what seemed to me this inadmissible theory [of induction], I decided to submit it to full discussion [in my lecture course]† and, I believe, demonstrated its lack of robustness. It is enough to reproduce the conclusion [to that discussion].

If it were possible for all induction to have the I as its ground and unique instrument, then it could, in the final analysis, give nothing but the I itself—that is,

---

* *1829 Lecture Course*, lectures 17, 18, 19.[53]
† *1829 Lecture Course*, lecture 19.[55]

voluntary and personal causes. And so, anthropomorphism would be the universal and necessary law of thought.

In accordance with such [a theory of] induction, every idea of an involuntary cause becomes impossible. There would be no forces in nature, but solely causes that were not just similar, but identical to [the cause] which we are. [On this theory,] the magnet would not just attract fire, but will to attract it and be able not to will it: *Fatum* would disappear and only freedom would exist. Such would be external nature.

The God of this induction is good, it is true—a personal and providential God; but what kind of personality, what kind of providence?[56] A personality full of suffering like our own, a providence necessarily limited and finite, a vain shadow of that eternal and infinite providence who humankind adores, whose omnipotence is equal to its wisdom and who comprehends in its counsels all times and all places. A God for whom the I acts as type and measure cannot participate in omnipotence, eternity, infinity.

A metaphysics that is so narrow in its foundation does not give rise to a robust morality. Personhood, voluntary and free activity, is certainly the proper subject of morality, and it is already a precious gift; but it is insufficient. The will cannot supply the rule that is imposed upon it, the laws which ought to govern acts of will, actions, and persons, both in the internal world of the soul and in the world of society and the State. The good and the law should, of course, conform to the nature of what must implement them; but they are based on a rejection of the idea that the subject is ever legislator.

Lastly, such a philosophy cannot make sense of the whole history of philosophy: it will necessarily shrink from any great dogmatism that tried to comprehend the universality of things. The most illustrious systems will appear to it as superhuman hypotheses, because they everywhere surpass the only measure applied to them—that of an incomplete psychology which, as a result of clipping its own wings when it comes to the three orders of real facts, neglects precisely the most important and most fruitful [order]—the one which, while appearing within consciousness, surpasses [consciousness], and opens up to man the only route leading him from himself to everything else.

It is with errors in philosophy as with faults in life: they are punished through their inevitable consequences. Any omitted or neglected order of real facts leaves a void in consciousness which can be filled with nothing but hypotheses. Every omission condemns it to some invention. Preoccupied with voluntary facts which he managed to abstract from the midst of the sensible facts which enveloped them to all other weary or dazzled eyes, [Biran] did not perceive rational facts.[57] This is a lacuna—I showed it to him and, to fill [this gap], he invented the hypothesis of an illegitimate induction. However, this hypothesis, which he never set out with much lucidity or precision, is too inconsistent and too vague to be enough, and so he gradually had recourse to another invention. In opposition to the scepticism which every idealism ordinarily brings in its wake, he took refuge in a kind of mysticism which we already see emerging in the long and curious note attached to the *Considerations of the Moral and the Physical*.[58] Here, he practically agrees that all the deductions or inductions that personality can make from itself are not enough for this personality,[59] and he appeals to divine intervention, to a non-accidental, but universal revelation by which God is united with man and teaches him the truth. He appeals to Plato's testimony in a dialogue on prayer which is in fact not by Plato; he cites some admirable passages from the *Republic* which are in need of much interpretation; he borrows from Proclus some passages in which more than one profound truth is hidden under an obscure covering; he invokes Van Helmont and Malebranche; and so, the author of a completely personal and completely subjective theory basically ends up with an appeal to grace.

This conclusion is far from any feeling of muscular effort, and this is of course an inconsistency; but it is a necessary inconsistency, an effect of remaining with the exclusive and the incomplete. Man suffocates in the prison of his self; he breathes easily only within a vaster and higher sphere. This sphere is that of reason—reason, that extraordinary faculty—human, if you like, in its relation to the I, but distinct in itself and independent of the I—which discovers for us the true, the good, the beautiful, and their opposites, sometimes to one degree and sometimes to another, sometimes in the form of reasoning, even syllogism (which does have its value and legitimate authority), sometimes in a more abstract and purer form, in the condition of spontaneity, inspiration, revelation.[60] This is the common source of all the most elevated truths, as well as the humblest; this is the light which illuminates the I but which the I does not make. Failing to recognize and follow this light, one replaces it with its shadow; one passes by reason without perceiving it; and then one despairs at science, and one hastens into mysticism, even though every truth of [mysticism] is still borrowed from this same reason which it imperfectly reflects and with which it often mixes deplorable extravagances.*

What would have happened to Biran, if we had not lost him in 1824? I knew him well enough and, if I may say so, I know well enough the history of philosophy and the hidden, but irresistible tendencies of all its principles to dare claim that the author of the note in question would have ended up like Fichte did.

Fichte is the major representative and genuine hero of the philosophy of the will and of the I, owing to the mould of his soul as well as that of his mind.[62] Fichte's theory is that of Biran's, but even more profound in its psychological foundations, more rigorous in its methods, more audacious in its implications. Just like Biran, Fichte also begins from the primitive act of willing, in which the I perceives itself as a free force, and is distinguished from everything which is not such. This I which first posits itself and which then goes on to continuously

---

* On reason, as distinct from both will and sensation, and as the unique principle of all truth, see the *Fragments*, *passim*, first and second preface, the 1828 lecture course and the 1829 lecture course.[61]

develop itself and reflect on itself, is the unique principle from which Fichte drew all his psychology, all his metaphysics, all his religion, all his morality, and all his politics. Having founded his entire system on this unique principle, he is not afraid to call it a subjective idealism.[63] Ah! This intrepid idealist, this theoretical and practical Stoic, of whom one could not truly say whether his system was made more for his character or his character for his system—only this head and this soul in so much accord, only this nature so unified and so firm, only this man so strong (and precisely because he was strong) could have maintained himself up until the end in the arid circle in which the rigour of his analysis and dialectic imprisoned him. Despite this, and although he said as much, he changed his doctrine: escaping from the I, he invoked divine intervention, a mysterious grace which descends from on high into man. However, in order for this grace to illuminate us and persuade us, it had to encounter something in us which could recognize it, welcome it,[64] comprehend it. This superior faculty is once again reason, which, if it had not been initially omitted by the spirit of his system, would naturally have revealed to the philosopher—as it has done to humankind—all the principal truths, those which scepticism cannot undermine and which mysticism disfigures, such as our own existence, attached to the will, and [the existence] of external nature, which certainly has some analogy with the I, but differs from it too, and, above the I and the not-I, a first and sovereign cause, of which the personal cause and external causes are but imperfect copies.*

This correspondence between Fichte's destiny and Biran's is striking. Such a doubled contemporary experience is a decisive lesson that history addresses to the systematic spirit.

In summary, Biran's theory, true in itself, is profound, but narrow. Biran rediscovered and restored a real order of facts that had been entirely misunderstood and effaced: he separated voluntary and free activity which characterizes the human person from sensation, and thereby re-established it in its independence. But, as if exhausted from this work, there no longer remained in him enough strength nor enough insight to investigate and discern a further order of phenomena buried beneath the first two. Such is human weakness. To one man one task alone: that which Biran accomplished has importance and grandeur and it was enough to honour his name. Profound minds are often exclusive, whereas extensive minds are sometimes superficial: they rarely leave so pregnant a mark on the intellect.

Such is the judgement I believe can be made about Biran's works. With their faults and their merits, they have served science; they must not perish. I have said it and will repeat it with complete conviction: Biran is the preeminent French metaphysician of my age. He is one of my teachers I was so fortunate to meet at the start

---

* On Fichte, see Tennemann, *Manual of the History of Philosophy*, Fr. trans., vol. 2, pp. 272–94.[65]

of my career; and, as unfortunate circumstances prevented me from closing his eyes,[66] I owe at least this monument to his memory.[67]

Paris, 1 March 1834
V. Cousin

Notes

1. First published as "Préface de l'éditeur" in P. Maine de Biran, *Nouvelles considérations sur les rapports du physique et du moral de l'homme*, ed. V. Cousin, Paris, Ladrange, 1834, pp. i–xlii (subsequently: *Fr. phil. 1838*, vol. 2, pp. 58–103; *Fr. phil. 1847*, vol. 4, pp. 288–322; *Fr. phil. 1855*, vol. 5, pp. 288–322; *Fr. phil. 1865*, vol. 5, pp. 302–34). We take the 1834 publication as our base text for this translation and note the significant modifications to later versions in the endnotes. We take the title, "Introduction to the Posthumous Works of Maine de Biran," from *Fr. phil. 1838*. We have omitted pp. i–v of this Introduction, since it consists for the most part in a long series of quotations of passages from Biran's executor, J. Lainé, on the condition of his literary estate on his death in 1824, as well as a few comments on the structure of the subsequent volume. As well as *Nouvelles considérations* (c.1820), which Cousin refers to as "the summary of all the author's works" (p. v), the volume also includes Biran's *Examen des leçons de M. Laromiguière* of 1817; some fragments: *Opinion de Hume sur la nature et l'origine de la notion de causalité, Sur l'origine de l'idée de force, d'après M. Engel*, then the *Exposition de la doctrine philosophique de Leibnitz* from 1819; and some replies to objections by P. A. Stapfer, *Réponse aux arguments contre l'apperception immédiate*. The Introduction constitutes Cousin's most extended attempt to present himself as Biran's successor—the logical next step in the progress of spiritualism; and this was, in many ways, one of Cousin's more controversial gestures, leading a generation of French philosophers, such as Ravaisson, to return to Biran, *pace* Cousin, in the name of a more authentic spiritualism. The delayed timing of Cousin's release of Biran's work—first in 1834 and then, under duress, in 1841, long after Biran's death in 1824—was also the subject of much controversy, so too Cousin's exclusion of Biran from university syllabi and curricula.
2. This was a salon at the home of P. Cabanis (in a house bequeathed him by Helvétius) which Destutt de Tracy, J. M. Degérando, Volney, and P. Laromiguière, as well as Biran, frequented during the first years of the nineteenth century.
3. The reference here is to the 1813 Commission which was the first formal body to express opposition to Napoleon at the height of the Empire, including, alongside Biran, J. Lainé (1768–1835), F. Raynouard (1761–1836), J. A. Gauvin-Gallois (1761–1828), and P.-F. Flaugergues (1767–1836).
4. The eighth year of the Revolutionary calendar (instituted in 1793).
5. Founded in 1795, the philosophy section of the Institut quickly became the home of *Idéologues*, like Cabanis and Tracy—and they exerted their power through, for example, setting prize-essay competitions on topics that furthered their agenda.
6. *Influence de l'habitude sur la faculté de penser*, awarded a prize by the Institut de France (including Cabanis and Tracy as judges) in 1802.
7. *Mémoire sur la décomposition de la pensée*, awarded a prize by the Institut de France in 1805.
8. See e.g. n. 3 above.
9. It is worth noting that Cousin had been elected to the Académie des sciences morales et politiques (part of the Institut de France) in 1832 and had begun organizing prize-essay competitions from 1833.
10. *Fr. phil. 1865*: "who has since become honourably known within philosophy" is omitted and to the end of the note Cousin adds a reference to his *Souvenirs d'Allemagne* for further information on Suabedissen. The references are to Biran's *De l'apperception immédiate*, submitted to the Berlin Academy in 1807; D. T. A. Suabedissen (1773–1835): German theologian and educational reformer; and to p. 5 of Biran's preface in the same volume as this Introduction first appeared (*Nouvelles considérations sur les rapports du physique et du moral de l'homme*, ed. Cousin).
11. *Sur les rapports du physique et du moral de l'homme*, awarded a prize by the Copenhagen Academy in 1812.
12. *Fr. phil. 1865*: "with all its attendant implications" replaced with "in the human mind."

13. By "physiology," Cousin is primarily referring to Cabanis's development of sensualism, but also to Broussais' and the early Comte's redeployment of it in the late 1820s to criticize Cousin himself (see n. 11 to the 1833 Preface above).
14. "It" likely refers to "activity" but could equally refer back to "sensation."
15. For example, on these three points Biran writes elsewhere of "that intimate sentiment or fact of consciousness, which constitutes the self as real cause, or immediate productive force of the movements brought about by the will." *The Relation between the Physical and the Moral in Man*, ed. and trans. D. Meacham and J. Spadola (London: Bloomsbury, 2016), p. 58.
16. *Fr. phil. 1865*: "the principle of Biran's theory" replaced with "Biran's entire theory."
17. *Fr. phil. 1865*: "Instead of all the arguments, which are scarcely worth more for than against, the spirituality of the I here appears to us in its unity and its identity" replaced with "It appears to us here in the unity and identity of the I."
18. That is, Condillac's project of accounting for all mental phenomena as transformations of sensations.
19. Perhaps most famously in the works of A. Bertrand (1795–1831), the student of Mesmer, who in 1823 published *Traité du somnambulisme et des différentes modifications qu'il présente*.
20. The debate that stemmed, in part, from La Mettrie's provocation in his 1745 *Histoire naturelle de l'âme* that humans are nothing more than complex animals.
21. The 1801 *Traité médico-philosophique sur l'aliénation mentale, ou la manie* by P. Pinel (1745–1826) and the 1828 *De l'irritation et de la folie* by F. J. V. Broussais.
22. We use the English "dementia" here to mirror the evident etymology in the French "démence."
23. *Fr. phil. 1865*: "the theological school" replaced with "De Bonald." L. de Bonald (1754–1840): the French counter-revolutionary thinker who makes the argument on the divine origin of language in a number of works including the 1802 *Législation primitive* and the 1818 *Recherches philosophiques sur les premiers objets des connaissances morales*.
24. A reference to the series of attempts by "the sensualist school" to explain the origin of language, beginning from Condillac's thought experiment of the two children in the desert in the 1745 *Essai sur l'origine des connaissances humaines*.
25. *Fr. phil. 1865*: "which must be recognized since it is the cause of all the acts of which these faculties are merely the generalization" replaced with "the common cause of all acts which are related to these manifold faculties."
26. *Fr. phil. 1865*: Cousin inserts the following footnote, "So speaks Biran and we leave to him the responsibility for this opinion. Of course, if Descartes had done what Biran here advises, he would have stopped Malebranche and Spinoza; but it is at least as indubitable that Descartes himself never misrecognized the free activity of man and the power of his will, and that he even saw the proof of the divine nature of the soul. Only he did not put it in the first plan of the *Meditations*, because he had a different goal and was above all proposing to demonstrate the spirituality of the thinking subject. It is the disdain for the authority of consciousness which, despite Descartes' precepts and examples, led Malebranche and Spinoza astray. See *Fragments de philosophie moderne*, first and section parts, *passim*; *Histoire de la philosophie*, lecture 8." The citations are to vols 3 and 4 of *Fr. phil. 1865*, as well as *Histoire générale de la philosophie* (Paris: Didier, 1863), pp. 360–444.
27. "It" could here refer back to "personality," but it is not clear.
28. *Fr. phil. 1847* and subsequent editions: Cousin inserts the following footnote, "I have already done justice to Biran for being the restorer of Leibniz." *Fr. phil. 1865* adds: "Leibniz's glory among us: History of Philosophy, lecture 9, etc." The citation is to *Histoire générale de la philosophie*, pp. 445–507.
29. *Fr. phil. 1865*: "something which, for different reasons, Descartes and Locke had almost equally failed to do or understand" is omitted and the footnote is moved earlier in the paragraph. Cousin is here quoting from Biran's translation of Leibniz's *On the Correction of First Philosophy and the Notion of Substance* from 1694. Biran's translation appears later in the volume that Cousin is editing, in his "Exposition de la doctrine philosophique de Leibnitz," pp. 319–20. Cousin cites from the 1768 edition of Leibniz's work by Louis Dutens (1730–1812).
30. *Fr. phil. 1865*: "with a less absolute and less elevated character which seems to come from the pen of Biran himself" replaced with "which confirms the preceding one." The Leibniz text, "On Nature Itself," is a fragment from 1698. Biran's discussion of this passage occurs in "Exposition de la doctrine philosophique de Leibnitz" (Cousin edition), p. 322.
31. *Fr. phil. 1865*: "Everywhere Leibniz distinguishes ..." to "... the same soul" is omitted. Biran cites it in "Exposition de la doctrine philosophique de Leibnitz" (Cousin edition), p. 340.
32. Biran cites this phrase in "Exposition de la doctrine philosophique de Leibnitz" (Cousin edition), p. 345.

33. A variation on the Aristotelian and empiricist dictum, roughly translated as: "There is nothing in the understanding that was not first in the senses, except for the understanding itself."
34. A biblical allusion to Wisdom 11:20.
35. Biran makes this claim in his text, "Réponses aux arguments contre l'aperception immediate," reproduced in the volume Cousin is introducing, p. 375.
36. Cousin is referring primarily to the section on history in Schelling's 1800 *System of Transcendental Idealism*.
37. *Fr. phil. 1865*: the passage from "... and this system is ..." to "... the whole edifice" is replaced with "As is well known, beginnings in all things and particularly in systems are always good; it is their entire development and above all their last word which require caution and a major examination before being accepted or rejected. By beginning from the I, from the I alone, and remaining within it, Biran should perhaps have proceeded to the monadology and to its necessary consequence, pre-established harmony. His prudence held him up before these famous hypotheses: he admired them without adopting them and limited himself to explaining their principle in the fact which consciousness immediately attests." To this Cousin adds a footnote citing Biran's *Exposition de la doctrine philosophique de Leibnitz* from later in the volume and his own *Histoire générale de philosophie*, lecture 9.
38. Hume's 1748 *Enquiry concerning Human Understanding* which also initially appeared under the title: *Philosophical Essays: Concerning Human Understanding*.
39. References to Locke, *An Essay Concerning Human Understanding*, bk II, ch. 26 and bk II, ch. 21, respectively.
40. The citation is to: *Cours de l'histoire de la philosophie. Histoire de la philosophie au XVIIIe siècle*, Vol. 2: *Ecole sensualiste* (Paris: Pichon and Didier, 1829), pp. 209-60.
41. Reid's criticisms are most fully developed in his 1788 *Essays on the Active Powers of Man*, particularly the essays "Of Active Power in General" and "Of the Will."
42. Cousin is referring his reader in particular to the section of the volume he is introducing which includes a fragment from Biran entitled, "Opinion de Hume sur la nature et l'origine de la notion de causalité" (pp. 273-90).
43. Thomas Brown (1778-1820): the *Lectures* were prepared for publication by his students and lecture 7 was devoted to concepts of power and causality.
44. A reference to Cousin's fragment, "Leçons de Laromiguière sur les facultés de l'ame" that was included in every edition—Cousin is referring to his analysis of the faculties which begins on *Fr. phil. 1833*, p. 78. The passage in question concludes, "What then is preference according to Laromiguière? It has the appearance of an exclusive desire, a predominant need—that is, a mere organic movement. Moreover, under the general term 'will' Laromiguière unites desire, preference and freedom." *Fr. phil. 1833*, p. 84.
45. e.g. elsewhere in the *Fragments*: in "Leçons de Laromiguière sur les facultés de l'ame" (*Fr. phil. 1826*, p. 32).
46. The French terms are *apercevoir*, *connaître*, and *savoir*, the latter two are, of course, often both translated as knowing (i.e. knowing as familiarity with and experience of vs knowing that or propositional knowledge).
47. *Fr. phil. 1865*: Cousin inserts the following footnote, "See Preface to first edition, pp. xiii-xxvi [pp. 66-7 above]."
48. *Fr. phil. 1865*: "*sui generis*" is omitted.
49. These are citations from Biran's "Examen des leçons de M. Laromiguière" printed later in the volume that Cousin is introducing.
50. e.g. in the 1817 "Exposition de la doctrine philosophique de Leibnitz," printed later in the volume Cousin is introducing, Biran writes, against the Cartesians, "Leibniz established the opposed thesis: every substance is completely and essentially active; every simple being has within it the principle of all its changes. Every substance is a force in itself, and every force or simple being is a substance" (p. 321).
51. *Fr. phil. 1847* and subsequent editions: Cousin inserts a footnote citing a footnote in his *Premiers essais*, translated in n. 173 to the 1826 Preface.
52. A reference to Cousin's lecture on Locke's theory of time from the *Essay on Human Understanding* as presented in the 1829 *Cours de l'histoire de la philosophie*, vol. 2.
53. *Fr. phil. 1865*: this footnote is omitted. The citation is to the three lectures on Locke's *Essay on Human Understanding* as analysed in the 1829 *Cours de l'histoire de la philosophie*, vol. 2.
54. Cousin is referring to "Réponses aux arguments contre l'aperception immediate," printed later in the volume he is introducing, where Biran speaks briefly of a "primary induction which transposes

causality from the I to the not-I." He goes on to "regret, for want of a better word, that I am employing the word induction in this new psychological sense" (pp. 393–4).
55. *Fr. phil. 1847* and subsequent editions: Cousin adds an additional citation to *Du Vrai, du Beau et du Bien*. The 1829 citation is to a lecture on Locke's theory of reflection.
56. *Fr. phil. 1865*: "but what kind of personality, what kind of providence?" replaced with "—this is much, without a doubt. But what is the personality of this God, what is his providence?"
57. *Fr. phil. 1865*: "rational facts" replaced with "facts which belong to reason."
58. The note is printed below in the volume Cousin is introducing, in *Nouvelles considérations sur les rapports du physique et du moral de l'homme*, pp. 147–64. The note begins, "Above the sphere of activity of the human soul and all the faculties of understanding and reason which it embraces, there is raised a creative faculty whose characteristics and products attest to a higher origin and bear on them the mark and, as it were, presentiment of an immortal nature" (p. 147). Biran continues by considering "the necessity of a divine revelation" (p. 151), which would be "internal" and addressed to "ineffable sentiment" and "the soul," rather than only the understanding (p. 152). Biran then goes on to look for evidence of it in "all those philosophers who have penetrated a little into the depths of the human soul," quoting at length from Proclus, van Helmont, Leibniz, the Gospel of John, Plato's *Theages*, both of his *Alcibiades* and the *Republic*, Bossuet, and Fénelon. Malebranche is not named in this note at all. The Plato dialogue whose authenticity Cousin doubts is the *Second Alcibiades* (but not the *Theages*).
59. *Fr. phil. 1865*: "this personality" replaced with "the human soul."
60. *Fr. phil. 1865*: "revelation" is omitted.
61. *Fr. phil. 1847* and subsequent editions: Cousin alters the footnote to provide different citations, including *Du Vrai, du Beau et du Bien*.
62. *Fr. phil. 1865*: Cousin inserts the following footnote: "On Fichte, see *On the True*, lecture 1, p. 7, and above, *Souvenirs d'Allemagne*, Jena" (*Fr. phil. 1865*, pp. 147–50).
63. *Fr. phil. 1865*: this sentence is omitted.
64. *Fr. phil. 1847* and subsequent editions: "welcome it" is omitted.
65. *Fr. phil. 1847* and subsequent editions: this footnote is omitted and replaced with brief citations to the lecture courses from 1818–19. It is noticeable that Cousin's claims about Fichte's turn to grace are not to be found in Tennemann's summary.
66. Biran died on 20 July 1824, when Cousin was setting out on a trip to Germany and from which, owing to his arrest in October that year (see Editors' Preface), he did not return until spring 1825.
67. In 1841, Cousin published three further volumes of Biran's works, penning a short prefatory note (reprinted in *Fr. Phil. 1847* onwards) which concludes, "I can now say to myself I have accomplished, as much as I could, the pious task I imposed on myself to conserve and expand the useful, earlier works of the man who had been one of my teachers and who I can today call, as I did in 1834, the first French metaphysician of our age" (*Fr. phil. 1865*, vol. 5, p. 340).

From Abelard[1]

I have elsewhere[*] determined scholastic philosophy's general character, charted its periods, recorded its great names, sketched its principal systems. I here add that scholasticism belonged to France, which produced, educated, or attracted the most illustrious doctors of this epoch. In the Middle Ages, the University of Paris was the principal European school. Moreover, it cannot be denied that the man who—through his faults as much as his qualities, through the audacity of his opinions, the dazzling nature of his life, the innate passion in his polemics, and his rare talent for teaching—contributed most to increasing and expanding the taste for study as well as this intellectual movement out of which the University of Paris arose in the thirteenth century[†] was Peter Abelard.

This name is assuredly one of the most famous, and renown is never bestowed in error; it is just a matter of rediscovering the reasons for it.

Abelard [was] from Pallet, near Nantes, and, after undertaking his first philosophical studies in this region and passing through the schools of most of the provinces to increase his learning, he arrived in Paris to perfect himself,[‡] and there, as a student, he soon became the rival of and victor over all the renowned masters there were: he reigned supreme in dialectic. Later, when he mixed theology with philosophy, he attracted such a great audience from all over France and even Europe that, as he himself said, the hostels were not enough to house them nor the earth enough to nourish them.[§] Everywhere he went, noise and crowds seemed to accompany him. The desert to which he withdrew gradually became an immense

---

[*] 1829 *Lectures*, 9th lecture, pp. 333–89. One could also consult Tennemann, *Manual of the History of Philosophy*, French translation, vol. 1, pp. 331–92.[2]

[†] It had already existed from the middle of the twelfth century, as the famous passage from John of Salisbury's *Metalogicon* proves; but Philippe-Auguste's edict dates from 1200 and Robert de Courçon's statute from 1215.[3]

[‡] Abelard, *Opera*, ed. Amb., *Hist. Calamit.*, p. 2. The most famous schools in the neighbourhood or on Abelard's route were those of Poitiers, Bec, Tours, Mans, Angers, and Chartres.[4]

[§] *Hist. Calamit.*, p. 19: "There was not enough room to house them or enough land to provide food for them." See also Fulk's letter to Abelard, Amb., p. 219: "Rome was sending its foster-children to you to be taught.... No expanse of land, no mountain peaks, no deep valleys, no roads—though they be blocked by difficult dangers and robbers—kept them from hastening to you. The terrible sea and the tempest of waves which lay in-between did not terrify the crowd of English youths ... [those from] far-off Brittany ... the men of Anjou ... the men of Poitiers, the Gascons, and the Iberians; Normandy and Flanders, German and Swabian.... I'll pass over all those living in the city of Paris."[5]

auditorium.* In philosophy, he was involved in the biggest controversy of the age—that between realism and nominalism—and he created an intermediary system. In theology, he marginalized the old school of Anselm of Laon,† which set out [passages] without explaining them, and he founded what today we would call rationalism. Moreover, he did not just shine within the schools; he affected Church and State; he was a member of two great councils,‡ had St Bernard for an adversary, and one of his disciples and his friends was Arnauld of Brescia.§ Finally, to ensure nothing was lacking from the singularity of his life and the popularity of his name, this dialectician—who had eclipsed William of Champeaux,[9] this theologian who provoked the Bossuet of the twelfth century[10]—was beautiful, a poet and a musician; he wrote songs in the common tongue which amused scholars and women; and, canon of the cathedral, professor of the cloister, he was loved with the most absolute devotion by that noble creature who loved like St Teresa, sometimes wrote like Seneca and whose grace must have been irresistible, since it charmed St Bernard himself.§§ A hero of romance in the Church, a beautiful spirit in barbarous times, leader of a school, and almost martyr for an idea—all of this contributed to make of Abelard an *extraordinary* character. But of all these aspects, the one which relates to our subject matter and which places him apart in the history of the human mind, as an inventor and man of genius, is the application of dialectic to theology.[12] Of course, before Abelard, there had been some rare attempts at this application—[attempts] that were perilous, but also useful, even in their deviations, to the progress of reason. However, Abelard established it in principle; it is he who therefore contributed the most to the establishment of scholasticism, for scholasticism is nothing but this. After Charlemagne and even before him, a little bit of grammar and logic had been taught in lots of places; at the same time there was no lack of religious teaching; but this teaching was reducible to a relatively standard exposition of sacred dogmas—it might have been enough for faith, but it did not bear fruit for the intellect. The introduction of dialectic into theology could alone result in that spirit of controversy which is both the vice and the honour of scholasticism. Abelard is, to a large extent,[13] the principal founder of the philosophy of the Middle Ages, such that France has given to

---

* *Hist Calamit*, p. 28: "I built, at first of reeds and thatch, an oratory dedicated to the Holy Trinity, hidden away there with one of my students.... When my former pupils learned where I was, they began to flock together here from every direction, leaving the cities and towns to live in this desert place."[6]

† *Histoire littéraire de la France*, vol. 10, p. 170.[7]

‡ The Council of Soissons in 1121 and the Council of Sens in 1140.

§ Condemned at the Council of Sens with Abelard. *Concil.*, vol. 6, pp. 11, 1219, ed. Hard.[8]

§§ *Histoire littéraire de la France*, vol. 12, p. 642, article "Heloise": "The greatest men of her time found glory in their relationship to her.... After his rupture with Abelard, St Bernard did not stop thinking highly of Heloise, despite the inviolable attachment that he knew she had for her spouse. Reciprocally, she always retained the same sentiments of veneration for the Abbé of Clairvaux. Hugus Metel, another adversary of Abelard, was no less zealous a partisan of the Abbess of Paraclete." See the two letters from Metel cited in this article and the letter from Peter the Venerable.[11]

Europe both the scholasticism of the twelfth century through Abelard and, at the beginning of the seventeenth century, the destruction of this same scholasticism in Descartes, the father of modern philosophy. And this is no mere inconsistency, for the same spirit which had raised ordinary religious teaching to this systematic and rational form called scholasticism could alone surpass this very form and produce philosophy in the strict sense. The same country could therefore certainly—some centuries apart—bear Abelard and Descartes. And between these two great men a striking resemblance can be noted, despite their differences. Both stand at the head of two great intellectual movements which seem to be at war with each other and which necessarily succeed each other.[14] Abelard tried to give an account of the only thing one could study in his time, theology; Descartes gave an account of what he was finally permitted to study in his time, man and nature. The latter recognized no other authority but that of reason; the former attempted to transpose reason into authority. Both of them doubted and both of them searched; they wanted to understand as much as possible and to rest only when there was evidence—this is the common trait that they lent to the French spirit, and this fundamental resemblance leads to many others: for example, that clarity of language which is born spontaneously from accuracy and precision of ideas. Add to this that Abelard and Descartes are not only French, but belonged to the same province, to that Brittany whose inhabitants distinguish themselves by means of such a lively sentiment for independence and such a strong personality. From the natural originality to be found in these two illustrious compatriots [emerges] a specific disposition to only grudgingly admire any achievement that had preceded them, as well as what was in the process of being achieved in their own epoch; a [sense of] independence often taken to the point of controversy; confidence in their own strengths and contempt for their adversaries; more consistency than solidity in their views, more wisdom than comprehensiveness [*l'étendue*],[15] more vigour imprinted on their mind and character than elevation[16] or depth in their thought, more invention than common sense, revelling in their own senses rather than elevating themselves to universal reason—stubborn, risky, innovative, revolutionary.

Abelard and Descartes are incontestably the two greatest philosophers that France has produced—one in the Middle Ages and the other in modernity. And yet, twelve years ago France did not have a complete edition of Descartes,[17] and it still awaits a complete edition of Abelard.[18] The volume prepared in 1616 by the Counsellor of State, Amboise,* contains the whole history of Abelard's relation to Heloise, the Commentary on St Paul's Letter to the Romans and the *Introduction to Theology*; but the very precious pieces found in this collection were published without any order or, I might add, any care. Some other of Abelard's writings were

---

* Petri Abaelardi, *Opera*, in 4, with notes by Duchesne.

scattered and almost lost in Benedictine collections.* A good number of works that were previously famous have now been buried under the dust of libraries in France and Europe.† I propose [to the Académie][21] with my heartfelt wishes, and second it with all the means at my disposal, a complete edition of the works of Peter Abelard. If I were younger, I would not hesitate to undertake it myself, and I will suggest this work, which is simultaneously patriotic and philosophical, to one of those young professors, full of zeal and talent, whose career I helped get started and in whom I have taken so much interest.[22] I would, at least, like to take responsibility for a part of this task by publishing and disseminating some works, unpublished until now, by this Descartes of the twelfth century.

Notes

1. This opening passage was first published in a report to the Académie des sciences morales et politiques on a proposed edition of Peter Abelard's work in early 1835; the report was published in full in *Frag. ph. 1838*, vol. 2, pp. 104–31 under the title, "Essay on the *Sic and Non* (Yes and No), an Unpublished Theological Writing by Abelard, based on Two Manuscripts from Saint-Michel and Marmoutiers, Read to the Académie des sciences morales et politiques at the sitting of the 1st March 1835." However, in parallel, this passage was also incorporated basically unchanged into a 200-page introduction to Cousin's *Abélard: ouvrages inédits, pour servir à l'histoire de la philosophie scolastique* (Paris: Imprimerie royale, 1836) and this 200-page introduction, along with the work's appendices, was further reproduced under the generic title, "Abelard," as the entire contents of *Fr. phil. schol.*, which subsequently became *Fr. phil. 1847*, vol. 2 (subsequently: *Fr. phil. 1855*, vol. 2; *Fr. phil 1865*, vol. 2, pp. 1–217). We have published the initial passage that is common to both, before they go on to diverge, and we take the 1838 publication as our base text for this translation and note the significant modifications to later versions in the endnotes. As is clear from the below, Cousin constructs Abelard as a French philosophical hero to sit alongside Descartes—one who mediated between extremes in the name of a rationalism hospitable to theology.
2. The citations are to V. Cousin, *Cours de l'histoire de la philosophie. Histoire de la philosophie au XVIIIe siècle*, vol. 1 (Paris: Pichon and Didier, 1829), pp. 333–89; W. G. Tennemann, *Manuel de l'histoire de la philosophie*, vol. 1, trans. V. Cousin (Paris: Sautelet, 1829), pp. 331–92.
3. John of Salisbury (1115–80) arrived in Paris in 1136 and studied there for the next twelve years, later providing an autobiographical sketch of his studies in his *Metalogicon*. The other references are to Philip II of France (1165–1223) who formally created the University of Paris by edict and Robert de Courçon (c.1160–1219) who proscribed Aristotle's metaphysical and physical treatises from being studied there.
4. The citation is to Abelard's public letter, *The History of my Calamities*, from c.1132. The reference to "Amb." is to the seventeenth-century edition by François d'Amboise (see below). The relevant passage reads, "As an imitator of the peripatetics, I wandered, debating as I went, through various provinces, wherever I had heard that the art of dialectic was actively cultivated. At last, I arrived in Paris, where the study of logic was already most flourishing, and I sought out as a teacher William of Champeaux." *The Letters of Abelard and Heloise*, ed. and trans. M. M. McLaughlin and B. Wheeler (Basingstoke: Palgrave Macmillan, 2009), pp. 17–18.
5. Cousin reproduces the original Latin; translations from: *Letters of Abelard and Heloise*, p. 31; "Fulk, Letter to Peter Abelard", trans. W. North (Internet Medieval Source Book, 1998: https://sourcebooks.fordham.edu/source/fulk-abelard.asp).

---

* The *Christian Theology* and the *Hexameron*, in the *Thesaurus novus anecdotorum* of Martenne and Durand, 1717, vol. 5; the *Ethics or the Book: Know Yourself* in the *Thesaurus anecdotorum novissimus*, vol. 3, pp. 626–88, by B. Pez, 1721.[19]

† In Berlin in 1831 appeared the *Dialogue of a Philosopher with a Jew and a Christian*, ed. Rheinwald.[20]

6. Cousin reproduces the original Latin; translation from *Letters of Abelard and Heloise*, p. 38.
7. This is the multi-volume history begun by Benedictine monks in the early eighteenth century and taken up once more by the Institut de France in Cousin's day. Cousin, however, is drawing solely on the earlier eighteenth-century volumes which cover the relevant time-period. The school of Anselm of Laon (d. 1117)—mentioned in the main text—was responsible for the *Glossa ordinaria* and focused on providing concordances of biblical passages and Patristic commentaries. Anselm expelled Abelard from his school in 1113.
8. Cousin is here citing the 1726 *Acta conciliorum* by Jean Hardouin (1646-1729). Arnauld of Brescia (1090-1155), mentioned in the main text, was a critic of papal power and preacher of Christian poverty and was ultimately hanged for rebellion. He and Abelard were condemned at Sens on the instigation of St Bernard for their proposals on monastic reform.
9. Abelard's first teacher in Paris—see n. 4 above.
10. A reference back to St Bernard. J. B. Bossuet (1627-1704): Preacher to Louis XIV, historian, and theological defender of orthodoxy. See also p. 242 below.
11. The citation is to the volume, *La suite du XIIe siècle de l'Église jusqu'à l'an 1167*, which had first appeared in 1763 and was reprinted in slightly revised form in 1830. The letter from Peter the Venerable is reproduced in *Letters of Abelard and Heloise*, pp. 293-302.
12. *Fr. phil. schol.* and subsequent editions: "as an inventor and man of genius, is the application of dialectic to theology" replaced with "is the invention of a new philosophical system and the application of this system to theology."
13. *Fr. phil. schol.* and subsequent editions: "to a large extent" is replaced with "the principal author of this introduction [of dialectic into theology] and."
14. *Fr. phil. schol.* and subsequent editions: this sentence is omitted.
15. *Fr. phil. 1847* and subsequent editions: "more consistency than solidity in their views, more wisdom than comprehensiveness" is omitted.
16. *Fr. phil. 1847* and subsequent editions: "elevation" replaced with "comprehensiveness [*l'étendue*]."
17. Until Cousin began preparing one himself in 1824.
18. See n. 22 below.
19. References to Abelard's *Theologia Christiana* (c.1120-40), the *Expositio in hexaemeron* and *Ethica seu liber: Scito te ipsum* (before 1140), respectively.
20. Abelard's *Dialogus inter philosophum, Judaeum et Christianum* from 1136-9.
21. This text originally formed part of a report Cousin presented to the Académie des sciences morales et politiques in 1835 to propose the preparation, under its auspices, of an edition of Abelard's work.
22. *Fr. phil. 1847* and subsequent editions: Cousin adds the following footnote: "No one came forward, so I took on this task myself, assisted by my two young friends, Jourdain and Despois. Two volumes in 4° soon appeared, which included all Abelard's works, with the exception of those which I communicate below and which I had already published under the title: *Ouvrages inédits d'Abelard*, 1 vol. in 4° (Paris: Imprimerie royale, 1836)." The collected works were published as *Œuvres d'Abélard*, 2 vols, ed. V. Cousin (Paris: Durand, 1849-59); for the *Ouvrages inédits*, see n. 1 above. Cousin's "friends" are Charles Jourdain (1817-86) and Eugène Despois (1818-76).

From Foreword to *On Pascal's Pensées*[1]

While at the beginning of the nineteenth century Chateaubriand encouraged [the introduction of] imagination and good taste into Christianity through the charm of the new beauties he discovered there; while the Abbé Frayssinous spoke before a learned and elect audience at Saint-Sulpice[2] on that favoured theme of the Gallican Church,[3] *obsequium rationabile*, an obedience that conforms to reason;[4] and while an accommodating philosophy, emerging out of the heart of the University,[5] struggled against materialism and atheism by attempting to rehabilitate among us the Cartesian tradition, purified and brought back to life by the light of our century; there appeared a man[6] who, instead of sharing in this reparative work, suddenly mutated it into a violent reaction—a vigorous but extreme mind hurrying with the blindness of logic to pursue every consequence of one principle, coming to a stop only at the bottom of an abyss from which he escaped only to throw himself again down the opposite path with the same ardour and the same blindness.[7] He was both obstinate and fluid, and always excessive, disdaining what the majority of men adore, pleasure and fortune, having no other passion than the renown of his name and the noise of his systems—not the St Bernard,[8] but the Jean-Jacques Rousseau of our century. Such is the man who renewed the project left incomplete by Pascal and the Jesuits,[9] while believing he had invented it and imagining himself to have made a decisive contribution to the Church, ending, with one blow, all its quarrels and suppressing one of the two principles that it had tried to harmonize.[10] The Abbé de Lamennais attacked all dogmatism; he no longer distinguished, as had been done previously, between good and bad, true and false philosophy. All philosophy became false and bad to him by the very fact that it was grounded on reason and laid claim to a certainty that was its own, [since he argued] all certainty arises from authority, which now had no other ground than itself: it is because it is and insofar as it is.[11] Lamennais is Pascal reduced to a system; he is the author of the *Condemnation of Cartesian Philosophy* and the *Philosophical Treatise on the Weakness of the Human Mind*[12]—less learned and less methodical,[13] but passionate, vehement, armed at once with the iron-clad logic of the *Social Contract* and the inflamed rhetoric of the *Heloïse*.[14] Subscribing to just one principle—authority—his new doctrine completely shattered exclusive systems; it seduced and got rid of the weak ones. Moreover, it linked itself to the very project of the Restoration, which it exaggerated and aggravated. However, after 1830, this ardent soldier of authority and Rome became one of the apostles of freedom. Representative monarchy,[15] which had previously appeared to him as fabricated licence, became unbearable tyranny. Lamennais is [now] a republican in politics, and his starting point in philosophy is no longer revelation, but reason.* The old Abbé de Lamennais is no more, but his earlier doctrine endures. This doctrine has permeated the clergy: the French Church, particularly its young fanatics, has received from him a dreadful and lasting imprint. The Church has rejected Lamennais but has retained—if not his system—than at least the spirit which animated it. It is Lamennais who was the first to attack modern philosophy in Descartes, its father; and once set in motion, everyone followed; and there is today no purportedly religious pamphlet that does not endlessly denounce Descartes and philosophy.

What are all these attacks which daily savage what they call the philosophy of the University, if not the consequence and monotonous echo of his old polemic in *On Indifference*? All that has now been invented is but one new word—pantheism;[17] such is the sole variation on Lamennais' argument. Lamennais said: All philosophy which wishes to be consistent ends in scepticism; today it is said to us: All philosophy which begins from reason (and so is called rationalism)[18] necessarily leads to pantheism, that is, to the identification of God with the world—that is, [it leads] to materialism and to atheism. Look at Descartes and all the Cartesians—including me and my friends, all of whom, I beg their pardon, must be affiliated with those great figures of the seventeenth century I mentioned above, if they are to be consistent. But who, in fact, will they make believe that my friends and me now confound the world and God, like Volney and Dupuis,[19] and have become belated admirers of the very same religion of the universe-God against which we have fought with all our might since youth? Let's speak directly: what is pantheism? It is no disguised atheism, as is claimed; no, it is a declared atheism. To say in the presence of this universe, which is as vast, as beautiful, as magnificent as it can be: God is entirely there—this is God, he is nothing else; this is also to clearly say that it is possible that there is no God, for it is to say that the universe has no cause that is essentially different from its effects. And some dare impute such a doctrine to us!

The relations which unite creation and creator constitute an obscure and delicate problem, and the two extreme solutions to it are equally false and dangerous: first, that a God passed so much into the world as to appear absorbed into it; secondly, a God separated so far from the world that the world appears to progress without him—two sides, but the same excess, the same danger, the same error. God is always and everywhere in the world; as a result—along with being and duration—the order and beauties of this world which come from God are mixed together with the inherent imperfections of the creature; for, as immense as it is, this world is finite in itself, compared to God who is infinite; it manifests him, but it also veils

---

* *Sketch of a Philosophy*, 3 vols (Paris, 1840)—vol. 1, Preface: "Philosophy has its roots in our nature and it is why one can assign it the beginning. Contemporaneous with man, this is nothing but *the very exercise of his reason*...." This does not prevent many propositions in the *Sketch* recalling those of the *Indifference* book. Two opposed spirits are endlessly at war here and it would take a third work to bring them into agreement.[16]

his grandeur, his intellect, his wisdom. The universe is the image of God, it is not God—something of the cause passes into the effect, it does not exhaust it, and remains completely whole in itself. The universe itself is so far from exhausting God that many of God's attributes are there converted into a near impenetrable obscurity and are discovered solely in the human soul. The universe is necessity, but the soul is free; it is one, simple, essentially identical to itself under the harmonious diversity of its faculties; it is capable of conceiving virtue and achieving it; it is capable of love and sacrifice. Moreover, it denies that the being, which is the first and last cause of this soul, is an abstract being, possessing less than it has given, and having itself no personality, freedom, intellect, justice, or love. Either God is inferior to man, or he possesses at least all that is permanent and substantial in man, with infinitely more.

This declaration is sufficient, I hope, [for those] who [read me] fairly and in good faith; but it is not [enough], I admit, [for those] with a need for accusations and a passion for harm.

Some will persist in repeating—using one or two phrases misappropriated from their natural meaning—that I admit only one substance, that the soul is necessarily a mode of this substance, and hence I am really a pantheist and a fatalist. But how could I make the human soul a mode of God, when, for me, the first maxim of both psychology and ontology is that the human soul has as its fundamental characteristic being a free force, that is, a substance—the concept of substance being comprehended in that of force, as I have so often demonstrated alongside Maine de Biran and Leibniz?[20] Either contest this demonstration, which is the principle of all my philosophy, or seek another ground for your accusation. I have pushed the freedom of man so far to have drawn from it a profoundly liberal politics, which I recommend to your attention. In my eyes, as in those of Leibniz, the external world is composed of forces and therefore of substances. If, then, I have spoken somewhere of God as the sole substance, as the sole being who is, is it not obvious that I wished to emphasize by this—in the way the Platonists and many Church Fathers did—the eternal substance and essence of God in opposition to our relative and limited existence?*

More than once I have complained that the seventeenth century and Cartesianism itself went too far by attributing too much to God's action and by not sufficiently respecting the personal power of man, the voluntary and free force which constitutes him. And as a result, my philosophy is associated with Malebranche's sublime mysticism which substitutes divine action for human action! Besides, Malebranche's would be a strange atheism to the extent he sacrifices man for God! It is rather an exaggerated theism; but, nevertheless, I have not

---

* See, for the most detail, the Prefatory Note to the third edition of *Philosophical Fragments*, p. xix [p. 130 above] and the *Lectures on Kant's Philosophy*, third lecture, p. 113 and the sixth lecture against the Transcendental Dialectic.[21]

hesitated in fighting against it* and showing in all my writings that man and nature are forces endowed with an activity of their own, that the human soul is a force that is as free as it is intelligent, that, on these two grounds, it is self-conscious, recognizes both itself and the rights, duties, and responsibilities of all its actions.

They do not fail to reply that, if I do not destroy God, I misrecognize him by refusing him freedom, since I take creation to be necessary. Let us understand each other. There is, in the jargon of the schools, two kinds of necessity—physical necessity and moral necessity.[23] It cannot be a question here of the physical necessity of creation; for, on this hypothesis, God—we repeat for the hundredth time—would be without freedom, that is, beneath man. Thus, there remains the moral necessity of creation. Ah! I have retreated from this expression, [since] by it alone [creation] can appear equivocal and compromise God's freedom. And as for that [expression] so much to your liking that I substituted for it, I will repeat the explanation I have given [elsewhere] and which a miserable dexterity always makes you overlook.†
I am free—this for me is an incontestable demonstration that God is so too and possesses all my freedom, with regard to what is essential to it and to a supreme degree, without the limits imposed on my nature by passion and a limited intellect. Divine freedom does not know the misfortunes of my [freedom], its disturbances, its uncertainties; it is naturally united with the intellect and with divine benevolence. God was perfectly free to create or not create the world and man, just as much as I am free to side with a certain party. Is this clear, I say, and do you find me explicit enough on God's freedom? But here is the knot of the difficulty: if God was perfectly free to create or not create, then why did he create? God created because he found that creation conformed more to his wisdom and to his benevolence. Creation is not God's arbitrary decree, as Ockham wished it to be; it is a perfectly free act in itself, but one that is grounded in reason—this is all surely agreed. Since God decided to create, he preferred [creation], and he preferred it because it appeared to him better than its opposite. And if it appeared better to his wisdom, he thus consented to this wisdom, and, armed with omnipotence, produced what appeared best to him. This is my optimism: accuse it of atheism and fatalism as much as you like, you cannot accuse me thus without doing the same to Leibniz—and that is even without mentioning St Thomas and many others: I consent to be a fatalist and an atheist like Leibniz. The God who made me could easily have not made me, and my existence does not lessen his perfection. However, on the one hand, if, when creating the world, he had not created my soul—this soul which can understand him and love him—creation would have been imperfect, for while reflecting God in some of his attributes, it would not have manifested the greatest and most holy ones, such as freedom, justice, and love; and, on the other hand,

---

* *1829 Lectures*, second lecture on Spinoza and Malebranche, p. 427 of the second edition. See also the two articles on Mairan's and Malebranche's correspondence in the *Journal des Savants* (1842).[22]
† Prefatory Note to the third edition of the *Fragments*, p. xxi [p. 132 above]. This edition is from 1838.

it was good that there was a world, a theatre in which he could deploy this being capable of raising himself to God through the passions and the sufferings which bring him back to earth. All things are good as God made them and as they are. I conclude from this—and you will not be displeased by it—that, without being *necessitated* either physically, which is absurd, or morally, which seems equivocal, remaining free and perfectly free, but finding it better to create than not to create, God created not only with wisdom, but in virtue of his wisdom, and that, in this great act, intellect and love govern freedom.

This explanation is not a concession; it is the further development of the fundamental thought which serves as our ground, my friends and me—that is, that the insights of high metaphysics lie within psychology. It is with the aid of consciousness, and the permanent elements which constitute it, that, by a legitimate induction, we raise man to knowledge of God's most hidden attributes. Man can understand nothing of a God of whom he does not possess some shadow in himself: he gives what he takes to be essential in himself, or rather he hands it back to him who gave it to him; and he can feel neither his freedom nor his intellect nor his love, with all their imperfections and their limits, without possessing an incontestable certainty of God's freedom, intellect, and love, grounded in infinity. If I am allowed to speak this way, my own work has been [to establish] a profound psychology as its starting point with a grand moral, religious, and, at the same time, liberal philosophy as its final goal, in opposition to the atheism which produces the superficial psychology of empiricism, and in opposition as well to the hypothetical metaphysics of the German school, born from the absence of all psychology.[25] If I have some renown in France, to what do I owe it, I ask you, if not the task I have persevered with for thirty years—that of combatting materialism and atheism as the extreme consequences of the philosophy of the previous century, not—it is true—by waging war on reason, but by trying to better direct it; not by abjuring philosophy, but by proclaiming, on the contrary, its supreme and benevolent mission. I bow down before revelation, the unique source of supernatural truths; I bow down also before the authority of the Church, nourisher and benefactor of humankind, to whom alone it has been given to speak to nations, to rule public mores, to fortify and contain souls. How many times have I not defended—both as a politician and as a philosopher—ecclesiastical authority within its necessary limits?* In so doing, I lost my old popularity[26]—but I do not regret it; I made it my duty and I am ready to do so again and to sacrifice everything for this holy cause— everything except this other portion of truth, justice, and my reflective conviction. I mean the sentiment of the excellence of human reason and the natural and legitimate power it has received from God to make known to man both himself and his divine author. Shed light on this power; do not try in vain to stifle it. Respect

---

* See particularly my *Report* to the Chamber of Peers on the law of primary teaching—a report in which I staunchly defended the legitimate role of the clergy in the overseeing of public schools.[24]

the accommodating direction and energy that Cartesianism gives to thought. Far from repeating, against the truth of things and against the evidence of history, that all philosophy leads to atheism, oh! I implore you, proclaim loudly that bad philosophy alone leads to this dreadful error, and that wisely cultivated reason bears within itself those beliefs without which those of the Church would lack a ground, and would no longer rest on anything but imagination or on an impious despair for truth, trying hard to deceive itself and disturb the Church instead of finding peace there. What benefit, tell me, does the haughty system I am fighting against gain for the Church of France? It has given it a day's triumph, then unhappy rifts, and now a fatal direction, contrary to its national traditions, to its interests at all times, to the declarations of the holy Councils, to the permanent genius of Catholicism. Instead of struggling against the University, let the Church of France join together with it to accomplish in harmony their different missions. University professors of philosophy do not teach religion; they have no right to; for they do not speak in the name of God; they speak in the name of reason. They should, rather, teach a philosophy which, so as not to betray reason itself, society, and the state, should contain nothing which is opposed to religion. Their roles are too different to be opposed and to be exchanged. But their ultimate end is the same: the rehabilitation of the dignity of the soul, faith in divine Providence, and service to the nation.

I ask the reader's pardon for these explanations which, in appearance, sit so awkwardly in a foreword on variants in Pascal's [texts].[27] However, it is Pascal, in the very book on which this work is going to focus, who first declared war on Cartesianism and on all philosophy. This war has been renewed today; it has now attained its ultimate pitch of violence. It was thus not unseemly to here formulate this response to the enemies of philosophy, and here is my last word: Let the government remain undecided and silent; let the exhausted public spirit become increasingly alien to those noble interests which made our forefathers' and our fathers' hearts beat and for so long made France the soul and intellect of the world; let unrestrained attacks shake weak convictions and [persuade] those who have no experience of the difficulties of life; for there is one man whose good conscience will keep him tranquil and firm; who will not fold under this coalition of all the wretched parties; who, God willing, will not let himself be either led astray by some of them or intimidated by others; who will never lack the profound respect he professes for Christianity and will never betray the sacred rights of freedom of thought and faith in the dignity of philosophy; unshakeably attached to this cause all his life, even if he is insulted every day, torn to shreds and blackened by calumny.

V. Cousin
15 December 1842

Notes

1. First published in *Des Pensées de Pascal: Rapport à l'Académie française sur la nécessité d'une nouvelle édition* (Paris: Ladrange, 1842), pp. i–lv. This text functions as the foreword to the collection of Cousin's reports to the Académie des sciences morales et politiques on the philological challenges facing any attempt at a new edition of Pascal's works. It is reproduced unaltered in the subsequent second (1843) and third (1847) editions, although a new preface is added that touches on some of this material. Because it was written so late, this is, however, one of the few short texts we include in this volume that did not appear in one of the *Fragments* volumes. In what follows, we reproduce the last eighteen pages of the Foreword (pp. xxxviii–lv), which had been preceded by a few pages (pp. i–iv) resuming the philological stakes of the book, before then undertaking an involved narrative that positions Pascal in the midst of the battles being fought between the Cartesians and the Catholic Church during the seventeenth century (pp. v–xxxvii). In the final pages extracted here, Cousin turns to the nineteenth century and spots resemblances with the persecution of his own Cartesian project by the Catholic Right—and takes up once more his defence against accusations of pantheism begun in the 1838 Preface.
2. Denis-Antoine-Luc, comte de Frayssinous (1765–1841), who delivered a popular series of lectures on dogmatic theology at Sant-Sulpice from 1803–9, before becoming court preacher to Louis XVIII during the Restoration. Cousin had already discussed Saint-Sulpice's relatively hospitable relation to Cartesianism in the seventeenth century (pp. xxxiii–xxxiv) and, as a result, mentions (just before the translated passage begins) Frayssinous as someone who "did not cease to pursue the principal object which the most authoritative theologians constantly proposed—the accord of reason and faith" (p. xxxvii). In an accompanying note, Cousin approvingly cites Frayssinous's *Défense du christianisme* as proving the existence of God "by means of *pure reason* and on the *faith of the human species*" (p. xxxvii).
3. Before it became a term for a particular Catholic denomination (much later in the nineteenth century), the Gallican Church merely referred to the Catholic Church in France, although often a form of that Church that worked closely with the state and in the state's interests. Frayssinous' most popular early work was entitled, *Les vrais principes de l'Église gallicane sur la puissance ecclésiastique* (1818).
4. *Obsequium rationabile* is used in the Vulgate translation of *Romans* 12:1 to denote Paul's idea of "reasonable service" to the Church.
5. i.e. Cousin's own eclecticism.
6. As will become clear, Cousin's reference is to Félicité de Lamennais (1782–1854), the Catholic theologian whose *Essai sur l'indifférence en matière de religion* (*Essay on Indifference in Matters of Religion*) became the most influential text of Restoration Catholicism.
7. At the end of the 1820s, Lamennais broke with his earlier conservative theological values and began a path marked by the rejection of the state, of orthodoxy and even of the authority of Rome. In the early 1830s, his journal, *L'Avenir*, received Papal censure and Lamennais developed a Christian anarchism. He was imprisoned in 1841 for his attacks on the state.
8. On Cousin's positioning of St Bernard, see pp. 238–9 above.
9. This project is of course the attack on Cartesian philosophy and, through it, on philosophical rationality itself, which had formed the subject matter of the earlier sections of this Foreword.
10. The two principles—"authority" and "reason"—are first introduced on p. xvi of the Foreword.
11. For example, in his *Essai sur l'indifférence*, Lamennais characterizes "the lamentable conclusion in which all philosophy necessarily ends" as a state in which philosophers "travel from abyss to abyss, passing by, in their descent, all degrees of error, without being able to stop themselves at any of them, sagging under the vengeful weight of the truths they blaspheme, falling and sinking into the stagnant lake of indifference." This, he continues, is the effect of, "instead of being led by a superior guide, by divine reason itself, undertaking to replace it with human reason and making it the ground of faith, with the result that [philosophy] ends up denying everything, because it can understand nothing and wants to practise nothing." Vol. 1 (Paris: Tournachon-Molin and Seguin, 1817), pp. xxxiii–xxxiv.
12. Two works by P. D. Huet: *Censura philosophiae cartesianae* (1689) and *Traité philosophique de la faiblesse de l'esprit humain* (1723). Cousin had discussed both these works at length earlier in the Foreword (pp. xvi–xviii)—positioning them as exemplary of the Jesuit attack on Cartesianism, which was in fact, Cousin reveals, a polemic "against reason itself ... against all species of dogmatism" (p. xvii).
13. i.e. than Huet.

14. i.e. Rousseau's 1761 *Julie; or The New Heloise* (alongside his 1762 *The Social Contract*).
15. i.e. the form of government first established in France by the July Revolution of 1830 and which Cousin passionately defended (see p. 25 below).
16. Lamennais' *Esquisse d'une philosophie* was ultimately published in four volumes from 1840 to 1846. Cousin here quotes the first words of the first volume (Paris: Pagnerre, 1840), p. i.
17. As Cousin implies, attacks on pantheism as "the heresy of the nineteenth century" (in the Abbé Bautain's words) were very common from the Catholic Right during this period, but Cousin is presumably thinking specifically of H. L. C. Maret's 1840 *Essai sur la panthéisme*. Maret (1805–84) had been close to the younger Lamennais and was a Professor at the Sorbonne, as well as a priest. Considering the extent to which Cousin defends his theory of divine creation in what follows, it is worth quoting Maret's criticism: "To create for Cousin is to cause; he wishes to give us an exact idea of creation by means of the faculty we have to produce specific effects, which are solely the exercise of our faculties. God is an absolute and necessitated cause; he creates with himself; he passes into his work, while remaining in himself. The world is thus created with the divine substance and created necessarily. Its existence is as necessary as that of God himself, since it is solely the expression of his life, the redoubling of his unity. [...] But in what way then can this doctrine differ from pantheism? Does not pantheism consist in making God pass into the world, in regarding the world as part of God himself? Indeed, if the world is necessary, if it is indispensable for the divine life, it is evidently an integral part of God." *Essai sur la panthéisme* (Paris: Debécourt, 1840), p. 9.
18. Maret's label for nineteenth-century pantheist philosophy, whose two main exponents, to his mind, are Cousin and Hegel, is indeed "rationalism": "modern rationalism" is equivalent to "nineteenth-century philosophy" (*Essai sur la panthéisme*, p. 48).
19. Constantin François de Chassebœuf, comte de Volney (1757–1820) and Charles François Dupuis (1742–1809)—two radical deists who argued, on the basis of comparative mythology, for the historical inexistence of Christ at the end of the eighteenth century.
20. See p. 228 above.
21. *Leçons sur la philosophie de Kant* (Paris: Ladrange, 1844), pp. 113, 158–262. The former passage runs (although it is in fact in the fifth lecture): "In a sublime and true sense, we are only phenomena, compared to the eternal and absolute being, since we are merely relative, dependent, limited, finite beings, who do not possess in themselves the principle of their existence, just as the causative force with which we are endowed presupposes a first cause in which everything participates, us and everything else."
22. The first reference is to material on Malebranche from the 1829 lecture course. Cousin writes, "Malebranche does not destroy the concept of cause, as Spinoza does; he retains it in God but he degrades it in man; he makes human freedom very weak and the action of the infinite God." *Cours d'histoire de la philosophie professé en 1828–29*, vol. 2 (Paris: Didier, 1841), p. 428. The second reference is to Cousin's "Méditations métaphysiques et correspondance de N. Malebranche avec D. de Mairan, publiées pour la première fois sur les manuscrits originaux" which appeared in the August and December 1842 issues of the *Journal des Savants* and was then anthologised in *Fr. phil. cart.*
23. A traditional distinction common in eighteenth-century theodicies—and given canonical form in Leibniz's comments at the beginning of the *Theodicy* on which Cousin is drawing: "Physical necessity is founded on moral necessity, that is, on the wise one's choice which is worthy of his wisdom; and both of these ought to be distinguished from geometrical necessity. It is this physical necessity that makes order in Nature and lies in the rules of motion and in some other general laws which it pleased God to lay down for things when he gave them being." *Theodicy*, trans. E. M. Huggard (La Salle, IL: Open Court, 1985), p. 74.
24. *Premier rapport fait à la chambre des Pairs au nom d'un commission spéciale chargée de l'examen du projet de loi sur l'instruction primaire, le 21 mai 1833* (reprinted in *Œuvres* 5th series, Vol. 1: *Instruction publique en France* (Paris: Pagnerre, 1850), pp. 23–61. The material on the ecclesiastical role in oversight of primary education is on pp. 47–9.
25. Cousin is drawing on his earlier criticisms of absolute idealism in the 1833 and 1838 Prefaces—see pp. 107–8, 127–8 above.
26. That is, the changing perception of Cousin from leader of the liberal movement of opposition during the Restoration to a statist conservative as the fortunes of the July Monarchy waned.
27. See n. 1 above.

Foreword to *Fragments of Cartesian Philosophy*[1]

Eclecticism is[2] not some kind of uncertain equilibrium between every system. If it discerns something true and good in the falsest of systems and excess and error in the truest of systems, if it attempts to guard against all irreflective and extreme movements, this is not to say that it is condemned[3] to that timid impartiality which watches the struggle between opinions without taking any part in them, from, as it were, the heavens. No: hospitable to all systems and blind to none, eclecticism has made its choice among systems; it very much prefers some to others, because of their principles and because of their consequences. We do not conceal it: in philosophy as in politics, we hold a deep-seated opinion, long chosen and professed.[4] In politics, we are openly in favour of the principles of the French Revolution. Its cause is ours; we have served it, and we will serve it to the end with unshakeable loyalty. We certainly do not mean that one must throw to the wind the traditions through which nations endure like families, and still less sacrifice order for freedom, which would be the first victim here. But ultimately, in the great controversy which today divides France, Europe, and the world, we belong to the liberal party in France, in Europe, and in the world. We declare that, since 1789, the sole true government for all civilized peoples is constitutional monarchy. This form of government best assures freedom; it is through it that [freedom] is cherished by us; for freedom is life; and without it peoples and individuals would languish as in the shadows of death. Our wish and our heartfelt desire are therefore that it be invoked everywhere someone fights for it or suffers for it. Likewise, in philosophy, although we work hard to remain clear of that slope which pulls idealism into mysticism,[5] we are declared partisans of every system[6] favourable to the holy cause of the spirituality of the soul, of freedom,[7] and of responsibility for one's own actions, of the fundamental distinction between good and evil, of disinterested virtue, of a creator-God, ruler of worlds, maintainer and refuge of humanity. It is for this reason that—without renouncing our own judgement and our own views[8]—in the struggle of opposed systems, in turn winners and losers, which is called modern philosophy, every one of our avowed preferences is for Cartesianism. We respect and we cherish philosophical freedom, but we are convinced that its best employment is in the Cartesian school.[9] This school is, in our view, far above all rival schools owing to its method which is the true one, owing to its independent and moderate spirit which is the genuine philosophical spirit,[10] owing to that character of spiritualism, both sober and elevated, which must always be our own,[11] owing to the moral grandeur and beauty of its principles of every kind, and finally owing to the fact that it is essentially French and has spread across our nation an immense glory, which there is no good in repudiating[12]—for, after truth, is not glory[13] something sacred?[14] It is this last and relatively patriotic aspect of Cartesianism that we wish to briefly rehearse in the below, since we have set out and developed the other aspects a hundred times before.[15]

Whatever is said in England, it is not Bacon, but Descartes who is the father of modern philosophy. Bacon is of course a very great mind; but he is an incomparable amateur in metaphysics, rather than a metaphysician in the strict sense of the term.[16] He proclaimed in magnificent language precepts that were excellent, if a little vague—precepts which were borrowed for the most part from Italian physicians and naturalists[17] and which he did not[18] himself put into practice. He left neither a general nor a particular theory; no discovery, whether large or small,[19] to which his name remains attached. Descartes is the author of a clear and precise method, and he applied it to two or three sciences, which he thereby renewed or created.

Try to take Descartes out of his time: the framework of the seventeenth century would not just be disturbed, it would be torn apart. Men and things—all of them would be altered and would fall down to their very foundations. It is likely that no considerable intellectual fact would remain intact, no great mind left standing. What would Malebranche, Arnauld, Fénelon, Bossuet, Spinoza, Leibniz, Locke himself have become [without Descartes]? All of them were in some feature marked by and visibly bore Descartes' stamp. Remove Bacon [from his time] and nothing changes; he exercised no influence on anyone, not even on Locke who scarcely cites him. It seems that the shame of his conduct[20] weighed on his reputation and for a long time obscured the authority of his genius. It is only—or at least, it is above all—in the middle of the eighteenth century that [Bacon] comes to be invoked, almost out of the depths of oblivion, to be joined to Locke, such that both of them are turned against Cartesianism.

Let me dare utter the truth: the eighteenth century in France—so rich in great men*—did not produce one in philosophy, at least if one understands philosophy to be metaphysics. Turgot is the only superior man with any taste for this kind of study, but he did not get very far;[22] such that Condillac is still the first and basically only French metaphysician of the eighteenth century. But who, I ask you, is Condillac if not an intelligent disciple of Locke? He possesses a little originality only when he exaggerates master's principles, as well as in their details and in some

---

* See the judgement I have made on the eighteenth century in France and in Europe as a whole in the first lecture of my *History of Philosophy in the Eighteenth Century*, vol. 2 of the second series of the lecture course.[21]

of his applications. Locke's great disciple is evidently Hume,* who wrote twenty years before Condillac.[24]

So, what happened? Whereas Voltaire, Montesquieu, Buffon, Rousseau, Quesnay took the whole of Europe as their school and whereas all the famous historians, journalists, economists, and naturalists were inspired by the genius of France, when it came to metaphysics France was, as it were, struck down with sterility. No one else imitated it; it imitated [them]; and its voice—so loud in everything else—was here met with merely a weak echo that did not reach the ears of posterity. To have some influence across distances and nations, novelty is required—a strength, a grandeur incompatible with the spirit of imitation.

However, turn your gaze towards the French metaphysics of the seventeenth century: what a different spectacle! The whole of Europe followed France, because in France there appeared an extraordinary man who followed no one.

Indeed, Descartes invented everything. He is without precursor or, at least, without model. The school he founded owes nothing to any foreign inspiration. It is a fruit of the earth, a work which, at bottom and in its form, is profoundly and exclusively French—and perhaps even more so, if I may say, than the poetry and arts of this great and incomparable epoch.

Moreover, to what movements did Cartesian philosophy give rise from one end of Europe to the other! Let us mention just one aspect: it is Descartes who produced Spinoza, Leibniz, Clarke, and Locke himself.

Of course, today we know that Socrates and Plato were familiar with, recommended, even practised Descartes's method, the psychological method. But Descartes knew nothing of this: he invented it, like Socrates had himself invented it; and this is why both of them moved, influenced, and subjugated their contemporaries and exercised such an unparalleled influence over the human mind.

Of course, neither of them was free from error. But what survived are the great truths that they put into the world.

Let me add that these truths have that positive characteristic of kindling and elevating souls, as much as they do enlightening and inspiring minds.

It is for this reason that, early on, both the Socratic school and the Cartesian school attracted me in such a lively and powerful manner, and that, for thirty years, I have not ceased invoking to the youth of our country these two inexhaustible sources of true ideas and rich inspirations.

To speak here solely of Descartes: from my earliest years and in my first lectures from 1815 to 1820,[25] I staunchly defended the principles of psychology and

---

* The treaty on *Human Nature* is from 1739. Even before Hume, Locke possessed a crowd of disciples, Collins, Dodwell, Toland, and others who exaggerated and aggravated some of the least happy propositions of the *Essay on Human Understanding*. It is into the midst of this active and daring society that Voltaire landed, guided by Bolingbroke, during his stay in London. Locke's school developed in England alone and elsewhere Hartley is his most famous representative after Hume and he directly produced Bonnet, Darwin, and Priestley.[23]

Cartesian theodicy against the Scottish school and against German philosophy. The first iteration of my lecture course included a lecture from 1816* devoted to demonstrating, against Reid, that the principle of Cartesianism, the famous: *I think, therefore I am*, is not stuck in a vicious circle; and there is another lecture from 1820† in which, in the process of refuting Kant's scepticism, I believe I established without reply that the Cartesian proof of the existence of God is free from paralogisms and is the legitimate foundation of all theodicy.

Later, in my second [period of] teaching from 1828 to 1830,[28] I did not limit myself to solely glorifying Descartes' name, genius, and method everywhere; I further endeavoured to bring to light the general character, the succession, the progress, the merits—and the faults—of the entire [Cartesian] school from its founder through to Leibniz, inclusively.[29] For Leibniz is the last and greatest of the Cartesians.‡

Since then, I have taken the time and the care to shed light on various points from the history and doctrine of Cartesianism: for example, in the second volume of the third edition of *Philosophical Fragments*, in the *Introduction* to the works of Pere André, and in my work, *On Pascal's Pensées*.[31]

Whereas England has long possessed magnificent editions of Bacon and Locke, France did not possess even a single complete edition of Descartes. I have remedied this damaging failure.§ It was also on the basis of my proposal that the Académie des sciences morales et politiques set a competition [for] a new examination of Cartesianism.§§

Finally, when an intelligent bookseller wished to ask me for advice on the composition of a philosophical library to be used by the young as well as people of society, I quickly undertook—and still undertake—to recover, for the sake of the commerce of ideas, the all-too-forgotten masterpieces of our beautiful philosophy of the seventeenth century. It is in order to furnish a useful complement to the editions of Descartes, Malebranche, Spinoza, Arnauld, and Leibniz that I have united in this volume[34] pieces that were scattered here and there and that shed some light—not on the principal, well-illuminated features—but on the inferior aspects and, as it were, neglected nooks of this immortal monument [of Cartesianism], which was erected by French genius alone and which alone [French genius] can repair and enlarge, without touching its foundations, in line with the progress of the centuries and the needs of the nineteenth century.[35]

---

  * Vol. 1, sixth lecture, p. 27.[26]
  † Sixth lecture, *Transcendental Logic*, pp. 237–54.[27]
  ‡ Vol. 2, eleventh and twelfth lectures.[30]
  § Edition of Descartes, 11 vols in 8°, with plates.[32]
  §§ See the speech of the President of the Académie in *Literary Fragments*, p. 52.[33]

Notes

1. *Fr. phil. cart.*, pp. v–xii (subsequently: *Fr. phil. 1855*, vol. 3, pp. v–xii; *Fr. phil. 1865*, vol. 3, pp. 1–8). We take the 1845 publication as our base text for this translation and note the significant modifications to later versions in the endnotes. Cousin's 1845 *Fragments of Cartesian Philosophy* consists for the most part in previously unpublished seventeenth-century manuscripts (particularly correspondence) relating to the history of Cartesianism in France, which we have not reproduced here. The following Foreword is Cousin's most explicit and unqualified avowal of Cartesianism—the text in which his self-image as the Descartes of the nineteenth century is fully on display.
2. *Fr. phil. 1865*: the following opening passage is added: "Yes, as I have been saying for a very long time, eclecticism is still the most general feature of the nineteenth century in all things, including in the arts, letters, and philosophy. However, it must be understood: the eclecticism we profess."
3. *Fr. phil. 1865*: the passage from "... that vacillates ..." to "... it is condemned ..." replaced with: "between opposites, and it is not condemned."
4. *Fr. phil. 1865*: the passage from "No ..." to "... and professed" replaced with "Hospitable to all systems, because it is familiar with the reasons which gave birth to them and which sustains them, an eclecticism worthy of the name is able to choose among them, and in the past as in the present, to distinctly prefer some over others, as much because of their principles as well as their consequences. We thus declare: we profess a deep-seated opinion in philosophy as in politics."
5. Idealism and mysticism are two of the four fundamental, but exaggerated systems that, according to Cousin, recur throughout the history of philosophy, and it is a natural tendency of the human mind for idealism to convert into mysticism—see p. 202 above and the accompanying notes.
6. *Fr. phil. 1865*: "declared partisans of every system" replaced with "sympathetic to every doctrine."
7. *Fr. phil. 1865*: "of the soul, of freedom" replaced with "and freedom of the soul."
8. *Fr. phil. 1865*: "without renouncing our own judgement and our own views" is omitted.
9. *Fr. phil. 1865*: this sentence is omitted.
10. *Fr. phil. 1865*: "genuine philosophical spirit" replaced with "philosophical spirit itself."
11. *Fr. phil. 1865*: "that character of spiritualism, both sober and elevated, which must always be our own" replaced with "its virile and elevated spiritualism."
12. *Fr. phil. 1865*: "there is no good in repudiating" replaced with "it would be insane and an admission of guilt to repudiate."
13. *Fr. phil. 1865*: "of the nation" is added.
14. *Fr. phil. 1865*: "for us" is added.
15. *Fr. phil. 1865*: this sentence replaced with "It is this too forgotten feature of Cartesianism which we wish to recall in a few words."
16. *Fr. phil. 1865*: "an incomparable amateur in metaphysics, rather than a metaphysician in the strict sense of the term" replaced with "not a metaphysician, properly speaking."
17. e.g. Bernadino Telesio (1509–88).
18. *Fr. phil. 1865*: "did not" replaced with "scarcely."
19. *Fr. phil. 1865*: "He left neither a general nor a particular theory, no discovery, whether large or small" replaced with "He undertook some fortuitous investigations of heat; he left no discovery."
20. In 1621, Bacon was accused of and pleaded guilty to twenty-three counts of corruption, involving taking gifts from litigants in political office.
21. *Fr. phil. 1865*: this footnote is omitted. The citation is to the first lecture of Cousin's 1829 course, entitled, "Tableau of the Eighteenth Century."
22. A. R. J. Turgot (1727–81): prior to his influential works in economics which began appearing in the mid-1750s, Turgot had planned a "universal history" and defended theses at the Sorbonne on the "continual progress of the human mind."
23. The allusion to Voltaire is to his stay in London between 1726 and 1728, where he renewed a friendship with Viscount Bolingbroke (1678–1751). The other relatively lesser-known figures mentioned are Anthony Collins (1676–1729), Henry Dodwell (1641–1711), John Toland (1670–1722), David Hartley (d. 1757), Charles Bonnet (1720–93), Erasmus Darwin (1731–1802), and Joseph Priestley (1733–1804).
24. *Fr. phil. 1865*: passage from "his master's principles" to "before Condillac" replaced with "principles of the English philosopher" (omitting the last sentence and the footnote on Hume). Condillac's *Essay on the Origin of Human Knowledge* was in fact written in 1746—only seven years after Hume's *Treatise on Human Nature* and two years before the publication of *An Enquiry concerning Human Understanding*.

25. i.e. the first period of Cousin's teaching, prior to his removal from teaching duties for liberal sympathies.
26. A reference to the opening page of Cousin's "On the True Meaning of Descartes' *cogito, ergo sum*" (pp. 144–9 above). This suggests that the 1816 essay is intended as a complex engagement with Reid and his followers (using the Reidian Stewart as a provocation against Reid).
27. *La philosophie de Kant* (Paris: Ladrange, 1844), pp. 237–54 (the material on the *cogito, ergo sum* begins on p. 242, after a similar defence of the Cartesian ontological argument against Kant). Here, Cousin makes use of much the same line of thinking as "On the True Meaning of Descartes' *cogito, ergo sum*," arguing, first, "the *cogito ergo sum* is an enthymeme that can be developed into a syllogism only on the condition of destroying it"; and secondly, the Kantian paralogisms solely apply to syllogisms, for "no major premise can cross the abyss which separates thought from being, phenomenon from substance" (pp. 242, 244).
28. i.e. the period of teaching between Cousin's return to his teaching posts and his taking up of ministerial appointments in the wake of the July Revolution.
29. *Fr. phil. 1865*: "inclusively" is omitted.
30. Cousin is referring back to the material on Leibniz in a new edition of his 1829 lecture course.
31. *Fr. phil. 1865*: this paragraph is omitted. In addition to his *Introduction aux oeuvres du père André* (Paris: Crapelet, 1843) and the opening to the "Foreword" of *On Pascal's Pensées* (not included in our translation below), Cousin is here referring to various fragments, such as newly discovered manuscripts on Descartes, Malebranche, and Leibniz and an essay, "On the Persecution of Cartesianism in France" (*Fr. phil. 1838*, vol. 2, pp. 174–206).
32. Descartes, *Œuvres*, 11 vols, ed. V. Cousin (Paris: Levrault, 1824–6).
33. *Fragments littéraire* (Paris: Didier, 1843), pp. 51–4, which summarizes the results of the Académie's competition on Descartes.
34. i.e. *Fr. phil. cart.*
35. *Fr. phil. 1865*: this final paragraph replaced with the following: "Today it is again under the invocation of Descartes that we are able to put forward these two volumes of particular dissertations intended to clarify, justify, and disseminate—by accommodating it to the progress of the age and the needs of the nineteenth century—an illustrious doctrine that France has given to the world and from out of which arose modern philosophy."

APPENDIX

Two Edicts Issued by the Royal Council of Public Education

Edict of 28th September 1832 to Determine the Philosophy Questions On Which Aspirants to the Title of Bachelor-ès Will Be Interrogated.[1]

Art. 1. The Latin programme of philosophy questions for the *baccalauréat-ès* examination is removed.[2]

Art. 2. It is replaced by the following programme:

Introduction

1. Object of philosophy.—Utility and importance of philosophy.—Its relations with the other sciences.
2. On the different methods which have been followed up to the present day in philosophical investigations.—On the true philosophical method.
3. Division of philosophy.—Order in which one must arrange its parts.

Psychology

4. Object of psychology.—Necessity of commencing the study of philosophy with psychology.—On consciousness and the certainty which pertains to it.
5. On the phenomena of consciousness and on our ideas in general.—On their different character and their diverse types.—Give examples.
6. On the origin and formation of ideas.—Take as examples some of the most important of our ideas.
7. Give a theory of the faculties of the soul.—What determines the existence of a faculty?
8. Sensibility.—Its character.—Distinguish sensibility from all the other faculties, and mark its place in the order of their development.
9. On the faulty of knowing, or reason.—Distinctive character of this faculty. On the faculties which are related to the general faculty of knowing:
   On consciousness.
   On attention.
   On external perception.
   On judgement.
   On argumentation.
   On memory.
   On abstraction.

On generalization.
On the association of ideas.
10. On activity and its diverse characteristics.—On voluntary and free activity.—Describe the phenomenon of the will and all its circumstances.—Demonstration of freedom.
11. On the I; on its identity; on its unity.—On the distinction between soul and body.

Logic

12. On method.—On analysis and synthesis.
13. On definition; on division and classification.
14. On certainty in general and different kinds of certainty.
15. On analogy.—On induction.—On deduction.
16. Authority of human testimony.[3]
17. On argumentation and its different forms.
18. On sophisms and the means to resolve them.
19. On signs and language in their relations to thought.
20. Characteristics of a well-formed language.
21. On the causes of our errors and the means of remedying them.

Morality

22. Object of morality.
23. On the diverse motives for our actions.—Is it possible to reduce them to one alone?—What is their relative importance?
24. Describe the moral phenomena on which rests what is called moral conscience, sentiment or the concept of desire, the distinction between good and evil, moral obligation, etc.
25. On praise and blame.—On punishment and recompense.—On moral sanctions.
26. Division of duties.—Individual morality, or the duties of man towards himself.
27. Social morality, or the duties of man towards others:
    a. Duties towards man in general;
    b. Duties towards the State.
28. Enumeration and evaluation of the different proofs for the existence of God.[4]
29. On the principal attributes of God; on divine Providence, and the plan for the universe.
30. Examination of objections drawn from physical evil and from moral evil.
31. Man's destiny.—Proofs of the immortality of the soul.
32. Religious morality, or duties towards God.

History of Philosophy[5]

33. What method must be applied to the study of the history of philosophy?
34. Into how many general epochs can one divide the history of philosophy?
35. Show familiarity with the principal schools of Greek philosophy before Socrates.
36. Show familiarity with Socrates and the character of the philosophical revolution he authored.

37. Show familiarity with the principal Greek schools after Socrates to the end of the school of Alexandria.
38. Who are the principal scholastic philosophers?
39. What is Bacon's method?—Analyse the *Novum organum*.
40. In what does Descartes' method consist?—Analyse the *Discourse on Method*.
41. Show familiarity with the principal modern schools after Bacon and Descartes.
42. What benefits can be drawn from the history of philosophy for philosophy itself?

Edict of the Royal Council, 12th August 1842
List of Books Recommended for the "classe de philosophie"[6]

Among the ancients:

Plato's dialogues;
Aristotle's analytics;
Cicero's philosophical treatises.

Among the moderns:

Bacon: *De Augmentis scientiarum* and *Novum organum*;
Descartes: *Discourse on Method*, *Meditations* with objections and replies;
The Port-Royal Logic;
Bossuet: *Treatise on the Knowledge of God and Oneself* and *Treatise on Free Will*;
Fénelon: *Treatise on the Existence of God* and *Letters on Diverse Metaphysical Subjects*;
Malebranche: *The Search after Truth, Christian Meditations* and *Dialogues on Metaphysics*;
Arnauld: *Treatise on True and False Ideas*;
Buffier: *Treatise on First Truths*;
Locke: *Essay on Human Understanding*;
Leibniz: *New Essays on the Understanding* and *Theodicy*;
Clarke: *On the Existence and Attributes of God*;[7]
Euler's letters to a German princess;[8]
Ferguson's *Institutes of Moral Philosophy*;
Reid's *Works*.

Notes

1. This translation is based on the text given in V. Cousin, *Défense de l'Université et de la philosophie* (Paris: Joubert, 1844), pp. 359–62. We have further consulted D. Rancière's reconstruction of the text in V. Cousin, *Défense de l'Université et de la philosophie*, ed. D. Rancière (Paris: Solin, 1977). An earlier translation exists in John I. Brooks III, *The Eclectic Legacy: Academic Philosophy and the Human Sciences in Nineteenth-Century France* (London: Associated University Presses, 1998), pp. 248–50. See Barancy's and Bernard Granger's essay for context. The *baccalauréat* was (and still is) the national diploma in France which permits students to access higher education; prior to 1852, the "baccalauréat des lettres," which culminated in the "classe de philosophie" and subsequent exam, was the secondary qualification passed through before accessing qualifications in the sciences, law, medicine, and theology. What is immediately evident in this edict is the proximity of the prescribed

questions to Cousin's own philosophical doctrines: the section on psychology closely follows the 1833 Preface to *Philosophical Fragments* and the section on morality follows Cousin's presentation of ethics in his lecture courses from 1818 to 1820. Hence, although formally published by the Royal Council of Public Instruction, this was one of the most significant ideological documents that Cousin—as its secretary—formulated, since it required aspiring students wishing to enter university to undertake a course in and then an examination on Cousinian philosophy. It served as one of the key means by which eclecticism came to function as the ruling form of thought in early nineteenth-century France. Moreover, since the training of philosophers at the École Normale, in particular, consisted in preparation to teach the *baccalauréat*, this edict also ensured Cousinianism was central to higher education too, such that (in addition to students) familiarity with it was necessary for professors. The strictness with which Cousin expected this syllabus to be applied can be discerned from a circular issued by the Royal Council on 8 April 1833, which reads in part: "This programme is merely the exact summary of philosophical teaching, such that it has occurred in the royal colleges. It is the natural and obligatory basis for the *baccalauréat* examination in this part of classical studies. Since it concerns a diploma which should give the same advantages to all students from royal and communal colleges indiscriminately, it is right that all of them should demonstrate the same degree of instruction.... It is intended to raise the teaching of philosophy in the communal colleges to the same heights as in the royal colleges and to introduce into the progress of the teaching a uniformity which is always compatible with freedom of discussion, but indispensable so that the merit of the teachers and the successes obtained by each of them can be appreciated comparatively. I have no need, I am sure, to insist on these considerations ... so as to make you feel the extent to which it is necessary that the programme of philosophy questions is faithfully followed in the examination of aspirants to the title of Bachelor of Letters. It should be conformed to not only in its fundamentals and its form, but also in the order of the questions posed" (*Défense*, pp. 355–6). The syllabus of questions for the *baccalauréat* examination had previously been set in 1823—during one of the more reactionary phases of the Restoration—by the then Minister of Public Education, Denis-Luc Frayssinous, Bishop of Hermopolis (see p. 242 above). The fifty questions were split into three sections: Logic, Metaphysics, and Morality, based on an Aristotelian logic (see *Défense*, pp. 352–5). Almost none of these 1823 questions are retained in the 1832 syllabus, and Cousin adds two new sections on Psychology and History of Philosophy.
2. One of the key features of secondary education under the Restoration had been the requirement to compose examination answers in Latin (the 1823 syllabus was set out in Latin). Under the July Monarchy, the opening up of education—and the reduction of the influence of the Church—was in part expressed through a series of edicts removing the Latin requirement. The Royal Council had added in 1830 that "the Latin language could only render many ideas in modern philosophy obscurely and imperfectly" and its use "corrupted the invention needed for new terms" (*Défense*, p. 357).
3. The Royal Council issued a further edict on 14 July 1840 concerning questions 16 and 17: These "two questions ... are to be replaced with the following:

16. On the syllogism and its rules.—Cite examples.
17. On the utility of the syllogistic form."

In an attached circular, the Royal Council write, "You will find no other changes than the introduction of some new questions in logic concerning that form of reasoning so abused in the Middle Ages and, since then owing to an extreme reaction, too neglected—that is, the syllogistic form. The syllogistic art is at the very least powerful fencing practice which habituates the mind to precision and rigour. It is in this manly [*mâle*] school that our fathers were formed; there is only benefit in retaining it for the current youth" (*Défense*, pp. 363–4).
4. These metaphysical questions came under attack in the early 1840s from the Catholic Right as part of the attempted reforms of secondary education by Abel Villemain (then Minister of Public Education), even though metaphysics was far less prominent in the 1832 version of the syllabus than the 1823 one. The metaphysical implications of some of these questions became emblematic of the challenge posed by Cousin's secular and rationalist metaphysics to the authority of the Church. As Charles de Montalembert, a sometime follower of Lamennais, put it to the Chamber of Peers, "This is the rule that has been outlined, praised, and defended by the honourable M. Cousin himself so many times before you! That one teaches metaphysics, not contrary to revelation, but outside of it, but independent of it, and brings to the aid of revealed truth demonstrations one attains solely by reason." *Trois discours sur la liberté de l'Église* (Paris: Waille, 1844), p. 151. On this basis, for instance, in his report on the new laws presented to the Chamber of Peers in April 1844, the Duc de Broglie argues for the suppression of all metaphysical topics in the curriculum, insisting that the Government "include in secondary teaching nothing which exceeds the studies of logic, morality,

and elementary psychology [and] defer to higher education any question which could shake, even for a moment, the data on which rests the unanimous and spontaneous conviction of the human race, [which could] alter to any degree the tranquillity and serenity of mind in early youth." *Écrits et discours* (Paris: Didier, 1863), vol. 3, p. 244. To these worries Cousin responds as follows to the Chamber: "It is in metaphysics alone that we teach pupils that they have a spiritual soul, which is the sole genuine cause and is responsible for all their acts, surrounded by these material beings endowed with movements that do not belong to them." He continues, "One will say: teach metaphysics to listeners who are fifteen or sixteen years old. I respond: yes certainly, [teach] the soul and God to fifteen or sixteen-year olds.... Do you believe that it is only at eighteen or nineteen years old ... that one can understand such simple and robust proofs as those that can be given for the principal natural truths!" (*Défense*, pp. 51, 54).

5. The addition of the history of philosophy to French philosophical teaching was a priority for Cousin, and the discipline had already been added to the *agrégation* syllabus in the weeks following the 1830 Revolution. As in the previous note, Villemain's proposed reforms were cause for a re-examination of the appropriateness of history of philosophy at this level of teaching. For example, having mentioned Descartes, Bossuet, and Fénelon on the existence of God, the Duc be Broglie wonders in his report (see previous note), "But are these the questions which can be posed without any peril before listeners who are fifteen or sixteen years old by hundreds of teachers who are themselves young and just starting off in their teaching career? What other questions, no less delicate and no less thorny, could they in turn raise at the same time? The role which, in philosophical teaching today, the history of philosophy itself has taken up—does it not (intentionally or not) place minds on a very slippery slope? In setting out before the youth the tableau of the principal aberrations of the human mind, who can respond that the distribution of praise and blame will always be undertaken with irreproachable discernment and in just measure?" *Écrits et discours*, vol. 3, pp. 241–2. Cousin responds to these worries in his speech to the Chamber of Peers on 2 May 1844: "Among the various parts of philosophical teaching there is one which seems to have above all alarmed some minds—that is the history of philosophy.... [But] it occupies two or three of the last weeks of the [*baccalauréat*] course, and it is composed of famous dates which cannot be forgotten, the titles of the principal monuments that have received universal admiration, and particularly sober and selective quotations from the best opinions of the most illustrious philosophers, as a sort of living demonstration of this consoling truth that all good beliefs which constitute the patrimony of common sense and which serve for the salvation of the soul arise from all countries and at all times." *Défense*, pp. 54–5.

6. This translation is based on the text given in V. Cousin, *Défense*, pp. 364–5 and corrected in Rancière's edition, pp. 83–4. We only clarify Cousin's citations in the following notes when his reference is somewhat unclear. The "classe de philosophie" referred to here is the final class of secondary education devoted to the introduction of philosophy that was mandatory for completion of the "baccalauréat des lettres," prior to entering university. This list of key texts had previously been formulated in September 1809 under Napoleon. The 1809 list included a number of texts that were removed in 1842: Pascal on proof, Wolff's logic's Gravesande's *Introduction to Philosophy*, Burlamaqui's *Principles of Natural Right*, Condillac's *Treatise on Systems*, *Art of Thinking*, and *Logic*, and Bonnet's *Analytic Essay on the Faculties of the Soul*. The 1842 list added the texts by Bossuet, Arnauld, Buffier, Ferguson, and Reid, as well as the Fénelon letters. The texts by Plato, Aristotle, Cicero, Bacon, Descartes, Fénelon on the existence of God, Malebranche, Locke, Leibniz, Clarke, and Euler remained unchanged. In the Chamber of Peers on 4 May 1844 Cousin defended "the true character of this list ... of classic books of philosophy which can be placed in the hands of teachers and pupils." He underlines the importance of a list of readings "which will plant insensibly into minds and souls the seeds of every thought that will come to develop there"; he points out that, while at first glance it might look like the seventeenth century is overrepresented, it is not and nor should it be, since the "system" of Cartesianism is no longer relevant and "is not taught in universities." He continues, "Just like the list adopted by the Imperial Council in 1809, the new list furnishes models and masters for all reasonable doctrines and, so as to enter fully into what is living and essential in it, I will say that it provides guarantees to all forms of worship by providing representatives for them all. Hence temperate and moderated, it can be applied to all schools and direct all minds without doing any violence to them. We encounter two pagans, but [pagans] who have no superiors, Plato and Aristotle; there is the founder of laic philosophy, Descartes; there are Catholic writers coming from different sides: Arnauld represents Port-Royal; Malebranche [represents] the Oratory; Fénelon [represents] Saint-Sulpice; then there is that incomparable man who presides over all orders, all congregations, all parties from the heights of his infallible good sense, Bossuet. Finally, we were not afraid of adding a Jesuit name—such was our impartiality; and so, after the names we have just cited, we have placed that of the judicious Father Buffier. But we have not presented solely French authors

of the seventeenth century—that would have been to repudiate an entire century of our history and that of the human mind. There are also several foreign and Protestant writers, Clarke and Leibniz; a man who sometimes doubted too much, but without ever falling into an abyss and who will forever remain a true sage, Locke, the circumspect leader of a daring school that should be watched over, not proscribed. Finally, one of the most robust and most sober of minds, Reid, closes this glorious and irreproachable list." *Défense*, pp. 185–6.

7. Samuel Clarke's 1705 *A Demonstration of the Being and Attributes of God*.
8. Leonhard Euler's letters to Friederike Charlotte of Brandenburg-Schwedt between 1760 and 1762.

Index

For the benefit of digital users, indexed terms that span two pages (e.g., 52–53) may, on occasion, appear on only one of those pages.

Abelard, P. xiii–xiv, xvi–xvii, xxv, 7, 237–41
Abel-Remusat, J.-P. 184
absolute, the xii–xiii, xix–xx, 68–70, 74, 75–77, 95–96, 97, 98–100, 101–2, 106–7, 130, 145, 151–52, 153, 154, 155, 156–57, 159, 163–64, 167, 169–71, 172–73, 174–77, 185–86, 187, 209–11
abstraction 40, 52, 107–8, 176–77, 181–82, 193–94, 257
　comparative abstraction 52, 176–77
Académie des sciences morales et politiques xvii, 16, 31, 239–40, 253
admiration 172–73
agrégation xv, 11, 16, 31, 259
anarchy xiii
André, Père 7–8, 253
Aquinas, T. 131–33, 245–46
aristocracy 79–80
Aristotle xvi, 25–26, 31, 61–62, 67–68, 102–3, 107–8, 128–29, 155–56, 169–71, 192–93, 259
Arnauld, A. 164, 251, 253, 259
atheism 21, 23, 27, 78–79, 101–2, 201–2, 242–43, 244–47
attention 5, 28–29, 92–94, 95–96, 97–99, 128–29, 150, 218, 226, 257
Austin, S. ix, 125–26

baccalauréat 16, 18, 257–59
Bacon, F. 5, 9, 10, 62–64, 220, 251, 253, 259
Barthélemy-Saint-Hilaire, J. xvi, 25–26
Bautain, L. 22
Beckers, H. 124, 134
Bernard, St 237–39, 242–43
Bonnet, C. 18–19, 251–52, 259
Bossuet, J.-B. 18–19, 237–39, 251, 259
Boureau-Deslandes, A.-F. 25
Brown, T. 225
Brownson, O. ix, 125–26
Brucker, J. J. xi, 25, 182–83, 184, 205
Buffier, C. 7, 18–19, 259
Buhle, J. G. 157
Burke, E. 173

Cabanis, P. 216, 233
Cartesianism vii–viii, xiii, 7–8, 21, 23, 28–29, 30, 31, 60–61, 67–68, 128–29, 155–56, 221, 242–43, 244–45, 246–47, 250–55
cause
　impersonal cause 46–47, 65–66, 222–24
　infinite cause *see* substantial cause
　personal cause 46–47, 65–66, 70–71, 72–73, 98–99, 222–24, 228, 229–30, 231–32
　substantial cause 46–47, 65–66, 74, 76–77, 98–99, 101–2
Chambre des Pairs 7–8, 246–47, 259
Charter of 1814 3, 20–21, 22, 34, 40–42, 115–16
Chateaubriand, F.-R. 242–43
choice ix–x, xi–xii, 27–28, 71–72, 73, 113–14, 160–61, 202, 209–10
Cicero 259
Clarke, S. 7, 252, 259
classe de philosophie 259
Collins, A. 201–2, 252
common sense xi, 7, 28–29, 53, 61–62, 77–78, 109–11, 112–13, 128–29, 142, 187, 209–10, 224–25, 237–39
Comte, A. xi–xii, 116
concours général xv
Condillac, E. B. de x, 5–7, 8, 9–10, 18–20, 28, 60–61, 62–64, 103–4, 201–4, 215, 218, 220, 251–52
constitutional monarchy 19, 20, 34, 108, 242–43, 250–51
construction 92–94
Cotten, J.-P. vii–viii, xix
Cousin, V.
　Abelard-edition xvi, 239–40
　biography xiv–xix, 103–8
　Descartes-edition xvi, 7–8, 25–26, 239–40, 251–52, 253
　General History of Philosophy xviii, 36, 37, 38, 40, 197–98
　Kant-lectures ix, 104–5, 244, 252–53
　lecture course of 1828 ix, 15, 115–16, 205–6, 216, 222–24, 253

Cousin, V. (*cont.*)
  lecture course of 1829 xviii, 26–27, 36, 130, 131–33, 204, 224–25, 228, 229, 231, 237, 245–46
  On the True, the Beautiful and the Good ix, 10, 45–46
  Plato-translation xvi, 26–27, 107–8, 197
  political and educational roles xvii–xviii, 3, 11, 14–19, 31–32
  Proclus-edition xvi–xvii, 25–26, 107–8, 197
Cratylus 191–92
creation 76–77, 101–2, 130, 131–33, 243–44, 245–46
critique 35, 38, 48–49, 60–61, 155–56, 205–6

D'Alembert, J. 6
D'Assas, N.-L. 71–72, 131–33
D'Holbach, P.-H. 201–2
Damiron, P. 15, 16–17
definition 185, 186
Degérando, J. M. xxv, 4–5, 100
deliberation 70–73, 131–33, 141, 160–61
democracy xviii, 20–21, 115–16
Descartes, R. x, 5–8, 10, 25, 28–29, 32–33, 39, 45, 53, 92–94, 102–4, 127, 128–29, 144–49, 155–56, 194–96, 220–22, 237–40, 242–43, 250–55, 259
  Discourse on Method xx–xxi, 8, 259
  Meditations on First Philosophy 8, 144–49, 259
  Principles of Philosophy 144–45
  see also Cartesianism
dialectic 5, 106–7, 147–48, 185, 191, 192–96, 201–2, 231–32, 237–39
Diderot, D. xi, 6, 25, 35–36
dissertation de philosophie générale ix–x, 11, 17–18
dogmatism 46–47, 50, 52, 81–82, 95–96, 100, 109, 125–26, 128–30, 218–19, 224–25, 230, 242–43
Douailler, S. vii–viii
Dubois, P. 11, 15

East, the 79–80, 181–84, 204
eclecticism ix, 3, 8–9, 17–18, 19–21, 34, 81–82, 112–16, 126, 133–34, 157, 194–96, 197–98, 202–4, 209–11, 222–24, 250–51
École Normale xv, 5, 15–16, 17, 31, 59, 64–65, 81–82, 103–4, 134, 207
effort *see* muscular effort
egoism 142–43
Eleaticism 100–2
Emerson, R. W. ix
enthusiasm 73, 104–5, 172–73, 192–94, 201–2

eternity xix, 30, 36, 40, 45, 46–47, 80–81, 100, 130, 141, 142, 167, 174–75, 185–86, 187, 191–92, 244
Euler, L. 75–76, 259
extensity xii–xiii, xxvii, 5, 48, 53, 62–64, 66, 134, 169–71, 192–93, 194–96, 209–10

facts of consciousness
  rational facts 9, 52–53, 65–67, 226, 230–31
  sensible facts 9, 10, 66–67, 225–26, 230–31
  volitional facts 9, 10, 65, 66–67, 225–26, 230–31
faith 10, 28, 29, 47, 60–61, 78–80, 99–100, 104–5, 109, 111–12, 115–16, 128–30, 141, 147, 181–82, 191–94, 200–1, 237–39, 246–47
fanaticism xiii–xiv, 29, 41, 202–4, 242–43
fatalism 6–7, 27, 71–72, 79–80, 112–13, 114, 131–33, 160–61, 244, 245–46
Fénelon, F. 251, 259
Ferguson, A. 18–19, 259
Fichte, J. G. xxvii, 5, 19–20, 72–73, 74, 96, 104–7, 127, 160–62, 163–64, 166, 231–32
Frayssinous, D. L. 18, 242–43
freedom xix–xx, xxiii, 11, 20, 26–27, 30, 38, 42, 46–47, 59–60, 73–75, 128, 130–33, 141–43, 160–61, 162–64, 167–68, 169–71, 183–84, 193–94, 217–18, 219, 230, 244, 245–47, 250–51, 258
free will 27, 28, 73, 141
French Revolution *see* Revolution of 1789

Galluppi, P. 126
Garnier, A. xv
Gassendi, P. 144–49
geometry 3–4, 102–3, 145–46, 147–48, 155, 176–77
grace 131–33, 194–96, 230–32
Greece 183–84, 192–96
Guizot, F. xiii, 3, 22

Hamilton, W. ix, 53, 107–8, 126–27, 128
happiness 79–80, 142–43
harmony 9, 59–60, 61–62, 75–76, 77–78, 101–2, 133, 172–73, 193–94, 197–98
Harris, W. T. ix
Hegel, G. W. F. xv, 25–27, 28–29, 48, 104–8, 128
  Encyclopedia of the Philosophical Sciences 105–6, 107–8
Hegelianism ix, 26–28, 194–96
Heloïse 237–40
Helvétius, C. A. 10, 28
Hobbes, T. 10, 131–33
Huet, P. D. 242–43
Humboldt, W. 184

INDEX 265

Hume, D. 47, 49, 70–71, 224–25, 251–52
hypothesis 9–10, 48, 49, 75–76, 92–94, 99–100, 106–8, 109–10, 129–30, 131–33, 176–77, 218–19, 220, 230–31

idealism 4–5, 10, 19–20, 29, 30, 37, 38, 106–7, 197–98, 230–32, 250–51
Idéologues 4, 6–7, 10, 27–28
impartiality xi–xiii, 29, 62–64, 81–82, 94–95, 202, 205–6, 209–10, 250–51
impersonal reason 50–51, 53, 67–69
induction 5, 38, 48, 51, 62–64, 69–70, 75–76, 81–82, 92–94, 100, 107–8, 112–13, 220, 229–31, 246–47, 258
Institut de France xvii–xviii, 215, 216
intellectual intuition 50–51, 107–8, 127
intention 143, 219–20

Jacobi, F. H. 104–6, 127
Janet, P. xvii–xviii, xix–xx, 21, 194–96
Jesuitism 202–4, 242–43
Jouffroy, T. S. 15, 25–26
July Monarchy xiv, 14, 15–16, 42, 115–16

Kant, I. xxvii, 19–20, 28–29, 38, 45, 47, 50, 60–61, 67–69, 95–96, 104–5, 106–7, 126, 127, 128–29, 145, 155–57, 169–71, 173, 187, 205–6, 252–53
Kierkegaard, S. xix
Kingdom of Heaven 141

La Mettrie, J. O. de 201–2
Lamennais, F. de 22, 110–11, 242–43
Laromiguière, P. xxv, 4–5, 28–29, 103–4, 202–4, 215, 226
Laurent, P.-M. 100
Leibniz, G. W. xix, 7, 25–26, 60–61, 62–64, 102–3, 107–8, 114–15, 128–29, 130–31, 187, 194–96, 221–25, 228, 244, 245–46, 251, 252, 253, 259
  monadology 221, 222–24
  pre-established harmony 61–64, 222–24
Leroux, P. 35, 40–41, 42–43
liberalism xv–xvii, xviii, 7–8, 20, 28–29, 47, 244, 246–47, 250–51
Locke, J. 5, 6–7, 19–20, 28, 30–31, 38, 47–48, 60–61, 92–94, 102–4, 155–57, 201–2, 220, 221–22, 224–25, 251–52, 253, 259
logic 46, 47, 51–53, 68–69, 125–26, 129, 144–45, 147–48, 151–52, 153, 154, 155, 159, 160, 167, 168–69, 202–4, 237–39, 242–43, 258
Louis Philippe xvii, 34
Louis XIV 8

Louis XVIII 34, 41, 42
Luther, M. 131–33

Macherey, P. vii–viii
Maine de Biran, P. x, 4–5, 70–71, 103–4, 130–31, 215–36, 244
Malebranche, N. 5, 7–8, 60–62, 103–4, 221, 230–31, 244–45, 251, 253, 259
Mancino, S. 126
Mandeville, B. 201–2
Martignac, Vicomte de xvii
materialism 10, 21, 27–28, 30–31, 60–61, 75–76, 100, 201–2, 225, 242–43, 246–47
Mauve, C. vii–viii
method vii–viii, xi, 3–4, 5, 8–9, 10, 17–18, 21, 23, 28–29, 35, 36, 47–48, 51–52, 53–54, 59–66, 67–68, 75–76, 77–78, 80–82, 91–96, 100, 102–3, 104–5, 107–8, 112–13, 125, 126–27, 128–29, 144–46, 154–56, 181–82, 191, 220, 221, 250–51, 252, 257, 258
Middle Ages 26–27, 40, 41, 200–1, 237–40
monarchy *see* constitutional monarchy
Montesquieu 35–36, 38, 252
moral necessity 245–46
muscular effort xix–xx, 70–71, 217–18, 225–26, 231
mysticism 29, 30, 37, 50–51, 100, 104–5, 111–12, 172–73, 191–94, 201–2, 205–6, 221, 230–32, 244–45, 250–51
mythology 182–84, 192–94

nationalism xiii
necessity *see* moral necessity
negation 50–51, 72–73, 96, 160–61, 167, 176

objectivity xix–xx, 29, 42–43, 49–51, 52, 68–69, 74–75, 95–96, 99–100, 125, 127–28, 150–51, 153, 154, 156–57
Ockham, W. 131–33, 245–46
ontology xix–xx, 8, 9–10, 21, 23, 45, 46–47, 48, 51–52, 53, 60–61, 65–66, 69–70, 74, 76–79, 91, 92–94, 95–96, 97, 99–100, 104–5, 107–8, 128, 151–52, 153, 197–98, 205–6, 229, 244
organism 70–71, 96–97, 98, 143, 163–64, 168, 216–17, 219, 222–24
origin of language 219–20

pantheism 22–23, 25–26, 100–2, 130–31, 243–44
paralogism 110–11, 145–46, 200–1, 252–53
Pascal, B. xix, 18–19, 102–3, 247, 248, 253
passivity 6–7, 70–71, 74–75, 131–33, 162–64, 218
patriotism xiii, 102–3, 239–40, 250–51

personality 5, 52, 66–67, 69–71, 74–76, 79–80, 95–96, 98, 103–4, 159–60, 217, 219–21, 230–31, 243–44
phenomenology 46, 52–53, 151–52
philology xvi, 29, 31–32, 205
philosophy of nature 46–47, 74, 104–8, 124, 127, 128
physics 9, 75–76, 92–94, 102–3, 106–7, 222
Plato xiii, 14–15, 25–26, 32–33, 61–62, 67–69, 78–79, 102–3, 107–8, 114–15, 128–29, 130, 131–33, 174–75, 185–90, 191–96, 197, 230–31, 252, 259
　Euthyphro 131–33
　Laws 14–15
　Meno 185, 186
　Parmenides 107–8, 185
　Phaedrus 185, 186, 187
　Republic 102–3, 185, 186, 230–31
　Theagus 230–31
Platonism xiii, 130–31, 244
Poli, B. 126
Poret, H. 51–52
practical philosophy 8–9, 10, 41, 43, 46–47, 59–60, 68–69
primary education 16, 22
Proclus xvi–xvii, 25–26, 107–8, 194–96, 197, 231
Protestantism 110–11
Providence 41, 46–47, 53–54, 74, 79–80, 131–33, 200–1, 230, 246–47, 258
psychology x, 6–8, 9, 18, 23, 32, 35, 36–37, 39, 45, 46–48, 51–52, 53, 64, 65–67, 68–70, 74, 76–79, 81–82, 91, 92–97, 99–100, 104–5, 106–8, 125–26, 127–30, 131–33, 151–52, 154–55, 160–61, 197–98, 205–6, 222–26, 228, 229, 230, 231–32, 244, 246–47, 252–53, 257–58
Pythagoras 61–62, 67–68, 78–79, 193–94

Ravaisson, F. xix, 124
reflection 6–7, 37, 47–49, 50–51, 52, 68–69, 71–74, 78–80, 92–94, 99–100, 104–5, 147, 150–52, 160–61, 166–71, 175–76, 181–84, 191–93, 194–96, 207, 220
Reid, T. 9, 18–20, 25–26, 39, 47, 50, 60–61, 145–46, 155–57, 202–4, 224–25, 252–53, 259
Reiffenberg, F. de 209–11
Renan, E. 11
revelation 21, 27, 53, 78–79, 96–97, 181–82, 230–31, 242–43, 246–47
Revolution of 1789 x, 26–27, 34–35, 40–42, 250–51
Revolution of 1830 xvii, 15–16, 115–16
Revolution of 1848 xviii
Richelieu, Duc de xvi
Ripley, G. ix, 125–26
Romanticism xix

Rosmini, A. 126
Rousseau, J.-J. 7, 25, 30, 35–36, 38, 39, 242–43, 252
Royal Council for Public Instruction xvii–xviii, 15–16, 257–59
Royer-Collard, P. P. xiii, 4–5, 8, 15, 28–29, 39, 59, 64–65, 103–4, 129, 202–4, 215, 229

Saint-Martin, L. C. de 30
Saint-Simon, H. de 100, 101–2
Saisset, E. 25–26
scepticism xix, 8, 18–19, 25–26, 37, 38, 40, 47, 49, 50, 60–61, 68–69, 92–94, 95–97, 106–8, 109, 115–16, 129–30, 147–48, 172–73, 193–96, 200–2, 205–6, 218–19, 224–25, 230–32, 243, 252–53
Schelling, F. W. J. ix, 28–29, 48, 52, 104–8, 124–25, 126–28, 206, 222–24
Schlegel, A. W. 184
Schleiermacher, F. D. E. 186
secularisation x, 21–23, 47, 200–1
severity xii, 205–6
Sevigny, Madame de 102–3
Simon, J. xv, 15–17
socialism 27–28, 115–16
Socrates xix, 39, 102–3, 127, 128–29, 191, 194–96, 252, 258
somnambulism 219
Sorbonne, the *see* University of Paris
Spinoza, B. 7, 10, 25–26, 32–33, 60–61, 100–2, 128, 145–46, 194–96, 221, 251, 252, 253
spiritualism xix, 3, 4, 10, 11, 18–19, 23, 28–29, 39, 46–47, 75–76, 100–1, 201–2, 218, 221, 250–51
spontaneity 37, 50–51, 52, 68–69, 71–74, 79–80, 131–33, 160–61, 166–71, 175–76, 181–82, 183–84, 231
Stewart, D. 144–45, 224–25
sublime, the 106–7, 111–12, 131–33, 173, 191, 192–96
substance xix–xx, 10, 22, 45, 47, 53, 65, 67–68, 69–70, 74, 75–77, 78–79, 95–96, 99–100, 101–2, 128, 130–33, 144–45, 147, 151–52, 163–64, 169–71, 174–76, 185–86, 187, 221–22, 228, 244, *see also* cause: substantial cause
syllogism 145–46, 231, 259
syncretism 112–14, 209–10

Taine, H. xix, 45
Tennemann, W. G. 29, 96, 104–5, 107–8, 124, 200–8, 231–32, 237
theocracy 200–1
theodicy 18, 46–47, 95, 100, 205–6, 252–53
theology 4, 7–8, 21, 22, 23, 46–47, 100, 108–10, 111–12, 115–16, 131–33, 219–20, 237–40

Thiers, A. xvii
Thomasius, C. xi
Toland, J. 251–52
tolerance xii–xiii, 204
Tracy, A. D. de 202–4, 216, 220
trademark argument 53
Trinity, the 109, 237–39
triplicity 75–77, 159
Turgot, A. 6, 7, 30, 38–39, 251–52

University of Paris xv, 3, 15–16, 19, 59, 237, 242–43

Van de Weyer, S. 209–10
Vera, A. 25–26
Vermeren, P. vii–viii
Voltaire 8, 30–31, 35–36, 38, 251–52

Wendt, A. 124–91, 206
will *see* freedom: free will
Willm, J. 124
Wolff, C. 60–61, 107–8

Xenophon 101, 130

Zeno 101, 130